THE WRIGHTSMAN COLLECTION

VOLUME IV

Porcelain

THE WRIGHTSMAN COLLECTION

VOLUME **IV** *Porcelain*

by CARL CHRISTIAN DAUTERMAN

Curator, Western European Arts, The Metropolitan Museum of Art

THE METROPOLITAN MUSEUM OF ART

Distributed by New York Graphic Society Ltd., Greenwich, Connecticut

The centers indicated by numbers on this map began significant production of porcelain between 1710 and 1756. This period embraces the earliest such production at each factory represented in this catalogue, beginning with Meissen and ending with Derby. Earlier factories had been established at Flórence (Medici porcelain, about 1575), Pisa (about 1619), Rouen (letters patent granted 1673), and Saint-Cloud (letters patent granted 1702). Various experiments with porcelain-making were attempted even earlier, but because of lack of documentation they are not recorded here; neither are experiments such as those at Alcora (1751) or St. Petersburg (1744).

The numbers in red on the map indicate factories represented in the Wrightsman Collection, in this volume or in Volume III.

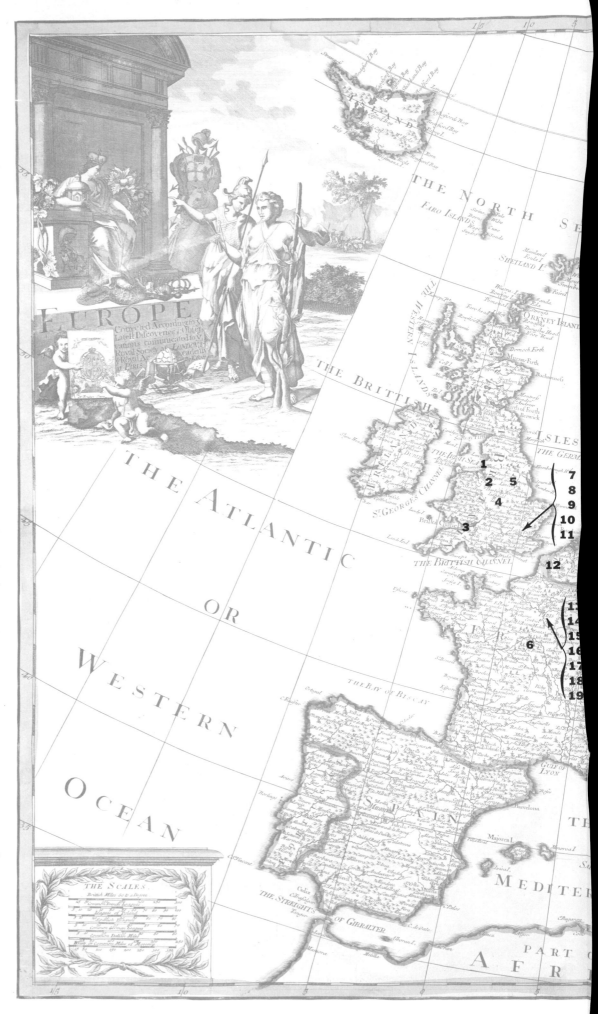

PREFACE

THE TEXT OF this volume has been divided into four geographical categories. European porcelains constitute the first three divisions, German, French, and English; Oriental porcelains, a numerically smaller group, the fourth.

Each of the European groups is further divided into subgroups consisting of sculptures, other ornamental porcelains, and tableware. Within each of these, as with the Oriental porcelains, the order is chronological. Virtually all the German porcelains are Meissen, and they are, almost without exception, of earlier date than the other European porcelains. The French porcelains fall into one major (Vincennes-Sèvres) and three minor (Saint-Cloud, Chantilly, and Mennecy) groups. The English porcelain section is richest in Chelsea, supplemented by Worcester, Derby, Longton Hall, and Bow.

The most important aspect of the Meissen section is the bird sculptures (Catalogue Nos. 1–43), the largest and most diversified collection known to the writer. The birds are given their English titles and subtitled with the eighteenth century German equivalents, taken mainly from Albiker, *Die Meissner Porzellantiere im 18. Jahrhundert*. In the section on Meissen porcelains, some comparable examples cited here as in the collection of Ernst Schneider, Schloss Jägerhof, Düsseldorf, have since been transferred to Schloss Lustheim, a division of the Bayerisches Nationalmuseum, Munich. The transfer was made after our text had gone to press; it applies only to pieces from that collection which have been published in Rückert, *Meissener Porzellan, 1710–1810*. The richness of the Sèvres factory records and their greater availability have made it generally possible to supply the equivalent French eighteenth century terms throughout the descriptions of the French porcelains. Of particular note among the Sèvres are the five candelabrum vases (Catalogue Nos. 80–83), the rose-pink vases (Catalogue Nos. 84 A and B, 86), and, of course, the large representation of the ambassadorial service made for Louis, Prince de Rohan (Catalogue No. 109). Everything in this section is of soft paste except for a pair of black and gold trumpet vases (Catalogue Nos. 91 A and B).

The order of description of each catalogue entry is: name of object; contemporary name, where known; dimensions; physical description; marks; attribution and date; references; exhibitions; former owners; comments; comparable examples. To avoid repetition, much detailed information concerning craftsmen, artists, and technical terms has been reserved for the Biographies and Glossary.

OPPOSITE: *Europe, Corrected According to ye Latest Discoveries & Observations comunicated to ye Royal Society at London & ye Royal Accademy at Paris, 1744–1752, by Emanuel Bowen (1720–1767), English. The American Geographical Society, New York*

It is hoped that the frequent references to auction sales in the text will be as helpful to future researchers as the eighteenth century records of Lazare Duvaux and others have been to the present generation of scholars and connoisseurs. Where noted, the sales have been set out in chronological order to give some indication of the frequency of occurrence and to offer a ready means of tracing the fluctuation of values for a particular type of object. Prices have been quoted for eighteenth and nineteenth century sales when known. Twentieth century prices, being more generally available, have not been included, as they can be readily traced in the priced catalogues of well-equipped art libraries.

The Sèvres porcelains in this collection have provided an unusual diversity of incised marks, which here, as well as in *Decorative Art from the Samuel H. Kress Collection at The Metropolitan Museum of Art*, I have treated as an item of catalogue description. The painted marks of the decorators appear in so many standard books of reference that they have not been reproduced, although they are described for identification in each case. I have, however, chosen to illustrate the sparsely documented incised marks, as there is a growing interest and intensification of research in such marks. During the preparation of the catalogue text, several previously unrecognized alphabetical marks occurring on the Wrightsman porcelains were attributed to specific workers at the factory. The relationship between the craftsmen and their marks was traced with the aid of a computer and confirmed by a comparison of the handwriting of the marks with that of signatures on Sèvres payroll records. Marks attributed to Bougon, Danet, and Liance are illustrated both in the text and under the biographies of these craftsmen. Other correlations of mark and signature, uncovered too late to be included in the catalogue section, are:

Bu   for Bulidon, a sculptor, working 1745–1759. Found on the statuette Catalogue No. 114 B.

cSn   for Charles Censier *jeune*, a *répareur*, working 1758–1775. Found on the stand for a jam pot, Catalogue No. 109.

CT   for Collot, a *répareur*, working 1754–1772. Found on plates in the dinner services Catalogues Nos. 97 and 102; a tray, Catalogue No. 102; and a plate in the dessert service Catalogue No. 109.

gP   for Claude-Jean-Baptiste Grémont *père*, a *répareur-acheveur*, working 1746–1775. Found on a tray, Catalogue No. 87; a pair of fruit dishes, Catalogue No. 102; and a tray in the dinner service Catalogue No. 109.

gtn   for Gautron, a *répareur*, working about 1767. Found on a cup, Catalogue No. 95.

M   for Marcillon, a *répareur*, working 1756–1758. Found on two plant pots, Catalogue Nos. 79 B and 88.

I LOOK UPON the preparation of this volume as a trust invested in me by Mr. and Mrs. Charles Wrightsman and the administration of The Metropolitan Museum of Art. My first thanks therefore go to them.

The undertaking could not have been realized, however, without the friendly cooperation of many others who helped to formulate the contents of these pages.

To Francis Watson, Director of the Wallace Collection, I am especially indebted for his careful scrutiny of the text and many valuable suggestions. The introduction to the French porcelains was written in collaboration with him. Mr. Watson has also supplied an essay on mounted Oriental porcelain, to which I have contributed a few technical facts.

The diverse international character of the Wrightsman porcelains has given me stimulating opportunities to consult with colleagues, collectors, dealers, and others having specialized knowledge of porcelains and related fields. Dr. Rainer Rückert, Oberkonservator of the Bayerisches Nationalmuseum, Munich, has given generously of his time and talents in connection with the Meissen porcelain. Dr. Jean Delacour, Research Associate, and Charles E. O'Brien, Assistant Curator, of the Department of Ornithology of the American Museum of Natural History have contributed by identifying the species of tropical birds represented among the Meissen porcelains. My colleague Dr. Helmut Nickel, Curator of Arms and Armor, also helped with problems affecting Meissen. Pierre Verlet, Conservateur-en-chef du Département des Objets d'Art at the Louvre, has given helpful advice with the French porcelains, and Svend Eriksen, Librarian of the Dansk Kunstindustrimuseum, Copenhagen, generously provided galley proofs of biographical notes on artists and craftsmen, compiled for his recently published book, *The James A. de Rothschild Collection at Waddesdon Manor: Sèvres Porcelain*. Mlle Marcelle Brunet, recently retired archivist of the Manufacture Nationale de Porcelaine de Sèvres, has graciously extended the facilities of her library and shared her own researches concerning the workers at Sèvres and their marks. Robert Charleston, Keeper of Ceramics at the Victoria and Albert Museum, was most helpful in his comments on the Chelsea scent bottles as well as the English enamel boxes in Volume III. Drs. John A. Pope, Director of the Freer Gallery, Washington, D.C., and Sherman E. Lee, Director of the Cleveland Museum of Art, have guided me with respect to the Oriental porcelains, as have also Fong Chow, Associate Curator in Charge, and Suzanne G. Valenstein, Curatorial Assistant, of the Metropolitan Museum's Department of Far Eastern Art.

Information concerning comparable pieces in public and private collections has been offered by Dr. S. Ducret of Zurich; Jeffrey Story of New York; William W. Winkworth of London; Geoffrey de Bellaigue, of the Lord Chamberlain's Office, London; Miss Rosamond Griffin, of Waddesdon Manor; Dr. I. Menzhausen, of the Porzellansammlung, Dresden; and Mr. J. P. Palmer of the Fitzwilliam Museum, Cambridge.

I wish especially to acknowledge the professional guidance received from Dr. Jack Heller, former Director of the Institute for Computer Research in the Humanities of New York University, in connection with preparing data on the incised marks of Sèvres for screening by the computer. The subject was treated as a pilot project in the use of computers in the field of art history. Through his dedication and the diligent work of Petrea Horner, a volunteer, the identification of potters has produced gratifying results of wide application.

Others who have worked with me from time to time, whose application to the endless minutiae of research and the daily pursuance of routines has added form and substance to this work, are Patricia FitzGerald Mandel, Deborah Stott, Barbara B. Wille, Alice Goldman, Karen Graham, Beatrice Guthrie, and Ronald Freyberger. They helped to shape this structure, detail by detail, as one would build a house.

Among my colleagues in the Department of Western European Arts, I gratefully acknowledge the encouragement received from John Goldsmith Phillips, Chairman, who acted as coordinator of the catalogue; Clare Le Corbeiller, Assistant Curator, with whom I collaborated in the introduction to the English section; Jessie McNab Dennis, Assistant Curator, for her help in heraldic research in connection with Volume III; and Margit Meyer, who skillfully typed the text.

The volume was edited by Anne MacDougall Preuss. Bibliographic references were checked and the bibliography compiled by Jean Gallatin Crocker and Joan Sumner Ohrstrom.

CARL CHRISTIAN DAUTERMAN

CONTENTS

ORIENTAL PORCELAIN

MEISSEN PORCELAIN

INTRODUCTION

Porcelain-making in Europe may be regarded as having developed in two schools or traditions, exemplified in the Wrightsman Collection by the wares of those two great factories, Meissen and Sèvres. The distinction is a technical one, expressed in the terms "hard-paste" and "soft-paste" porcelain. The ingredients of "hard-paste" porcelain are drawn directly from nature; in "soft-paste" porcelain various materials, some of which may have been previously processed, are combined with an artificial compound: glass. The distinction is also an aesthetic one, for there is a very real difference in the behavior of colors when applied to the differing glaze of each. With Meissen "hard-paste," the colors remain upon the surface of the glaze after firing, but with Sèvres "soft-paste" the colors tend to fuse with the glaze.

Meissen, the leading exponent of "pure" or hard-paste porcelain, was the first European factory to be successful in overcoming a monopoly enjoyed by Oriental potters for half a millennium or more. From the late sixteenth century until the beginning of the eighteenth, European porcelain experiments had produced only various types of soft-paste or artificial porcelains. At the instigation of his advisor Ehrenfried Walther von Tschirnhaus (1651–1708), Frederick Augustus, Elector of Saxony and King of Poland (1670–1733), established an experimental laboratory on the left bank of the Elbe at Dresden, not far from the royal palace.

Augustus, known as "the Strong," was an insatiable collector. While he was making the Grand Tour as a young man, the sight of the great art treasures of Europe had given him the desire to emulate his namesake, the first Elector Augustus (reigned 1553–1586), who had accumulated an extensive library and a wealth of cabinet objects to supplement the princely silver treasury he had inherited. The collection had been well preserved by succeeding electors, so that the second Augustus came into possession of numerous paintings, prints, jewels, arms and armor, curios, and objects of art, the whole comprising a *Kunstkammer*, or "private collection," in the best royal tradition of its day.

But his ruling passion was for Oriental porcelain, and his extravagance in these purchases—he spent 100,000 talers on this collection during the first year of his reign—led Tschirnhaus to pun wryly "China has become the bleeding-bowl of Saxony." Tschirnhaus was a mercantilist, who was convinced that salvation for Saxony lay in exploiting the natural resources of that area. As a result, a variety of products, including faïence, glass, and carved agate, issued from the workshop at Dresden. This was also the place where the Elector's alchemist, Johann Friedrich Böttger (1682–1719), conducted his gold-making experiments. Under the pretext of employing him, Augustus kept the youthful Böttger in close custody. In the mind of the Elector, dreams of gold were apparently uppermost; but for the more hard-headed

Tschirnhaus, aware of the immense volume of Oriental porcelain pouring into Europe, the prospect of cornering this lucrative and limitless market was even more promising.

After enormous amounts had been spent on attempts to make gold, the Elector's advisor and alchemist pooled their talents in the direction of making porcelain, which in the eighteenth century acquired the sobriquet of "white gold." As a chemist and physicist, Count von Tschirnhaus had interested himself in experimenting with glass. His efforts to combine glass with gold and other metals were in part directed toward the simulation of gemstones, and this interest very likely contributed to the production in 1707, with Böttger, of red stoneware of such hardness and compact texture that it possessed qualities close to those of jasper, permitting it to be cut and polished by a lapidary. This success so pleased Augustus that he provided a factory in the Venusbastei in Dresden (used until 1710) and arranged to increase the funds available for the pursuance of experiments toward porcelain. Tschirnhaus, however, is reported to have begun experiments involving kaolin as early as 1675, evidently in the realization that this was an essential material, since it retained its whiteness after being fired at high temperatures. Knowledge of this fact was indeed fundamental to the Chinese secret, which was not made known to the European world until 1712 in the letters of the Jesuit missionary Père d'Entrecolles.

Apparently the two collaborators shared the conviction that the principle behind true porcelain lay in the ability to combine a fusible mineral substance with a non-fusible one. Böttger found the answer in using alabaster as a flux, in combination with a non-fusible white-burning clay from Colditz. The basic formula for the paste, however, did not become commercially practicable until 1713, when a kaolin or *weisse Erde* from Aue was substituted for the Colditz clay.

The enormous prestige of finding an equivalent for Chinese porcelain by means of independent invention thus came to Saxony through the acumen of Tschirnhaus and the assiduity of Böttger. Although Tschirnhaus barely lived to see it, the great dream eventually materialized. Böttger's notebooks show that on January 15, 1708, he actually achieved his first success. It must have been Tschirnhaus, however, who was the first to announce to the Elector that the experiments promised success, for in July 1708 he was appointed privy councilor and director, probably as a reward for his participation in this project. But we know that on March 20, 1709, Böttger made the momentous announcement to Augustus that he knew "how to make the good white porcelain with the finest glaze and all suitable painting to such perfection that it equals, if not surpasses, the East Indian."[1] His boast that his new porcelain displayed the "finest glaze and all suitable painting" must be taken as a reference to his use of unfired lacquer, as he had difficulty mastering ceramic colors comparable to those of the Chinese, either in the form of underglaze blue or of overglaze enamels.

The interval between recording the first true porcelain in January 1708 and the announcement to Augustus in March 1709 had doubtless been spent in experimenting with glazes and colored decoration. Böttger kept voluminous notes on the materials and formulas for the body and glazes used in these

1. Schnorr von Carolsfeld, *Porzellan der europäischen Fabriken*, pp. 59–60.

experiments. The exact share played by each partner is hard to document: because of Tschirnhaus's death, and since all of the detailed notes of work undertaken in this interval are in Böttger's hand,[2] he is often given credit for the major contribution; on the other hand, Tschirnhaus in his earlier experiments, had made much use of burning glasses and prisms to concentrate the heat of the sun in testing the fusibility of various days and stones. The long exposure required for the porcelain paste to "fix" could, however, be provided only by a kiln, and it was apparently Böttger's knowledge of kiln construction that helped to bring his noble partner's theories to fruition. The consideration that Tschirnhaus carried the news of the first success to the Elector is really only an indication of his superior rank at court.

Augustus released a public announcement on January 23, 1710, stating his intention to establish a porcelain-making enterprise that would use the natural resources of the realm for the general prosperity. His statement, printed in four languages, was posted on the doors of all the churches in Saxony.[3] On June 2, 1710, operations were started at the Albrechtsburg Castle, about a dozen miles from Dresden at Meissen. He also dispatched a letter to various European courts, announcing enthusiastically:

> We are assured of being able to make a porcelain that for its transparency and its other qualities will be able to rival that of the East Indies, and we have every reason to think that in handling this white material judiciously we shall be able to surpass it, not only in beauty and quality but also in the diversity of forms and in the fabrication of large, massive pieces such as statues, columns, services. . . .[4]

In what was doubtless a combination of extraordinary enthusiasm for porcelain and a desire for commercial exploitation, Augustus conceived of a huge display that would demonstrate the success of the Meissen enterprise. Therefore he provided not merely a gallery but another palace as the most fitting home for his porcelain. In 1717, he acquired an impressive building in Dresden-Neustadt, on the right bank of the Elbe. Built by Matthias Daniel Pöppelmann (1662–1736) for Count Flemming and called the Dutch Palace because first tenanted by the Dutch envoy, it was remodeled for its new purpose and somewhat more appropriately renamed the Japanese Palace. Here the Elector mounted a great exhibition of what were then modern porcelains, eventually exceeding 35,000 examples, with installations reaching from floor to ceiling. His vast collection of Chinese and Japanese imports was disposed according to color on the ground floor, and the fruits of the Albrechtsburg were similarly grouped on the floor above. The plans included a throne room and a chapel, each to feature decorative elements of porcelain, and the latter to have life-size figures of the Apostles and an organ with porcelain pipes. A central gallery was reserved for over-sized vases, large animal figures, and birds.

A working relationship existed between this palatial repository and the factory, in that Oriental porcelains from the former were transferred to Meissen, about a dozen miles away, to serve as models.

2. Ducret, *Germain Porcelain*, p. 12.

3. Ducret, *op. cit.*, p. 13.

4. Rüdt de Collenberg, *La Porcelaine en Europe*, p. 6.

An order from the Elector directing such a removal during November and December of 1729 still survives. (It may well be that one purpose of the so-called Johanneum inventory numbers—see under Catalogue Nos. 2 A and B—the earliest of which seem to date from 1721, was to make the bookkeeping of such transactions easier.) That Augustus took an active role at this period in furnishing the Japanese Palace is revealed by the official Meissen records.[5]

Our picture of the Japanese Palace remains shadowy, since we are left without adequate visual records of what was undoubtedly the greatest porcelain extravaganza of the eighteenth century. At the time of the Elector's death in 1733, the installation was still unfinished, and his ambitious dreams for it died with him. Augustus III shared few of the interests or enthusiasms of his father, and under his successor the collection was dismantled and packed away in storage in 1775.[6]

Despite the vicissitudes of almost 250 years, including the severe bombing of 1945, the visitor to Dresden today can still find the Royal Saxon Collection immensely rich and varied. Its several categories are divided, different buildings housing, respectively, early paintings, later paintings, prints, objects of decorative art (at the Grünes Gewölbe), and numismatics. The Japanese Palace still stands—it was gutted during World War II—but the porcelain collections are today displayed in the Zwinger, another storybook palace, designed by Pöppelmann to include grottoes, fountains, and garden walks surrounded by high walls, which has now been effectively restored.

THE WRIGHTSMAN Collection is particularly rich in the wares of the early years of Meissen, especially the second quarter of the eighteenth century, when materials and techniques only recently mastered were still being used daringly and imaginatively. The collection avoids the later products, which too often are characterized by a mechanical perfection born of the potters' established confidence in their technique and of Meissen's success in the market.

Meissen porcelain presented Western European man with an entirely new substance in which to express his artistic creativity. The unpredictability of the material lent excitement to his efforts as well as glamour and prestige to his success. The Meissen works in this collection give rich evidence of the achievement of the early artists. Although Meissen porcelain was influenced during the earliest period of the manufactory by the forms and decoration of Oriental prototypes, the Meissen decorators and technicians lost little time in going beyond imitation. They even managed to surpass their Eastern contemporaries in some technical respects, as in the elaborate use of gilding and of purple lustre, the latter previously untried on porcelain (in this collection see Catalogue Nos. 49 A and B, 50, and 51).

IN THE century before the advent of Meissen, European artists had often displayed their fascination with parrots and other exotic birds, using a variety of media. Notable examples are found in the engrav-

---

5. Sponsel, *Kabinettstücke der Meissner Porzellan Manufaktur von Johann Joachim Kändler*, pp. 37–38.
6. Schmidt, *Porcelain as an Art and a Mirror of Fashion*, p. 60.

[6]

ings of Nicolas Robert (1640–1685), the paintings of Adam Pynaker (1622–1673), the chased designs on Restoration silver, and among Indian embroideries made for the European market. Meissen went beyond all these with a combination of qualities that porcelain alone could provide: pronounced plastic versatility, brilliant coloration against a foil of jade-like white, and a glistening envelope of clear glaze to augment the sense of vitality and tension.

The bird sculptures of Meissen rank among the most striking achievement of the porcelain ceramist's art, and the Wrightsman examples take second place to none. Meissen birds show scant indebtedness to Oriental sources even though they were antedated by Chinese and Japanese birds in porcelain. One usual difference is that Meissen parrots rest on tree-stump bases, Chinese parrots on stylized rockwork. In this catalogue a single allusion to an Oriental prototype exists: the pair of white eagles (Catalogue Nos. 1 A and B).

In a manner peculiar to Meissen, the birds reflect the Elector's interest in natural history. While Augustus enjoyed the hunt, his interest in birds and animals went far deeper; the porcelains of his factory featured the wild creatures, not their hunters. Natural history was a popular topic of discussion at his court, and by no means revolved solely around the stuffed specimens in his *Kunstkammer*. At his hunting lodge, the Moritzburg, near Dresden, the Elector kept a menagerie and an aviary, stocked in part through an African expedition he financed during the years 1730–1733.

The report of the Elector's commission dated December 17, 1731, mentions that the first figures of birds and animals for the Japanese Palace were then in a favorable state of progress. Among them were nine parrots, "well-fired pieces, white," and five parrots in enamel colors. Gröger[7] tells that in June of 1734 the model master Johann Joachim Kaendler (working 1731–1775) was to be found at the Moritzburg, translating with either pencil or wax his impressions of several species of birds, including the cockatoos represented by Catalogue Nos. 7 A and B, and 8.

One can readily picture the Meissen sculptors Kaendler, Kirchner, and Ehder on their visits to the Elector's zoological gardens, sketching from life the wide variety of birds they would transmute into glistening porcelain. An insight into the number of birds produced may be gained by an order from Augustus dated Warsaw, April 2, 1732, requesting that "214 animals of all kinds, large and small, and 218 porcelain birds of all kinds in various sizes," be supplied for the New Front Gallery of the Japanese Palace. It is recorded that most of these were completed and delivered,[8] although not before Augustus's death in the following year.

Among the modelers of birds and other figures Kaendler was the most prolific. As *Modellmeister* from 1733 onward, he was in charge of all plastic design, which encompassed not only figures and groups, but also the shapes and relief decoration of utilitarian wares. Production of life-size birds, however, antedated Kaendler's arrival. Several models are known: a parrot roughly the size and type of Catalogue No. 18 (though posed in the manner of Catalogue Nos. 22 B and 28); an ostrich; and a bird

7. Gröger, *Johann Joachim Kaendler*, p. 33.
8. Schmidt, *op. cit.*, p. 278.

of an unnamed and perhaps imaginary species. These figures are believed to have derived from Oriental models; but, unlike Oriental porcelain birds, they are white and gold. Other early models are decorated in a variety of colors, among them a long-tailed bird perched upon rockery and some peacocks in standing and squatting poses. All of these are described and illustrated in Albiker, *Die Meissner Porzellantiere*, 1935, nos. 240–243, 245.

Of the seventy bird figures included in this collection, the majority represent tropical species, mainly parrots, which were especially favored by the factory. Their native habitat ranges from Africa to India and the Americas. South America is represented by species from various countries, including Venezuela, Ecuador, Peru, Bolivia, Paraguay, and Argentina. Most of the species are identifiable through the researches of Albiker, and with the help of Jean Delacour and Charles E. O'Brien of the American Museum of Natural History, New York, the list of identifiable species was extended. Nature was sometimes charmingly modified by the Meissen enamelers when they departed from the colors observed in the aviary to create combinations with original decorative qualities. Thus the pair of African gray parrots, Catalogue Nos. 21 A and B (the species as it occurs in nature), may be compared with its many color variations, all from a single pair of molds. These include a blue-headed parrot (Catalogue No. 24); one with barred wings (Catalogue No. 25); another with piebald head (Catalogue No. 27); ones in yellow-green (Catalogue Nos. 22 A and B); one in gray and black (Catalogue No. 26); and a type with an imbricated pattern (Catalogue Nos. 23 A and B). The repeated use of a basic model was highly efficient, as the preparation of each new and often complicated mold was a costly undertaking.

Complementing the tropical birds, actual and fanciful, are numerous examples of European ones, lending a remarkable diversity to the collection. Among them are models only infrequently seen, such as thrushes, hoopoes, kingfishers, herring gulls, bitterns, and mallard ducks. Swans also are represented in a range of sizes and poses, including miniature figures and others exquisitely mounted as candelabra in Louis XV gilt bronze (Catalogue Nos. 9 A and B, 33–38).

Among figures reported in 1731 as "formed and finished in raw paste" were three eagles almost certainly corresponding to the model of Catalogue Nos. 1 A and B. Large pieces were left "in the white" at this time because it was feared that the additional firing required by the coloring might be destructive. There was another distinction based on size: the larger pieces, requiring thicker walls, had to be made of clay of a special formula, to withstand the tendency toward fissuring during the firing that was increased by the greater mass and weight.

Rückert, in his comprehensive catalogue, *Meissener Porzellan 1710–1810*, of an exhibition held in Munich in 1966, mentions the installation of new ovens, double the former size, in 1732. This improvement made it possible to accommodate objects considerably larger than the above-mentioned eagles, such as goats more than two feet long or peacocks almost four feet high. It also made possible the expanded production of smaller "bread-and-butter" articles.

The 1735 report[9] on the status of the Japanese Palace collection provides a detailed account of the

9. Berling, *Das Meissner Porzellan und seine Geschichte*, II, p. 184.

[8]

kinds of birds and animals still in current production. From this source it is evident that eagles were among them. Seven were described as "completed," as also were sixteen small swans, "finished but not ordered." The latter reference deserves special attention as evidence that small swan sculptures were made in advance of the famous Swan Service (1739–1741), to which the earliest swans have sometimes been attributed.

Not much is discoverable about the earliest prices charged for Meissen birds. Perhaps the largest sculptures were not meant to be sold at all, but rather to be used as showpieces at the Japanese Palace. In the Commission's report for 1734,[10] however, figures that may be prices—although they may also be factory costs—are given opposite the listings. The following list, excerpted from the report, refers only to those species represented in the Wrightsman Collection:

6 Eagles	[at] 136 [Talers][11]
6 Parrots	" 14
5 Cockatoos	" 24
3 Parakeets	" 8¼
13 Birds of Paradise	" 4⅓
14 Magpies	" 11¼
6 Yellow birds [Orioles]	" 6

Little information has been made available concerning the sales prices of birds appearing during the important thirty years from 1735 to 1765. A most informative list exists for the latter year, however, as published by Berling;[12] it refers to a number of the species represented in this catalogue. By 1765 most of these models had been in production for a decade or two, and in consequence there may have been some adjustment of the prices at which they were originally offered. The following representative examples will help to indicate the range:

Miniature swans, cockatoos, and parrots	12 Groschen	
Small eagles and medium-sized swans	1 Taler	
Small swans	2 "	
Canaries	2 "	12 Groschen
Guinea hens and small parrots	4 "	
Large cockatoos	8 "	
Small eagles	12 "	
Ducks	18 "	
Jays and large parrots	30 "	

10. Sponsel, *op. cit.*, pp. 56 ff.

11. The Saxon taler was equal in 1753 to approximately one gram of fine gold (Sedillot, *Toutes les Monnaies du Monde: Dictionnaire des Changes*, pp. 166, 189).

12. Berling, *op. cit.*, p. 199. Berling has also published some undated bookkeeping sheets illustrating that there were two scales of prices: one for commercial buyers (*Kauff Leuthe*), and one for private individuals (*Particulier*).

That porcelain was indeed a luxury commodity can be seen by comparing these prices with the salaries paid to workers at the factory. The Meissen personnel record for April 1731 reveals that flower painters received only four to five talers, and figure painters about nine to thirteen talers, per month.

On the death of the Elector, February 1, 1733, hundreds of porcelains were still in preparation for his Japanese Palace. His impatience with the progress, and his ambitious planning, are from time to time revealed in the factory archives. For example, on February 25, 1732, he ordered various large vases, large animals, tureens, and dishes (Kaendler often objected to his fondness for large porcelains as threatening to force the material beyond its natural capacity). These were supplemented six weeks later by his order from Warsaw, previously mentioned, for some 432 birds and animals of all sizes and kinds. Augustus, sharing the baroque abhorrence of a spatial vacuum, was apparently determined to fill every nook and corner, and every wall from floor to ceiling.

ORNAMENTAL pieces other than birds in the Wrightsman Collection are relatively few but significant. It is with vessels of this nature that the careful observer may best become aware of some of the subtle distinctions between Meissen porcelain and its Oriental counterpart. The first of these is the color of the material itself. The German ware is usually whiter, because of its higher kaolin content, and for the same reason it is also somewhat harder. The colors used in its decoration are not so varied or sparkling, partly because of differences in the technique of their application, and partly because of their composition.

The Meissen decorator had only two methods of applying color decoration: under the glaze, or over the glaze. For the former, color applied directly to the once-fired ware or *biscuit*, he was limited to cobalt blue, because no other color would survive the intense heat of the second firing. For color over the glaze, he used a small palette of enamel colors before subjecting the porcelain to a third firing, which fixed the glaze and decoration.

The Chinese, on the other hand, could control both cobalt blue and copper red under the glaze, because the paste, less rich in kaolin, required less intense heat to give it permanence. They painted these colors on air-dried but unfired clay. Secondly, they had at their command a variety of colored glazes for painting upon the previously fired ware (*émail sur biscuit*). Third, like the Meissen artists, they used enamel colors for decorating over the glaze. Some of their enamels, in addition to being more brilliant, were rather thick and impasto-like, therefore having more tactile quality than Meissen, with its flat and scaly brush strokes. Yet the first true porcelain of Europe scored a great success despite its technical limitations in capturing the essential forms, colors, and decorative motifs not only of the Chinese, but also of the Japanese.

In the early ornamental pieces there was much borrowing from Far Eastern sources. Evidence is to be seen, for example, in the shape and decoration of the two bowls Catalogue Nos. 45 A and B, of Japanese Kakiemon derivation, or in the slender beaker forms of Catalogue Nos. 47 A and B, and 48 A and B, after Chinese K'ang Hsi models. Beginning about 1720, there issued from the Albrechtsburg a wide range of

"Kakiemon" vessels, including hexagonal jars, bowls, and vases. It is curious that the influence of Japanese designs during the formative years of Meissen should fall within the period 1683–1759, when Japan's ports were virtually closed to European traders. The Dutch, however, did have some access to the ports, and they provided the channel for a small flow of Japanese porcelain. Augustus the Strong's enterprise as a collector assured a good representation of Kakiemon porcelain in the Japanese Palace: Soame Jenyns noted[13] about 130 pieces when he saw the Royal Saxon collection in 1936. The delightful sketchy decoration of the Meissen "Kakiemon," including that of the table porcelains (especially Catalogue No. 63), may also represent to some degree the transfer of designs taken at second hand from Chinese imitations of the Japanese, and made expressly for export to Europe.

Literally millions of examples of Chinese porcelain had arrived in Holland before the Meissen factory came into existence. These were collected widely throughout northern Europe, and Augustus II's passion for them is well known. Thus, the preponderant influence upon Meissen was Chinese, especially in a number of vases ambitiously reflecting *famille verte* shapes and decoration of the K'ang Hsi period. Not that absolute literalness was always the rule. For example, a distinction frequently observed between the original and the adaptation is that, among covered vases, the K'ang Hsi example will show the neck fully glazed on the interior, and a ring of glaze on the underside of the overhanging flange of the cover; the Meissen example, conversely, tends to be without glaze just inside the lip, on the entire underside of the flange, and on the insetting rim of the cover.

Similarly, more Chinese than Japanese porcelain is to be found today with mounts of costly bronze, gilded and chased (see Introduction to Oriental porcelain, pp. 375 ff.). The prestige of such mounts was at times extended to both the Chinese- and Japanese-inspired vases of Meissen. In addition to examples listed above, the tureens Catalogue Nos. 61 A and B, the deep plant pots Catalogue Nos. 55 A and B, and the thoroughly westernized pair of vases Catalogue Nos. 52 A and B may be noted. In the last, the use of pictorial reserves within a solid field is an echo of a Chinese practice.

Finally, it must be admitted that no very sharp distinction between Chinese and Japanese porcelains was insisted upon by Europeans in the eighteenth century. Thus, decorative motifs as well as the shapes of vessels were modified and combined in a way that became more identifiable with Meissen than with either foreign source. The "Kakiemon style," so called, affords the best illustration. Popular from about 1730, it has few immediate Japanese prototypes. The arrangement of the decorative elements so that they float freely without background or horizon line and the peculiar "shorthand" method of representation are more suggestive than literal. The most characteristic "Kakiemon" motif is a fantastic winged animal: the shape of its back and tail belong to the Chinese *ch'i-lin*, the head and feet to some species of dog, the wings to a dragon, and the stripes to a tiger. The swooping bird, possibly a crane or heron, resembles Kakiemon birds, but again it is not a literal copy; the same may be said of the floral decoration.

13. Jenyns, *Japanese Porcelain*, pp. 153–154.

EARLY MEISSEN encouraged an enormous increase in the number of vessels designed for specialized purposes. The very novelty of porcelain as a European medium stimulated the desire to experiment with forms entirely new, to take their place beside silver in an ever-expanding pattern of courtly living. At times there was some borrowing from the more established field, as evidenced in the shapes of teapots, tureens, and snuffboxes. Yet the versatility of porcelain soon made available, and on a vastly grander scale, an expanded repertory of luxury objects. Silver, in the main, suffered from the disadvantage of remaining a custom-made commodity, each piece being fashioned slowly and laboriously as an individual creation. Table porcelain, on the other hand, though not for the common man, was almost immediately channeled into volume production of some diversification. Evidence for this is the Meissen price list of 1731, which itemized close to four hundred kinds of objects.[14]

Before the end of its first twenty-five years, the Meissen manufactory had agents in Paris, Amsterdam, Warsaw, and thirty-two German cities. Within this same period the products of the factory had traveled to Sweden, Denmark, and Russia in the form of munificent gifts presented by Augustus, and there are records of extensive trade, as with the Greek dealer Manasses Athanas, whose orders included one for 36,000 coffee cups for the Turkish market. Such instances could only have led to ever more efficient ways of turning out useful wares.

The growing popularity of porcelain engendered especially the expansion of large and varied services, whether for dining, for the dressing table, or for the newly fashionable beverages tea, coffee, and chocolate. Obviously, the greatest volume consisted of objects to be used at table. Long before mid-century, there was a porcelain dish or vessel for almost every conceivable refinement in the art of dining. The huge Swan Service made between 1737 and 1741 for the administrator of the factory, Count Brühl, estimated to consist of almost two thousand pieces, was created with such fertility of imagination that the design of only one item—a figural candlestick after a project for silver by Juste-Aurèle Meissonnier (about 1693–1750)—has ever been traced to a source in any other medium. This service for one hundred diners included, in addition to plates and platters of several sizes and types, an assortment of vegetable dishes, tureens, sauce boats, stemmed cups for oranges, and even a monteith. Wall sconces and fountains of matching design were also a part of the order. While the service was in preparation, the count ordered other specialized equipment for his table, the most remarkable being a great centerpiece. This consisted of a cartouche-shaped stand supporting a fruit bowl and four dishes for sweetmeats, around which were placed spice boxes and four pairs of vessels for vinegar, olive oil, and mustard, modeled in the form of grinning Orientals, some astride grotesque birds. Thus porcelain design, which at its inception had depended somewhat upon silver for its ideas, assumed the initiative before the end of the 1730s.

Again, because porcelain could be produced more quickly and inexpensively than silver, it could more readily cater to the changing whims and foibles of courtly life. More than any other medium, porcelain had the capacity to express, through form and color, the frivolity, the sheer joy of life, that

14. Rakebrand, *Meissner Tafelgeschirre des 18. Jahrhunderts*, p. 6.

was the chief reason for being of the rococo. Witness the imaginative production of "toys" in porcelain: cane handles, scent bottles, needle cases, sometimes modeled in bizarre fashion, or exquisite snuff boxes painted with miniatures, like those described in Volume III of this catalogue.

The essential contribution of Meissen—its inexhaustible inventiveness—may be summed up in terms of a characteristic item: the teacup. The early eighteenth century had known cups of silver, although they were doubtless never very numerous; some, like those in the amazing service by Dinglinger at the Grünes Gewölbe, were decorated with enamel, and were practically unavailable except to the royal family. But the porcelain cup made at Meissen was, next to the imported Oriental one, the most appropriate answer to the need for a suitable vessel in which to enjoy the exotic beverage. In the charm of the teacup's gilded or multicolored decoration, in its capacity to retain the heat of the liquid, in its variety of shape, in the absence or presence of handles (one or sometimes two), it expressed endless improvisation. It was soon supplemented by other cups designed for coffee and chocolate, each with its own capacity for variety of form and decoration. It may fairly be said of the porcelain cup that its combination of fragility with strength was symbolic of an emergent technological society; and it may further be noted that the symbolism, as well as the porcelain cup itself, has not become outmoded even in our day of plastics.

CARL CHRISTIAN DAUTERMAN

1 A, B Pair of Eagles

(Adler)

1 A: H. 22⅜ (56.9); W. 8⅜ (21.3); D. 11⅛ (28.3).

1 B: H. 22 (55.9); W. 8½ (21.6); D. 10 (25.5).

EACH bird with wings furled and tail lowered is perched rigidly erect upon a flat-topped rock of irregular shape and roughly indented sides. The head is slightly turned and inclined, the beak wide open. In three-quarter view, the shoulders of the wings break the profile sharply. One toe of each foot overlaps its counterpart on the other foot, and the talons curl over the edges of the perch. The modeling is crisp and stylized, especially on the head and neck, where the feathers taper sharply, and on the under parts, where they are represented as rounded imbrications; the wings are similarly treated.

The bird is white, except for patches of brown at the sides of the head, surrounding the deep-set eyes, which have brownish-black pupils and are ringed with pale coral. Traces of streaked and mottled brown also occur upon the legs and the rocky base. All of these areas are colored in lacquer, which flakes off readily.

Each plinth, about six inches high, consists of a rough outer wall and an inner core. The latter resembles a cylindrical flower pot, fitting tightly within the base; it has a flat bottom with a large, roughly oval opening, from which broad fissures radiate to the outer edge. A thick white glaze has accumulated on the underside around the outer edges. Within the upper half of each cylinder are six triangular ribs, arranged radially, which help to support the weight of the bird. The entire interior of the base presents a brownish biscuit surface.

No. 1 A is marked on the unglazed underside of the core with crossed swords painted in black:

[15]

This unconventional mark is probably not complete. No. 1 B is marked on the underside of the core with straight crossed swords painted in deep green:

Models created in 1731, attributed to Johann Gottlob Kirchner (during his second period of employment at Meissen, 1730–1733).

REFERENCES: Connolly, *Art News*, Christmas edition 1957, p. 116 (illustrated).

Formerly in the collection of Lord Hastings, Melton Constable, Norfolk.

There can be little question that the marks were added some time after Nos. 1 A and B had left the Meissen studio.

The species is an eagle or gyrfalcon of uncertain classification, probably an idealized creation of the type seen in Oriental paintings. Dating among the earliest of the life-size sculptures attempted at Meissen, many of which were left in the white, these birds were decorated with unfired colors, most of which have worn off or been removed.

The model was recorded at the Dresden Schloss (Albiker, *Die Meissner Porzellantiere im 18. Jahrhundert*, 1935, nos. 258, 260, pl. LXIII; 1959, fig. 23), and the Staatliche Porzellansammlung, Dresden (*ibid.*, 1935, no. 259, pl. LXIII), at the latter in an entirely white version. During a visit to that collection in 1962, the writer saw a white eagle with unglazed buff-colored under parts.

Comparable examples, with variations in the coloring, were in the collections of F. Mannheimer, Amsterdam (sold at F. Muller, Amsterdam, October 14–15, 1952, lot 269 [illustrated in catalogue], and also illustrated in *Connaissance des Arts*, December 15, 1952, p. 65); Mrs. Basil Ionides, Buxted Park (sold at Sotheby's, London, July 2, 1963, lot 58 [illustrated in catalogue]). A

[16]

single eagle was illustrated as the frontispiece of the catalogue for the Coronation Exhibition, 1953, held by the Antique Porcelain Company, London.

According to Albiker (*op. cit.*, 1935, p. 108), the eagle molds were numbered 1 and 2. A further explanation of these mold numbers, which are of the greatest importance in dating Meissen groups, is given by Rückert in his catalogue of an exhibition in 1966 at the Bayerisches Nationalmuseum (*Meissener Porzellan 1710–1810*, pp. 40–42): in 1749 Christian Heinrich Kaendler, assembler and brother of the sculptor Johann Joachim Kaendler, was commissioned to inventory and number the existing molds in the factory. These he attempted to arrange chronologically, beginning with number 1 for the first mold made in 1731 and ending with 1090 for a mold made in December 1748.

The Oriental prototypes from which Nos. 1 A and B derive have been variously identified as Chinese and Japanese. Albiker (*op. cit.*, p. 124) describes the birds as copies after an unknown Chinese model. A somewhat similar pair of polychromed and gilded eagles formerly in the Ionides Collection was reproduced in color by Reinaecker in *Country Life Annual*, 1956, p. 55, among "Fantasies of Chinese Ceramic Art," but when sold six years later at Sotheby's (see above), they were called "Japanese, 17th Century." A pair of Oriental eagles at Waddesdon Manor, Buckinghamshire, is classified as "Chinese, c. 1700." One of these, with closed beak, is illustrated in Eriksen, *Waddesdon Manor, The James A. de Rothschild Bequest to the National Trust*, p. 64. The Waddesdon examples are 21⅛ and 22 inches in height, and therefore close in size to Nos. 1 A and B, as are also the Ionides eagles. The likelihood of Japanese rather than Chinese provenance for the prototype of Nos. 1 A and B seems the stronger of the two possibilities.

A pair of comparable Oriental eagles from the collection of Louis-Jean Gaignat (1697–1768), secretary to the king and Receveur des Consignations, was sold by Pierre Rémy, Paris, February 14–22, 1769, lot 120. Gabriel de Saint-Aubin sketched four views of these eagles, which were

modeled in two different poses, in the margins of his catalogue of that sale (see below). They appear on p. 70, in the section devoted to Chinese and Japanese porcelains. The whole was reproduced in 1921 under the title *Catalogues des Ventes et Livrets de Salons Illustrés par Gabriel de Saint-Aubin*, XI, with a foreword by Émile Dacier. The drawings show two views of an eagle in the pose of Nos. 1 A and B, in which the shading suggests pigmented markings. The description reads:

> Deux beaux Aigles de grandeur naturelle, fond gris panaché de brun, sur leur troncs; les pieds sont de bois doré.
> L'un des deux est admirable par sa fierté & le fini de son plumage.

Facsimile of page 70 of the Gaignat sale catalogue from Catalogue des Ventes et Livrets de Salons Illustrés par Gabriel de Saint-Aubin. The Metropolitan Museum of Art Library

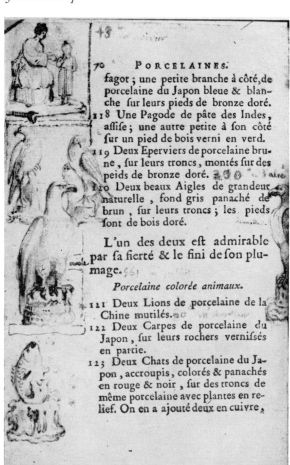

2 A, B Pair of Birds of Paradise

(Paradiesvögel)

2 A: H. 12 (30.5); W. 4¼ (10.8); D. 3¼ (8.3).

2 B: H. 12⁹⁄₁₆ (31.8); W. 4¼ (10.8); D. 3⅜ (8.6).

EACH bird, with one wing sharply upraised and its black beak wide open, is perched on a tall slender tree stump. The plumage is brilliantly painted with orange-red on the primaries, turquoise-blue on the upper parts, yellow-green on the breast, and maize-yellow on the under parts. There are conspicuous fanlike puce tufts under the wings, and the tail has extraordinary quill appendages, longer than the bird's body and terminating in violet whorls. The white tree stumps are enlivened with leafy green branches and tufts of mottled grass.

Each is marked on the unglazed underside of the base in black ink: No 280 over W; on No. 2 B a black dot follows the mark, and crossed swords painted in blue are barely discernible nearby.

Models created in January 1733 by Johann Joachim Kaendler (working 1731–1775).

REFERENCES: Connolly, *Art News*, Christmas edition 1957, p. 116 (illustrated).

Formerly in the Royal Saxon Collection, Dresden (probably), and that of Armand Esders, Paris.

The marks on these birds appear to be inventory marks identifying the porcelains as having belonged to the Royal Saxon Collection, Dresden. However, they differ from the earliest of the so-called "Johanneum" marks that relate to an inventory begun in 1721: they are painted black, without having first been cut into the porcelain; and they employ the abbreviation "No" in place of the usual "N." Considering that the models for Nos. 2 A and B were not created until 1733, this alternative method of marking may be assumed to represent a later, unrecorded inventory. For a further discussion of Johanneum marks (the name is anachronistic), see note under Nos. 61 A and B.

Although these birds have been called quetzals in other catalogues, they are, in fact, largely fanciful, and were perhaps inspired by the South American birds of paradise.

Comparable birds were formerly in the collection of Ole Olsen, Copenhagen (Schmitz, *Generaldirector Ole Olsens Kunstsamlinger*, II, no. 1359 a, b, pl. XXXI). Others are now in the collection of Irwin Untermyer, New York (Hackenbroch, *Meissen and Other Continental Porcelain in the Irwin Untermyer Collection*, p. 14, fig. 15) and in the Staatliche Porzellansammlung, Dresden (Albiker, *Die Meissner Porzellantiere im 18. Jahrhundert*, 1935, no. 102, pl. XXVII; 1959, fig. 102).

A pair from the Royal Saxon Collection was sold at R. Lepke, Berlin, October 7–8, 1919, lots 115, 116 (illustrated in catalogue, pl. 13); another pair was sold by Ball – Graupe, Berlin, March 15, 1933, lot 49 (illustrated in catalogue, pl. 2).

The Meissen manufactory *Jahrbuch* for January 1733, XIX, p. 51, records under Kaendler's name:

> Another small bird the size of a finch, with 2 large and 2 small wings, a long bill, and the tail consisting of 2 long feathers which develop at the end into a double ring (noch ein kleinen Vogel in Grösse eines Finken, hat Flügel 2 grosse and 2 kleine, einen langen Schnabel, und der Schwanz bestehet in 2 langen Federn, welche sich am Ende in einen doppelten Ring verwandeln).

3 A, B   Pair of Magpies

(Elstern)

3 A: H. 22¼ (56.5); W. 9 (22.9); D. 4¼ (10.8).

3 B: H. 21¼ (54.0); W. 10 (25.4); D. 5⅝ (14.4).

EACH bird, with long tail erect and wide-open beak, is perched in a highly animated pose on a spiral tree stump. The plumage is largely black, relieved with a broad band of white running from the shoulder to the rump, and narrow stripes of white marking the primaries and encircling the eyes. There is a subtle and barely noticeable veining of olive green on the upper wing coverts. The perches are molded with leafless twigs, moss, and tufts of grass; on No. 3 A these are yellow-green and soft turquoise, and on No. 3 B they are left uncolored.

Each is marked at the lower edge of the base with crossed swords painted in blue under the glaze; No. 3 A is marked on the unglazed underside of the base in black ink: IIE; and No. 3 B: No. 281 over W.

Models created in February 1733 by Johann Joachim Kaendler (working 1731–1775).

These birds are representations of the European magpie, *Pica pica*.

The numerical mark suggests that No. 3 B was formerly in the Royal Saxon Collection, Dresden (see under Nos. 2 A and B for an explanation of this type of "Johanneum mark").

A single magpie is in the collection of Ernst Schneider, at the Schloss Jägerhof, Düsseldorf (Rückert, *Meissener Porzellan 1710–1810*, no. 1105, pl. 271). A pair is in the collection of Irwin Untermyer, New York (Hackenbroch, *Meissen and Other Continental Porcelain in the Irwin Untermyer Collection*, p. 5, fig. 4). Others were in the Royal Saxon Collection, now the Staatliche Porzellansammlung, Dresden (Albiker, *Die Meissner Porzellantiere im 18. Jahrhundert*, 1935, nos. 60, 61, pl. XX; 1959, figs. 80, 81).

Some from the Royal Saxon Collection, Dresden, were sold at R. Lepke, Berlin, October 7–8, 1919, lots 103, 104 (illustrated in catalogue, pl. 9). One from an unidentified collection was sold at Ball – Graupe, Berlin, June 28, 1932, lot 146 (illustrated in catalogue, pl. 22). A pair from the collection of Ole Olsen, Copenhagen (Schmitz, *Generaldirektor Ole Olsens Kunstsamlinger*, II, no. 1358 a, b, pl. XXXII), was sold at Winkel-Magnussen's, Copenhagen, May 10, 1948, lot 243 (illustrated in catalogue, p. 39).

An entry in the Meissen manufactory *Jahrbuch* for February 1733 under Kaendler's name appears to refer to this model:

1 Magpie, lifesize (1 Aelster in Lebensgrösse).

4 A,B Pair of Golden Orioles

(Pirole)

4 A: H. 10¼ (26.1); W. 6 (15.3); D. 4 (10.2).

4 B: H. 10¼ (26.1); W. 5¾ (14.7); D. 4½ (11.4).

EACH bird, its head sharply turned toward the tail, its body painted a pale yellow with black wings dappled with the same color, is perched on a gnarled and foliated tree stump of medium height from which spring sprays of yellow-green leaves. The long beak is copper-colored, and the legs are barred with the same color. The pose of each is not identical, for No. 4 B's wings are slightly extended, the right farther than the left, thus displaying more of the yellow underside.

No. 4 B is marked on the unglazed underside of the base with crossed swords painted indistinctly in blue; No. 4 A is unmarked.

Models created in March 1734 by Johann Joachim Kaendler (working 1731–1775).

REFERENCES: Connolly, *Art News*, Christmas edition 1957, p. 117 (4 A illustrated).

The species represented is *Oriolus oriolus*, native to Europe, Asia, and Africa.

Schnorr von Carolsfeld, in *Porzellansammlung Gustav von Klemperer*, p. 211, mentions an earlier model completed in July 1733 by Kaendler. The model was clearly popular, for derivative versions by J. G. Ehder (see No. 14) and P. O. Reinicke are also known.

Comparable golden orioles are recorded in the collections of Ernst Schneider at the Schloss Jäger-hof, Düsseldorf (illustrated in Hackenbroch, *Keramik-Freunde der Schweiz*, April 1960, opp. p. 6); Mr. and Mrs. Lesley G. Shaefer, New York; and the Duke of Windsor, Paris.

Others are recorded by the Staatliche Museen, Berlin (*Verzeichnis der Neuerwerbungen seit 1933*, p. 162, nos. 120, 121, formerly in the Feist Collection). Examples in the Staatliche Porzellansammlung, Dresden, are illustrated in Albiker (*Die Meissner Porzellantiere im 18. Jahrhundert*, 1935, no. 112, pl. XXIX; 1959, figs. 104, 105); and in Handt and Rakebrand, *Meissner Porzellan des Achtzehnten Jahrhunderts, 1710–1750*, pl. 72. The model is also represented at the State Hermitage Museum, Leningrad (*Staryé-Gody*, May 1911, pl. 29).

Still others are recorded in the C. H. Fischer Collection, Dresden, sold at J. M. Heberle, Cologne, October 22–25, 1906, lots 192, 193 (illustrated in catalogue, pl. 5); the Royal Saxon Collection, sold at R. Lepke, Berlin, October 7, 1919, lots 107, 108 (illustrated in catalogue, pl. 12); the Erich von Goldschmidt-Rothschild Collection, Berlin, sold at Ball – Graupe, Berlin, March 23–25, 1931, lot 453 (illustrated in catalogue, pl. 80); and in an anonymous sale at Ball – Graupe, Berlin, June 28, 1932, lot 140 (illustrated in catalogue, pl. 20). One from an unidentified collection was sold at Christie's, London, March 22, 1965, lot 157 (illustrated in catalogue).

The Meissen manufactory *Jahrbuch* contains two references to orioles by Kaendler, cited by Schnorr von Carolsfeld (*op. cit.*, p. 211). For July 1733:

> A bird of moderate size, called an oriole, sitting on a base (einen Vogel von mittelmässiger Grösse, eine Bier Eule genannt, auf einem Postament sitzend).

For March 1734:

> 1 bird of medium size finished, called an oriole (1 Vogel von mittelmässiger Grösse gefertigt, welcher eine Bier Eule genannt wird).

5 Golden Oriole

(Pirol)

H. 10¼ (26.1); W. 5⅜ (13.7); D. 3¾ (9.5).

COMPARABLE to No. 4 A, but differing in minor details. The beak is slightly open, revealing a rippling tongue. The wings, solid black at the shoulder, have elongated C-scrolls in yellow outlining the tips of the principal feathers. The legs are black. Three coral-red cherries and sprigs of small blue blossoms spring from the supporting tree stump.

The bill has been restored and is slightly shorter than in other known examples.

Impressed on the unglazed underside of the base: 6.

Model created in March 1734 by Johann Joachim Kaendler (working 1731–1775).

No. 5 was cast from the same mold as No. 4 A; the base has been modified by hand tooling.

For comparable examples in other collections, see under Nos. 4 A and B.

6 A, B Pair of European Kingfishers

(Eisvögel)

6 A: H. 8⅜ (21.3); W. 5¼ (13.4); D. 3¼ (8.3).

6 B: H. 9 (22.9); W. 5 (12.7); D. 3¼ (8.3).

EACH stub-tailed green bird, with a long black bill, is perched on a base of rockwork. The dappled, grass-green upper parts have two oval patches of pale blue at the center of the back. In the male (No. 6 B), the wing primaries are striped in black, edged in russet-brown, the latter matching the under parts. In the female (No. 6 A) the primaries are green, tipped with black, and the under parts are streaked with chestnut-brown. Bulrushes and tufts of vegetation in turquoise and jade-green spring from the jagged bases.

Unmarked.

Models created in 1735 by Johann Joachim Kaendler (working 1731–1775).

REFERENCES: Connolly, *Art News*, Christmas edition 1957, p. 117 (illustrated).

Formerly in the collection of Baron and Baroness C. G. von Seidlitz, Paris.

Another version, by J. F. Eberlein (working with Kaendler 1735–1749), was executed in 1739. The species depicted is the kingfisher, *Alcedo atthis*.

Another example is in the collection of Ernst Schneider at the Schloss Jägerhof, Düsseldorf. A modern copy, fashioned after the Kaendler original, is recorded at the Schauhalle, Meissen (Albiker, *Die Meissner Porzellantiere im 18. Jahrhundert*, 1935, no. 122, pl. XXXI).

A single kingfisher, varying somewhat in coloration, in the collection of Baron von Born, Budapest, was sold at R. Lepke, Berlin, December 4, 1929, lot 135 (illustrated in catalogue, pl. 7). A comparable example from an unidentified collection was sold at Ball – Graupe, Berlin, June 28, 1932, lot 139 (illustrated in catalogue, pl. 21).

7 A, B   Pair of Cockatoos

(Kakadus)

7 A: H. 7⅝ (19.4); W. 8⅜ (21.3); D. 6⅛ (15.6).

7 B: H. 8¼ (21.0); W. 6¹¹⁄₁₆ (17.0); D. 3⅝ (9.3).

EACH bird, vigorously modeled and boldly colored, with a "war bonnet" crest, is perched on a gnarled tree stump. No. 7 A is posed with unfurled wings, lowered head, and gaze directed downward. No. 7 B is in an alert pose with open beak and closed wings. The vivid crests are green, orange-red, and blue, colors repeated in the wing tips and tails. On No. 7 A the area surrounding the eyes is a pale mottled yellow-green; on No. 7 B it forms a circle of bright orange-red. The legs and claws of both are pale flesh-pink and on No. 7 B are additionally barred in orange. The perch of No. 7 A is encrusted with splotched gray-green and yellow leaves, while No. 7 B has tiny red berries on a branch with pea-green leaves.

Unmarked.

Models created in June 1737 by Johann Friedrich Eberlein (working 1735–1749).

REFERENCES: Connolly, *Art News*, Christmas edition 1957, p. 116 (illustrated).

Formerly in the collection of Catalina von Pannwitz, Hartekamp, the Netherlands.

The model does not appear to represent a known species.

A cockatoo that seems to represent the type of No. 7 B, although described as 35 cm. high and by Kaendler, 1732, is in the collection of Aimé Martinet, Geneva (illustrated in color in Ducret, *German Porcelain and Faience*, no. 9). An example comparable to No. 7 B (one of a pair) is in the collection of Baron Edward de Rothschild, Geneva. A modern cast is recorded at the Schauhalle, Meissen (Albiker, *Die Meissner Porzellantiere im 18. Jahrhundert*, 1935, no. 100, pl. XXVII; 1959, fig. 129 [only one bird illustrated]).

An example comparable to No. 7 B, from the collection of Walter von Pannwitz, Munich, was sold at H. Helbing, Munich, October 24–25, 1905, lot 306 (illustrated in catalogue, pl. LV). A duplicate of No. 7 A, from an unidentified collection, was sold at Ball – Graupe, Berlin, March 15, 1933, lot 58 (illustrated in catalogue). Two examples from the same mold as No. 7 B, with Louis XV gilt-bronze mounts, were sold from the collection of Prince Henckel-Donnersmarsch, Sweden, at Sotheby's, London, May 20, 1958, lot 144 (illustrated in catalogue); they were subsequently sold from the collection of René Fribourg at Sotheby's, June 25, 1963, lot 30 (illustrated in catalogue). Two other examples were sold at Sotheby's, February 24, 1959, lot 138 (illustrated in catalogue). A pair of cockatoos from the Palmer estate was sold at Christie's, London, November 2, 1964, lot 119 (illustrated in catalogue).

These models are not to be confused with a slightly larger version (35 cm. in height), combining the stooping pose of No. 7 A and the closed wings of No. 7 B. That model was created by Kaendler in 1734 and was reissued in 1780. An example of the Kaendler version is at the Rijksmuseum, Amsterdam; a later version is at the Schauhalle, Meissen (Albiker, *op. cit.*, 1935, no. 98, pl. XXVII).

For another example, cast from the same mold as No. 7 B, see No. 8.

8 Cockatoo

(Kakadu)

H. 8½ (21.6); W. 6½ (16.5); D. 3⅝ (9.3).

THE COMPACTLY modeled bird, with open brown beak, is perched on a low stump. Its lowered head bristles with a panache of long feathers enameled orange-red, sky-blue, puce, yellow, and green, matching the wing primaries and the tail; the orange-red is repeated in the eyes. The secondaries and the legs, which are barred, are canary-yellow. The back is yellow delicately streaked in gray, while the under parts are reserved in white. On the base below the supporting branches a sparse cluster of blue-green foliage emerges from a clump of moss.

Unmarked.

Model created in June 1737 by Johann Friedrich Eberlein (working 1735–1749).

REFERENCES: Connolly, *Art News*, Christmas edition 1957, p. 116 (illustrated).

Formerly in the collection of Baron and Baroness C. G. von Seidlitz, Paris.

The model does not appear to represent a known species.

For comparable examples, see under No. 7 B, which was cast from the same mold.

[30]

9 A, B Pair of Miniature Swans, Mounted in Gilt Bronze

(Schwäne)

9 A: (overall) H. 4½ (11.4); W. 3¾ (9.5); D. 3 (7.7).
(porcelain) H. 3⅞ (9.8); W. 3½ (8.9);
D. 2 (5.1).

9 B: (overall) H. 4⅕ (11.4); W. 3¾ (9.5); D. 3 (7.7).
(porcelain) H. 3⅞ (9.8); W. 3½ (8.9);
D. 2⅛ (5.4).

EACH bird, with sharply S-curved neck and a black mask that pales into white behind the head, rests on an oval mound molded with leaf imbrications. The open beak is bordered by a narrow white band of teeth with flat crowns. The legs and feet are lustrous, solid black. Each bird is mounted upon a modern gilt-bronze plinth of rococo design, stamped with the initials JB on the underside.

Each is marked at the lower edge of the base with crossed swords painted in blue under the glaze.

Models possibly created 1737–1741; by Johann Joachim Kaendler (working 1731–1775) or Johann Friedrich Eberlein (working 1735–1749).

The species represented is the mute swan *Cygnus olor*, native to Europe and Asia.

A similar pair of miniature swans from the collection of René Fribourg, New York, was sold at Sotheby's, London, June 25, 1963, lot 14 (illustrated in catalogue).

It seems reasonable to suppose that free-standing swans may have constituted a part of that famous *chef-d'oeuvre* of the Meissen factory, the monumental Swan Service, made for Count Heinrich von Brühl between 1737 and 1741 by Kaendler and Eberlein working in collaboration. Savage (*18th-Century German Porcelain*, fig. 19b) illustrates two models of swans, which he assigns to this great service, one of them corresponding

to No. 34 in this catalogue, later in date than Nos. 9 A and B. Swans adapted for a functional purpose are illustrated by two bonbon dishes formerly at the Berlin Schloss (illustrated in Albiker, *Die Meissner Porzellantiere im 18. Jahrhundert*, 1935, nos. 271, 272, pl. LXVIII; 1959, figs. 228, 229). These were modeled in the full round with little concession to their function as containers. A matching swan-shaped sauceboat by Eberlein, in the collection of Ernst Schneider at Schloss Jägerhof, Düsseldorf (Rückert, *Meissener Porzellan 1710–1810*, no. 514, pl. 129), is generally considered to have been made for Count Brühl's service. The same swan motif appears in a vigorously modeled sugar caster and a teapot in the Untermyer Collection, New York (see Hackenbroch, *Meissen and Other Continental Porcelain in the Irwin Untermyer Collection*, p. 142, fig. 132, and p. 157, fig. 148, where they are also assigned to the Swan Service).

It is generally accepted that every one of the 2,200 pieces made for the Swan Service bore the von Brühl arms, yet none of the above-mentioned objects carries them. It may be conceded, however, that it would have been impractical to paint arms on objects having such uneven bases.

At any event, the forceful modeling of Nos. 9 A and B is stylistically close to that of the examples mentioned as associated with the Swan Service (compare the more suavely modeled swans Nos. 33 A and B, dating from 1747). Therefore, a date of about 1737–1741 is tentatively assigned to this pair of miniature swans.

10 A, B   Pair of Jays

(Eichelhäher)

10 A: H. 15⅜ (39.1); W. 10 (25.4); D. 8½ (21.6).

10 B: H. 17 (43.2); W. 10⅜ (26.4); D. 8¾ (22.3).

EACH vigorously modeled bird, with lowered head and open beak, is perched on a stout tree stump. The male (No. 10 A) has a speckled buff crown grading into streaks of pale blue and then into brown pencilings on the neck. The wings are cobalt-blue at the shoulder, the primaries black and white, and the back powder-blue. The blue wing coverts are barred in black and white. The rump is brown and white, and the tail black. The female (No. 10 B) has finer markings on the crown; the back is a grayer blue, and the effect of the wing colors is one of less contrast. The base of each has patches of vegetation including oak leaves and acorns. On No. 10 A there is a large red squirrel with a plumed tail; on No. 10 B caterpillars and a large brown beetle enliven the composition.

No. 10 A is marked on the unglazed underside of the base with crossed swords painted indistinctly in blue, and impressed: 26; No. 10 B is unmarked.

Models created in October 1739 by Johann Joachim Kaendler (working 1731–1775).

REFERENCES: Connolly, *Art News*, Christmas edition 1957, p. 117 (illustrated).

Formerly in the collections of J. Pierpont Morgan, London; Baron and Baroness C. G. von Seidlitz, Paris.

The species represented is *Garrulus glandarius*.

Comparable jays are in the collections of Ernst Schneider at Schloss Jägerhof, Düsseldorf, and of Irwin Untermyer, New York (Hackenbroch, *Meissen and Other Continental Porcelain in the Irwin Untermyer Collection*, p. 4, fig. 3). Others are in the Bayerisches Nationalmuseum, Munich (Hofmann, *Das Europäische Porzellan des Bayerischen*

[34]

Nationalmuseums, nos. 223, 224; see also Albiker, *Die Meissner Porzellantiere im 18. Jahrhundert,* 1935, no. 106, pl. XXVIII; 1959, fig. 88); the Museo "Duca di Martina," Villa Floridiana, Naples; and the Residenz, Munich (Rückert, *Meissener Porzellan 1710–1810,* no. 1108, pl. 272).

A comparable pair from the collection of Walter von Pannwitz was sold at H. Helbing, Munich, October 24–25, 1905, lots 354, 355 (illustrated in catalogue, pl. LXXII, erroneously numbered 355, 356). A jay of the model represented by No. 10 A was in the C. H. Fischer Collection, Dresden, sold at J. M. Heberle, Cologne, October 22–25, 1906, lot 455 (illustrated in catalogue, pl. XXVII). Another in the pose of No. 10 B, though with a squirrel below, was in an unidentified collection sold at Ball – Graupe, Berlin, March 15, 1933, lot 30 (illustrated in catalogue, pl. 6). A pair comparable to Nos. 10 A and B, with modern gilt-bronze mounts, was sold from the collection of Virginia M. Rosenthal, New York, at Parke-Bernet, New York, April 13–14, 1945, lot 231 (illustrated in catalogue). Another pair, also with modern gilt-bronze mounts, formerly in the collection of F. Mannheimer, was sold at F. Muller, Amsterdam, October 14–15, 1952, lot 272 (illustrated in catalogue). An example comparable to No. 10 A was sold from the collection of Ole Olsen, Copenhagen, at Winkel-Magnussen's, Copenhagen, May 4–8, 1953, lot 699 (illustrated in catalogue); still another in the collection of Thelma Chrysler Foy was sold at Parke-Bernet, New York, May 23, 1959, lot 622 (illustrated in catalogue); it was dated "about 1760." An example from an unidentified collection (formerly in that of Baron Gustave de Rothschild, Paris) was sold at Christie's, London, May 30, 1963, lot 45 (illustrated in catalogue, pl. 8). A pair with Louis XV gilt-bronze mounts was sold at Sotheby's, London, November 20, 1964, lot 134 (illustrated in catalogue).

Two entries in the Meissen manufactory *Jahrbuch* under Kaendler's name refer to this model. One is mentioned under January 1740, XXXI, p. 253, supplement:

[35]

1 lifesize jay sitting on a stump, represented as in nature, next to which is a squirrel, lifesize, sitting on a branch, modeled in clay, in addition to other embellishments also to be found there (1 Eichel Gabicht in Lebensgrösse auf einem Stock sitzend, natürlich vorgestellet, neben dem ist ein Eichhorn in Lebensgrösse auf 1 Ast sitzend in Thon poussiert, nebst anderen daran befindlichen Zierrathen).

The other is a listing for May 1740, XXXIII, p. 101:

Divers oak leaves along with other appurtenances, with which to adorn the jays, modeled in clay (Annoch unterschiedliche Eichel Blätter nebst anderem Zubehör, die Eichel Gabichte damit zu verzieren, in Thon poussieret).

In Kaendler's own list of fees, the *Taxa*, 1740–1748, is the entry:

1 jay also sitting on a stump, next to which a squirrel, lifesize, sits on a branch. 5 Thalers (1 Eichel Gabicht gleichfalls auf einem Stocke sitzend, neben welchem ein Eichhorn in Lebensgrösse auf einem Aste sitzet. 5 Thlr).

Evidence of a similar model by Ehder is given in the *Jahrbuch* for October 1743 (from Rückert, *op. cit.*, p. 196):

A stump on which the jays come to sit, newly modeled (1 Stück Baum, worauf die Eichel Gabichte zu sitzen kommen, neu bossirt).

11 Parakeet

(Sittich)

H. 13 (33.0); W. 6¾ (17.2); D. 4½ (11.4).

ALERTLY posed upon a tall tree stump, the figure turns its head sharply over its left shoulder. Its long straight tail is supported upon a truncated branch springing from the lower part of the tree stump. The plain ivory-yellow neck and breast are in marked contrast to the multicolored head, wings, and tail, which show areas of puce, pale turquoise, yellow, and blue. The colors and modeling of the head create the effect of a hood. The brown legs, strongly barred with black, straddle the top of the stump from which three-lobed yellow-green leaves emerge. There is a single flower on the rocky base.

Unmarked.

Model created in 1740 by either Johann Joachim Kaendler (working 1731–1775) or Johann Gottlieb Ehder (working 1739–1750) (see below).

REFERENCES: Connolly, *Art News*, Christmas edition 1957, p. 116 (illustrated).

Formerly in the collection of Catalina von Pannwitz, Hartekamp, the Netherlands.

The records at Meissen are ambiguous in assigning this model to both Kaendler and Ehder during 1740. It is not clear whether collaboration is implied, or whether two similar figures were made. The species is apparently fanciful, at least as far as its coloring is concerned.

A comparable example in the Hermitage collection was published in *Staryé-Gody*, May 1911, pl. 29. Another, at Schloss Moritzburg, is illustrated in Albiker, *Die Meissner Porzellantiere im 18. Jahrhundert*, 1935, no. 88, pl. XXVI; 1959, fig. 94.

Two examples of the same model (each one of a pair) from an unidentified collection were sold at Ball – Graupe, Berlin, March 15, 1933, lots 52, 57 (illustrated in catalogue, pls. 11, 13).

[37]

Three entries in the Meissen manufactory *Jahrbuch* mention the model, calling it a parrot, however. Two refer to Kaendler, dated June 1740, XXXIII, p. 101:

> 1 parrot modeled in clay, the large type for Mons. Huiet, that it may be seen as a companion to the parrot made earlier by me (1 Pappagoy in Thon poussieret, grosse Sorte für Mons. Huiet, dass solcher gegen den ehemals von mir gefertigten Pappagoy siehet);

and p. 111:

> 2 parrots of proper size sitting on a large branch, modeled in clay for Mons. Huiet. To be sure these are to be seen as a pair (2 Pappagoyen von ziemlicher Grösse auf einem grossen Ast sitzend in Thon poussieret für Mons. Huiet. Zwar dass solche gegeneinander sehen).

Another, under the same date and volume, p. 114, is claimed for Ehder:

> 3 parrots in clay finished with all accessories (3 Papageien in Ton verputzt nebst allem Zubehör).

12 Amazon Parrot

(Amazonenpapagei)

H. 5⅞ (14.4); W. 6⅝ (16.8); D. 3⅝ (9.2).

THIS boldly modeled figure, with lowered head, unfolding wings, and sharply drooping tail, is poised, its body almost horizontal, as if it were peering at the foliage below. Its plumage is in a low key of green, with streaked olive areas interrupted by patches of yellow and gray-blue in the crown, wings, and tail. A black beak and legs of rust-brown further characterize the figure. The perch is a short conical stump with green foliage and three brown fungus growths.

Marked on the underside of the base with crossed swords, painted in deep blue, accompanied by an M in black.

Model created about 1740 by Johann Joachim Kaendler (working 1731–1775).

Formerly in the collection of Baroness Renée de Becker, New York.

Allowing for slight artistic license in the coloring, the figure may be taken to represent the blue-fronted Amazon parrot (*Amazona aestiva*), native to Brazil, Argentina, Paraguay, and Bolivia.

Comparable Amazon parrots are recorded in the collections of Irwin Untermyer, New York (Hackenbroch, *Meissen and Other Continental Porcelain in the Irwin Untermyer Collection*, p. 10, fig. 9); and at the Staatliche Museen, Berlin (*Verzeichnis der Neuerwerbungen seit 1933*, p. 160, no. 116).

An example mounted with several other species of Meissen birds, on a gilt-bronze clock, from an unidentified collection, was sold at Ball – Graupe, Berlin, March 15, 1933, lot 62 (illustrated in catalogue, pl. 1).

[38]

13 A, B   Pair of Thrushes

(Drosseln)

13 A: H. 8 (20.4); W. 7¼ (18.5); D. 3¾ (9.5).

13 B: H. 8 (20.4); W. 7⅛ (18.2); D. 3½ (8.9).

EACH thrush has a blue-green head and back, and outer wing feathers in canary-yellow bordered with black. The male (No. 13 B) has a large patch of chestnut-brown at the throat, which is paler on the female (No. 13 A). The coral color of the sharp, strong bills matches the legs, which are barred in black. Low, gnarled stumps emerging from rocks and partly covered with dappled green shrubbery serve as supports. There are small blue flowers with yellow centers below the left foot of No. 13 B.

Each is marked at the lower edge of the base with crossed swords painted in blue under the glaze.

Models created about 1740; attributed to Johann Joachim Kaendler (working 1731–1775).

REFERENCES: Connolly, *Art News*, Christmas edition 1957, p. 117 (illustrated).

Formerly in the collections of the Earl of Beau-champ, Madresfield Court, Malvern Link, Worcestershire; Baron and Baroness C. G. von Seid-litz, Paris.

The species represented is one of the many common varieties of thrushes.

The model is known with several color variations. A pair in a private collection at Dresden is represented in Albiker, *Die Meissner Porzellantiere im 18. Jahrhundert*, 1959, figs. 133, 134. A comparable pair, differently colored, is in the collection of Ernst Schneider, at Schloss Jägerhof, Düsseldorf (Rückert, *Meissener Porzellan 1710–1810*, nos. 1119, 1120, pl. 275). Another is in the collection of Irwin Untermyer, New York (Hackenbroch, *Meissen and Other Continental Porcelain in the Irwin Untermyer Collection*, p. 7, fig. 6).

A single thrush in the pose of No. 13 A was in the collection of C. H. Fischer, Dresden, sold at J. M. Heberle, Cologne, October 22–25, 1906, lot 694 (illustrated in catalogue, p. 102). A similar example from an unidentified collection was sold at Ball – Graupe, Berlin, June 28, 1932, lot 145 (illustrated in catalogue). Another, also from an unidentified collection, was sold at Ball – Graupe, Berlin, March 15, 1933, lot 28 (illustrated in catalogue, pl. 5); a date of about 1745 was assigned to it.

14 Golden Oriole

(Pirol)

H. 11⅜ (28.9); W. 6⅛ (15.6); D. 4 (10.2).

THE YELLOW and black figure, with head raised and sharply turned toward the tail, is perched upon a tall, slender tree stump. The chestnut-brown beak is open, revealing a rippling brown tongue. The wings, thrust slightly forward and outward at the shoulders, are patterned with yellow V shapes outlining the ends of the larger feathers; their tips overlap the tail, which terminates in a yellow bar. Legs and feet are gray, closely barred with black.

Marked at the lower edge of the base with crossed swords painted in blue under the glaze.

Model created 1740–1741; attributed to Johann Gottlieb Ehder (working 1739–1750).

This is a later version of the model by Kaendler represented by No. 4 B.

Schnorr von Carolsfeld (*Porzellansammlung Gustav von Klemperer*, no. 782) attributes a further variant, completed in January 1747, to P. Reinicke. The height is given as 26 cm.

A pair of golden orioles by Ehder, formerly in the Royal Saxon Collection, Dresden, is in the collection of Irwin Untermyer, New York (Hackenbroch, *Meissen and Other Continental Porcelain in the Irwin Untermyer Collection*, p. 6, fig. 5). For a single example mounted on a chandelier, see *ibid.*, p. 144, fig. 133.

Comparable orioles have been attributed to Kaendler, although they appear to be closer to the work of Ehder. See a model from the Siegfried Salz Collection, sold at Cassirer—Helbing, Berlin, March 26–27, 1929, lot 48 (illustrated in catalogue, pl. III). Another example of the Ehder type is an oriole from a private collection (Geheimrat W., Dresden), which was sold at R. Lepke, Berlin, February 24–26, 1937, lot 469 (illustrated in catalogue, pl. 16).

The Meissen manufactory *Jahrbuch*, XXXIII, p. 8, records under Ehder for January 1740:

1 oriole cast in clay (1 Bierohle in Thon verputzt).

For November 1741, p. 290:

1 oriole precisely modeled (1 Bierohle rein bossiert).

The Reinicke version is described in the notices for January 1747, p. 36:

1 oriole modeled in clay (1 Bier-Ohle in Thon boussiert).

See also Nos. 4 A and B and 5.

15 A, B Two Hoopoes

(Wiedehopfe)

15 A: H. 12 (30.5); W. 7 (17.8); D. 4⅞ (12.4).

15 B: H. 12 (30.5); W. 7 (17.8); D. 5¼ (13.4).

THE BIRDS are identically posed, varying only slightly in their patterning. Each has a prominent V-shaped double crest of erect plumes, and the head and neck are finely streaked with rufous brown and black. The wings are barred with black and white, in a pattern continuing across the back, while the tail is solid black. The legs are gray-blue, striped with black. Oak leaves and acorns, painted green and brown, ornament the stumps, one of which (No. 15 B) is further decorated with a large black and brown stag beetle.

Each is impressed on the unglazed underside of the base: 46. No. 15 A is also marked on the underside of the base with crossed swords painted in blue (faintly discernible).

Model probably created in August 1741 by Johann Gottlieb Ehder (working 1739–1750).

REFERENCES: Connolly, *Art News*, Christmas edition 1957, p. 117 (illustrated).

Formerly in the collection of Catalina von Pannwitz, Hartekamp, the Netherlands.

The birds are of the species *Upupa epops*, widely distributed throughout Europe, Africa, India, and elsewhere.

Comparable hoopoes by Kaendler and Ehder are in the collections of Irwin Untermyer, New York (Hackenbroch, *Meissen and Other Continental Porcelain in the Irwin Untermyer Collection*, p. 3, fig. 2); the Landesgewerbemuseum, Stuttgart (Albiker, *Die Meissner Porzellantiere im 18. Jahrhundert*, 1935, no. 114, pl. XXIX); the Museo "Duca di Martina," Villa Floridiana, Naples; a single hoo-

poe, formerly in the Royal Saxon Collection, Dresden, is illustrated in Berling (*Dissertation Programme . . . Meissen*, p. 37, fig. 75); another is in Schloss Moritzburg (Albiker, *op. cit.*, 1935, no. 113, pl. XXIX; 1959, fig. 132 [different view]).

Other examples were sold from the collection of Walter von Pannwitz, Munich (H. Helbing, Munich, October 24–25, 1905, lots 270, 271 [illustrated in catalogue, pl. XLV]); at an anonymous sale, Ball – Graupe, Berlin, March 15, 1933, lot 44 (illustrated in catalogue, pl. 10); and from the collection of Virginia M. Rosenthal, New York (Parke-Bernet, New York, April 13–14, 1945, lot 226 [illustrated in catalogue]).

A model for a single hoopoe was created earlier by Kaendler. An entry in the Meissen manufactory *Jahrbuch* under his name for July 1736 reads:

> 1 bird finished, the hoopoe so-called, life-size, as if he rests on a branch overgrown with leaves (1 Widehopffen den sogenannten Vogel in Lebensgrösse gefertigt wie er auf einem Aste mit Blättern bewachsen ruhet).

A pair of hoopoes is assigned to Ehder in the same source, under the date August 1741:

> 2 birds, called the hoopoe, on trees, modeled in clay (2 Vögel, der Wiedehopp genannt, auf Bäumen, in Thon bossirt).

The authorship of such models must be decided mainly on stylistic grounds, although references to the modeling of accessories, as in the *Jahrbuch* entries above, sometimes shed light, here in favor of Ehder.

16 A, B Pair of Indian Parakeets, Mounted in Gilt Bronze

(Sittiche)

16 A: (overall) H. 13⅟₁₆ (33.1); W. 9 (22.8);
　　　D. 7½ (19.0).
　　　(porcelain) H. 11½ (29.1); W. 7 (17.8);
　　　D. 6 (15.3).

16 B: (overall) H. 14 (35.6); W. 8¾ (22.2);
　　　D. 7½ (19.0).
　　　(porcelain) H. 12¼ (31.1); W. 8 (20.4);
　　　D. 5⅝ (14.4).

EACH long-tailed parakeet has predominantly lettuce-green plumage, except at the tips of wings and tail, where delicate brown pencilings shade to a gray-blue toward the end. At the back of the head a crescent of mottled chalky blue is bordered by a thin purple line. The purple beak shades into dark stone gray at the tip. One bird (No. 16 A) raises a morsel of food to its beak with its left foot, while its companion clasps the perch with both feet. Each tall tree stump is represented as a gnarled and spiraled shaft from which jut branches bearing almond-shaped pale green leaves, dappled with yellow, interspersed with red and purplish cherries. The perches are further enlivened with a variety of insects including green and yellow caterpillars, brown beetles, and flies. Springing from the base of each are low green plants bearing amethyst-purple blossoms, and clusters of speckled brown fungi. A rococo mount of gilt bronze serves as a base. It consists of jagged rockwork and tumbled vegetation bordered by serpentine scrolls.

The mounts may conceal marks on the porcelain; each mount is stamped with the crowned C (see below) on the base of one of the scrolls.

Models created in June 1741 by Johann Joachim Kaendler (working 1731–1775); the mounts are French, dating from 1745–1749.

Formerly in the collections of Baron Max von Goldschmidt-Rothschild, Frankfurt am Main; Baroness René de Becker, New York.

The figures represent the Indian ring-neck parakeet (*Psittacula krameri*), native to India, Africa, and China.

For a comparison with another pair in the collection, see Nos. 17 A and B. The model represented by No. 16 A is again seen in No. 25.

Comparable Meissen parakeets are recorded in the possession of Irwin Untermyer (Hackenbroch, *Meissen and Other Continental Porcelain in the Irwin Untermyer Collection*, p. 8, fig. 7); the Dresden Schloss (Albiker, *Die Meissner Porzellantiere im 18. Jahrhundert*, 1935, no. 89, pl. XXVI; 1959, fig. 95 [one only, relates to No. 16 A, and shows a different view from that in the earlier edition]); the Historisches Museum, Bern (*Weltkunst*, April 1, 1953, p. 7, fig. 1, formerly in the Kocher Collection); the Staatliche Museen, Berlin (*Verzeichnis der Neuerwerbungen seit 1933*, p. 158, no. 113, formerly in the Feist Collection); and the Staatliche Porzellansammlung, Dresden (colored yellow-green, orange-red, and yellow).

Others appear in the sale catalogues of the following collections: C. H. Fischer, Dresden (sold at J. M. Heberle, Cologne, October 22–25, 1906, lot 408 [illustrated in catalogue, pl. 5]); Siegfried Salz, Berlin (sold at Cassirer – Helbing, Berlin, March 26–27, 1929, lots 44, 45 [illustrated in catalogue, pl. 11]).

The Meissen manufactory *Jahrbuch*, XXXV, p. 172, records under Kaendler's name for June 1741:

For the Countess of Moschinska, an Indian bird of suitable size, modeled from life at her residence [presumably her palace at Dresden], and presented as if

he sits on a cherry branch and eats a piece of sugar from his claw (Für die Gräfin von Moschinska einen Indianischen Vogel von ziemlicher Grösse in dero Logis nach dem Leben in Thon poussieret und solchergestalt vorgestellet, wie er auf einem Kirschast sitzet und ein Stücklein Zucker aus der Pfote frisst).

Although Nos. 16 A and B and 17 A and B are products of the same molds, the feathers of the wings and tail were tooled after the casting, giving an individual appearance to each bird.

The crowned C was once interpreted as the mark of Caffiéri, Cressent, and Colson. However, Nocq (*Le Figaro Artistique*, April 17, 1924, pp. 2–4) suggested that it was a hallmark used on bronzes made during the period from March 5, 1745, to February 4, 1749. During these years taxes were levied on works made of various materials, stamped accordingly. Tin, for instance, was stamped F (for *étain fin*) or CE (for *claire étoffe*), according to the quality; lead was stamped Ier p V (for *premier plomb vieux*). The C probably stands for *cuivre*. Verlet was later able to show (*Apollo*, July 1937, pp. 22, 23) that the crowned C cannot be the mark of a *ciseleur*, but must refer to the date of execution.

See also Volume II of this catalogue, Nos. 273 A and B.

17 A, B   Pair of Indian Parakeets

(Sittiche)

17 A: H. 11¼ (28.6); W. 6⅝ (16.8); D. 3⅝ (9.2).

17 B: H. 12⅜ (31.5); W. 6 (15.3); D. 3⅞ (9.8).

THE jade-green birds, except for coloring and minor details of modeling, are similar to Nos. 16 A and B. The female (No. 17 A), slightly more yellow than its companion, raises a morsel of food to its beak; its neck is ringed with a narrow band of rose-violet hatchings, broadening to a patch of pale blue at the back of the head. Some of the wing and tail feathers are tinted apple-green. The male (No. 17 B), with head turned sharply over its left shoulder, has a brilliant purple beak. A mantle of short feathers covering its head is edged with purple that grades into black at the front of the head. Its wing primaries are blue-green, penciled in brown, and the undersides of the wings and tail are canary-yellow. A tall, spiraling tree stump serves as a perch for each bird and carries sparse foliage of several varieties. Grape leaves edged in yellow conceal the top of the stump of No. 17 A, which is also decorated with a large brown and black beetle and a barred yellow caterpillar above some yellow flowerettes and mushrooms. The perch of No. 17 B is hung with three dark aubergine cherries and almond-shaped yellow-green leaves.

Unmarked.

Models created in June 1741 by Johann Joachim Kaendler (working 1731–1775).

REFERENCES: Connolly, *Art News*, Christmas edition 1957, p. 116 (illustrated).

Formerly in the collection of Baroness Renée de Becker, New York.

For other examples in the collection, see Nos. 16 A and B (where additional comments on the models are made), and No. 28.

18 South American Parrot

(Papagei)

H. 5⁵⁄₁₆ (13.5); W. 3⅞ (9.8); D. 2⅛ (5.4).

THE FIGURE is compactly modeled, with predominantly leaf-green plumage and iron-red wing tips. The upper plumage of the body is overlaid by a faint net-like pattern of pale aubergine color extending from the base of the open yellow mandibles to the pale clay-yellow tail. The bird stands on a low stump decorated with a cluster of gray mushrooms and a clump of leaves.

Marked on the unglazed underside of the base with crossed swords painted indistinctly in blue.

Model created about 1741 by Johann Joachim Kaendler (working 1731–1775).

REFERENCES: Connolly, *Art News*, Christmas edition 1957, p. 116 (illustrated).

Formerly in the collection of Herbert Gutmann, London.

The figure resembles the species *Pionospitta pileata* of southeastern Brazil and Paraguay.

This model was produced in varying colors and patterns of plumage; see, for example, No. 19. A version in a Dresden private collection is illustrated in Albiker, *Die Meissner Porzellantiere im 18. Jahrhundert*, 1935, no. 95, pl. XXVI; 1959, fig. 96. Others are recorded in the collections of Ernst Schneider, at Schloss Jägerhof, Düsseldorf (Rückert, *Meissener Porzellan 1710–1810*, no. 1084, pl. 267), and the Staatliche Museen, Berlin (*Verzeichnis der Neuerwerbungen seit 1933*, p. 161, no. 115).

An example from an unidentified collection was sold at Ball – Graupe, Berlin, June 28, 1932, lot 149 (illustrated in catalogue, pl. 21). Parrots in several sizes were being made by 1741 as shown by the following extract from the Meissen manufactory *Jahrbuch*, XXXV, p. 172. The entry is dated October of that year, and is under Kaendler's name:

> Another parrot of the smallest kind, newly modeled so that two may be seen as a pair (Annoch einen Pappagoy kleinste Sorte neu pouss. damit auch 2 gegeneinander sehen).

19   South American Parrot

(Papagei)

H. 5⁷⁄₁₆ (13.8); W. 3¾ (9.5); D. 2⅛ (5.4).

IN SIZE and pose this figure is similar to No. 18. The body plumage is green, with olive overtones that contrast with the deep lapis-blue of the wing primaries and the iron-red of the tail. Dark green foliage studded with a single aubergine flower embellishes the stump.

Unmarked.

Model created about 1741 by Johann Joachim Kaendler (working 1731–1775).

REFERENCES: Connolly, *Art News*, Christmas edition 1957, p. 117 (illustrated).

For comparable examples, see under No. 18.

20 South American Parrot

(Papagei)

H. 5⅝ (14.4); W. 4 (10.2); D. 2³⁄₁₆ (5.6).

THIS stubby figure turns its head sharply over its right wing. The crown, back, and shoulders, of soft grass-green, are abruptly demarcated from the unfigured white throat and under parts. The shoulders are penciled with muted aubergine and dappled with cream; the wing tips show a zone of pale blue deepening to lapis, repeated upon the tail.

Marked on the unglazed underside of the base with crossed swords painted indistinctly in blue.

Model probably created about 1741 by Johann Joachim Kaendler (working 1731–1775).

REFERENCES: Connolly, *Art News*, Christmas edition 1957, p. 117 (illustrated).

Allowing for some liberty in the coloring, the bird is derived from the black-headed caique (*Pionites melanocephalia*) of Brazil, Venezuela, and the Guianas.

Two examples of this model were sold as a pair from an unidentified collection, at Ball – Graupe, Berlin, March 15, 1933, lot 60 (illustrated in catalogue, pl. 14). Another from an unidentified collection (Geheimrat W., Dresden) was sold at R. Lepke, Berlin, February 24–26, 1937, lot 470 (illustrated in catalogue, pl. 16).

21 A,B   Pair of Parrots

(Papageien)

21 A: H. 8 (20.4); W. 5 (12.7); D. 2⅞ (7.4).

21 B: H. 7⅝ (19.4); W. 5½ (14.1); D. 3¼ (8.3).

EACH multicolored small bird with head sharply turned sits upon a low tree stump; No. 21 A clasps a deep aubergine-colored cherry in its beak. The head and most of the body of each is patterned with scale-like imbrications in gray, outlined in white. In No. 21 A, the lower wing feathers are ochre-yellow, the leg coverts olive-green, and the tail puce. In No. 21 B, the longer wing feathers are puce, the leg coverts ochre-yellow, and the tail grass-green. The pale pink legs and feet of each are barred in black. The perch of No. 21 A displays a pair of red cherries and pointed green leaves; that of No. 21 B is encrusted with notched triangular green leaves.

Unmarked.

Models created about 1741 by Johann Joachim Kaendler (working 1731–1775).

Formerly in the collection of Baroness Renée de Becker, New York.

The figures resemble the African species *Psittacus erythacus*.

Similar figures, somewhat different in scale and coloring, are recorded in the collections of Irwin Untermyer (Hackenbroch, *Meissen and Other Continental Porcelain in the Irwin Untermyer Collection*, p. 10, fig. 10); and the Staatliche Museen, Berlin (*Verzeichnis der Neuerwerbungen seit 1933*, p. 161, nos. 118, 119).

Others appear in the sale catalogue of Erich von Goldschmidt-Rothschild, Berlin, Ball – Graupe, Berlin, March 23–25, 1931, lot 199 (mounted as candelabra, illustrated in catalogue, pl. 49), and lot 451 (illustrated in catalogue, pl. 79). A pair mounted as candelabra figures appearing on the Berlin art market in 1935 was recorded in Albiker, *Die Meissner Porzellantiere im 18. Jahrhundert*, 1935, no. 96, pl. XXVI; 1959, fig. 239 (only one illustrated). Other examples were sold from the collection of Emma Budge, Hamburg, at P. Graupe, Berlin, September 29, 1937, lot 769 (illustrated in catalogue, pl. 121); from an unidentified collection, Sotheby's, London, November 15, 1955, lot 65 A (illustrated in catalogue); and from the collection of Mrs. Edward Hutton, Sotheby's, London, November 23, 1965, lots 57 and 60 (illustrated in catalogue).

Nos. 21 A and B are popular models, which exist in a variety of color combinations. Compare Nos. 22 A and B, 23 A and B, and 24–28.

22 A, B Pair of Parrots

(Papageien)

22 A: H. 7⅝ (19.4); W. 5½ (14.1); D. 3⅜ (8.6).

22 B: H. 7⅝ (19.4); W. 5½ (14.1); D. 3¼ (8.3).

EACH sturdy yellow-green parrot turns its head sharply over the shoulder. Head, neck, and breast are covered with a mantle of rounded scale-like feathers concentrically patterned in green and yellow, their outlines penciled in purple. A zone of variegated moss-green extends across the back from one wing shoulder to the other and descends to the tip of the tail. On the wings it yields to areas of periwinkle and powder-blue. The stubby tail is marked with a narrow stripe of iron-red at either side. Pale flesh-colored claws clasp the gnarled tree stump, decorated with curling stems bearing grape leaves in pale turquoise.

No. 22 B is marked on the unglazed underside of the base with crossed swords painted in blue; No. 22 A is impressed on the unglazed underside of the base: 26 and what may be a Y.

Models created about 1741 by Johann Joachim Kaendler (working 1731–1775).

Formerly in a private collection (sold at Sotheby's, London, April 10, 1951, lot 101 [illustrated in catalogue]).

The plumage resembles that of *Pionites leucogaster* of Peru, Ecuador, and Brazil.

For these models in other color combinations, see Nos. 21 A and B, 23 A and B, and 24–28.   [57]

23 A, B Pair of Parrots

(Papageien)

23 A: H. 7⅞ (20.0); W. 4⅞ (12.4); D. 3⅜ (8.6).

23 B: H. 7½ (19.0); W. 5 (12.7); D. 3½ (8.9).

THE ROBUST green birds are almost identical to Nos. 21 A and B, and were apparently cast from the same molds. A soft yellow-green is predominant in the plumage, with details lightly penciled in a darker tone shading to a brilliant iron-red on the lower wings and tail. The beaks are gray, the legs flesh-pink. The low rustic stumps forming the perches are brown-stained and decorated with large leaves edged with pale turquoise. A cherry nestles amid the leaves of No. 23 B.

Each is impressed on the unglazed underside of the base: 26 (twice on No. 23 B).

Models created about 1741 by Johann Joachim Kaendler (working 1731–1775).

Formerly in the collections of Baroness Mathilde de Rothschild, Grünburg; Baroness Renée de Becker, New York.

In color, the figures resemble certain Amazon species in a general way, although they do not follow nature closely.

For these models in other color combinations, see Nos. 21 A and B, 22 A and B, and 24–28.

24 Blue-Headed Amazon Parrot

(Blaustirnamazone)

H. 7⅞ (20.0); W. 5⅜ (13.7); D. 3½ (8.9).

IN THIS compactly modeled figure the prevailing lettuce-green plumage shades to olive-yellow. The head, which is sharply turned over the right shoulder, is cobalt-blue, as are the shoulders. Primaries and tail feathers are burnt-orange. The low tree stump is decorated with green oak leaves interspersed with other foliage.

Unmarked.

Model created about 1741 by Johann Joachim Kaendler (working 1731–1775).

Formerly in the collection of Lord Biddulph, Under Down, Ledbury, Herefordshire.

In color, the figure suggests the blue-headed Amazon parrot (*Amazona aestiva*).

For the model in other color combinations, see Nos. 21 A, 22 A, 23 A, 25, and 26.

25 Amazon Parrot

(Amazonenpapagei)

H. 7⅝ (19.4); W. 5¼ (13.4); D. 3⅜ (8.6).

THIS parrot holds a small round seed in its speckled brown beak and is perched with its head turned over its right shoulder on a short stump decorated with a spray of turquoise foliage. The plumage is basically leaf-green, darkening upon the wings, which are crossed by a broad band of iron-red. The tail is cobalt-blue, and the under parts cream-yellow.

Marked on the unglazed underside of the base with crossed swords painted indistinctly in blue.

Model created about 1741 by Johann Joachim Kaendler (working 1731–1775).

Formerly in the collection of Lord Biddulph, Under Down, Ledbury, Herefordshire.

Although the figure suggests a species of *Amazona* in size and form, its coloring is fanciful.

For the model in other color combinations, see Nos. 21 A, 22 A, 23 A, 24, and 26.

26 Gray Parrot

(Graupapagei)

H. 7¾ (19.7); W. 5⁷⁄₁₆ (13.8); D. 3⅜ (8.6).

THE POSE and modeling of this gray parrot are very close to those in the preceding five descriptions (Nos. 21–25). This example has basically gray plumage, with black outlines on the wing feathers, and a brilliant iron-red tail. The beak is black and slightly open. The perch is modeled with stumps of branches and a cluster of spreading, mottled turquoise leaves.

Marked on the unglazed underside of the base with crossed swords painted in blue.

Model created about 1741 by Johann Joachim Kaendler (working 1731–1775).

Formerly in the collection of Lord Hastings, Melton Constable, Norfolk. Its companion is owned by Mrs. David Gubbay, Little Trent Park, Herefordshire, and was inherited from Sir Philip Sassoon, of Trent Park, Herefordshire.

The color of the bird is close to the species *Psittacus erythacus*, of Africa.

For the model in other color combinations, see Nos. 21 A, 22 A, 23 A, 24, and 25.

27 Amazon Parrot

(Amazonenpapagei)

H. 7½ (19.0); W. 4¾ (12.1); D. 3⅜ (8.6).

THIS piebald parrot, gazing over its left wing, has pale apple-green plumage with a peculiar development of markings about the white head, which is crossed by a cobalt-blue band passing through the eyes. Cobalt-blue occurs again in the wing primaries and some of the feathers of the tail. The sturdy yellow feet grasp the low perch, which is decorated in front with a spiraling twig bearing three purple berries and grape-like leaves bordered with pale turquoise.

Unmarked.

Model created about 1741 by Johann Joachim Kaendler (working 1731–1775).

Formerly in the collection of Lord Biddulph, Under Down, Ledbury, Herefordshire.

The color of the bird resembles that of the parrot *Amazona albifrons* of Mexico and Central America.

For the model in other color combinations, see Nos. 21 B, 22 B, 23 B, and 28.

28 Parrot and Parakeet with Clock, Mounted in Gilt Bronze

Overall: H. 24 (60.9); W. 18 (45.7); D. 13 (33.0).

Parakeet: H. 11½ (29.1).

Parrot: H. 7½ (19.0).

A SINUOUS spray of scrolled gilt bronze rises from a rococo base to support a drum-shaped clock and a variety of multicolored porcelain flowers. Two green birds are perched beneath the dial. At left is a parakeet, nibbling on a morsel of food raised in its left claw. A narrow band of puce encircles its neck; the color is repeated on its wings, which are tipped with blue; its long tail is blue and clay-yellow. Cherries and strawberries dangle from its two-branched perch. At right is a parrot with green upper parts and a short, dark blue tail. The wing feathers are puce, repeated in a paler tone on the under parts. The low stump is decorated with berries and pastel-colored flowers.

The parakeet is marked at the lower edge of the base with crossed swords painted in blue under the glaze; the parrot is unmarked.

The model for the parakeet created in June 1741; that for the parrot probably in the same year. Both by Johann Joachim Kaendler (working 1731–1775). The mounts are French, dating from about 1750.

Formerly in the collection of Lady Cynthia Pole-Carew, Torpoint, Cornwall.

The parakeet is a modified version of the Indian parakeets Nos. 16 A and 17 A. The parrot duplicates, except in color, the model shown as Nos. 21 B, 22 B, 23 B, and 27. For further comment on each bird see under Nos. 16 A and B and 21 A and B.

See also Volume II of this catalogue, No. 263.

29 A, B   Pair of Bohemian Waxwings

(Seidenschwänze)

29 A: H. 9¾ (24.8); W. 5⅝ (14.4); D. 4⅛ (10.5).

29 B: H. 9 9/16 (23.4); W. 5¾ (14.7); D. 3⅛ (8.0).

THE FIGURES are similarly posed, except for the position of their heads. One bird (No. 29 A) preens its partially extended right wing; the other (No. 29 B) cocks its head to the opposite side. Graduated ash-brown and gray tones predominate in the plumage, contrasting with black masks over the eyes and black in the wings and yellow-tipped tail. A zone of henna appears on the head, under the tail, and upon the tips of the secondaries. The delicate black legs and feet of each rest upon a tree stump decorated with serrated yellow-green leaves and multicolored blossoms, to which are added on No. 29 B russet-brown berries.

Unmarked.

Models begun in 1741 by Johann Joachim Kaendler (working 1731–1775); completed in that year by Johann Gottlieb Ehder (working 1739–1750).

REFERENCES: Connolly, *Art News*, Christmas edition 1957, p. 117 (illustrated).

Formerly in the collection of W. Johnson.

The species represented here is the Bohemian waxwing, *Bombycilla garrulus*, native to Europe and Asia.

Kaendler prepared another set of waxwing models in June 1774 (see Albiker, *Die Meissner Porzellantiere im 18. Jahrhundert*, 1935, p. 122, no. 116, for entry in the *Jahrbuch*).

Comparable Bohemian waxwings are recorded in the collections of Irwin Untermyer, New York (Hackenbroch, *Meissen and Other Continental Porcelain in the Irwin Untermyer Collection*, p. 19, fig. 21); the Cecil Higgins Museum, Bedford, Bedfordshire (illustrated in Savage, *18th-Century German Porcelain*, pl. 40); the Meissen Schauhalle (Albiker, *op. cit.*, 1935, no. 116, pl. XXX [figure at right, modern cast]).

Others are found in the sale catalogues of Baron von Born, Budapest (sold at R. Lepke, Berlin, December 4, 1929, lot 134 [illustrated in catalogue, pl. 7]); and of an unidentified collection (sold at Ball – Graupe, Berlin, March 15, 1933, lot 53 [illustrated in catalogue, pl. 10]).

A pair mounted in eighteenth century gilt bronze (as candelabra) from the collection of John Coventry was sold at Christie's, London, March 22, 1965, lot 158 (illustrated in catalogue).

Overall: H. 11¾ (29.8); W. 9⅞ (25.1); D. 5¾ (14.6).

Birds: H. 6 (15.3); W. 4½ (11.4); D. 2½ (6.4).

Jar: H. 6¾ (17.2); W. 5½ (14.1).

THE PIERCED, melon-shaped jar with a cover is flanked by a pair of guinea fowl, each component being mounted on an individual tree stump support resting upon a base of scrolled and foliate gilt bronze. The cover of the white jar is pierced with five tapering "windows" and surmounted by a finial in the form of a blue hydrangea. Cover and jar are joined by threaded mounts of gilt bronze. The vessel is molded with alternating convex and concave lobes to which are applied scrolling brown branches supporting green and chalky blue hydrangeas and heart-shaped turquoise leaves, all modeled in the round. The cover and shoulders are heightened with gilding. The vessel is joined to its stem by means of a metal foliate mount, painted olive green. At either side stands a guinea fowl, its red comb and wattles, striped violet neck, and black body relieved by a white rump and scattered white speckles. Broad-petaled flowers in pastel tints of orange, green, blue, and yellow rise on metal stems between the birds. Porcelain leaves spring from the tops of the left and right tree stumps, and trefoil leaves of green-painted metal trail across the gilt-bronze base. The bird at the left of the jar lacks the outer toe of its right foot. The missing toe is a factory defect, remedied by painting in the form against the white base.

The mounts may conceal marks on the porcelain. The mounts are stamped on the right forefoot with the crowned C (for a note on the crowned C, see under Nos. 16 A and B).

Models of guinea fowl created in September 1741 by Johann Joachim Kaendler (working 1731–1775); the jar created about 1745. The mounts are French, dating from 1745–1749.

The species represented appears to be the com-mon guinea fowl, *Numida meleagris*, native to West Africa.

A comparable pair of guinea fowl is in the collection of Ernst Schneider, Schloss Jägerhof, Düsseldorf (Rückert, *Meissener Porzellan 1710–1810*, nos. 1129, 1130, pl. XXXI). One in a Dresden private collection is illustrated in Albiker (*Die Meissner Porzellantiere im 18. Jahrhundert*, 1935, no. 136, pl. XXXIII; 1959, fig. 126). A smaller pair is in the Staatliche Porzellansammlung, Dresden.

A single guinea fowl was in the collection of C. H. Fischer, Dresden (sold at J. M. Heberle, Cologne, October 22–25, 1906, lot 62 [illustrated in catalogue, pl. 5]). A pair belonging to Erich von Goldschmidt-Rothschild, Berlin, was sold at Ball – Graupe, Berlin, March 23–25, 1931, lot 450 (illustrated in catalogue, pl. 78). A single example from the Emma Budge Collection, Hamburg, was sold at P. Graupe, Berlin, September 29, 1937, lot 774 (illustrated in catalogue, pl. 122). A pair from an unidentified collection was sold at Christie's, London, April 20, 1959, lot 114 (illustrated in catalogue).

The jar, which was used as a perfume burner, is of a type represented in the collections of Irwin Untermyer, New York (Hackenbroch, *Meissen and Other Continental Porcelain in the Irwin Untermyer Collection*, pl. 11, fig. 11) and Erich von Goldschmidt-Rothschild, Berlin (sold at Ball – Graupe, Berlin, March 23–25, 1931, lot 198 [illustrated in catalogue, pl. 48]).

The Meissen manufactory *Jahrbuch*, September 1741, XXXV, p. 253, mentions under Kaendler's name:

> A guinea hen of moderate size, modeled in clay, which is meant to be a companion to another guinea hen, in order that such pieces may always be seen as a pair (Eine Perl Henne in Thon poussirt von mittelmässiger Grösse, welche ebenfalls Compagnon gegen eine andere Perlhenne abgeben soll, damit solche Stücke allzeit gegeneinander sehen).

See also Volume II of this catalogue, No. 268.

31 A,B Two Canaries

(Kanarienvögel)

H. 4⅛ (10.5); W. 3⅛ (8.0); D. 1⅝ (4.2).

IDENTICALLY posed, with the head turned over the left shoulder, each bird is perched upon a low tree stump of smooth contours, from which springs a gnarled leafy branch. No. 31 A is white, with touches of pale sulphur-yellow about the wings and tail, and a most delicate yellow tint on the crown; the legs are flesh-colored. No. 31 B shows an abundance of yellow in its plumage, with gray pencilings on the head, shoulders, a single feather of the wing coverts, and along the edges of the wings and tail. Each has barred legs.

No. 31 A is marked on the unglazed underside of the base with crossed swords faintly painted in blue; No. 31 B is unmarked.

Model created in the early 1740s, probably by Johann Joachim Kaendler (working 1731–1775) or Peter Reinicke (working 1743–1768).

The figure represents the domestic canary or finch (*Serinas canaria*), native to the Canary Islands.

The model appears, along with five other Meissen birds of various species, on a mantel clock mounted in gilt bronze, in an anonymous collection sold at Ball – Graupe, Berlin, March 15, 1933, lot 62 (illustrated in catalogue, pl. 1). The clock movement is by Gilles *l'aîné* of Paris, active about 1760–1790. A canary comparable to No. 31 B was sold anonymously at Sotheby's, London, March 12, 1968, lot 192A (illustrated in catalogue).

32 Parrot Group

(Papageien)

Overall: H. 15¼ (37.8); W. 9¾ (24.8); D. 5¾ (14.7).

TWO PARROTS are posed under a forked tree bearing deeply notched gray-green leaves and coral-red fruit. The bird at left is perched upon a rock; its plumage is soft yellow-green except for the wing tips and tail, which are puce and purplish blue. It cocks its head over its companion, whose colors are ochre-yellow and puce, with purplish blue primaries and tail. This second bird stands in front of the base of the tree decorated with a profusion of vines interspersed with blue convolvulus and other blossoms of various colors. The rockwork base is further enlivened by a yellow-winged fly and a multicolored caterpillar.

Unmarked.

Model created in 1745 or 1747 by Johann Joachim Kaendler (working 1731–1775).

Formerly in the collection of F. Mannheimer, Amsterdam (sold at F. Muller, Amsterdam, October 14–15, 1952, lot 270 [illustrated in catalogue]).

The species of the birds is unidentifiable, as their colors are not apparently taken from nature.

A comparable parrot group in the collection of Baroness Renée de Becker, New York, was shown at an exhibition at The Metropolitan Museum of Art, New York, 1949 (see Avery, *Masterpieces of European Porcelain*, no. 309, pl. v). This group was earlier in the collection of Erich von Goldschmidt-Rothschild, Berlin (sold at Ball – Graupe, Berlin, March 23–25, 1931, lot 452 [illustrated in catalogue, pl. 79]).

Other groups with the birds colored differently are recorded in a Dresden private collection (Albiker, *Die Meissner Porzellantiere im 18. Jahrhundert*, 1935, no. 97, pl. XXVII; 1959, fig. 130); and in an anonymous collection (Geheimrat W., Dresden), sold at R. Lepke, Berlin, February 24–26, 1937, lot 535 (illustrated in catalogue, pl. 15).

The Meissen manufactory *Jahrbuch*, April 1745, p. 201, records under Kaendler's name:

> For the Queen 2 Indian birds modeled in Dresden, to sit next to each other, with which are also found branches with cherries and other fruit (Für die Königin 2 Indianische Vögel in Dressden poussirt, wie solche nebeneinander sitzen, darbey Bäume mit Kirschen und anderen Früchten befindlich).

A later reference from January 1747, p. 25, refers to the preparation of wax originals for the making of molds:

> 1 new small group cut up, on which various parrots are found (1 neues Groupgen zerschnitten, woran unterschiedliche Pappagoys befindlich sind).

33 A–C Three Miniature Swan Groups, Mounted in Gilt Bronze

(Schwäne)

33 A: (overall) H. 5⁹⁄₁₆ (14.1); W. 4⅝ (11.7);
D. 3½ (8.9).
(porcelain) H. 4¹³⁄₁₆ (14.0); W. 4¾ (12.1);
D. 3¼ (8.2).

33 B: (overall) H. 5¾ (14.7); W. 4⅛ (10.5);
D. 3⅜ (8.6).
(porcelain) H. 5 (12.7); W. 4⅛ (10.5);
D. 2½ (6.4).

33 C: (overall) H. 5¾ (14.7); W. 4 (10.2);
D. 3¼ (8.2).
(porcelain) H. 5⅛ (13.0); W. 4 (10.2);
D. 2½ (6.4).

THE THREE white swans, with erect heads and black beaks, consist of a male (No. 33 C) and two females (Nos. 33 A and B), each of the latter having a cygnet upon its back and another under its breast. Each rests on a rustic oval mound, splashed with turquoise and molded with a stunted aquatic plant that presses against the right side of the bird. Each stands in a modern gilt-bronze mount of rococo design.

No. 33 B is marked on the unglazed underside of the base with crossed swords painted almost [75]

imperceptibly in blue; Nos. 33 A and C are un-marked.

Models of Nos. 33 A and B created in November 1747 by Johann Joachim Kaendler (working 1731–1775) and/or Peter Reinicke (working 1743–1768); model of No. 33 C probably created about 1747, perhaps by Kaendler.

The species represented is the mute swan (*Cygnus olor*), native to Europe and Asia.

An example of the swan and cygnets, in the castle at Stuttgart, is illustrated in Albiker (*Die Meissner Porzellantiere im 18. Jahrhundert*, 1935, no. 141, pl. XXXIV; 1959, fig. 230).

A group similar to Nos. 33 A and B, from the collection of Mrs. Edward Hutton, New York, was sold at Sotheby's, London, November 23, 1965, lot 50 (illustrated in catalogue).

Two entries in the *Jahrbuch* of the Meissen manufactory seem to relate to the model of Nos. 33 A and B; both are under notices for November 1747. One, p. 396, is under Kaendler's name:

> 2 models of small swans displayed with young and set in appropriate postures (2 Modelle zu kleinen Schwanen mit Jungen ausgestellt und in gehörige Positur gesetzt).

The other, p. 408, is under Reinicke's name:

> 1 swan with 2 young precisely modeled in clay to go with the preceding [swans mentioned in the work-book] (1 Schwan mit 2 Jungen zu vorhergehenden in Thon rein boussiert).

For comparison with a model of apparently earlier design see Nos. 9 A and B.

34 Miniature Swan Group, Mounted in Gilt Bronze

(Schwäne)

Overall: H. 5⅛ (13.0); W. 4 (10.2); D. 3½ (8.9).

Porcelain: H. 4¾ (12.1); W. 4½ (11.9); D. 3¼ (8.2).

A FEMALE swan, white with a black beak, with wings slightly raised, supports a cygnet upon its back, and shields another beneath it. The base in the form of a mound is molded with turquoise water plants and patches of green vegetation bordered with yellow. It rests in a modern gilt-bronze mount of rococo design, stamped with the initials J D.

Marked on the unglazed underside of the base with crossed swords painted faintly in blue.

Model possibly created about 1747 by Johann Joachim Kaendler (working 1731–1775) and/or Peter Reinicke (working 1743–1768).

The species represented is the mute swan (*Cygnus olor*), native to Europe and Asia.

This model is illustrated in Savage, *18th-Century German Porcelain*, pl. 19b, where it is said to have formed part of the famous Swan Service made for Count Heinrich von Brühl between 1737 and 1741. As such, it might be the work of Johann Joachim Kaendler, though the modeler Johann Friedrich Eberlein (working 1735–1749) was also working on the same commission. The suave modeling of No. 34, however, suggests that it may be a later work. Two somewhat similar groups, Nos. 33 A and B, may be compared. For a discussion of the Swan Service, see under Nos. 9 A and B.

35 Pair of Swans with Pot-Pourri Jar, Mounted in Gilt Bronze

Overall: H. 10½ (26.7); W. 9⅜ (23.8); D. 6³⁄₁₆ (15.7).

Birds: (both) H. 5 (12.7); W. (left) 2¼ (5.7); (right) 2½ (6.3); D. (both) 4 (10.2).

Jar: H. 4½ (11.4); Diam. 4½ (11.4).

THE COVERED white bowl is flanked by swans, and is molded in relief with a plum-blossom motif. It has been converted into a pot-pourri jar by a pierced rococo mount, which separates the domed cover from the vessel. A foliated spray of gilt bronze serves as a finial. Below it to the left and right two black-faced swans sit on domed oval bases, one base tinted with mottled leaf-green, the other with pale turquoise-blue. All three units are supported on an irregularly shaped gilt-bronze plinth of sweeping rococo scrolls. The group is further enriched with bulrushes in painted metal.

The jar is marked on the unglazed underside with crossed swords painted in blue, and impressed: 10; the swans are unmarked.

Models of the swans probably created about 1747; attributed to Johann Joachim Kaendler (working 1731–1775); the jar created 1735–1745. The mounts are French, dating from about 1750.

Formerly in the collection of Stella S. Hausman.

The species represented is the mute swan (*Cygnus olor*), native to Europe and Asia.

The bowl and cover, of about 1735–1745, may have been molded directly from a Fukien porcelain example. In this connection, Hofmann (*Das Porzellan*, fig. 44) illustrates a covered porcelain box in the Landesmuseum, Kassel, thought to be an experimental piece made at Dresden by Ehrenfried Walther von Tschirnhausen in 1702. Like the bowl and cover of No. 35, both parts of this box are molded with plum motifs in relief.

The swans appear to represent a model illustrated in Savage, *18th-Century German Porcelain*, pl. 19b (end figure, right), where it is said to form part of the Swan Service. For a discussion of the possible inclusion of swans in the Swan Service of Count Brühl, see under Nos. 9 A and B.

For the contemporary French terminology relating to the separate parts of the gilt-bronze mounts, see Volume II of this catalogue, under No. 269.

For comparable examples of swans, see No. 177.

36 A,B Pair of Swans, Mounted in Gilt Bronze as Candelabra

36 A: 23 (overall) H. (58.4); W. 16½ (41.9);
  D. 10¼ (26.1).
  (porcelain) H. 10⅝ (27.0); W. 8¾ (22.3);
  D. 5¾ (14.7).

36 B: (overall) H. 22 (55.9); W. 16¾ (42.6);
  D. 11 (28.0).
  (porcelain) H. 10⅝ (27.0); W. 8¼ (21.0);
  D. 6⅜ (16.2).

EACH large white swan, about one-half natural size, is seated upon a flat-topped circular mound of pale blue water plants. The pose is one of arrested action, the head is turned toward the observer, and the furling of the wings is tentative, as if the bird were about to rise in flight. The beak is striated with Venetian red at the knob and shiny black at the tip. Details of the plumage are precisely yet delicately modeled, especially upon the body, to suggest a soft texture. Three spiraling candle arms of gilt bronze of foliate design rise behind each swan and spring from a pierced gilt-bronze plinth of scrolling acanthus leaves, etc.

The mounts may conceal marks.

Model probably created 1745–1750; attributed to Johann Joachim Kaendler (working 1731–1775); the mounts are French, dating from about 1750.

REFERENCES: Connolly, *Art News*, Christmas edition 1957, p. 120 (No. 36 A illustrated).

The species represented is the mute swan (*Cygnus olor*), native to Europe and Asia.

A swan closely similar to No. 36 B, in the collection of Baroness Renée de Becker, was exhibited at The Metropolitan Museum of Art, New York, 1949 (see Avery, *Masterpieces of European Porcelain*, no. 285, pl. IX, where it is dated "about 1748/50").

A slightly varying and somewhat larger pair is known, which Schnorr von Carolsfeld (*Porzellansammlung Gustav von Klemperer*, p. 211, nos. 783, 784, pl. 81) assigns to Kaendler with the suggestion that the model was created the summer of 1748. Albiker illustrates the same pair in *Die Meissner Porzellantiere im 18. Jahrhundert*, 1935, nos. 143, 144, pl. XXXIV; 1959, fig. 231 (only one reproduced).

A comparable pair exists in the collection of Ernst Schneider, at Schloss Jägerhof, Düsseldorf; and there are two pairs at the Rijksmuseum, Amsterdam, where they are mounted in French gilt bronze set with blossoms of Vincennes porcelain.

An unmounted pair from the Siegfried Salz Collection, Berlin, was sold at Cassirer – Helbing, Berlin, March 26–27, 1929, lots 42, 43 (illustrated in catalogue, pl. V). A single mounted example resembling No. 36 A, from a private collection (Geheimrat W., Dresden), was sold at R. Lepke, Berlin, February 24–26, 1937, lot 537 (illustrated in catalogue, pl. 15). Another comparable to No. 36 A, from the collection of René Fribourg, New York, was one of a pair at Sotheby's, London, June 25, 1963, lot 15 (illustrated in catalogue).

A life-size swan (about 55 cm.), completed in June 1735 by Johann Friedrich Eberlein (working 1735–1749), was among the several large-scale white porcelain sculptures first attempted at Meissen in that decade. An example of this model from the Royal Saxon Collection, Dresden, is illustrated in Albiker, *op. cit.*, 1935, no. 55, pl. XVIII.

The model of Nos. 36 A and B, apparently undocumented, is repeated in Nos. 37 A and B. For a slightly smaller version, compare Nos. 38 A and B.

See also Volume II of this catalogue, Nos. 258 A and B.

37 A, B Pair of Swans

(Schwäne)

37 A: H. 10⅝ (27.0); W. 8¾ (22.3);
D. 5¾ (14.7).

37 B: H. 10⅝ (27.0); W. 8¼ (21.0);
D. 6⅜ (16.2).

EACH figure is posed as if about to rise from the circular mound-shaped base, decorated with low turquoise-tipped water plants, and turns its head warily toward the observer, revealing the black and jasper-red markings of its bill and ringed eyes. The plumage is white, save for a touch of black penciling on the secondary feathers on the right wing of No. 37 A. The subtly modeled surface is coated with a faintly blue-tinted glaze, contrasting strongly with the intense vitreous black of the legs. In No. 37 B, the glaze shows "teadust" fleckings.

Each is marked at the lower edge of the base with crossed swords painted in blue under the glaze.

Model probably created 1745–1750; attributed to Johann Joachim Kaendler (working 1731–1775).

The species represented is the mute swan (*Cygnus olor*), native to Europe and Asia.
The models repeat those of Nos. 36 A and B.

[83]

38 A, B   Pair of Swans

(Schwäne)

38 A: H. 8½ (21.6); W. 6⅝ (16.8);
D. 4½ (11.4).

38 B: H. 8½ (21.6); W. 6⅞ (17.5);
D. 4¾ (12.1).

EACH is a smaller version of Nos. 36 A and B and 37 A and B, with minor variations, chiefly in the more twisted aspect of the neck, and the position of the head. The bases are low, circular plinths fringed with the curling leaves of aquatic plants tipped with pale turquoise.

Each is marked at the lower edge of the base with crossed swords painted in blue (somewhat blurred) under the glaze.

Model created about 1745–1750 by Johann Joachim Kaendler (working 1731–1775).

The species represented is the mute swan (*Cygnus olor*), native to Europe and Asia.

A comparable pair of swans in the collection of Baroness Renée de Becker, New York, was shown at The Metropolitan Museum of Art, New York, 1949. One was illustrated in the catalogue (Avery, *Masterpieces of European Porcelain*, no. 285, pl. IX). Another pair is in the collection of Ernst Schneider at Schloss Jägerhof, Düsseldorf (Rückert, *Meissener Porzellan 1710–1810*, nos. 1117, 1118, pl. 275).

A single matching swan from the collection of Baron von Born, Budapest, was sold at R. Lepke, Berlin, December 4, 1929, lot 14 (illustrated in catalogue, pl. 17).

Kaendler is known to have been modeling swans in November of 1747; see under Nos. 33 A–C.

For additional comments on the larger swans, see under Nos. 36 A and B and 37 A and B.

39 A, B   Pair of Mallard Ducks

(Enten)

39 A: H. 11¼ (28.6); W. 10¼ (26.1); D. 5½ (14.1).

39 B: H. 11 (28.0); W. 10⅛ (25.8); D. 5¼ (13.4).

EACH stands among low water plants on a circular base. The drake (No. 39 B), its head thrown slightly backward, opens its flesh-tinted bill to reveal a row of toothlike serrations on the upper mandible. The head and upper neck are painted in varying shades of violet, the breast and back in dead-leaf brown streaked and barred in black, and the wings are minutely patterned in brown and black, partly reserved in white. No. 39 A is similarly marked, though the head is a purple *flambé*, there is a pale yellow band at the base of the neck, and the breast is of violet minutely dotted with black. The ducks nestle amid the short curling turquoise leaves of rushes springing from circular mound-shaped bases, dappled in yellow and green.

Each is marked at the lower edge of the base with crossed swords painted in blue under the glaze.

Models created in 1749; attributed to Johann Joachim Kaendler (working 1731–1775).

REFERENCES: Connolly, *Art News*, Christmas edition 1957, p. 117 (illustrated).

Formerly in the collection of Sir Philip Sassoon, Trent Park, Herefordshire.

The ducks are the domestic mallard of the northern hemisphere, descended from the wild species, *Anas boschas*.

Meissen ducks are especially rare. Several exist in the collection of Ernst Schneider, at Schloss Jägerhof, Düsseldorf (Rückert, *Meissener Porzellan 1710–1810*, no. 1112, pl. 273); others are in the Rijksmuseum, Amsterdam; one with closed beak, but otherwise close to the type of No. 39 A, is in the Staatliche Porzellansammlung, Dresden.

40 A, B Pair of Young Herring Gulls

(Möwen)

40 A: H. 11 (28.0); W. 10½ (26.8); D. 5⅝ (14.4).

40 B: H. 11 (28.0); W. 9¾ (24.8); D. 5¹³⁄₁₆ (14.8).

EACH bird is posed in an attitude of wary alertness, one (No. 40 A) with its left leg upraised. Each stands with its head sharply turned, amid tall blue-green rushes springing from a round base. The long brown bill and black wing tips contrast with the fawn and sepia penciling of the rest of the plumage, which is delicately modeled to convey the softness of a warm living form. The legs and feet are an ivory-white.

Each is marked at the lower edge of the base with crossed swords painted in blue under the glaze.

Models created about 1753 by Johann Joachim Kaendler (working 1731–1775).

REFERENCES: Connolly, *Art News*, Christmas edition 1957, p. 117 (illustrated).

Formerly in the collection of Catalina von Pannwitz, Hartekamp, the Netherlands.

The species represented is the herring gull (*Larus arentatus*), common in many parts of the northern hemisphere.

Comparable gulls are to be found in the collections of the late Mrs. Jacques Balsan, Lantana, Florida; the State Hermitage Museum, Leningrad (*Staryé-Gody*, May 1911, pl. 29); the Rijksmuseum, Amsterdam (a pair); the Staatliche Porzellansammlung, Dresden (Albiker, *Die Meissner Porzellantiere im 18. Jahrhundert*, 1935, nos. 130–132, pl. XXXII; 1959, fig. 91 [a gull corresponding to No. 40 A]); Irwin Untermyer, New York (Hackenbroch, *Meissen and Other Continental Porcelain in the Irwin Untermyer Collection*, p. 18, fig. 19).

A single gull from an unidentified collection was sold at Christie's, London, June 21, 1965, lot 155 (illustrated in catalogue).

[89]

41 A, B   Pair of Bitterns

(Rohrdommeln)

41 A: H. 14¾ (37.5); W. 7¾ (19.7); D. 6¼ (15.9).

41 B: H. 14⅜ (36.5); W. 6½ (16.5); D. 5 (12.7).

EACH long-necked, ungainly bird with long legs stands beside a tall cluster of turquoise-green water plants springing from a circular mound base. The modeling accentuates the disheveled fluffiness of the plumage, which varies from white to stippled brown and black. The dark sepia crown is demarcated by a curving white area that begins just in front of the eye and terminates in short tufts near the back of the head. Under each eye is a long, pointed streak matching the color of the crown. The legs are speckled and barred.

No. 41 B is marked at the lower edge of the base with crossed swords painted in blue under the glaze; No. 41 A is unmarked.

Models created about 1753 by Johann Joachim Kaendler (working 1731–1775).

REFERENCES: Connolly, *Art News*, Christmas edition 1957, p. 116 (illustrated).

Formerly in the collection of Baron Max von Goldschmidt-Rothschild, Frankfurt am Main. The birds were confiscated by the Nazis during World War II and stored in the Frankfurt Museum für Kunsthandwerk.

The birds represent the species *Botaurus stellaris*, native to Europe and Asia.

Other examples of this rare model are in the collections of Charles E. Dunlap, New York (formerly in the collection of Robert von Hirsch, Basel); Gustav von Klemperer, Dresden (illustrated in Albiker, *Die Meissner Porzellantiere im 18. Jahrhundert*, 1935, no. 124, pl. XXXII; 1959, fig. 90, and again in Schnorr von Carolsfeld, *Porzellansammlung Gustav von Klemperer*, no. 785, pl. 78); Mr. and Mrs. Lesley G. Shaefer, New York; the Henry E. Huntington Library and Art Gallery, San Marino, California (Wark, *French Decorative Art in the Huntington Collection*, fig. 97, mounted as candelabra); the Museum für Kunsthandwerk, Frankfurt am Main (illustrated in the catalogue of the exhibition *Figürliche Keramik aus Zwei Jahrtausenden*, 1963–1964, fig. 89); the Rijksmuseum, Amsterdam.

A pair from the collection of Siegfried Salz, Berlin, was sold at Cassirer—Helbing, Berlin, March 26–27, 1929, lots 40, 41 (illustrated in catalogue, pl. IV). These were later sold from an unidentified collection at Ball – Graupe, Berlin, March 15, 1933, lot 42 (illustrated in catalogue, pl. 9). Another pair, from the collection of Mrs. Edward Hutton, New York, was sold at Sotheby's, London, November 23, 1965, lot 58 (illustrated in catalogue).

42 Miniature Cockatoo

(Kakadu)

H. 2³⁄₁₆ (5.6); W. 1¹¹⁄₁₆ (4.3); D. 1 (2.6).

THE SMALL white-breasted bird perches upon a tree stump of more or less conical shape. A pointed crest of medium height rises, tiara-like, from the back of the head. The upper parts are yellow-green with darker pencilings, the crest and wings yellow, splashed with orange-red. A small white ring surrounds each eye.

Unmarked.

Model possibly created about 1745–1750.

There is no available record of this model at the Meissen manufactory.

A comparable figure, apparently a companion to this one, in the collection of C. H. Fischer, Dresden, was sold at J. M. Heberle, Cologne, October 22–25, 1906, lot 901 (illustrated in catalogue, pl. XXII).

43 A, B Miniature Parakeet and Parrot

(Sittich und Papagei)

43 A: H. 2⅛ (5.4); W. 1¾ (4.5); D. ¹⁵⁄₁₆ (2.4).

43 B: H. 2¼ (5.7); W. 1⅜ (3.5); D. ¹⁵⁄₁₆ (2.4).

THE parakeet is speckled, with gray-green upper parts and buff under parts, yielding to puce at the wing tips and tail. The parrot (No. 43 B) has a bright yellow body and wings with bands of orange-red, green, and blue. Each rests on a tree stump, sparsely encrusted with green leaves.

Unmarked.

Models possibly created in 1745–1750.

Formerly in the collection of Herbert Gutmann, London.

There is no available record in the Meissen manufactory of these models, which represent indeterminate species.

Two comparable birds from the collection of Mrs. Edward Hutton, New York, were sold at Sotheby's, London, November 23, 1965, lot 42 (illustrated in catalogue). Several miniature birds of other species are illustrated in the sale catalogue of the collection of C. H. Fischer, Dresden (J. M. Heberle, Cologne, October 22–25, 1906, pl. XXII).

44 Beaker

H. 3⅟₁₆ (7.8); Diam. at lip 2¾ (7.0); Diam. at base 2 (5.1).

THIS is a cone-shaped beaker, swelling toward the out-turned lip, and molded at the base with a band of gadrooning. It is decorated with a gilded chinoiserie vignette of seated and kneeling figures flanking a palm tree. The figures rest upon a platform ornamented with a baroque arabesque from which is suspended a blossom hung with two drapery festoons. A pair of serrated gold bands, bordered by alternating arabesques, C-scrolls, pearlings, and other ornament, encloses the vignette. The interior and gadrooned base are also gilded.

Marked on the underside with the monogram

 painted in gold.

Dating from about 1720; the decoration *Hausmaler* work of the workshop of Bartholomäus Seuter, Augsburg, dating from about 1730–1735.

A comparable beaker in the Staatliche Porzellansammlung, Dresden, is illustrated in Zimmermann, *Meissner Porzellan*, p. 49. Another, in a private collection in Munich, appears in Rückert, *Meissener Porzellan 1710–1810*, pl. 16, no. 48.

A Meissen cup and saucer (location not recorded) with gilding bearing the inscription "A. Seite, 1736 Augusta" (Honey, *European Ceramic Art*, p. 555) affords documentary evidence of chinoiserie having been done there (Augusta Vindelicorum is the Roman name for the locality; the signature is that of Abraham Seite [1690–1747]). The Augsburg gilder Bartholomäus Seuter (1678–1754), the brother of Abraham Seite, is identified with the chinoiserie and other ornament employed in No. 44. Augsburg hausmalers were partial to the use of chinoiserie scenes adapted from engravings by Martin Engelbrecht (1684–1756), also of Augsburg (see Honey, *op. cit.*, p. 407).

45 A, B Two Bowls, Mounted in Gilt Bronze

45 A: (overall) H. 8⅝ (21.9); W. 12 (30.5);
      D. 7⅞ (20.0).
      (porcelain) H. 6 (15.2); Diam. 7¹³⁄₁₆ (19.9).

45 B: (overall) H. 7⅜ (18.7); W. 11 (27.9);
      D. 7 (17.8).
      (porcelain) H. 4¾ (12.0);
      Diam. 7¹³⁄₁₆ (19.9).

EACH deep circular vessel with swelling walls is enameled with a collar of turquoise-blue *rinceaux* interrupted by iron-red plum blossoms. The broad white field below is painted in the Kakiemon manner with zigzag stems supporting chalky blue and turquoise leaves, and iron-red peonies with round gold centers. On No. 45 A the foliage springs from a mound of deep blue and turquoise rockery. There is a spray of three red blossoms, with leaves in turquoise and blue in the center of the interior of each.

Each bowl is mounted with chased and gilded bronze, consisting of a rim mount tooled with foliage in relief; a pair of rococo C-scroll handles, each surmounted by a winged dragon; and a substantial base of *rocaille* design, resting upon three points.

Each is marked on the underside with the "caduceus," painted in blue under the glaze.

The porcelain dates from about 1725; the mounts are French, dating from 1735–1745.

It is to be noted that these bowls do not match, although they are very similar; one is markedly more shallow than the other.

The *Merkurstab* or caduceus made its first appearance about 1723, and its use continued or was resumed in the early 1730s, especially in connection with small coffee cups destined for the Turkish market. Zimmermann in his *Meissner Porzellan* (p. 340) tells of a Greek exporter Manasses Athanas, who in 1731 requested that the caduceus be used instead of the crossed swords, apparently because the latter mark might be mistaken in Turkey for a Christian cross. The same source (p. 166) reveals that in 1734 when Athanas repeated his request (which earlier had been granted), offering at the same time to order as many as 3,000 dozen coffee cups if the factory would grant him exclusive rights to porcelain so marked, the Meissen authorities declined to discontinue the crossed swords.

See also Volume II of this catalogue, Nos. 256 A and B.

46 Beaker

H. 5⅞₆ (13.9); Diam. 3¹³⁄₁₆ (9.7).

OF MODIFIED Chinese beaker shape, the vessel
has gently incurving walls expanding toward the
lip and rising from a bulbous octagonal base that
rests upon a sloping circular foot. The upper
portion is painted most conspicuously with puce,
iron-red, pea-green, and touches of gray-blue,
with a continuous panoramic band of chinoiserie
figures. On one side is a scene of a mandarin
holding an audience, with a screen and architecture in the background, and on the other a lady
of high station is seated at a table equipped with a
tea service and flanked by attendants. Gilded
baroque lacework encloses the scene above and
below.

The lower portion is gilded, and each of its
eight facets is reserved with an ovoid panel enclosing a single figure, standing, kneeling, or sitting,
each holding an attribute of his rank.

Marked on the underside with crossed swords
(the hilts having pommels) painted in deep blue
under the glaze.

Dating from about 1725–1730; the decoration
probably by Johann Gregor Herold (working
1720–1765).

A pair of covered beakers dating from about
1740 (as indicated by the European harbor scenes
featured in the decoration) was in the collection
of Gustav von Klemperer, Dresden (see Schnorr
von Carolsfeld, *Porzellansammlung Gustav von
Klemperer*, nos. 203, 204, illustrated). Together
with a similar pair of purple-ground beakers in
the collection of Ernst Schneider at Schloss Jägerhof, Düsseldorf, they offer interesting evidence for
the survival of this unusual form into the 1740s
(see Rückert, *Meissener Porzellan 1710–1810*, nos.
410, 411, pl. 104).

The problem of ascribing chinoiserie to J. G.
Herold is made difficult by the paucity of au-
thenticated examples. Only two signed pieces
are known. One, a vase formerly in the Royal
Saxon Collection, Dresden, was destroyed in
World War II. It was signed "Johann Gregorius
Höroldt inven: Meissen, den 22, Janu. anno 1727"
(see Pazaurek, *Meissner Porzellanmalerei des 18.
Jahrhunderts*, figs. 3, 4). The other, also a vase, in
the Meissen Stadtmuseum, is inscribed "J.G.
Höroldt fec. Meissen, 17 Augusti 1726" (see
Ducret, *German Porcelain and Faience*, no. 6, illus-
trated p. 61).

Among objects that may reasonably be attributed to Herold are a teacup and a presentation goblet
at The Metropolitan Museum of Art, New York
(acc. nos. 54.147.75, 66.63 a–c). The former is part
of a breakfast service made for Victor Amadeus,
King of Sardinia, mentioned in the Meissen archives as a project upon which Herold himself
worked in March and June of 1725. The goblet
was made for Sophia Dorothea, Queen of Prussia,
in 1728. There is little question that the painting of
this goblet was done by Herold; its painted detail
agrees very closely with other examples accepted

as his work. On the cover of the Metropolitan Museum's goblet, a vessel of the same type is depicted within a cartouche, evidence, it would seem, of the prestige of the goblet as a gift. When it is remembered that Herold's work at this period was limited to only the most important products of Meissen, i.e., those commissioned by the Elector, this seems to strengthen the attribution, especially in view of the recipient (see Dennis, *Metropolitan Museum of Art Bulletin*, Summer 1963, pp. 10–21, figs. 3, 5–8, and color plate).

Like these two objects, the beaker No. 44 is decorated with attenuated figures in light-colored robes, sparsely patterned, the men wearing complicated headgear, the women with varying high coiffures. The decoration on these three objects is also characterized by a lively inventiveness, an emphasis on small utensils, the presence of openwork pedestals, and the painterly approach of the artist, showing little reliance on outline, as associated with the work of Herold.

This type of vessel is usually furnished with a flat-domed cover having eight sloping sides and a gilded finial in the shape of an urn. Sometimes the basic design of a covered beaker was adapted for a *Pokal*, or presentation goblet, by setting it upon a high, spreading foot. An elaborate example of such a covered goblet with chinoiserie decoration, attributed to Herold, about 1725–1730, is in the Rijksmuseum, Amsterdam. It is illustrated in *Keramos*, April 1963, p. 37, fig. 5.

47 A, B   Pair of Beaker Vases

H. 11⅞ (30.2); Diam. 5¼ (13.4).

EACH cylindrical vase, with gently incurving walls, fashioned in the manner of a K'ang Hsi beaker, is decorated with scattered Oriental motifs, including a turquoise and gold *fu*-lion, an acolyte in cobalt-blue and turquoise robes, and several sprays of flowers in the Kakiemon manner, with colorful butterflies and other insects in the intervening spaces. The modern mounts are of carved and gilded wood.

Each is marked on the underside with the "caduceus," painted in blue under the glaze.

Dating from about 1725–1728.

Formerly in the collection of Sir Bernard Eckstein, London.

The decoration is closely similar to that of a vase recorded in Handt and Rakebrand (*Meissner Porzellan des Achtzehnten Jahrhunderts, 1710–1750*, pl. 16), presumably at the Staatliche Porzellansammlung, Dresden.

A cup and saucer decorated in this pattern are in the Hans Syz Collection, Smithsonian Institution, Washington, D.C.

For a note on the caduceus mark, see under Nos. 45 A and B.

48 A, B Pair of Beaker Vases

H. 11⅞ (30.1); Diam. 5¼ (13.4).

EACH cylindrical vase, with gently incurving walls, is fashioned in the manner of a K'ang Hsi beaker. The decoration, adapted from the Chinese, is an informal composition of iron-red and aubergine blossoms amid leaves of green, turquoise, and starch-blue. Interspersed among the blossoms are exotic birds, some in flight, some perched, and others standing beside conventionalized rockery. The modern mounts are of carved and gilded wood.

Each is marked on the underside with the "caduceus," painted in blue under the glaze.

Dating from about 1725–1730.

Formerly in the collection of Mrs. von Friedlaender-Fuld, Berlin.

The Chinese aspect of the colors and the painting serve to place the decoration within Herold's first decade at Meissen.

A related pair of vases is in the Hans Syz Collection at the Smithsonian Institution, Washington, D.C. (see his article in *Antiques*, June 1960, p. 571, fig. 12).

For a note on the caduceus mark, see under Nos. 45 A and B.

49 A, B Pair of Beakers

H. 5¼ (13.4); Diam. 4¾ (12.1).

EACH trumpet-shaped vessel curves to a broadly flaring lip and somewhat less flaring foot. A narrow molded and gilded ring encircles the vase about an inch above the base. One side of each is painted with a chinoiserie scene depicting a pair of figures who flank, on No. 49 A, a stand with a radiant mask emerging from a vase, and, on No. 49 B, a drum table supporting a bowl. The scenes are bordered with four-lobed frames (*Laub und Bandelwerk*) of gilding and iridescent purple luster.

Each is painted on the reverse with a delicately tinted, richly floriated spray of *Indianische Blumen* (chrysanthemums and lotuses executed in the Oriental manner) in iron-red, purple, and pale green. Scattered blossoms in the Kakiemon style are painted in the band above the gilded foot ring. Inside the lip of each is a gilded lacework border.

Each is marked on the underside with crossed swords, painted in blue under the glaze.

Dating from about 1730; the figure painting is in the manner of Johann Gregor Herold (working 1720–1765).

The popularity of chinoiserie decoration, launched at Meissen by the art director J. G. Herold, led to a rapid increase in the number of artists employed. It was almost inevitable that the painters under Herold's direction should assimilate a number of the master's idiosyncrasies. Conspicuous among these is the employment of hats with broad, double brims, found on several pieces attributed to J. G. Herold, who in turn appears to have copied them from engravings by the Augsburg engraver Martin Engelbrecht (1684–1756).

50 Beaker

H. 5¼ (13.4); Diam. 4⅛ (10.5).

THE trumpet-shaped vessel, with a broadly flaring lip and molded base, is painted at each side with a four-lobed panel of a chinoiserie scene. In one panel a corpulent male figure waves a beribboned fan or wand; and in the other a nobleman and his page gaze at steaming utensils upon a circular table having tall spindly legs. A palm tree and stalks of pink hollyhock rise behind the central figure.

Each panel is enclosed within an elaborate border of iridescent purple luster and gold scroll-work *(Laub und Bandelwerk)*, into which are worked minuscule Chinese figures and baroque motifs in purple and iron-red.

Marked on the underside with crossed swords, painted in blue under the glaze.

Dating from about 1730.

The figure appearing in the illustration is reminiscent of the hand of Johann Ehrenfried Stadtler (working 1723/1724 onward), in its iron-red and black outlining and in the artist's preoccupation with corpulent Chinese, pinwheel-like flowers, huge fans, and the like. A comparable example attributed to Stadtler is a cup and saucer in the collection of Ernst Schneider at Schloss Jägerhof, Düsseldorf (Rückert, *Meissener Porzellan 1710–1810*, no. 218, pl. 59).

51 Bowl

H. 3⅛ (8.0); Diam. 6¹¹⁄₁₆ (17.1).

THE DEEP round bowl has a flaring rim and a sharply defined ring foot. The exterior is painted on each side with a panel, one showing a European harbor scene, the other a view of a river with a windmill, both with many figures. Each scene is set within a baroque cartouche of iridescent purple luster, gold scrollwork, and puce volutes of foliage *(Laub und Bandelwerk)*. Alternating with the cartouches are sprays of lotuses and other flowers painted iron-red and purple, in the Oriental manner. The interior is painted with a harbor scene somewhat similar to that on the exterior, showing standing figures in the foreground and a tall yellow tower looming above the distant shore. Inside the lip is a rich border of gilded lacework.

Marked on the underside with crossed swords (their hilts distinctly S-shaped), painted in blue under the glaze. There is also a large 2, painted in gold, presumably the mark of the gilder.

Dating from about 1730–1735; the painting is in the manner of Christian Friedrich Herold (working 1725–1778).

The decoration is typical of the period when interest in Chinese subjects was beginning to yield to European scenes.

52 A, B Pair of Vases, Mounted in Gilt Bronze

Overall: H. 13⅝ (34.6); W. 10¾ (27.3); D. 7 (17.8).

Porcelain: H. about 6¾ (17.2); W. about 6⅛ (15.7).

EACH ovoid vase, with incurving cover, is of the so-called "Mayflower" type. The surface, except for two panels on each, is covered with small starch-blue flowers, their white centers dotted brown and yellow. Each panel is enclosed by a cusped white border in low relief, and is painted with scenes in the manner of Antoine Watteau. On No. 52 A is a group of three figures, including a youth who plays a lute, and on the reverse a seated couple holding hands; on No. 52 B are pairs of romantic figures. Each vase is richly mounted in chased and gilded bronze of rococo design. The cover is ornamented with a pierced cluster of scrolls and flowers; it is separated from the vessel by an openwork band of related design, from which two floriated scroll handles descend to the high spreading foot of swirling leaf scrolls. The interior of each vessel and its cover is lined with gilded metal.

No marks are visible on the porcelain. The mounts are stamped on the base and cover (and on No. 52 B on the scroll of the handle also) with the crowned C (for a note on the crowned C, see under Nos. 16 A and B).

The porcelain dates from about 1740; the mounts are French, dating from 1745–1749.

A pair of related vases mounted as ewers, the mounts thought to be by Caffiéri (1674–1755), is in the Wallace Collection, London (Watson, *Catalogue of Furniture*, p. 76, nos. F 103–104). Other examples are in the Louvre (where the blossoms are white; acc. nos. 8061–8062), and the Cleveland Museum of Art (illustrated, *Handbook*, 1966, p. 138; acc. no. 44.230). Still another mounted pair is in the Henry E. Huntington Library and Art Gallery, San Marino, California (illustrated in Wark, *French Decorative Art*, fig. 99).

The vogue for "Watteau subjects" (the term also applies to illustrations derived from his master Claude Gillot, and his followers, Nicolas Lancret and J.-B. Pater) began in 1738. In that year they appeared on an armorial service made for the daughter of Frederick Augustus II, Elector of Saxony (1696–1763), Maria Amalia Christina, among a wedding gift of seventeen services. This truly royal service, now in the Museo Arqueológico Nacional, Madrid, was decorated with park scenes in green with black underpainting, interspersed with opulent panels of gold bordered by gold scrollwork.

See also Volume II of this catalogue, Nos. 267 A and B.

53 A–C   Garniture of Three Vases, Mounted in Gilt Bronze

53 A: (overall) H. 12¼ (31.1); W. 7 (17.8);
     D. 6 (15.2).
     (porcelain) H. 8½ (21.6);
     Diam. 5³⁄₁₆ (13.1).

53 B, C: (overall) H. 9¼ (23.5); W. 5⅛ (13.0);
     D. 5 (12.7).
     (porcelain) H. 6¾ (17.2);
     Diam. 4½ (11.4).

THE GARNITURE consists of one large (No. 53 A) and a pair of smaller (Nos. 53 B and C) baluster-shaped vases. The ground of each is decorated with applied delicate green stems and small multi-colored blossoms, framing, on each vase, a pair of cartouche-shaped panels painted with scenes in the manner of Watteau, against a field of gold. Painted sprays of naturalistic poppies, anemones, tulips and other blossoms are interspersed among the molded and applied flowers.

The panel on the larger vase No. 53 A depicts a scene in a park, with a couple admiring a flower chain while a youth watches furtively from behind a stone pedestal, and on the opposite side, an amorous couple is seated before an arbor, with a rival suitor standing at the left holding a shepherd's staff. The scenes on No. 53 B show seated couples, one with a lute; those on No. 53 C show on one side a pair of seated lovers and an eavesdropping harlequin, and, on the other side, a young man and woman standing in conversation before a garden statue. The smaller vases have an additional gold band at the base of the neck.

Each vase is mounted in chased and gilded bronze with two upswept scrolled and foliate handles that clasp opposite sides of the vase and spring from a spreading base of rambling strap scrolls overlaid with flowers.

Each is marked on the underside with crossed swords, painted in blue under the glaze.

The garniture dates from about 1745; the mounts are French, and slightly later in date.

Formerly in the collection of Harvie Morton Farquhar, and Baroness Nellie Lisa Helles Burton, both of Needwood House, Burton-on-Trent, Staffordshire (sold Christies's, London, November 23, 1950, lot 201 [illustrated in catalogue]).

A comparable pair is in the Cleveland Museum of Art. The type appears in Hofmann, *Das Europäische Porzellan des Bayerischen Nationalmuseums*, no. 128, pl. 7.

Another pair with gilded and painted reserves, from the collection of the Staatliche Museen, Berlin, was sold at J. Böhler, Munich, June 1–2, 1937, lots 467 and 468 (illustrated in catalogue, pl. 35). These, however, were encrusted with mayflowers. One from an anonymous collection was sold at Weinmüller, Munich, March 18–19, 1964, lot 30 (illustrated in catalogue, pl. 54). A pair from the René Fribourg Collection was sold at Sotheby's, London, May 4, 1965, lot 176 (illustrated in catalogue).

The largest vase in this garniture is fitted with mounts identical to those of the corresponding vase in a garniture at the Victoria and Albert Museum, London; illustrated in the *Catalogue of the Jones Collection*, Part II, pl. 38, no. 181.

See also Volume II of this catalogue, Nos. 271 A–C.

54 A,B Pair of Chinese Figures, Mounted in Gilt Bronze as Candelabra

54 A: (overall) H. 12¾ (32.3); W. 11½ (29.2);
D. 6 (15.2).
(porcelain) H. 8⁷⁄₁₆ (21.5); W. 3⅜ (8.6);
D. 3⅝ (9.2).

54 B: (overall) H. 13½ (34.3); W. 11 (27.9);
D. 6¾ (17.2).
(porcelain) H. 8¼ (20.9); W. 3¼ (8.2);
D. 4 (10.2).

EACH dancing Chinese boy wears a cabbage-leaf hat, loose lavender robes, and a flower-patterned cape-like garment over his shoulders. He is rotund, with puffy cheeks, and his mouth is open as if in song. Each raises one hand and the opposite knee. One has a pair of black slippers, the other yellow. A circular mound-shaped base with sides irregularly notched, its top strewn with blossoms and leaves, serves as a support.

Each figure is framed by a cluster of white and tinted porcelain flowers supported on leafy metal stems painted green. On either side a serpentine candleholder of gilt bronze in a foliate design rises from an elevated platform of openwork rococo scrolls.

Unmarked.

The porcelain dates from about 1745–1750; the mounts are French, dating from about 1750.

Formerly in the collection of Mrs. Jacques Balsan, Lantana, Florida.

A similar model, attributed to Kaendler, and dated about 1745, is in the Cecil Higgins Museum, Bedford, Bedfordshire (see Palmer, *Apollo*, Febru-

ary 1950, p. 41, fig. VI).

Five figures of Chinese dancing boys in two sizes are in the collection of the State Hermitage Museum, Leningrad, and one is in the Forsyth Wickes Collection of the Museum of Fine Arts, Boston.

A comparable pair, unmounted, from an anonymous collection, was sold at Sotheby's, London, June 2, 1959, lot 153 (illustrated in catalogue). Another pair, slightly larger and of a somewhat varying design, is illustrated in the same catalogue, lot 154.

A third pair, from the collection of Robert Goelet was sold at Parke-Bernet, New York, October 13–15, 1966, lot 373 (illustrated in catalogue).

A variant but related form, with nodding head and pronounced Oriental features, was in the collection of Ole Olsen, Copenhagen, where it was described as dating from about 1735 (see Schmitz, *Generaldirektor Ole Olsens Kunstsamlinger*, II, p. XXXVI, fig. 1367).

See also Volume II of this catalogue, Nos. 257 A and B.

55 A,B Pair of Plant Pots, Mounted in Gilt Bronze

Overall: H. 5⁹⁄₁₆ (14.2); W. 7 (17.8); D. 5 (12.7).

Porcelain: H. 4⁷⁄₈ (12.4); Diam. 4⁵⁄₈ (11.7).

EACH tub-shaped vessel has a gently flaring lip, and sides that bulge toward the base, which is constricted to form a flaring foot. The surface is molded in low relief with five horizontal bands of floral sprigs, each sprig bearing three blossoms, and each blossom four rounded petals. The flowers of the upper, middle, and lower bands are tinted soft blue flecked with yellow; the alternate bands are reserved in white. Beneath the lip of each are painted nosegays of roses, convolvulus, anemones, and star flowers. Under one gilt-bronze handle of each vase a cluster of small flowers has been applied.

Each vase is mounted in gilt bronze with a pair of horizontal loop handles applied with leaves and flowers, and springing from a gadrooned rim. A molded and gadrooned mount surrounds the foot.

Each is marked on the underside with crossed swords, painted in blue under the glaze.

The porcelain dates from about 1750; the mounts may be German, dating from about 1750–1775.

See also Volume II of this catalogue, Nos. 266 A and B.

56 A, B   Two Leaf Dishes

56 A: H. 1¾ (4.5); W. 6½ (16.5); D. 5¼ (13.4).

56 B: H. 1⁷⁄₁₆ (3.7); W. 6⅝ (16.8); D. 5⅜ (13.7).

EACH dish, in the form of a fig leaf, has three larger and two smaller lobes, all with sharply serrated edges. A scrolling stem, springing from the underside and resting upon the rim, serves as a handle. The interior is molded with delicate veinings, painted with naturalistic sprigs, and an irregular border of deep green.

Each is marked on the underside with crossed swords, painted in blue.

Dating from about 1755.

A comparable pair is in the collection of the Bayerisches Nationalmuseum, Munich.

57 A–D Set of Four Cups

H. 3¼ (8.3); W. 4 (10.2); D. 2¹⁵⁄₁₆ (7.5).

EACH cup is of deep tulip shape, with a flaring rim and a pair of delicate scrolled handles. Each is painted on either side with an exotic Oriental figure within a gilded four-lobed border, heightened with scrollwork and pairs of kidney-shaped panels of pink luster, and with an outer border of iron-red and deep purple feathery scrolls. There is gilded lacework inside the lip. The following figures are depicted:

57 A: (obverse) a court lady with fan; (reverse) a tall courtier standing under a breadfruit tree.

57 B: (obverse) an official in puce robes, holding a small tray with burning incense; (reverse) a stooping servant carrying a bird on a perch.

57 C: (obverse) an ambassador unrolling a scroll; (reverse) a servant standing before a round tripod table supporting flasks.

57 D: (obverse) a court lady with parasol and censer; (reverse) a kneeling figure holding a teacup and saucer; at left a steaming kettle rests upon a tall stove.

Each is marked on the underside with the numeral 1 in German script followed by a dot, painted in gold, probably the mark of the gilder.

Dating from about 1724–1725; the figure painting is in all probability by Johann Gregor Herold (working 1720–1765).

A pair of closely similar cups and saucers are in the collection of Gustav von Klemperer, Dresden (Carolsfeld, *Porzellansammlung Gustav von Klemperer*, nos. 87, 88, pl. 10). A comparable cup, claimed as "certainly by J. G. Höroldt" was in the collection of M. Salomon, Dresden (illustrated in Pazaurek, *Meissner Porzellanmalerei des 18. Jahrhunderts*, figs. 5, 6).

The attribution to J. G. Herold is reinforced by, among other considerations, that artist's predilection for figures with hats and parasols with a pronounced radial pattern (see Nos. 58 A–D). The motif is conspicuous in two of his six chinoiserie etchings, dating from 1726, reproduced in Ducret, *Keramik-Freunde der Schweiz*, July 1957, figs. 49, 51. Another characteristic associated with this master is the interruption of the gold bands on the foot rings of his cups by a fleur de lys type of ornament, immediately under the center of each pictorial panel (Wark, *Keramik-Freunde der Schweiz*, July 1957, figs. 25, 27, and 28).

58 A–D   Set of Four Cups

H. 3 ¼ (8.3); W. 4 (10.2); D. 2 ¹⁵⁄₁₆ (7.5).

EACH cup is of deep tulip shape, with a flaring rim and a pair of delicate fret handles of the same design as those on Nos. 57 A–D. Each is painted on either side with an exotic Oriental figure within a cartouche-shaped gold border heightened with variously shaped panels in a darker tone of gold, all within an outer border of puce and iron-red conventional sprigs. Gilded lacework decorates the inside of the lip. The following figures are depicted:

58 A: (obverse) a gray-robed official seated beside a chest of drawers inlaid with plaques painted with landscapes; (reverse) a walking figure with a large bird at his feet.

58 B: (obverse) a figure with a parasol, standing before a tripod table supporting a smoking urn; (reverse) an alchemist at a furnace inset with a tile decorated with a landscape.

58 C: (obverse) a figure in puce robes kneeling beside a tall tripod table supporting a smoking censer; (reverse) an orange-robed figure holding a staff.

58 D: (obverse) an alchemist raising a flask to eye level against a background of blue clouds above a harbor scene; (reverse) a servant with tray; a table and stand at the right.

Each is marked on the underside with the numeral 2 in German script followed by a dot, painted in gold, probably the mark of the gilder.

Dating from about 1724–1725; the figure painting is in all probability by Johann Gregor Herold (working 1720–1765), for reasons noted under Nos. 57 A–D.

59 Cup

H. 3³⁄₁₆ (8.2); W. 3⅞ (9.8); D. 2⅞ (7.4).

THIS two-handled cup, of the type of Nos. 57 A–D and 58 A–D, is painted on one side with a female servant in yellow and puce robes holding a tray of jars and vases, and, on the reverse, with a seated man in a figured russet gown dyeing a length of silk. The vignettes are framed with gilded cartouches highlighted with panels of iridescent gold and foliate scrolls of puce and russet. Gilded lacework decorates the inside of the lip.

Marked on the underside: 17, painted in gold; and J.B. 173, painted in black.

Dating from about 1725; the figure painting is in all probability by Johann Gregor Herold (working 1720–1765), for reasons noted under Nos. 57 A–D.

60 Cup and Saucer

Cup: H. 2⅝ (6.7).

Saucer: Diam. 5⅛ (13.0).

THE HANDLELESS cup is spade-shaped, and the rim of its deep saucer is boldly undulating. Each is painted with pairs of pomegranates on angular stems, the saucer with additional lotus and hawthorn motifs, all in the Kakiemon manner. The colors are iron-red, soft green, and pale cobalt, heightened with gilding; the rim of each is painted chestnut-brown.

The cup is marked on the underside with crossed swords, and the saucer with a version of the "caduceus," both painted in blue under the glaze. The saucer is impressed on the inner slope of the foot ring with a small cross.

Dating from about 1725.

For a discussion of the caduceus mark, see under Nos. 45 A and B.

61 A, B   Pair of Tureens, Mounted in Gilt Bronze

Overall: H. 12⅜ (31.4); W. 10 (25.4);
D. 7⁷⁄₁₆ (18.9).

Porcelain: H. 12½ (31.8); Diam. 7½ (19.0).

EACH is a deep cylindrical jar contracting at the base to form a molded round foot, and fitted with a sloping cover, topped with a finial in the form of an artichoke. Both parts are decorated in the Kakiemon manner, with the "yellow tiger" pattern, representing a flesh-tinted tiger charging around a broken stalk of blue bamboo and leafless branches bearing multicolored star-like blossoms. Alternating with this motif is a gnarled aubergine tree trunk, suggesting a dragon with his head thrown back, standing before an angular shrub of blue and turquoise, which bears highly conventionalized iron-red and straw-yellow plum blossoms.

Each tureen is ornamented with mounts of chased and gilded bronze. The rims of the cover and bowl are enclosed by narrow beaded bands. At either side of the bowl is a mask of a bearded faun from whose head a scrolling horn rises to meet the lower band. The base is supported by a broad molded band, pierced and tooled with acanthus leaves in its upper portion.

Each is marked on the underside with crossed swords, painted in blue under the glaze, accompanied by N = 172 cut through the glaze and filled with black pigment. The latter, repeated inside the cover of each, is an inventory mark of the Royal Saxon Collection, Dresden, "N" being the usual abbreviation for "number."

The porcelain dates from about 1730; the mounts may date from 1775–1785 or later.

Formerly in the Royal Saxon Collection, Dresden.

The decoration agrees in every detail with that on a twelve-sided dish in the Royal Saxon Collection (see Hannover, *Pottery and Porcelain*, III,

European Porcelain, p. 59, fig. 79; also Schmidt, *Porcelain as an Art and a Mirror of Fashion*, fig. 24).

Inventories of the Royal Saxon Collection were extended from time to time as additions were made. Under the original system, a W, for *Weiss*, designated white Saxon (Meissen) porcelain. Other symbols were used for the several varieties of Chinese, Japanese, and Meissen wares that constituted the collection, while it was housed in the Japanese Palace, Dresden.

William Chaffers, in his *Marks and Monograms on European and Oriental Pottery and Porcelain* (p. 481), advances the engaging theory that these ineradicable marks were cut through the glaze of both Meissen and Oriental porcelains in order to discourage visitors to the Japanese Palace collection from appropriating royal property.

In the opinion of Dr. Menzhausen-Handt of the Staatliche Porzellansammlung at the Zwinger, the earliest surviving inventory was made in 1721 and extended to cover the period 1722–1727. This information also appears in Jenyns, *Japanese Porcelain*, p. 241, where it is further stated that a second volume of the inventory, presumably containing higher numbers, is lost. The same source explains that "a record in the Meissen factory says that the delivery of the last porcelains from the factory to the palace took place in 1741." This information provides a *terminus ante quem* for the dating of porcelains bearing these inventory marks anachronistically referred to as "Johanneum" marks, after the name of the museum in Dresden where they were housed during the nineteenth century.

The "yellow tiger" pattern is derived from the Kakiemon school of Japanese seventeenth and eighteenth century potters. It is represented in most major museum collections. At The Metropolitan Museum of Art, New York, it is found on a large dish and a teapot (George B. McClellan Collection, acc. nos. 42.205.125, 42.205.130). A dinner service in this pattern was made for Augustus the Strong, from which a tureen and platter, and possibly other surviving pieces, are at the Staatliche Porzellansammlung, Dresden.

The "yellow tiger" pattern was first introduced at Meissen about 1728. It has been suggested that the tiger (often erroneously called a lion), which occurs with great frequency in the designs of Kakiemon ware, is a reflection of the tales of destruction wrought by these beasts in Korea as a result of their having increased in number during the long wars with the Japanese at the end of the sixteenth century (see Dingwall, *The Derivation of some Kakiemon Designs on Porcelains*, p. 21). The pattern often incorporated a dragon. In the decoration of Nos. 61 A and B, the contorted tree trunk may be a purposeful suggestion of a dragon, inas-much as that animal was emblematic of imperial and royal qualities. A tea service in the "yellow tiger" pattern at the Victoria and Albert Museum, London, is exceptional in its representation of additional figures flying kites or carrying parasols, pennants, and the like.

Animals, birds, and plants in the Kakiemon tradition were employed in delightful variations, not only at Meissen but also at Vienna before 1730: an example is a Du Paquier *bourdalou* in the Kakiemon vein (see Ducret, *Keramik-Freunde der Schweiz*, July 1959, fig. 13). A Meissen tankard at the Rijksmuseum, Amsterdam, depicts a galloping *fu*-lion whose rider is seated in reverse position (Wark, *Keramik-Freunde der Schweiz*, April 1956, pl. 1, fig. 1).

See also Volume II of this catalogue, Nos. 270 A and B.

62 Cup

H. 2 (5.1); Diam. 2½ (6.4).

THE SMALL cup is cone-shaped, swelling out toward the out-turned lip, with a gilded and gadrooned foot. It is painted in delicate colors with
a continuous panorama of a harbor showing
numerous vessels, figures of stevedores and others,
including a pair of turbaned figures in conversation on a pile of cargo. Inside and outside the lip
is a gilded border of baroque scrolls in a lacework
pattern.

Marked on the underside with crossed swords,
painted in blue under the glaze.

Dating from about 1730–1735; the painting by
Johann Georg Heintze (working 1720–1749) or an
early follower of his style.

The style of the painted decoration of this cup
appears to be early and recalls the manner of
Johann Georg Heintze, generally acknowledged
to be the inventor of Meissen harbor scenes. The
only signed example of this artist's work is an
enamel plaque in the Stuttgart Landesgewerbemuseum, dated 1734. It depicts a view of Meissen
from a bend in the Elbe, with the Albrechtsburg
castle (where Meissen porcelain was made) as the
center of interest. The refinement of the painting,
and the almost unbelievably minute scale of the
figures to be seen on the plaque and on later work
ascribed to Heintze, suggest that the cup No. 62
was decorated by Heintze or an early follower of
his style.

A somewhat similar cup with a harbor scene
and rich gold embellishments is at the Rijksmuseum, Amsterdam (illustrated in Den Blaau-
wen, *Saksisch Porselein*, fig. 16).

THE SERVICE consists of 141 items. It is chiefly distinguished from the following services Nos. 64 and 65 by its borders. On No. 63 these are broad and have a molded basketry pattern simulating a bold diagonal weave, divided into oblong panels bordered with beading, the outer rims resembling cording. It shares with these other two services a decorative scheme generally called the "flying dog" pattern, after a winged animal prominent in the design. The principal motifs are broadly scattered and arranged somewhat at random. Besides the flying dog, they consist of a swooping crane, and a cluster of flowers with a beetle or other insect at the base. Tiny flowers and sprays of leaves are scattered thinly over the field. Overlying the molded borders are small moths or butterflies, and rather stiff floral sprigs of the type called *Indianische Blumen*. The basic colors of the painted enamels are yellow-green, iron-red, and pale blue, with accents of yellow and chestnut-brown.

The service comprises the following:

TUREEN

The body is hemispherical, with bearded mask handles and a painted domed cover having an orb finial.

PAIR OF TUREENS

Each is of drum shape, with female mask handles and domed covers with artichoke finials.

123 PLATES

The border of each is divided into twelve panels, delicately notched at the rim. Fifty-six of the smaller plates have rims painted chestnut-brown as in No. 65.

Many are marked with crossed swords of the "dot" period (1763–1774), painted in blue under the glaze, and accompanied in some instances by

L or DD in blue, or in others impressed with a Maltese cross, an L, 16, 32, or 52. Some are incised with the letter E. Several are incised with a dotted cross and a crescent, for the molders Schiefer and Petzsch Junior, respectively.

QUATREFOIL OVAL TRAY
Impressed on the underside: 54.

SIX ROUND DISHES, in three sizes
Two impressed on the underside: 2, and 22, respectively.

PAIR OF OVAL PLATTERS

SIX BASKETS
Each has two handles rising from male and female masks.

Unless otherwise indicated, all pieces are marked with plain crossed swords, painted in blue under the glaze.

Major portions of this service date from the period 1735–1740, although some replacements of later eighteenth century date have been made, as for example plates marked with crossed swords of the Punct period; others dating from the nineteenth century are marked with the letters L or DD painted in blue.

The name "flying dog," usually applied to this pattern, is a misnomer inasmuch as the winged animal from which it takes its name is a composite creature. Fantastic animals of this type were borrowed from Chinese and Japanese sources. As depicted in this service, the winged creature shows the head and feet of a dog, the back and tail of a Chinese *kylin*, the wings of a dragon, and the stripes of a tiger. It is therefore arbitrary to name it after any of these.

This pattern and its cognate, the "flying squirrel" or "flying fox," are widely represented in museum collections. The Metropolitan Museum of Art, New York, possesses a plate and a mustard pot in the "flying dog" pattern (acc. nos. 17.26.1 and 42.205.94, respectively), and the Hans Syz

Collection at the Smithsonian Institution, Washington, D.C., contains a variety of objects of matching design.

The diagonal basketry pattern used for the borders of this service represents a Meissen innovation. It is the earliest of the osier patterns, first used extensively in the Count Alexander Joseph Sulkowski service dating about 1735. The name derives from the common osier, a species of willow used for basketmaking.

THE SERVICE consists of twenty-three items. Its painted decoration matches that of Nos. 63 and 65, although it lacks both the basketry-molded borders of No. 63 and the chestnut-brown painted rims of No. 65. The octagonal, fluted, and lobed outlines of the major vessels are more closely akin to the shapes of Japanese "brown-edge" Arita ware than are the Europeanized forms of Nos. 63 and 65.

The service comprises the following:

EIGHT DINNER PLATES
Each is marked on the underside with the baton of Berlin, painted in blue under the glaze.

TWO MEAT PLATTERS
Each is cartouche-shaped, with an oval center.

Each is marked on the underside with the baton of Berlin, painted in blue under the glaze, and incised: K over 22; in addition, three short parallel lines are cut into the foot ring.

PAIR OF SERVING DISHES
Each is of octagonal shape.

One is impressed on the inner side of the foot ring with three small dots forming a triangle, presumably marks of the Meissen craftsmen Müller, Seidel, or Grund Junior, during the period 1730–1740; the other is incised with a modified 4, an unrecorded mark.

CIRCULAR BOWL
The sides are molded as chrysanthemum petals.

Impressed on the underside: 23.

TWO PAIRS OF LEAF-SHAPED DISHES
Each is modeled with bent twig handles, heightened with yellow-green and applied with small blossoms.

One pair is deeply notched and painted with crossed swords in blue under the glaze; the other marked on the underside with the baton of Berlin painted in blue under the glaze, and impressed: 29; two notches are cut into the inner edge of the foot ring.

PAIR OF DOUBLE LEAF-SHAPED DISHES
Each is molded in the form of two overlapping almond-shaped leaves with serrated rims.

TEAPOT

The body is pear-shaped, with a double scroll handle, domed cover having a floral finial, and a dolphin-head spout with a bearded mask at the base.

VASE

The oblate pear-shaped vase has two reverse scroll handles.

SPRINKLER VASE

The body is balloon-shaped with a slender knopped neck.

TRENCHER SALT

Oval with vertically ridged sides.

Unless otherwise specified, the pieces are Meissen, marked with crossed swords, painted in blue under the glaze.

The Meissen portion of the service dates from the second quarter of the eighteenth century; the Berlin portion from the last quarter.

The knife and fork handles Nos. 73 A–JJ are related in design.

65 Dinner Service

THE SERVICE consists of ninety-four items. It differs from Nos. 63 and 64 in the absence of a basketry-molded pattern as on No. 63, and in the presence of a chestnut-brown fillet along the rims.

The service comprises the following:

THREE TUREENS, with covers, in two sizes

THIRTY-SIX PLATES, in four sizes, ranging from 9¼ (23.5) to 10⅛ (25.8)
Impressed on the underside, from smallest to largest: 16, 36, 52, 21.

NINETEEN SOUP PLATES, in two sizes
Of the ten smaller plates, nine are impressed on the underside: 16. The larger plates are replacements of recent date.

OVAL DISH

EIGHT ROUND DISHES, in four sizes

TWO OVAL PLATTERS

SIX ROUND PLATTERS, in two sizes
The three larger platters are impressed on the underside: 20; incised with triple parallel lines.

FISH PLATTER

THREE ROUND FLUTED DISHES, in two sizes

COVERED ROUND BOWL, with rooster finial

TWO CASSEROLES, with covers and turned walnut handles

TWO TEAPOTS

THREE SAUCEBOATS
Two are impressed on the underside: 44.

PAIR OF PEAR-SHAPED SALT AND PEPPER CASTERS
Each has a gold rim and is of recent date.

FIVE CARTOUCHE-SHAPED TRENCHER SALTS

Virtually all pieces are marked with crossed swords, painted in blue under the glaze.

The service dates, in part, from the second quarter of the eighteenth century, and includes replacements of recent date.

66 A–Z Dessert Service

66 A–D (platters): H. 2⅜ (6.0); L. 14¾ (37.5);
    W. 11 (28.0).

66 E–H (dishes): H. 1½ (3.8); L. 12¼ (31.1);
    W. 8⅞ (22.6).

66 I–Z (plates): Diam. 8⅞ (22.6) to 9 (22.9).

THE SERVICE comprises four platters, four serving dishes, and eighteen plates.

Each platter and dish, of oblong shape with eight sides (Nos. 66 A–H), is painted with five park scenes in the manner of Watteau. At the center is

an oval medallion depicting three or more persons, including a fortune teller, musicians, and children. Each of the four principal sides of the border is painted with an elliptical cartouche depicting a romantic couple, with occasionally the third figure of an interloper. The scenes are enclosed by ornate gold borders of foliate scrolls and hatched strapwork, picked out in umber. The space between them is interspersed with loosely scattered blossoms and nosegays including roses, tulips, anemones, and columbines, painted in the predominating colors of the figural medallions: orange, puce, and violet-blue. The rims are edged with umber.

Each octagonal plate is decorated in a similar manner, the five cartouches containing pairs of lovers, or actors from the *commedia dell' arte* in park settings.

Each is marked on the underside with crossed swords, painted in blue under the glaze. The plates are impressed under the glaze: 22; the dish No. 66 E is impressed: 27. The plates Nos. 66 W and Y are also impressed: 27.

Dating from about 1740–1745.

Formerly in the collection of Lady Burdett-Coutts, Foremarke, Derbyshire.

A cup and saucer of comparable design are in the Hans Syz Collection in the Smithsonian Institution, Washington, D.C.

The style of the decoration of these plates and dishes is related to that of the salts Nos. 67 A–D, and to the porcelain handles of the flatware service Nos. 74 A–X.

67 A–D Set of Four Salts

H. 2 (5.1); W. 3⅝ (9.2); D. 3⅜ (8.6).

EACH vessel, in the shape of a stylized clam shell, has an undulating rim and rests upon three splayed scrolls. At the narrow end of the interior is a four-lobed panel painted with a rural scene including tiny figures of huntsmen and riders. The miniature view is intricately bordered with valanced panels of gilded trelliswork, enriched with linear scrolls and flowers picked out in umber. Sprigs of purple and other flowers occupy the center. The rim and feet of each are also outlined with gilding, and there is gilded lacework along the inner border.

Marked on the underside with crossed swords, painted in blue under the glaze.

Dating from about 1740–1745.

The style of the decoration is related to that of the dessert service Nos. 66 A–Z, and to the porcelain handles of the flatware service Nos. 74 A–X.

THE SERVICE consists of ninety-six items. It is decorated with nosegays and floral sprigs, sometimes overlapping or repeated in the edges of the borders, which are molded with a close-knit "old osier" basketry pattern in low relief. The rims are painted chestnut-brown.

The service consists of the following:

OVAL TUREEN, with rose finial
TWO ROUND TUREENS, with lemon finials
FORTY-FIVE DINNER PLATES
EIGHTEEN SOUP PLATES, lacking basketry molding
NINE OVAL DISHES
SIXTEEN ROUND DISHES
LEAF-SHAPED DISH
PAIR OF SHELL-SHAPED TRENCHER SALTS, lacking basketry molding
PAIR OF FLUTED OVAL SALTS

Virtually all pieces are marked with crossed swords, painted in blue; some of the plates are marked with impressed numerals: 22, 36, 51, 54, 56, 61. The oval dishes are impressed 30 and 36; the round dishes 16, 20, 21, 46, 61, and 67.

Dating chiefly from about 1750–1755.

The oval tureen was formerly in the collection of Lady Bettine Abingdon, London.

A matching tureen in the State Hermitage Museum, Leningrad, is illustrated in *Staryé-Gody*, May 1911, pl. 38.

A cup and saucer in this pattern are at the Victoria and Albert Museum, London (no. C1001 + A 1919).

The "old osier" pattern, characterized by its simulation of fine parallel weaving, is often di-

vided into sections by molded radial ribs, as on No. 68. It was introduced shortly after the first osier pattern (see No. 63). When in 1742 a more rococo version with spiral ribs, called the *Neuozier*, appeared, this version became known as the *Altozier*.

69 A–D   Two Pairs of Dishes

69 A, B: Diam. 11¾ (29.8).

69 C, D: Diam. 13 (33.0).

THE CHANNELED border of each circular dish, with gilded rim, is painted with four pairs of perched songbirds, each enclosed in a rococo gilded cartouche. Between them are triple flutings molded in relief with uncolored anthemia and floral scrolls in the "Dulong" pattern. The center of each dish is painted with a large nosegay, mainly of tulips and anemones, and several small sprigs of naturalistic blossoms, scattered in a random pattern.

Each is marked on the underside with crossed swords, painted in blue under the glaze. Nos. 69 C and D are impressed: 20.

Dating from about 1750.

The "Dulong" border was introduced in 1743 and is named after the Amsterdam firm of Dulong, Godefroy, and Dulong, which had had business relations extending over many years with the Meissen factory. It is characterized by four cartouche-shaped areas alternating with molded scroll and floral decoration, which, unlike basketry molding, is not confined to the borders, and extends slightly into the cavetto.

70 Sweetmeat Dish

H. 5⅞ (15.0); W. 8⅜ (21.3); D. 6¾ (17.2).

THE DISH is in the form of a luxuriant cluster of purple grapes veined and mottled with milky blue. The upper half is fitted with a looped and foliated green vine handle, and serves as a cover. The lower part rests upon a small oval base from which emerges a double scrolling vine at one end. The foliage on the cover and body is tinctured with brown.

Marked on the underside with crossed swords, painted in blue under the glaze.

Dating from about 1750.

EXHIBITED: Antique Porcelain Company, London, *English and Continental Porcelain of the 18th Century*, 1951, p. 94 (illustrated in catalogue).

Formerly in the collections of Sir Philip Sassoon, Trent Park, Herefordshire; the Marchioness of Cholmondeley, London.

A similar Meissen dish, varying somewhat in shape, is part of a collection of boxes modeled as artichokes, pears, pomegranates, and melons in the State Hermitage Museum, Leningrad. Eight of these, including the dish in the form of a bunch of grapes, are illustrated in *Staryé-Gody*, May 1911, pl. 31. A comparable pair from the collection of James Donohue, New York, was sold at Parke-Bernet, New York, November 2–4, 1967, lot 127 (illustrated in catalogue).

Several pieces in the famous Möllendorf service in the Victoria and Albert Museum, London, employ the grape cluster motif: compotiers and jugs (C 248–250-1921 and C 242, 243-1921). The service was made during the Seven Years' War, 1756–1763, to the order of Frederick the Great, when the Prussians occupied Dresden.

Other factories, working in porcelain and faïence, made similar vessels. One example is a jam jar made at Chelsea (see Gardner in *Transactions of the English Ceramic Circle*, II, no. 8, pl. L). A similar dish of Delft faïence, from Frankfurt an der Oder, is at the Fitzwilliam Museum, Cambridge; another, from the Delft factory of Hendrik van Hoorn, is at the Musées Royaux d'Art et d'Histoire, Brussels (illustrated in Helbig, *Faïences Hollandaises*, I, fig. 59), where it is identified as a *beurrier*.

The color of No. 70 suggests an attempt to duplicate the subtle hues of the Chinese ceramic product *Chûn Yao*, an outstanding accomplishment of the Sung dynasty. It is rarely seen in Meissen porcelain.

71 Lobster-Shaped Dish

H. 1½ (3.8); L. 5¹¹⁄₁₆ (14.5); D. 2⅛ (5.7).

THE DISH is in the form of a lobster painted red, shading to black at the head and tip of tail. Its great claws are extended before it, and the weight rests on four pairs of folded legs. The back is designed as an oblong cover, opening to a small chamber within the body.

Marked on the underside of the body between the legs with crossed swords, painted in deep blue under the glaze.

Dating from about 1750.

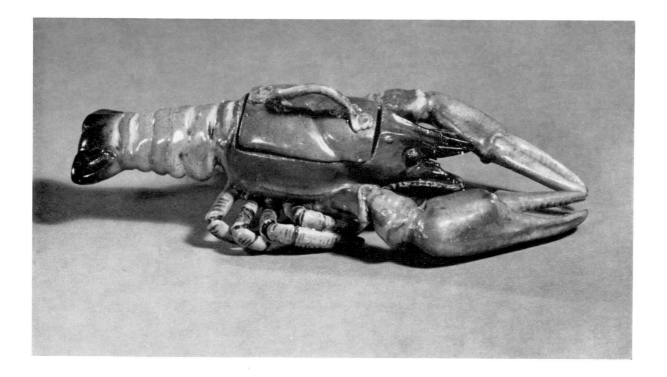

72 Sweetmeat Dish

H. 2⅛ (5.4); W. 7½ (19.0); D. 7⅜ (18.7).

THE DISH is triangular in shape, with a gilded rim, rounded contours, and a looped stem handle terminating in a bud. The interior is molded with superimposed petal motifs and leaf forms, reserved in white except for a large greenish leaf springing from the handle, bordered with mottled yellow and pea-green. Sprays of flowers, including an anemone, a fringed tulip, and three puce roses, are painted upon the white interior.

Marked on the underside with crossed swords, painted in pale blue under the glaze; impressed: K.

Dating from about 1770.

A closely similar example, and another that varies somewhat, are represented in the George B. McClellan Collection at The Metropolitan Museum of Art, New York (acc. nos. 42.205.187,188). Two other examples are at the Residenzmuseum, Munich.

Such dishes, known as *Päonienschalen*, were made at various times during the eighteenth century. The presence of the impressed K relates No. 72 to a similar dish, regarded as about 1770 in date, in the Bayerisches Nationalmuseum, Munich. An entry in the Meissen manufactory *Jahrbuch* for September 1746, under Ehder (working 1739–1750), sets an early date for the form:

1 Confectionery dish made of clay in the form of a sunflower. (1 Confect Schale in Gestalt einer Sonnen-Rose von Thon bausirt.)

THE SERVICE consists of eighteen pairs of knives and forks, each fitted with a porcelain handle (and twelve modern silver-gilt spoons). Each porcelain handle is round in section, expanding gradually toward the bulbous terminal. A narrow panel of simulated basket weave is molded in low relief at either end. The painted decoration, in the Oriental manner, depicts on one side of each handle a flying crane and a fanciful winged quadruped; on the other side is a flowering peony stalk with a winged insect at its base. The metal parts are of silver gilt. The knives have saber-shaped blades, the forks have three tines, and the shaft of each terminates in a cartouche-shaped globular ferrule.

The porcelain is unmarked.

Twelve each of the knives and forks are marked with the oval pinecone stamp over an o for Augsburg, 1759–1761 (Rosenberg, *Der Goldschmiede Merkzeichen*, no. 261).

The conjoined initials AW in an oval (Rosenberg, *op. cit.*, no. 920) for Johann Abraham Winkler (working 1736–1768).

The remaining six knives and six forks are stamped with a crab in a cartouche, the warranty

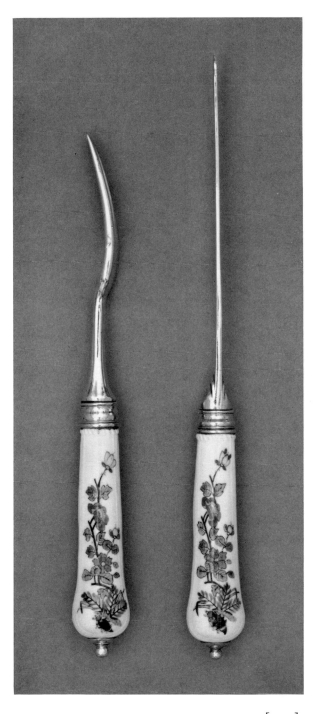

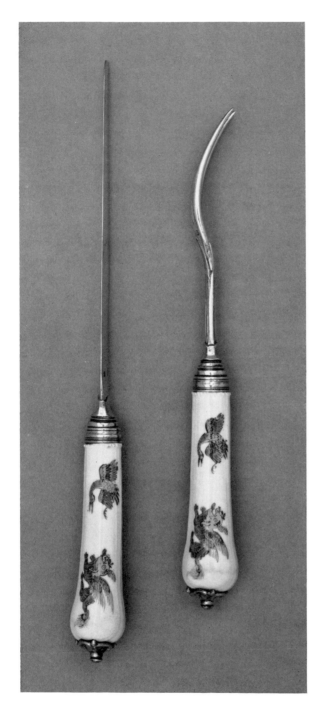

mark in use in the French provinces since 1838.

An anvil mark of an insect appears on the reverse of each strike.

The porcelain, though decorated in the Meissen manner of 1735–1740, may be of later date.

An antique black leather case with the gold monogram IC accommodates thirty-six pieces of this service.

The decoration of the porcelain handles is closely related to that of the services Nos. 63, 64, and 65.

THE SERVICE consists of twelve each of knives, forks (and modern silver-gilt spoons). The knives and forks are fitted with cylindrical porcelain handles, painted with miniature cartouches of Watteauesque figures enclosed by elaborate borders of hatched gold strapwork, shells, and scrolls. Near the ferrule is a band of minute oval scenes in puce, richly bordered with gold lacework. The metal parts are of silver-gilt.

Neither the porcelain nor the gilded silver is marked.

The porcelain dates from about 1740–1745; the metal parts are of recent date.

Compare the dessert service Nos. 66 A–Z for related decoration.

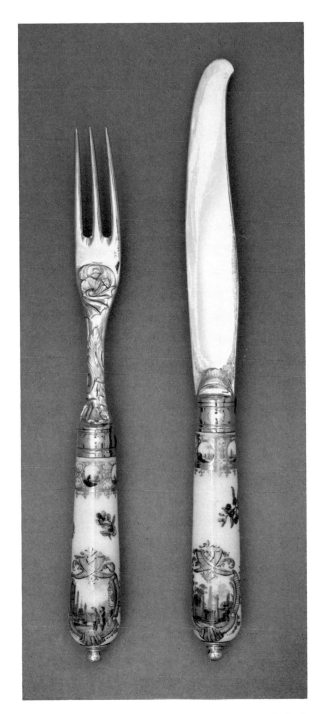

SÈVRES AND OTHER FRENCH PORCELAIN

INTRODUCTION

Isolated specimens of Chinese porcelain seem to have reached Europe at least as early as Marco Polo's travels in the East, and by the end of the fifteenth century the term *porcelaine* begins to appear sporadically in inventories. Ming porcelains were made for King Manoel I "the Happy" of Portugal (1469–1521), and the Emperor Charles V (1500–1558) actually ordered a service painted with armorial bearings from China, pieces from which still survive. In France a few pieces of Oriental porcelain were certainly owned by François I. But such things were rare and valuable curiosities. It was only in the second half of the seventeenth century that Oriental porcelain began to reach Europe in quantity, and when it did so it was welcomed with the highest enthusiasm. Every sovereign ruler or minor princeling found that fashion demanded he have a "China cabinet," a room where hundreds, even thousands of vases, generally of blue-and-white porcelain, stood on every conceivable ledge and shelf, chimneypiece or sill, as well as on innumerable brackets on the walls, and larger vases on the floor.

From the beginning there had been speculation on the nature and composition of porcelain. Sporadic attempts to manufacture it were made, of which the best known and most successful was the short-lived factory set up by the Medici at Florence about 1575 by the Grand Duke Francesco I. Here a few pieces of "artificial" porcelain in tolerable imitation of Ming blue and white were created—about fifty of them survive. In the second half of the seventeenth century such experiments received a huge fillip from the greatly increased quantity of porcelain arriving in Europe. At first this was brought almost exclusively in Dutch bottoms. During its voyage in 1698 the *Amphitrite*, the first French ship to bring imports directly from the Orient, had on board 186 packing cases filled with porcelain, though much Chinese porcelain had already reached France from Holland. The story has often been told, with varying degrees of romance, how the scientist Walther von Tschirnhaus, with the aid of the alchemist Johann Friedrich Böttger, succeeded in making true hard-paste porcelain at Dresden in 1708 as a substitute for his attempts to find the "philosopher's stone" and transmute base minerals into gold and silver, and how Augustus the Strong set up at Meissen what was to become the most famous and economically the most successful porcelain factory in Europe (see Introduction to Meissen porcelain, pp. 3 ff.). Soon every prince and great nobleman began to find it necessary to follow the example of the Elector of Saxony both for economic reasons and for prestige, and Karl Eugen, Duke of Württemburg, who acquired the Ludwigsburg factory in 1758, is recorded as saying that "A porcelain factory is an indispensable accompaniment of splendor and magnificence."

In France the manufacture of porcelain did not arise in quite this way, and it was more than half a century after the granting of the first patent for making porcelain in France before the Crown began to take a serious interest in its manufacture. In any case, it was not until 1769 that "true" or hard-paste porcelain of the type manufactured at Meissen was created at the royal Sèvres manufactory. Even after this the beautiful soft-paste porcelain continued to be used at Sèvres down to the Revolution for many vases, decorative and other pieces that are the factory's greatest glory, as well as for much of the table ware—in fact for the greater part of the establishment's output. Its use, although diminished, was continuous until 1804.

Two French factories have serious claims to have been making soft-paste porcelain before the end of the seventeenth century, those of Rouen and Saint-Cloud. Rouen, through a patent granted in 1673 to Louis Poterat, has priority. Poterat was asserted by the *intendant* of Rouen in 1694 to have "le secret de faire de la porcelaine," though he appeared to make very few pieces. A little earlier, in 1692, the *Livre Commode des Adresses de Paris* recorded that the Poterat family "a trouvé le secret de faire en France . . . la porcelaine semblable à celle des Indes." A few pieces of this early soft-paste porcelain have been identified. They are decorated in blue and white in much the same style as the faïence being made contemporaneously at Rouen. Only about thirty are recorded by Brébisson.[1]

The origins of the Saint-Cloud factory are more obscure. Nothing about such a factory is noticed in the *Livre Commode* mentioned above though later documents refer to experimental porcelain as having been made there by a certain Pierre Chicaneau as early as 1677 or 1678. The earliest account of the factory is given by an Englishman in 1698, and by that time the factory was evidently in active production. Dr. Martin Lister writes in his account of his visit to Paris in 1698: "I saw the potterie of St. Clou, with which I was marvellously well pleased, for I confess I could not distinguish betwixt the Pots made there, and the finest China Ware I ever saw," adding that he "found it . . . to equal, if not surpass the Chinese in their finest Art."[2] A conversation he had with a scientist, François de Morin, suggested that the secret had been discovered three years earlier, in 1695. The family of Pierre Chicaneau (died 1678) claimed to have improved upon Chicaneau's process and to have made porcelain since 1693. The products of Saint-Cloud were rare and highly prized. They were sold, Lister declared, "at excessive rates," quoting "some furnitures of Tea Tables at 400 Livres a Sett." By 1700 the Saint-Cloud factory was under the patronage of the Duc d'Orléans, and its proprietors, Pierre Chicaneau II and his family, had opened an establishment near the Place des Victoires in Paris, "pour la vente de leurs Porcelaine."

The earliest Saint-Cloud porcelain, like that made at Rouen, was decorated in blue on white in much the manner of contemporary faïence. Gilding, probably first attempted on French porcelain at Saint-Cloud, was already being used by the time of Lister's visit to France, and polychrome decoration, generally inspired by Oriental models, was soon introduced. The productions of the Saint-Cloud factory are represented in the catalogue below by a pair of white jars with sprays of plum blossom in relief (Catalogue Nos. 123 A and B), imitated from Japanese originals. They must date from around 1725.

1. Brébisson, *La Porcelaine Tendre de Rouen*.

2. *A Journey to Paris in the Year 1698*, by Dr. Martin Lister, pp. 139–141.

Such jars were produced in considerable quantity at the factory in the first half of the eighteenth century and seem to have been intended for toilet use.

Various other attempts to manufacture porcelain, mostly abortive, short-lived, and of lesser importance than those mentioned above, were made in France early in the eighteenth century, perhaps at Passy about 1700 and at Lille about 1711 as well as in a purely scientific and experimental spirit by the physicist Réaumur at Paris about 1717. But only two factories, both established a little later than these, are of any importance. These are the Chantilly factory set up under the patronage of the Duc de Condé at Chantilly and the factory at Mennecy under the protection of the Duc de Villeroy, and examples of the products of both factories are to be found in the catalogue below.

Louis-Henri de Bourbon-Condé was a first cousin of the king who had made an immense fortune out of speculation before the collapse of the System of Law. In 1726 he was exiled from Versailles to his great estates at Chantilly, where he occupied his leisure partly in collecting Japanese and other Oriental porcelain. Chemistry was among his numerous hobbies. The two interests combined in his protection of Ciquaire (or Sicaire, Cicaire) Cirou, who appears to have been manufacturing porcelain on a small scale at Chantilly from 1725, though it was not until 1735 that he was granted royal letters patent to do so. The first productions of Chantilly were copied closely from Japanese originals in the duke's collection and decorated in the Kakiemon style. It is recorded that it amused the duke to intermix these Chantilly pieces with his own collections to see if his guests could distinguish the Japanese originals from the French copies. The factory continued to flourish down to the end of *ancien régime* (and was purchased by an Englishman, Christopher Potter, during the Revolution), but its main importance in this brief historical survey is that two of its workers, the brothers Robert and Gilles Dubois, deserted the factory, claiming to take with them certain of its secrets, and played an important role in the foundation of the Vincennes, later the royal Sèvres, factory. They were joined shortly afterward by François Gravant, a greengrocer from Chantilly.

The origins of the Mennecy factory are somewhat obscure. They involve a certain François Barbin, described as a *faïencier*, but who seems to have been making porcelain in the Rue de Charonne at Paris in 1734 (and perhaps earlier) and who was protected by Louis-François de Neufville, Duc de Villeroy. By 1737 Barbin was living at the duke's château at Mennecy, but the porcelain manufactory was not moved there until 1748, though faïence had been made there for some time. Later in the century, in 1773, the porcelain manufactory was moved to Bourg-la-Reine. In effect, these three centers form a single establishment. That there was some stylistic relationship between Mennecy and Chantilly is evident from the five Chinese figures in the collection made at the Mennecy factory (Catalogue Nos. 127 A and B, 128 A and B, 129), all of them mounted in gilt bronze. These small grotesque figures, like the snuff- and sweetmeat boxes, *pots à fard*, small candlesticks, and such-like objects that the factory produced in profusion for use on the toilet table, are charmingly unsophisticated rather than subtly modeled. They owe their attraction to their artlessness; in this they resemble the English figures produced at Bow and are quite different in conception from most French and German eighteenth century porcelain. The same interrelationship between the Mennecy and Chantilly factories is to be seen here in a Chantilly pomegranate mounted as a perfume burner (Catalogue No. 124) to which parallels can readily be found among models of fruit created at the Mennecy factory.

The majority of pieces of French porcelain catalogued below were created at Sèvres. It would therefore be necessary to discuss it at greater length than the work of the other factories, even were it not the most famous of all French porcelain factories. The origins of the Vincennes-Sèvres factory, which was ultimately to become the celebrated Manufacture Royale de Porcelaine, are rather different from any so far mentioned and date from a good deal later than any of them except the Mennecy factory. Although it was eventually to be the chosen instrument of the French Crown for the production of what was to become famous throughout Europe as *porcelaine de France*, it did not begin under royal or even noble patronage. In its first tottering steps it was supported by financiers and bankers, and at that date it would have needed great foresight to believe that it would ultimately challenge the economic dominance of Meissen on the European market and become an instrument of national prestige and propaganda. That it was not even to succeed for many years in making the true or hard-paste porcelain which had given Meissen its pre-eminent position for about half a century after Böttger's discovery is in part a tribute to the care with which the technique was kept secret at Meissen, though the failure to discover any source of kaolin in France before 1768 was the principal factor.

Chance played a large part in decreeing that the beautiful soft-paste porcelain should be what brought fame and success to Sèvres. During the first thirty years of the factory's existence its scientists and technical advisers dreamed of creating "true" porcelain, and it is not without significance that Sèvres porcelain as a material does not even obtain a mention in the first edition of Diderot and d'Alembert's *Encyclopédie* (1751–1765). Its name was admitted into this great treatise only in the supplement of 1777 after the kaolin beds at Limoges had been discovered, and hard-paste or "true" porcelain had become a reality. The *Encyclopédie* makes no reference at any point to the soft paste on which the aesthetic fame of the factory now rests (as indeed it did then). And it is from the soft-paste productions of the Vincennes-Sèvres *manufacture* that all but the pair of vases Nos. 91 A and B in the catalogue below are drawn, most of them having been made in the two decades which followed the transfer of the manufactory from Vincennes to Sèvres in 1756 (see below).

The documents relating to the beginnings of the Vincennes factory are somewhat contradictory, and the actual date of its foundation cannot be given precisely. It is sufficient to record here that sometime around 1738 the brothers Orry de Vignory and Orry de Fulvy, both wealthy financiers and important servants of the state, were allowed by the king to install the brothers Gilles and Robert Dubois in rooms in the old royal château of Vincennes on the eastern outskirts of Paris. There these two escapees from the Chantilly factory were given finances (apparently from the resources of the Crown—Orry de Vignory was *controlleur-général des Finances* and his brother *Intendant*) to the tune of ten thousand livres in order to make porcelain, the technique of which they claimed to have learned during their earlier employment at Chantilly. Both the brothers Dubois were later accused of leading irregular lives, and Robert, at any rate, was dismissed by Orry de Fulvy on these grounds in 1741 though Gilles may have continued in a subordinate position at the factory until about 1746 (Eriksen, *Waddesdon Manor: Sèvres Porcelain*, p. 13, note 1). On the other hand, Chavagnac (*Histoire des Manufactures Françaises de Porcelaine*, p. 122) says Orry de Fulvy dismissed the brother Dubois in 1741. But it is at least likely that the dismissal was due more to the failure of their attempts to make porcelain than to their dissipation.

The Dubois brothers were succeeded in 1741 by their assistant from Chantilly, François Gravant, with whom was associated a certain Charles Adam who has recently been shown merely to have been the *valet de chambre* of Orry de Fulvy.[3] Adam was more than merely a puppet, for he had well-furnished apartments at Vincennes and seems to have spent a considerable amount of time there. But his master seems also to have spent a surprising length of time there and must have kept a watch on the experiments. Through Adam the financier advanced a further sum of nearly sixty thousand livres to the new establishment during the years 1741 to 1745. François Gravant seems to have been a good deal more successful than the Dubois brothers, and by 1745 had produced a sufficiently convincing soft-paste porcelain experimentally to apply for a royal patent to manufacture it for thirty years. In the event a twenty-year patent was granted to Charles Adam on July 24, 1745, "de fabriquer en France des porcelaines de la même qualité que celles qui se font en Saxe, pour dispenser les consommateurs de ce royaume de faire passer leurs fonds dans les pays étrangers," a phrase that fairly sums up the technical and economic aims of all experimental attempts to make porcelain in France. The aesthetic aims are more briefly hinted at in the definition (which comes farther on in the patent) of what the new establishment was to produce, viz. "porcelaine façon de Saxe, c'est à dire peinte et doré, à figure humaine . . . ." The right to use apartments in Vincennes was continued. It was made a penal offense for workmen to leave the factory without permission and for other factories to engage their services. The original loan of 10,000 livres was extinguished, and a new company was set up with a capital of 93,000 livres divided into twenty-one shares held by seven shareholders, all of them wealthy tax-farmers, bankers, and businessmen. A considerable part of the capital (24,000 livres and the promise of a pension for his family) went to pay Gravant for his "secret," so that it is clear that he had produced porcelain of a quality to satisfy the shareholders, who seem to have been fairly hard-headed businessmen. Three years later a further large sum of 24,000 livres was paid to a Benedictine monk, "frère Hippolyte," who appears to have possessed the secret of the technique of applying gilding to porcelain. He was also permitted to furnish the gold used at the factory. Thenceforward other French factories were forbidden to make use of gold. Various other appointments were made at this time and point to the factory's growing importance.

In 1745 Orry de Vignory fell from power and was succeeded by Jean-Baptiste Machault as *controlleur-général des Finances*. Machault clearly took a very great interest in the porcelain factory, and much of

---

3. André Sergène, quoted in Chapu, *Les Porcelainiers du XVIIIe Siècle Français* ("Collection Connaissance des Arts"), p. 154; the term *valet de chambre* hardly bore the same social implications at this date that it did later.

its success was due to him.[4] Nevertheless he seems to have permitted Orry de Fulvy to continue his immediate supervision until his death in 1751. Under him the newly constructed manufactory was thoroughly reorganized. Jacques-René Boileau de Picardie, an officer from the army commissariat, was appointed as managing director; a certain François Blanchard was made *garde-magasin*, in charge of the storage and sales side of the business, and Jean Hellot, a distinguished chemist and member of the Académie des Sciences, was appointed advisor on technical matters concerning the composition of paste, colors, etc. On the aesthetic side a certain "M. Hults [i.e., Hulst] dont le goût est connu et constant" was made artistic advisor;[5] Jean-Claude Duplessis, the well-known goldsmith and *fondeur-doreur* (see Volume II of this catalogue, pp. 565–566) was entrusted with the task of creating new models; and in 1748 Jean-Jacques Bachelier, a flower-painter, was entrusted with the supervision of all painted decoration as well as the duty of instructing apprentices in drawing and painting. With him was associated Jean-Antoine Mathieu, *émailleur du Roi*.

By 1750 there were over a hundred craftsmen (about half of whom were women) employed on various tasks at the Vincennes factory. In the following year a minor financial crisis arose in consequence of the death of Orry de Fulvy and the need to repay his shares in the business. As a result the company was dissolved and reconstituted in 1752, and in the next year the privilege granted to Orry's man, Charles Adam, was transferred to Éloy Brichard, the future *sous-fermier* whose tax mark appears on several gold boxes in the collection (Volume III of this catalogue, pp. 154, 155, 156). In this new company, the king, whose interest in work at Vincennes had hitherto been intermittent and more or less concealed, became a major shareholder. In the articles of the new company the factory was designated officially for the first time as a Manufacture Royale, and it was given the right, indeed the duty, to use the royal monogram of the interlaced L's on every piece made, together with a letter (A for 1753, B for 1754, and so on) to indicate the year of manufacture.[6] In addition, the monopolistic character of the manufactory was embodied in the patent. Other French factories were forbidden to make porcelain.

4. Chavagnac (*op. cit.*) in particular emphasizes the crucial role played by Machault in developing the factory. But, as Eriksen has pointed out (*The James A. de Rothschild Collection at Waddesdon Manor*, p. 14, note 3), the Comte de Chavagnac was descended from Machault and may possibly have overstressed his importance from motives of family pride. But it cannot be doubted that Machault provided both economic and aesthetic advice of great value.

5. Eriksen (*Waddesdon Manor: Sèvres Porcelain*, p. 17) has identified this man as a cultivated Dutch gentleman, Hendrik Van Hulst, an *amateur* member of the Académie de Peinture et Sculpture and a friend of the influential Le Normant de Tournehem.

6. At the same time the small, stick-on labels printed with the interlaced L's were also produced. These were intended as price tickets, and examples are occasionally still found surviving on Sèvres porcelain today, e.g., on the back of the porcelain plaques set into a *secrétaire à abattant* (Volume I, No. 105) in this collection. It seems worthwhile to put on record here that since Volumes I and II of the catalogue appeared, Verlet has drawn attention to the fact that in the latter part of 1776 Poirier and Daguerre bought from the Sèvres factory plaques corresponding to those on the *secrétaire* at the prices written on the tickets (Verlet, *Apollo*, March 1967, p. 210).

   The interlaced L's had, in fact, been occasionally used on Vincennes porcelain before 1753 but seemingly without any royal authority, e.g., enclosing a fleur de lys on a large uncolored chinoiserie group in the English Royal Collection (illustrated in *Burlington Magazine*, August 1962, p. 349, fig. 32).

At the same time the decision was taken to move the factory from Vincennes to Sèvres where it would be nearer the court at Versailles and no farther from the fashionable heart of Paris. At Sèvres the factory would be quite close to Bellevue, the small château that Mme de Pompadour had acquired and made her principal country residence in 1750 (see Volume I of this catalogue, p. 207), and it may be that the move was inspired by the king's mistress herself. Her precise role in the early days of the Manufacture is not easy to define. She was certainly to become one of its principal patrons and unquestionably helped to maintain the king's interest in it. As early as July 24, 1748, the anonymous author of the *Journal historique ou fastes du règne de Louis XV* declared "Le succès de cette entreprise . . . est du principalement à la protection et aux secours que la marquise de Pompadour a accordés dans les commencements toujours laborieux," but as the *Journal* was not published until 1766, one might suspect it of having been edited with some degree of hindsight if corroborative evidence was not available from elsewhere. From 1749 onward, before the factory's sales registers begin, we find her buying considerable quantities of Vincennes porcelain from Lazare Duvaux. Two years later Hellot noted that the *fermier* de Verdun was a philistine who had only taken up his five shares and displayed an interest in the company "afin de faire sa cour à M. de Machault et à Mme de Pompadour." D'Argenson's often quoted assertion that she declared that "not to buy as much of this porcelain as one can afford, is to prove oneself a bad citizen," cannot be entirely credited, for he was her sworn enemy. But by 1755 we find a *pot-pourri Pompadour*, *urnes Pompadour*, and a *broc Pompadour* appearing on the sales registers; and the fact that Bachelier, a favorite painter of Mme de Pompadour, was put in charge of the *ateliers de peinture* in 1748 seems to be indicative of her interest in the factory at this early date (see pp. 170–171). Finally, the land on which the new factory buildings were put up at Sèvres in 1753 belonged to Mme de Pompadour.

The enormous building, erected below the woods of Saint-Cloud by the architect-engineer Perronet to the designs of the architect Lindet, took three years to complete and even then was not particularly well planned to house a porcelain factory.[7] It was a four-story building, and no thought seems to have been given to the provision of easy methods of intercommunication, an important consideration when moving the fragile ware from one section of the factory to another. In spite of the large amount of capital now made available (it was on the order of 100,000 livres), the cost of the new building and the transference of the factory was high, and by 1759 there were fresh financial difficulties. Thereupon Louis XV stepped in and bought out the other shareholders. Thenceforward the Sèvres factory became the exclusive property of the Crown, administered on the same lines as the other Manufactures Royales at the Gobelins and the Savonnerie factories (see Volume II of this catalogue, pp. 523–532). Any deficit, for the future, was made up by the Crown, and even in 1792 Louis XVI refused to part with it, replying proudly to an offer to purchase: "Je garde la Manufacture de Sèvres à mes frais," regardless of the fact that he had no funds with which to support it. In the event the factory was confiscated by the Convention two days after the invasion of the Tuileries. Since that date the organization has been a national rather than a royal

7. An interesting contemporary description of the building and the organization of the factory is contained in the *Mémoires* of the Duc de Luynes, XVI, pp. 77–78.

porcelain manufactory, even though the titles *Impériale* and *Royale* were incorporated in its title during certain subsequent regimes.

The history of the factory in the years after the move to Sèvres will emerge when its productions are considered and need only be dealt with briefly here. In 1759, when the factory became the exclusive property of the king, a *commissaire-administrateur* was appointed to supervise the factory in much the same way that Orry de Fulvy had until his death. This was the Sieur de Barbarie de Courteille who, like Orry before him, was also *controlleur-général des Finances*. His *directeur-régisseur* at the factory was Boileau de Picardie. At Courteille's death in 1767 his duties were taken over by Henri-Léonard-Jean-Baptiste Bertin, *ministre de la maison du Roi*. Boileau continued to direct the factory down to his death in 1772, when he was succeeded by Melchior-François Parent, a much less successful administrator who was responsible for many of the financial troubles that beset the factory in the years preceding the Revolution. He was dismissed in 1778 and was replaced by the energetic Charles-Claude de Labillarderie, Comte d'Angiviller, *Controlleur des Bâtiments* and a most able administrator, whose hard work and careful economies were felt in all the artistic activities of the Crown during the last decade before the Revolution. He was represented at the factory by Régnier, who endeavored to correct the balance by once again restricting the activities of other French factories. Their competition had been harming Sèvres ever since the original prohibition of the setting up of rival factories had been relaxed when hard-paste porcelain was discovered. In this Régnier was not very successful. A Swiss, Jean-Jacques Hettlinger, was associated with Angiviller in order to push the sales side of the business. Nevertheless these last years of the Manufacture Royale's history can only be regarded as a period of decline from the first two successful decades.

Experimentation continued actively after 1756. It was in these years that some of the most famous ground colors were invented, dark blue *(bleu lapis)* before 1753, yellow and turquoise-blue *(bleu céleste)* in 1753, green in 1756, pink in 1757, king's blue *(bleu du roi* or *bleu nouveau)* in 1763.[8] In 1757 Pierre-Joseph Macquer, another member of the Académie des Sciences, was associated with Hellot as chemist at the factory. It was he who explored the Limousin for deposits of the kaolin from which the first successful hard-paste porcelain was made in 1769.

The use of gilding was greatly developed after 1756. Highly accomplished engraving and burnishing were used to impart vitality and variety to its surface appearance. The application of gilding in regular or irregular allover patterns variously described as *caillouté* and *vermiculé* was developed to relieve too monotonous areas of color (see below, p. 160). On the aesthetic side the modeling was strengthened by the appointment of the sculptor Étienne-Maurice Falconet as administrator of the sculpture studio in 1757. Many of the models for the popular *biscuit* figures (e.g., Catalogue Nos. 117–121) were created by him in the years preceding his departure for Russia in 1766. He was succeeded by Bachelier from 1766 to 1774, and in 1774 by Louis-Simon Boizot, who continued to supervise the sculpture workshops down to 1802.

Apart from the invention of the new colors, the years between 1756 and 1779 were the most successful

8. The range of colors available, their terminology, and the dates of invention of the various ground colors used at Sèvres have been so authoritatively discussed by Verlet (*Sèvres*, pp. 21–22) and recently, in greater detail, by Eriksen (*Waddesdon Manor: Sèvres Porcelain*, Introduction, pp. 28–31) that it has not been thought necessary to repeat the information here.

and the most prosperous in the factory's history. A wide range of new models was devised. The king interested himself closely in its work. Orders were placed for numerous large services as diplomatic and royal presents. At the turn of each year he personally conducted a sale of the factory's productions at Versailles, at which important courtiers were expected to make purchases. If the economic effect of this was probably not very great it undoubtedly had the effect of making Sèvres porcelain highly fashionable with the rich and powerful.

A more important role in supporting the factory financially and making its productions popular was played by the *marchands-merciers*. Verlet has shown (*Sèvres*, I, chart on p. 47) that their purchases were more than double the value of those made by the Crown, the factory's other principal patron. Lazare Duvaux's *Livre-Journal* in particular (as well as the sales registers of the factory) shows him to have been a lavish purchaser and regular retailer of Sèvres porcelain on which he was allowed a mere nine per cent discount (it was later increased first to twelve per cent and then to fifteen per cent). It has recently been suggested by several writers that Duvaux exercised some direct aesthetic influence on Sèvres. This is perhaps to overstress his role at the factory, where he was consulted on commercial rather than artistic matters. On July 7, 1771, it was decided that "il ne sera pas moins nécessaire d'y faire trouver un des marchands dont la Compagnie aura fait choix pour avoir son avis sur les choses usuelles dont la vente poura être plus moins facile." Later in the month, on July 28, the documents (Ms Y, vol. I) mention "comme il est nécessaire pour satisfaire le goût du public de consulter un marchand sur le choix desd. modèles elle a prié ces Messieurs d'engager le S. Duvaux dont le zèle lui est connu de s'y trouver. . . ."[9] But the mention in the *Livre de Ventes* for 1753 of "Pièces de service formes Hébert, Duvaux, Bouillard etc.," might seem to suggest that certain *marchands-merciers* did exercise some aesthetic as well as commercial interest. Thomas-Joachim Hébert seems definitely to have played some artistic role at Sèvres, for a *plateau Hébert* is mentioned in the sales register as early as 1753 and a *gobelet Hébert* appears in the following year. The Duc de Luynes tells us in his *Mémoires* that a Sèvres vase was named after this famous *marchand-mercier*. This may possibly (but by no means certainly) be the type for which a plaster model is preserved at the factory labeled *vase à cartels, modèle d'Hébert* (Troude, *Choix des Modèles de la Manufacture Nationale de Porcelaine de Sèvres*, pl. 108). An "écritoire Hébert, vert et fleurs, 216 l." is also listed in the sales registers in 1759. Eriksen has pointed out that Hébert was by no means a lavish purchaser from the Sèvres factory. But he was a *marchand suivant le Cour* and actually had his establishment within the confines of the Palais de Versailles (see Introduction to Volumes I and II of this catalogue, p. LIV), which perhaps put him in closer touch with its most influential patrons.

Poirier (and likewise his partner and successor Daguerre) was another *marchand-mercier* who certainly influenced the factory's creations. He popularized, though he did not invent, the practice of mounting furniture with plaques of Sèvres porcelain.[10] It was almost certainly he who devised those circular *plateaux* and curved *quarts de cercle* from which the *ébéniste* Martin Carlin made so many *tables en chiffonnière*

9. Documentation kindly communicated by Svend Eriksen.

10. On the origins of the practice, see Watson, "A Possible Source for the Practice of Mounting French Furniture with Sèvres Porcelain" in *Opuscula in Honorem C. Hernmarck 27.12.66*, pp. 245–254.

(Volume III of this catalogue, No. 297), and he seems to have had a monopoly or near monopoly in purchasing them from the factory. Sèvres, in addition to marketing its wares through the various fashionable *marchands-merciers* and selling them at the factory itself, set up before 1774 an establishment for retailing the products of the factory in the old Rue de la Monnaie in the fashionable heart of Paris. Two other depots were later opened in the capital.

Abroad, too, Sèvres was in demand. Large orders were received from Russia, and the names of many Englishmen appear on the factory's books. Foreign comments on Sèvres porcelain usually praise its qualities highly. Thus, on a visit to the factory in 1765 the Rev. William Cole noted in his *Journal*, "It is of a most admirable Beauty & Texture: the White has no Glassyness, as many of our Manufactures established in England has; but its Whiteness excells that of the true Porcelaine, as much as the Dresden Manufacture exceeds all other in the Beauty & Elegance of its make, Fashion and colouring."[11] He also describes purchasing a few pieces of Sèvres from the *marchand-mercier* Dulac's establishment in the Rue Saint-Honoré. Cole's only complaint concerned its price. "Indeed," he wrote, "it ought to be superabundantly eminent & excellent, as the Price is excessive," and he goes on to express shocked horror that his companion Horace Walpole should give "10 Louis or Guineas for a single Coffee Cup, Saucer & a little square Sort of *Soucoupe* or under-*Saucer*, to set them on." Nearly a quarter of a century later the same complaints were being made. Thus in 1791 the 2nd Viscount Palmerston, visiting the Sèvres factory, noted "The things are beautiful . . . dearer than I could have conceived. A service of desert china which though handsome was neither very large nor very fine, 270 guineas. I have bought two or three cups."[12]

THAT THE Vincennes-Sèvres factory had already attained fame at home and abroad well before the discovery of the kaolin beds at Saint-Yrieux and elsewhere in the Limousin region permitted the chemists Macquer and Montigny to create hard-paste porcelain, has already been noted above. This renown was a piece of the greatest good fortune, for it has never been seriously doubted that the factory's soft-paste ware is far more aesthetically satisfying than the true porcelain, first achieved in 1769. A great deal of capital both monetary and experimental had been invested in building up the soft-paste organization. By 1783 there were some 274 persons employed at Sèvres on its manufacture. The mastery of the difficult art of manipulating this fragile material, which the craftsmen had acquired so laboriously over several decades, could not be jettisoned overnight without serious economic loss. Nor could the years of experimentation which had produced the favorite ground colors. So soft-paste porcelain continued to be included in the factory's production into the early nineteenth century (see p. 150 above).

The soft-paste porcelain of Sèvres had unrivaled technical qualities. Even when ground colors were applied in the Meissen manner to cover all or almost all of the surface, it gave a soft, slightly uneven,

11. Rev. William Cole, *A Journal of My Journey to Paris in the Year 1765*, ed. Stokes, pp. 232–233.

12. *Portrait of a Whig Peer*, compiled from the papers of the 2nd Viscount Palmerston, by Brian Connell, p. 237. These complaints were echoed by Frenchmen. The Duc de Luynes (*Mémoires*, XVI, p. 92) complains of "le prix actuellement trop considerable des porcelaines de celle manufacture."

almost vibrant quality to the washes of color owing to the slightly porous quality of the paste. The effect was quite different from the brilliant uniformity of the hard-paste glaze. The unique whiteness of the Sèvres paste on which Cole commented at some length in 1765 was very different from the stony white of hard-paste porcelain. This quality was exploited with great skill by reserving large areas of white as a foil for smaller areas of color and decoration, especially in the early years at Vincennes and the first decade of the factory's existence at Sèvres. Scattered birds naturalistically painted in polychrome colors or conventionally treated in gilding told with great effect against large cartouche-shaped areas of white (e.g., Catalogue Nos. 76 A and B). Trophies (e.g., Catalogue No. 99) and playing infants (e.g., Catalogue Nos. 82 A and B) were similarly used, as they were added to the repertory of subjects.

Gilding, of which the factory enjoyed a national monopoly in its formative years (and indeed much later), was used to impart a very special quality to Sèvres porcelain. Even at a distance Sèvres can be distinguished from all other French porcelains by its sparkling rims, which were emphasized by a simple narrow line of gold (see Catalogue No. 88) or a discreetly toothed (see Catalogue No. 87) or more boldly scrolled (see Catalogue No. 110) border. On the main surfaces and especially around the white areas reserved for painted decoration, gold was used decoratively with greater elaboration (e.g., Catalogue No. 88), though never with the overwhelming allover effect of the large areas of plain burnished or matte gold that were to be developed at the factory in the Napoleonic era.

The gold itself was applied with a combination of fine and coarser brushes. Contrast and liveliness were produced by burnishing certain parts with an agate tool and leaving others matte. This technique, adapted from goldsmiths' work and applied later by Gouthière to gilt bronze, gave great vitality of surface appearance. In addition, pictorial effects were produced by engraving details on the surface of the gold with a sharp-pointed tool, giving both realism and sparkle to the scrolls, flowers, fruit, leaves, and ribbons from which the border decoration was so often composed (most of these features can be found on the various component parts of the Rohan service, Catalogue No. 109 below). The use of gilding on porcelain is analogous to the use of gilt-bronze mounts on contemporary furniture to set off the sober colors of the wood and still more so to that of gilded metal mounts applied with such success in France to Oriental porcelain, a fashion which rose to its height in the middle of the century (see Introduction to Volumes I and II, pp. LX, LXI, and Introduction to Oriental porcelain in this volume, pp. 375 ff.). This parallel becomes particularly evident in the second half of the century, when many of the vases of neoclassic design produced at the factory in the Louis XVI period were given handles in the form of gilded terminal figures of women imitating contemporary gilt-bronze mounts quite precisely.[13] Candlesticks of *biscuit* porcelain gilded all over and quite evidently intended to ape gilt bronze were produced in small numbers at the factory in 1773 (a pair from the Wallace Collection are illustrated by Verlet [*Sèvres*, pl. 75]). Lazare Duvaux frequently mentions French porcelain mounted with gilt bronze

13. There are no examples in the Wrightsman Collection, but the various types of *seau* included in the great dinner service ordered by Catherine II of Russia provide a particularly obvious example. A reproduction is to be found in *Les Porcelainiers du XVIIIᵉ Siècle Français* ("Collection Connaissance des Arts"), p. 221.

in his *Livre-Journal*. Some of this was probably mounted outside the factory to the *marchand-mercier*'s own specifications. Pages XXXIII and LXXXIX of the printed edition of Duvaux's daybook point to a working relationship with the eminent *bronzier* Jean-Claude Duplessis, co-director of art at Sèvres. In addition to making bronze mounts for ornamental porcelains at the factory he maintained his own foundry in Paris for this purpose. After his death in 1783, he was succeeded at Sèvres by Pierre-Philippe Thomire.[14]

Another ingenious use to which gold was applied at Sèvres was in the form of an openwork allover pattern to break large areas of ground color. These were generally referred to in the factory records as *caillouté*, or "pebbled," which describes their appearance sufficiently well. Variations are known as *pointillé d'or* (perhaps what is now referred to as *œil de perdrix*; see Catalogue Nos. 105 A to O), *sablé d'or*, *en briques d'or*, and *pois d'or*. *Vermiculé*, which better describes certain "wormy" types of patterning, is apparently a nineteenth century term, adapted from architectural usage. These allover patterns were, however, more regularly used after the first decade of the factory's existence at Sèvres, and examples in the Wrightsman Collection are rare. A form combining *caillouté* and *sablé d'or* decoration is, however, to be seen on the undated knife and fork handles Catalogue Nos. 113 A–JJ.

Very little that can be assigned with certainty to the earliest period at Vincennes is identifiable today. Bachelier in his *Mémoire historique sur la manufacture nationale de Porcelaine de France*, drawn up in 1781,[15] tells us that in 1748 Chinese porcelain was being copied at Vincennes as it had been at Chantilly whence had come François Gravant and the Dubois brothers who made the first experimental porcelain that led to the foundation of the factory. Oriental porcelain, especially that decorated in the Kakiemon style, provided some of the most popular types of decoration at Meissen, which the royal French factory was deliberately aiming to rival. The Comte de Chavagnac possessed two lobed bowls decorated in this style, which had descended to him from his forebear Machault, appointed administrator of the factory in 1745. An *écuelle* and stand of the same type is in the Musée National de Céramique, Sèvres. These were probably copied, not directly from Japanese models but from imitations of these made at Meissen. A figure of a parrot in the Musée des Arts Décoratifs, Paris, which Verlet (*Sèvres*, pl. 5) has assigned to Vincennes and dates from about 1745, was undoubtedly imitated from a Meissen original of a type similar to Catalogue No. 20 above. We know, too, that a series of sixteen plaques of porcelain was copied at the factory from Canton enamels in Machault's collection and used in 1748 to decorate a pair of commodes made by Bernard II Van Risamburgh. But if the earliest shapes and decorations were mostly inspired by "Chinese" (generally, in fact, Japanese) porcelain as interpreted at Chantilly and Meissen, currents of a more purely Western idiom soon began to submerge these characteristics.

14. Under the heading *Extraits des Livres de Ventes*, Chavagnac (*op. cit.*, p. 186) cites among listings for 1779, "À Mme Royale: Garniture, 3 vases chinois, fond Taillandier, montés en bronze, 2,400 l." In 1781, we find a reference in the sales registers to a "Table montée en bronze, l'histoire d'Achille, 6,000 l," and in the following year the king's aunts bought "Trois vases gris agathe, montés en bronze, 960 l." Surely these and many earlier bronzes were created by Duplessis or under his direction. The same source (pp. 206, 207) gives a list of payments to Thomire for providing mounts for Sèvres vases.

15. Bachelier's manuscript of 1781 was edited by Gustave Gouellain and printed in 1878.

The appointment of Jean-Claude Duplessis in 1745 to supervise the modeling workshops at Vincennes was crucial for the evolution of the rococo forms to which soft-paste porcelain was so admirably adapted. Duplessis, a *bronzier* and an *orfèvre*, had developed an individual rococo style which was far better suited to porcelain than those of either of the two great exponents of the rococo idiom in the middle years of the century, Charles Cressent and Jacques Caffiéri. Cressent's style, somewhat angular and based on a combination of rockwork, human forms, and strapwork, was not at all well adapted to the semi-fluid nature of the unfired paste. Caffiéri's on the other hand, as exemplified, for instance, by two chandeliers in the Wallace Collection dated 1751 (*Wallace Collection Catalogues: Furniture*, nos. F 83, 84), or the Passemant clock at Versailles of the same period, was altogether too open, too cage-like in construction, to be suitable for adaptation to the fragile soft paste, so inclined to warp and crack in the firing.

Duplessis had shown a mastery of a quite different rococo idiom to these in the pair of gilt-bronze *braseros* he had created in 1742 for Louis XV to present to the ambassador to the Sublime Porte and which are his earliest known masterpieces in gilt bronze. The smoothly flowing, linear character of their wholly abstract forms was excellently adapted to the nature of soft paste. It comes nearer in style to the work of Juste-Aurèle Meissonnier, one of the two founding fathers of that phase of the rococo known as the *style pittoresque*, than does the work of either Cressent or Caffiéri. The swirling, stepped terrace of gilt bronze that provides a base for a celebrated vase containing 470 Vincennes flowers presented by the Dauphine to her father, the Elector of Saxony, in 1749 was certainly the work of Duplessis, and its design comes very close to certain of Meissonnier's engraved designs for silver.[16] It is still in the Zwinger at Dresden.

The rococo indeed undoubtedly entered the factory's repertory first through the copying of contemporary silver, as it did in so many porcelain factories outside France. The fluent forms, with their undulating rims and "combed" or fluted motifs derived from exotic shells, found on so much contemporary silver, were admirably adapted to the nature of soft-paste porcelain. But the intricate surface decoration was less so. Under Duplessis's guidance this feature was suppressed and generally replaced by plain straight walls (as in the cups and saucers), or, in the case of vases, by rotund volumes with clean, smooth surfaces quite different from the often overwrought surfaces of contemporary works in hard-paste porcelain created at Meissen and elsewhere.

But in spite of the need for simplification, silversmiths' work continued to provide a basis and inspiration for Sèvres for a long time to come. The tureens especially are more or less direct transpositions from silver into porcelain. This appears particularly in their stands with "celery" type legs (cf. Catalogue

16. There is a considerable number of drawings for vases, inkstands, etc., by Duplessis in the archives of the Musée National de Céramique, Sèvres. Some have been published and discussed by Mme Levallet-Haug in *La Renaissance de l'Art Français et des Industries de Luxe*, February 1922, pp. 60–67. In addition, illustrations of a number of the plaster models of vases in the same museum have been published by Troude, *op. cit.* Several of these models bear the name of Duplessis, e.g., *vase gobelet Duplessis* (Troude, pl. 93). Unfortunately, few of the names now inscribed on these vases are to be found in the factory archives of the eighteenth century. They cannot therefore be accepted with complete confidence.

No. 97.6) and in their lids surmounted by a knop of vegetable form, an artichoke or the like. The rare but celebrated *bras de cheminée* produced in the 1760s are very evidently derived from metal examples and were perhaps originally designed by Duplessis to be executed in gilt bronze. Other examples of borrowings from metal can be found among the illustrations in Verlet's *Sèvres*: in the chamber candlestick (pl. 9), watering can (pl. 17), wall fountain and basin (pl. 20), and jug with basin (pl. 24). Even the famous elephant-headed candelabra-vases, the original plaster model for which is attributed to Duplessis (Catalogue Nos. 80–83), derive at least in part from metalwork, for the bases are of a form frequently found in gilt bronze. So is the foot of the *vaisseau à mât*. But there is clearly an attempt here to develop forms independent of silver and other metalwork (though perhaps not a wholly successful one; there is something too exotic, even bizarre, about the *vases à éléphants*). Eriksen has noted resemblances to an unusual type of Chinese vase, and the curious Oriental conceit of the elephants' heads may derive partly from Meissen, where J. J. Kaendler had produced candelabra supported on such heads as long ago as 1733.

The elephant-headed candelabra seem to have made their first appearance about 1756. The great creative moment in the history of Sèvres came in just this decade from the mid-fifties to the mid-sixties. It was in these years that the designers began to develop models totally new to the medium. Somewhat naturally the principal innovations were in the range of vases; there was little opportunity for evolving really new forms of domestic or useful ware. Some of the most striking of the new models appearing in these years are dual-purpose objects. The *vase à éléphants* is an example of this; so is the *pot-pourri gondole* with its pierced recesses to hold narcissus or hyacinth bulbs, which seems to have first appeared in the second half of the 1750s also.[17] Two entirely new models differing from anything produced at any other factory and analogous to this last object are the *vases hollandais*, which appeared as early as 1754 (Catalogue Nos. 84 A and B and 85 A and B), and the pot-pourri vase known as a *vase vaisseau à mât*, the earliest known version of which is dated 1754. The former, of a most ingenious design, is composed in two parts. The lower is a shallow vessel intended to hold water with narcissus bulbs accommodated in holes around the border. Into this fits the splay-sided or fan-shaped upper part, designed to hold cut flowers in the conventional manner. The celebrated *vaisseau à mât*, in the form of a masted ship, is traditionally said to derive from the single-masted ship that appeared in the armorial bearings of the City of Paris. Although it was not a dual-purpose piece like the *vases à éléphants*, its design was of unique character unlike anything previously produced at any porcelain factory. That it should have been attempted at all in the fragile soft-paste porcelain is remarkable. To fire such a piece with its elaborately pierced sides and yet avoid warping is evidence of the consummate technical skill available at Sèvres. Even so the fact that only fourteen of these vessels (of which only twelve seem to have survived) are known to have been sold from the factory suggests that there were a good many failures in firing these extremely complex and delicate pieces. The two-part *vase à Dauphins*, which first appears in the sales books of the factory in 1755,

17. A *pot-pourri gondole* in the Wallace Collection (*Illustrated Catalogue of the Furniture . . . and Objects of Art*, 1920, no. IV-B-162) purchased by Louis XV from Lazare Duvaux in 1758 is illustrated by Verlet, *Sèvres*, pl. 25.

is another original and complex piece with analogies with those mentioned above and is a sort of circular version of the *vase hollandais*.

If such totally original designs as the *vases à éléphants* and the *vaisseaux à mât* and the other vases mentioned seem to meet the second and third of the three qualities *gentilesse, nouveauté, variété* that Hulst laid down as a desirable guiding maxim for the factory's products (though in fact he was referring to painting rather than modeling), the first two vases bring to mind another of his dicta: "en fait de porcelaine surtout les dessins les plus bizarres, et les plus chimériques, l'emporteront souvent sur les dessins les plus élégants et les mieux raisonnés." His first quality *gentilesse* is better seen in the wide range of jardinières bearing a variety of different names in the factory's records: *caisses à fleurs, cuvettes Mahon,* or the vases with pierced lids and shoulders intended to hold pot-pourri, such as the type going under the name of *vase Tesniers* in the sales registers, though this may possibly refer to a type of decoration *à la Teniers* rather than to the shape. Some of the purely decorative vases intended to garnish a chimneypiece or table like the *vase Boileau* or the still rarer *vase à têtes de bouc,* the *vase à oreilles* or the goblet-shaped vase probably known as a *vase à cartels, modèle d'Hébert,* were of a supreme elegance, and a specialty of the factory. More *bizarres* and *chimériques* designs returned with the rise of neoclassicism. Such is the curious type known as the *vase ferré,*[18] which seems to have been created about 1763. In this, painted plaques are made to appear clamped to the sides with metal tie rods and suspended by feigned ropes and a sort of naval cleat. But if such decorative vases were the most original, the most impressive and the most costly products of the factory, they, in fact, represent only a relatively small proportion of its total output.

At first the Vincennes factory concentrated chiefly on the production of porcelain flowers in a deliberate attempt to compete with the Meissen factory. There can be little doubt that the mounted vase filled with porcelain flowers given by the Dauphine to her father in 1749 was sent as an impressive demonstration of how successfully the King of France's factory was able to rival or even surpass the Elector of Saxony's in one of its principal specialties. It was at just this time, in fact, according to Bachelier's *Mémoire Historique,* that "la manufacture commençoit à être en concurrence avec celle de Saxe."

Such bouquets of flowers set into vases, pots, or miniature tubs enjoyed a great popularity down to about 1755 and not only in France. In a somewhat affected letter addressed from Paris in August 1752 by the 10th Earl of Huntingdon to Lady Chesterfield, he writes ". . . I take the liberty of sending your Ladyship a flower-pot by the *voiturier* that sets out to-morrow for Calais; containing an ever-blooming nosegay, that braving the vicissitudes incident to terrestrial flowers, pretends to keep pace with any evergreen of them all; and promises to preserve as unfaded a lustre in the bleak months of December as any garland a British florist can provide in the more friendly month of June. So far, madam, I may safely advance; and if I carry the parallel no further, I console myself and my nosegay for its want of sweetness, from the consideration of its being destined for the perfumed atmosphere of a lady's chamber: where musk satchets, *et les eaux mystérieuse de Cithère, de miel, et de bergamot,* must triumph over the feeble

18. Troude, *op. cit.,* pl. 104.

pretensions of any real flowers whatsoever."[19] After 1755, however, the fashion for such things seems to have declined, though as isolated blossoms and sprays they continued to be used to ornament vases (especially as knops on the lids), wall lights, chandeliers, etc. More rarely they were used in *biscuit* porcelain on those plaques with molded frames inlaid with *biscuit* portrait heads (e.g., lot 122, Sotheby's, London, March 20, 1956 [illustrated in catalogue]). Verlet (*Sèvres*, p. 24) has also drawn attention to the fact that the *marchand-mercier* Darnault later ordered a number of such bouquets in the 1770s and 1780s.

The principal category of porcelain produced at Sèvres, as indeed at all other large-scale porcelain factories, was the useful wares. These ranged from huge dinner services down to single cups and saucers and even spoons. The finest services were made as diplomatic presents for Louis XV to give to foreign ambassadors and royalty. A wide selection of these was displayed at the exhibition *Les Grands Services de Sèvres* held at Sèvres in 1951, and is discussed in detail by Verlet in the catalogue. In placing them on public display in this way the organizers were merely following eighteenth century precedent. In an entry in her *Journal* dated June 24, 1784, an English visitor to Paris, Mrs. Cradock, wrote "We went this morning after breakfast, to see a splendid service of Sèvres porcelain, which the King is giving as a present to the King of Sweden. The whole service . . . is gilded and excellently painted."[20] After describing the decorative porcelain figures which went with it, she concludes "We returned full of admiration." Part of this service was included in the 1951 exhibition cited above, catalogue no. 8. It was given by Louis XVI to Gustavus III.

Orders for services were also placed by private individuals, both Frenchmen and foreigners. The Rev. William Cole tells us in his *Journal* that "The Duke and Duchess of Richmond . . . while I was at Paris . . . bespoke a Service of this Manufacture for their Table which was to cost 500 Pounds: I mean Mr. Walpole went with their Graces to Sève."[21] Another service of some eighty pieces decorated with pale blue *œil de perdrix* was delivered on March 20, 1771, to the dealer Lambert for the first Lord Melbourne and still remains in the hands of his descendants. It cost 5,197 livres, 19 sols.[22] Two services ordered from the factory by individuals were particularly prestigious. The first of these was the service decorated in a pronouncedly neoclassic style that was ordered for Catherine II, Empress of Russia. Verlet[23] itemizes 616 pieces delivered by June 1779 costing the prodigious sum of 202,572 livres, while more than a hundred more remained on order. The other commission (if it can properly be called

19. Historical Manuscripts Commission, Report on the Manuscripts of the late Reginald Rawdon Hastings, Esq., ed. Bickley, III, p. 77

20. *La Vie Française à la Veille de la Révolution (1783–1786)*, Journal Inédit de Madame Cradock Traduit de l'Anglais par Mme O. Delphin Balleyguier, p. 53. The manuscript of this interesting diary appears to be located in France and has never, curiously enough, appeared in the language in which it was written.

21. Cole, *op. cit.*, p. 234.

22. See Watson, "Annotated Handlist of the Sèvres and Other Porcelain in the Possession of Viscount and Viscountess Gage at Firle Place" (typescript manuscript at Firle and in Wallace Collection archives).

23. Full particulars are given by Verlet, Grandjean, and Brunet, *Les Grands Services de Sèvres*, catalogue no. 11.

a private one) was ordered by Louis XVI himself. This was decorated principally with scenes taken from the illustrations to Ovid's *Metamorphoses* and *Les Adventures de Télémaque*. On account of its cost, its component parts were delivered only in small selections each year, the first consignment being delivered at Christmas 1783. The king kept a record of his annual acquisitions and the price in a small notebook written in his own hand, which survives in the Archives Nationales. The onset of the Revolution prevented the completion of either of these two services. The Louis XVI service was completed only in 1803, long after the execution of the king, and was subsequently sold by the French government, passing ultimately into the possession of the English Crown.[24] The final payment for Catherine the Great's service was not made until 1793, but both provided valuable employment and financial support to the factory at a moment of increasing economic difficulty.

On account of the considerable cost of the large dinner services, the type of tableware most commonly bought by contemporaries was probably the small tea and coffee services, or even single cups and saucers. The former usually consisted of a tray with a varying number of cups and saucers, a sugar bowl, a cream jug, and a tea or coffee pot (more rarely a *chocolatière*), but could also comprise merely a small square tray with a single cup or cup and saucer. All were known as *déjeuners*, with various qualifying adjectives added, e.g., *déjeuner Duvaux*, *déjeuner Dauphin*, *déjeuner Bouret*, *déjeuner Hébert*, etc., the differences seeming to depend on the shapes of the cup or tray. The square tray and single cup and saucer mentioned above was known as a *déjeuner carré*, for the tray was a *plateau carré* (Catalogue Nos. 99, 103 below).

Another popular form of useful ware was the *écuelle*, a two-handled soup bowl with cover and stand. In 1752 Lazare Duvaux was retailing these at an average price of 120 livres. Later in 1758 he sold much more costly examples, prices as high as 432 livres (no. 3011) and 480 livres (no. 3083) being recorded. These last were perhaps of a specially rich character (though nothing in the accounts suggests this) as they were supplied to the Dauphin and the Prince de Soubise, respectively.

Single cups and saucers, too, were sold in great numbers from the factory. These also had varying names: *gobelet Bouret*, *gobelet Bouillard*, *gobelet Hébert*, *tasse forme litron*, etc., some of which can be identified from inscribed drawings surviving in the records at Sèvres.[25] The so-called *trembleuses* (a modern term)

24. The best account of this service is that included in the catalogue of the exhibition *George IV and the Arts of France* held at The Queen's Gallery in 1966, catalogue no. 51. It does not, however, deal with the iconography of the paintings. Pieces from the service are reproduced in Laking, *Sèvres Porcelain at Buckingham Palace and Windsor Castle*, pl. 59, in Verlet, *Sèvres*, pl. 88 (both in color), and elsewhere. The numerous paintings in reserves are, in fact, for the most part taken from the engravings by Le Mire and Basan after drawings by Eisen, Moreau, Boucher, Leprince, Monnet, et al., in the four-volume edition of the *Metamorphoses* issued 1767–1771 (Cohen, *Guide de l'Amateur de Livres à Gravures du XVIIIᵉ Siècle*, no. 769–772), or from those by Tilliard after Monnet illustrating the 1783 edition of Fénelon's *Télémaque* in two volumes (Cohen, no. 384). We are indebted to Geoffrey de Bellaigue for this information. Louis XVI's notebook recording his piecemeal purchases is reproduced by Verlet in *Faenza*, XXXIV, nos. 4–6, 1948, pp. 120–121. The completion of the service in 1803 is documented in the Archives Nationales and the archives at Windsor.

25. See Eriksen, *Waddesdon Manor: Sèvres Porcelain*, catalogue no. 32.

were very popular. These consisted of a cup of tapering conical shape usually supplied with a lid *(gobelet à cuvier)* and fitting into a deep saucer. They are said to have been made particularly for elderly people, as they would not easily overturn, but were certainly used by younger people also.[26] An immense range of useful tableware was available in Sèvres porcelain ranging from sauce ladles and skimming spoons to knife handles (cf. Catalogue Nos. 113 A–JJ below) and egg cups. It was with satisfaction that d'Angiviller was able to write about 1780 that "la manufacture de Sèvres . . . dans l'espace de 20 ans à rendu l'usage de la porcelaine française plus commune sur nos tables que ne l'était pour nos pères il y a cent ans l'usage de faïence."

Allied to the production of tableware was that of articles for the toilet. The most numerous were *pots à fard, pots à rouge,* and *pots à pommade* of differing sizes to hold various creams, rouge, etc. Toilet mirrors were rarely produced, but an exceptionally fine example was given to Grand Duchess Marie Feodorovna of Russia (see Volume I of this catalogue, No. 105) by Marie-Antoinette in 1784. For ablutions there were jugs and basins *(broc et sa jatte)*, sponge *(boite à éponge)* and soap holders *(boite à savonette)*, as well as shaving bowls *(bassins à barbe)* and numerous spittoons *(crachoirs)*, presumably for male use. Brushes and brush holders *(vergettes)* are rare, but a unique complete dressing table set dated 1763/1764 (with its *pots à pommade)* survives in the Wallace Collection (illustrated in Verlet, *Sèvres*, pl. 46). Even eye cups *(baignoires d'yeux)* were made, and a few survive (there is a collection of them in the C. L. David Collection, Copenhagen), as do a number of *pots de chambre* and *bourdalous* of Sèvres porcelain, objects that find frequent mention in the sales registers of the factory and the *Livre-Journal* of Lazare Duvaux.

Related to the lidded *pots à fard* are the numerous snuff boxes produced at the factory at least from 1756 onward and certainly made in emulation of Meissen (though they had also been made at Chantilly, Saint-Cloud, and Mennecy). There were two types. The earlier were generally oval or circular, made in two parts, a flanged body with a fitting lid to which a simple rim and hinge of metal were applied. A little later were boxes composed of six painted plaques of porcelain, intended to be mounted *en cage* in gold (see Introduction, Volume III of this catalogue, pp. 103–104). Tobacco jars and even porcelain pipes are recorded. But the miscellaneous uses to which Sèvres porcelain was adapted are far too numerous to be all mentioned here. Shuttles *(navettes)*[27] for "knotting" and the popular *parfilage* ("drizzling" in contemporary English) were particularly popular and produced in large numbers. The bodies of opera glasses and spyglasses are met with; so are inkstands and standishes. The most popular form of these latter seem to have been the large rectangular examples made up from rectangular plaques of porcelain mounted in gilt bronze. More rarely we find those entirely of porcelain, like a remarkable *écritoire* in the Wallace Collection (illustrated in color in Verlet, *Sèvres*, pl. 56) designed by Duplessis and probably given by the king to one of his daughters.

The former type of inkstand of plaques mounted in gilt bronze (three are illustrated in Eriksen,

26. See Eriksen, *Waddesdon Manor: Sèvres Porcelain*, catalogue no. 63.

27. Illustrated in the portrait of Mme Danger by Louis Tocqué (see *Country Life*, February 6, 1953, p. 338).

Waddesdon Manor: Sèvres Porcelain, nos. 64–66) were supplied regularly from 1764 onward to the *marchand-mercier* Simon-Philippe Poirier, who seems to have been the sole purchaser. He, too, was the principal buyer of plaques of Sèvres porcelain for mounting on furniture, an important specialty of the factory, which is discussed at some length in Volumes I and II of this catalogue (e.g., pp. LVII, LVIII, 282). Here it is sufficient to note that the earliest examples of *quarts de cercle*, sold to Poirier from the factory for mounting around the frieze of a *chiffonnier* by the *ébéniste* Martin Carlin, who specialized in this technique, are to be found in the Wrightsman Collection (see Volume III of this catalogue, No. 297). Other types of "furnishing object" made at the factory included clock and watch cases, lamps, and those plaques painted with figure subjects intended to hang on the wall like pictures. Perhaps the most famous of these are the series after Oudry's *Chasses du Roi* ordered to hang in the rooms where Louis XV dined at Versailles. Numberless objects must have been made only occasionally to special order. Such, for instance, was the *bénitier* made for Mme de Pompadour as a gift to the Pope.[28] Even sword hilts and, more extraordinarily, powder flasks, were occasionally made of Sèvres porcelain. Sculpture, mostly in *biscuit* porcelain, another important product of Sèvres, is discussed separately below.

LIKE ALL the artistic activities of the French Crown in the eighteenth century, the Garde-Meuble, the Menus-Plaisirs, the Gobelins tapestry factory, and the carpet-making establishment at the Savonnerie, the daily operations of the Vincennes-Sèvres factory are exceptionally well documented. Better so than any other porcelain factory. Not even at Meissen are such complete archives available. The principal repository of these documents is the archives of the present Manufacture Nationale de Sèvres. Here numerous files of manuscript notes (albeit many of them tantalizingly incomplete) are to be found, mostly bound in faded blue paper or yellowed vellum (occasionally scribbled on scraps of paper or even on playing cards). All these disclose valuable information about the management of the establishment and the organization and personnel of the principal ateliers where the modeling, the painting, the gilding, and the sculpture were carried out. They also tell much about the firing in the kilns, and the terminology used for various types of object as well as providing much information on matters of human interest concerning the personalities of individual craftsmen employed. The registers of sales, though also incomplete, throw an immense amount of light on taste, production, prices, patrons, etc., and quite frequently enable surviving pieces to be traced to the moment of their creation (see pp. 270–271 below, where pages from the sales records of the Rohan service, Catalogue No. 109, are reproduced).

Other records relating to the factory's creations and activities are to be found in the Archives

28. Bought from Lazare Duvaux on January 30, 1756 (*Livre-Journal*, no. 2392). "Il partira dimanche par les voitures, à votre addresse, le bénitier de Vincennes que vous avez commandé. Je l'ai trouvé beau, quoique simple. Offre-le-lui [i.e., the Pope] de votre part. Je ne veux jamais qu'il sache que c'est de la mienne. Demandez-lui en payement un petit morceau de la Vraie Croix. Envoyez-le-moi par le premier courrier extraordinaire." Mme de Pompadour to the Comte de Stainville (the future Duc de Choiseul), while he was French Ambassador at Rome (quoted without a date by Nolhac, *Mme de Pompadour et la Politique*, p. 69).

Nationales, in the Bibliothèque de l'Arsenal, and, as Eriksen has recently shown, an important group of kiln records has strayed into the library of the Institut de France. Printed records, notably the *Livre-Journal* of the *marchand-mercier* Lazare Duvaux (the manuscript existing in 1873 seems to have vanished without trace) and Chavagnac's printed extracts from the sales registers of the factory, throw interesting light on the retail side of the taste for Sèvres porcelain. Verlet, in particular, has done most valuable work in identifying surviving pieces sold by Duvaux and linking them with the *marchand-mercier*'s purchases from the factory, while the catalogue of *Decorative Art from the Samuel H. Kress Collection at The Metropolitan Museum of Art* illustrates (see nos. 32, 35, 37, 43, 52, and 58) how the sales records may be used as a guide to purchases made by royalty and other notables.

Many other scholars have made valuable use of these records, among them, *primus inter pares*, the Comte de Chavagnac. In his *Histoire des Manufactures Françaises de Porcelaine*, published in 1906 in collaboration with the Marquis de Grollier, Chavagnac made very extensive use of this archival material in the long section, running to almost 250 pages, he devoted to the history of the Vincennes-Sèvres factory. This article is the foundation stone on which all subsequent writers have built and is unlikely to be entirely superseded. Others who have made profitable use of these documents in their publications include Mlle Marcelle Brunet, until recently the indefatigable archivist of Sèvres, and Svend Eriksen in his highly important catalogue of the Sèvres porcelain in the Rothschild Collection at Waddesdon Manor. Serge Grandjean, too, has delved deeply into the records relating to the Napoleonic period.

Some idea of the range and value of the information contained in these documents can be obtained merely by listing the names of the more important ones and giving some brief description of their contents. The most fascinating reading, perhaps, is provided by the *Régistres Matricules*, which contain personal records of the various craftsmen working at the factory and their specialties. Their short titles as they appear on the spines of the volumes at Sèvres are often somewhat misleading. Thus the *Régistre Matricule des Arts de Doreur* contains, in addition to those of specialist gilders, the names of many sculptors and those workmen responsible for applying the grounds. Among other things, the document reveals that many of the leading gilders started as painters at the factory. The most famous of these, the gilders Noël and Le Guay, did so, and Louis Massue, appointed head of the gilding atelier in 1755, had started at the factory as a painter and gilder in 1745. This fact accounts for the pictorial skill with which such motifs as gilded birds were applied to the early porcelains produced at Vincennes, as well as the skilled draughtsmanship of the purely decorative gilding. Nothing more quickly betrays redecorated eighteenth century or genuine nineteenth century soft-paste Sèvres porcelain than the inferior quality of the gilding as compared with the work done at the factory in the eighteenth century. The same criterion applies with equal or greater force to the forgeries produced in both soft and hard paste later in the nineteenth century.

Another volume entitled *L'Atelier de Tourneurs et Répareurs* contains, in addition to the names of many of these key workers in the factory, much information on the employees who prepared the glazes, ground the ingredients for the paste, and looked after the furnaces. The *tourneurs*, or throwers, shaped the vessels by turning them on a wheel. Others, called *mouleurs*, created forms by pouring or pressing the paste into molds. After this the work was handed over to the *répareurs*, who refined it by chasing the molding, executing any pierced work, and generally giving the piece a finished appearance, before its first firing. This was most important work and contributed as much to the elegance and decorative effect of the finished piece as the work of the painters and gilders, though most of it still remains anonymous (see below, pp. 177–178). Duplessis was responsible for the work of all three classes of potters from 1745 onward, and there is a close analogy between the final delicate chasing and burnishing of gilt bronze, in which the craftsmen in Duplessis's own bronze foundry must have specialized, and the minute attention to detailed finish of the decorative features, particularly of the larger vases and display pieces, carried out by the *répareurs*. Eriksen has drawn attention to the fact that a *répareur* would sometimes spend as much as two to three weeks finishing a single vase. It is a measure of their importance that these *tourneurs*, *mouleurs*, and *répareurs* were regarded as the social equals of the painters in the factory's hierarchy. Justly so, but as the work of very few potters has been identified with certainty, it is only the names of the painters which have evoked the interest of collectors.

The registers of painters contain not merely records of employment, the basic details of their lives, assessments of their abilities, and particulars of their pay, etc., but sometimes physical descriptions of their appearance and often amusing character sketches. The flavor of these entries is given by this typical extract taken from the *Régistre Matricule des Peintres* for 1755 concerning Dodin, one of the leading figure painters at the factory:

> Le S [i.e., Le Sieur] Dodin (Charles Nicolas)
>   Du 1.e Janvier 1755.
>   Natif de Versailles agé de 21 ans. Sa taille n'est point encore décidée, a Le visage Blanc et agreable,
>   les Chevaux blonds, est garçon, avant d'entrer a la Manufacture, il aprenoit le génie, Son Genre
>   de talens est la Peinture en figure qu'il possede passablement bien, Et promet beaucoup de progrés.
>   Il est entré a La Manufacture en avril 1754, apointé d'abord à 24# et aujourduy il L'en à 42#.
>   Du 1.e Juillet 1755
>   Le talent de Dodin se perfectionne Sensilblement il vient d'etre augmente de 6#.
>   Du 1. Janvier 1756
>   Dodin promet tout ce qu'un talent de cette espèce peut promettre, il est Sage et assidu, ses
>   apointemens sont ajourdhuy de 60#.
>   Du 1. Janvier 1757
>   nouvelle augmentation de 6#.
>   Du 1 Janvier 1758
>   nouvelle augmentation de 9. Ses apointements sont de 75#. (Mort en Mars 1803 le 20 fevrier 1803
>   à Sèvres). [These are later additions; the actual date of Dodin's death was February 10.]
>   Charles-Nicolas Dodin
>   Né le 1 Janvier 1734—baptisé le 3 paroisse Saint-Louis à Versailles fils de Nicolas Dodin épicier
>   épouse en 1762, Jeanne Chabry, fille de Jean Chabry sculpteur (voir f° 176 du présent régistre). [This
>   notation is a modern addition to the manuscript.]

Informative and entertaining as much of this information is, it also omits much we should like to know: the curious fact, for instance, that Dodin studied military engineering as a young man before becoming a painter, and why, since his first names were Charles-Nicolas, he adopted the letter "k" as his mark on porcelain.

Surprising facts about other painters emerge from the Sèvres archives. Thus Jean-Louis Morin, the most accomplished painter of military and naval subjects at the factory, was originally trained as a surgeon, while the painter Charles-François Bequet had begun his career as a *marchand-mercier*. He seems therefore to have come down in the world.

When the factory first started, fan painters (almost twenty of them) were called in to supplement the few artists accustomed to the specialized technique of working on porcelain who had been enticed from factories at Chantilly and Saint-Cloud. The only professional painter of any great merit to be attached to the factory in the eighteenth century, and the only one to be elected a member of the Académie Royale, was Jean-Jacques Bachelier. His appointment in 1748 to supervise the *atelier de peinture* was certainly intended to raise the standard of painting at the factory. Regarded as a promising young artist (he was only twenty-four at the time of his appointment) specializing in the minor genre of flower (and later animal) painting, he was perhaps engaged under pressure from Mme de Pompadour, whose protégé he was. It may be on this account that, three years later, we find Hellot, the factory's chief chemist, writing of Bachelier in disparaging terms: "Bachelier . . . coute beaucoup et me paroit fort inutile." Nevertheless, there is no doubt he made an excellent job of training the minor painters of whom the atelier was composed. As he wrote of himself in 1781, "Son premier soin fut de former les sujets; ensuite il meubla les ateliers de tableaux, modèles et estampes dans tous les genres pour remplacer les productions chinoises qu'on copioit encore." It was probably by means of these engravings, etc., quite as much as by any direct intervention by the artists themselves, that subjects after Boucher and Oudry became so highly popular at the factory.[29] For many years, beginning in 1753, Bachelier directed his own school of painting in Paris where the pupils were encouraged ". . . en faveur des sujets destinés à entrer dans la manufacture," and, from this time onward, he received frequent payments recorded in the factory's accounts, for "tableaux pour servir de modèles aux peintres."

Apart from Bachelier himself none of the painters employed at the factory were independent artists of any great merit. Nor was it desirable that they should be. What Bachelier was required to do (and what indeed he did with conspicuous success) was to impose a "factory style." It was not desirable that the painters should develop obviously individual styles when half a dozen painters might be employed to paint flowers on a single large dinner service (see Catalogue No. 109 below).

Nevertheless, the style and quality of the work of different specialists was differentiable within limits,[30] and they were in fact differentiated into three classes, presumably according to their abilities. Jacquemart and Le Blant, writing in 1862, listed many of these craftsmen by class. Among those whose

29. On the use of Boucher's engravings by the Vincennes-Sèvres factory, see Zick, *Keramos*, July 1965, pp. 3–47.

30. In his introduction to the catalogue of the Sèvres porcelain in the Kress gift to the Metropolitan Museum, the author of the present catalogue has analyzed the differing styles of certain painters whose work is represented among the Hillingdon porcelain (*Decorative Art from the Samuel H. Kress Collection*, pp. 180–192).

work appears in this catalogue, Chappuis, Fallot, Rosset, Pierre, Taillandier, and Tandart were ranked in the first class. Some of the more familiar names were placed, rather unaccountably as it seems to us today, in the second class. Among these Levé, Evans, Cornailles, Aloncle, Morin (next to Dodin, the most successful figure painter to work at Sèvres in the entire eighteenth century), and Vieillard are all represented in the Wrightsman Collection. Others, Théodore, Méreaud, and Thevenet (to restrict the names to those mentioned in the catalogue), are not assigned to any class at all.

In addition to supervising the painting workshop, upon his appointment as art director in 1748 Bachelier was put in direct charge of one of the most important workshops in the factory, the *atelier de sculpture*; Duplessis, a co-director, seems to have concentrated on other specialties, for example the work of the potters and the rare *bronziers*. As one of the aims of the Sèvres factory was to rival or surpass Meissen,[31] glazed figures of the type that the Meissen factory had made so popular were attempted from the beginning. Mention has been made above (p. 160) of the parrot copied from a Dresden original that is in the Musée des Arts Décoratifs. Such parrots are mentioned several times in Lazare Duvaux's *Livre-Journal* in the years immediately before and immediately after 1750. A few models of dogs were also produced in glazed porcelain (in the *Livre de Ventes*, "Chiens 2 l. 5 s."[32] appears in 1758, and in 1766 a "Chien coloré") as well as a certain number of human figures: Lazare Duvaux mentions "un Hercule" in 1749 (presumably one of the "6 modèles des dieux" for which Depierreux was paid ninety livres in 1748),[33] "deux figures fauconniers" in 1750, "un group de Vincennes, sujet de Boucher, joueur de flute"[34] in 1752, for example.

But these figures do not seem to have attracted the public in the way Meissen figures continued to do. As late as 1767 Poirier, the *marchand-mercier*, was buying birds that were evidently surplus stock, for they are indicated in the sales registers as being still of Vincennes porcelain, and the prices are very much reduced as compared with those of 1750.

Soon after 1750, however, Bachelier thought up the ingenious idea of making figures from unglazed *biscuit* porcelain, the soft white color and matte surface of which resembled the marble employed for most indoor sculpture in the eighteenth century. This caught the imagination of the patrons of Sèvres far more successfully than the glazed figures and continued to be a staple product of the factory down to the end of the century and later. After hard-paste porcelain had been produced, it tended to be used (particularly after 1777) for these *biscuit* figures as being a whiter material resembling statuary marble

31. It is interesting to note that de Bastide, in describing the ultrafashionable interior of *La Petite-Maison*, first published in 1752 (see Introduction to Volumes I and II of this catalogue, p. XXXVI), several years before the transfer of the factory to Sèvres, mentions only Meissen porcelain vases among the decorative objects. French porcelain is not referred to at all.

32. The dogs are exceedingly rare today. An example of Vincennes porcelain dating from about 1750 is in the Fitzwilliam Museum, Cambridge (Louis Clarke bequest). A later example is in the possession of the Earl of Rosebery at Mentmore.

33. Groups of the deities from this series by Depierreux appear on the base of the mounted bouquet of Vincennes flowers given by the Dauphine in 1749 to Augustus III and mentioned below.

34. Presumably taken from the engraving L'Agréable Leçon by R. Gaillard after Boucher. A number of figures produced in the early years at Vincennes were taken from Boucher engravings. On the whole subject see Zick, *op. cit.*, pp. 3–47.

even more closely than the soft, very slightly warmer tone of the soft paste and also because it took the most delicate modeling of the molds exceedingly well.

Unfortunately the written archives at Sèvres are a good deal more sparse where the sculpture workshop is concerned than are those relating to the *atelier de peinture*. The sculptor Étienne-Maurice Falconet was appointed in charge of sculpture in 1757 (though he already worked for the factory as early as 1754) and remained there until he left Paris for Russia in 1766. He was succeeded, though not immediately, by Louis-Simon Boizot who was appointed as head of the sculpture workshop only in 1774. Under these two, various lesser sculptors worked on modeling at the factory. The minor sculptors Fernex and La Riche and several others were regularly employed in the modeling studios, and at one time or another more famous sculptors such as Pigalle, Bouchardon, Clodion, Pajou, Houdon, etc., all provided models.[35]

If the written records of the sculpture workshop are scanty at Sèvres, a very large number of models and molds still survive from the eighteenth century, though a number have been broken or lost. Examples of almost the entire range of *biscuit* sculpture has been published in the two volumes of *Le Biscuit de Sèvres* by Bourgeois, Lechevallier-Chevignard, and Savreux, the one illustrating all the eighteenth century models, the second those produced after the Revolution. And many of the plaster models are illustrated by Troude (*op. cit.*), where a number of the models for vases are reproduced also.

The most popular models in the early days of *biscuit* were probably those after François Boucher. For some, but not all of these, the painter prepared drawings from which figures or groups in the round were made in the modeling *atelier* (see under Catalogue Nos. 114 A and B, 115, 120 A and B below). Some, on the other hand, such as the popular Leçon de Flûte and the Mangeurs de Raisins, were merely adapted from engravings after Boucher's paintings.[29] Even when he was not responsible for the design himself, Boucher's influence was pervasive, and Falconet's La Lanterne Magique and La Marchande de Plaisirs (Catalogue Nos. 117 A and B) are very close to Boucher in conception and quite different from Falconet's own neoclassic manner as represented, for instance, by his famous L'Amour Menaçant (Catalogue Nos. 118, 119 B), the marble for which had been begun two years before he was appointed at Sèvres, and became exceedingly popular in *biscuit* reproductions.

Jean-Baptiste Oudry, the animal painter (who had much experience in working for the decorative arts at the Beauvais and Gobelins tapestry factories), was another who produced designs for sculpture that became popular in the form of *biscuit* figures, though here again some of the models were probably adapted from engravings. On a quite minor scale, Charles-Antoine Coypel and Carle Van Loo also provided designs for use at the factory.

The *biscuit* figures were widely used as table decorations. Most of the great presentation services given by the king were furnished with them (generally on stands of glazed and painted porcelain), though they rarely survive with the glazed tableware today. A service presented to the Duchess of

---

35. The fullest discussion of the history of the production of *biscuit* and other statuettes at Sèvres is contained in Chavagnac, *op. cit.*, pp. 251–260; see also Sainsbury, *Antiques*, January 1956, pp. 46–51, April 1965, pp. 430–433, and December 1965, pp. 824–828.

Bedford by Louis XV in 1763 is an exception and still retains its *biscuit* groups (the majority of animals after Oudry).[36] For the most part such figures were probably discarded in the nineteenth century as old-fashioned, unattractive objects likely to collect dust (which in fact they do and for this reason many were often kept under quite "Victorian" glass domes in the eighteenth century). In an age that preferred floral decorations and large *épergnes* filled with fruit on the dining table, these *biscuit* figures seemed superfluous. But when in 1789 Mrs. Cradock went to see the presentation service made for Gustavus III of Sweden she particularly remarked on the "ornements de table."[37]

Mrs. Cradock's further reference to "des hommes célèbres: généraux, littérateurs ou autres" was, of course, to the reductions of the life-size statues of the Grands Hommes de France that Angiviller commissioned from the principal contemporary sculptors over the period 1776–1787. The small statuettes, which Angiviller had made at Sèvres from 1782 onward, proved highly successful, especially as the hard-paste *biscuit de Sèvres* matched the statuary marble of the originals so well. The inspiration of the series undoubtedly derived from Rousseau and his enthusiasm for Plutarch, for Angiviller was a great admirer of Jean-Jacques. But they also contributed to the Directeur des Bâtiments' campaign to make the Crown once again a conscious patron of "serious" art as it had been under Louis XIV. Painters were to select subjects "propres à ramener les vertus et les sentiments patriotiques." The doctrinaire character of the series as well as its success with the king is very apparent in a description of the Grand Cabinet du Roi as it was in the 1780s, left us by the Comte d'Héziques, one of Louis XVI's pages. In this room, he tells us, there was:

> . . . multitude de figures de porcelaine, de vingt pouces de haut, copies exactes des statues des guerriers
> et des grands hommes du siècle de Louis XIV que le gouvernement faisait exécuter. Je citerai une statue
> à cheval de Frédérick II, remarquable au double point de vue de la ressemblance et de la delicatesse. . . .[38]

But this discussion of the production of *biscuit* porcelain at Sèvres has led us rather far from the consideration of the archives of the factory and their value. Much useful information is to be obtained from the financial records, which survive in considerable quantity. Thus the volumes entitled *Recettes et Dépenses* contain annual wage lists recording the monthly earnings of the workers, each countersigned by the recipient. Each employee is listed according to his occupation, and mention is sometimes made of whether he worked in soft or hard paste. The files however are far from complete. They run, for instance, continuously from 1761 to 1769, are sporadic during the 1770s, while only the lists for 1789 survive from the 1780s. During the troubled period of the Revolution down to 1794 the records are very fragmentary. A special section of these papers is concerned with *Travaux Extraordinaires* (overtime work) and describes

36. The service is discussed at some length and illustrated by Eriksen, *Apollo*, December 1965, pp. 484–491.

37. *Journal*, p. 53: "Les ornements de table consistent en statuettes et en groupes de porcelaine hauts de 2 pieds. Les premières représentent en différentes attitudes des hommes célèbres: généraux, littérateurs ou autres; les seconds, des sujets d'histoire." They are not mentioned by Verlet in his catalogue of *Les Grands Services de Sèvres* (catalogue no. 11) and have probably disappeared.

38. *Souvenirs d'un Page de la Cour de Louis XVI*, by Félix, Comte de France, d'Héziques, ed. le Comte d'Héziques, p. 155. Héziques perhaps means the Bibliothèque du Roi by the *grand cabinet* (see Verlet, *Versailles*, p. 602).

more fully than other records certain special projects carried out by several classes of workers. One, entitled *Travaux extraordinaires des peintres, répareurs, et autres ouvriers de la Manufacture Royale des Porcelaines établie à Sèvres pendant l'année 1776*, carries the names and signatures of sixty-three workers opposite the listing of the objects or special operation for which each was responsible. A few examples from this record are:

> Danet père (soucoupes, gobelets)
> Liance père (vases colonnes, vases à oreilles)
> Humbert fleuriste (bouquets de roses, vases à pied de biche)
> Paulin graveur (noyaux d'assiettes, assiettes)

Wage lists appear in a rather different form in the *États de Payements*, which exist for 1774 and again for 1780. In the earlier of these, separate columns are reserved for workers in soft paste *(La Porcelaine de France)* and in hard paste *(La Porcelaine Royale)*. Both books also contain the signatures of workers, or their marks in the case of the more illiterate employees. The partial shift from soft to hard paste after the latter was launched commercially between 1770 and 1772 can, to a limited extent, be studied in the *Journal des Ateliers en Pâte*, one volume of which begins in November 1773, and another is dated 1792. This describes the daily output of each worker among the *tourneurs*, *mouleurs*, and *répareurs*, as well as the assemblers (e.g., the *anseurs* who attached the handles, and the *becteurs* who molded the lips and spouts), and the flower makers. It also reveals that the technical skills of the throwers and molders were interchangeable, and that the workers sometimes moved from one occupation to the other, as the demand for the factory's productions fluctuated.

Among the other volumes available in the Sèvres archives, the *Sommier des Personnel* is concerned with vital statistics. Others deal with purely financial matters. Such are the *Comptes*, which run from 1773 to 1775, and the *Comptes des Effets Marchandes*, which contain charts of expenses.

Of far greater general interest, however, are the sales records of the factory, labeled *Ventes* on the spine of each volume, which constitute a broken sequence from 1752 onward. Written in a clear copperplate hand, they record the names of purchasers, the date, what they buy, and the price. In multiple purchases, the unit cost of each item is also recorded in separate columns. Two pages reproduced below (pp. 270, 271) give a clearer idea of their character than any verbal explanation. With the aid of these documents and the date-letters with which the porcelain is marked, scholars such as Chavagnac, Verlet, Eriksen, etc., have succeeded in tracing the origin of many surviving pieces of Sèvres porcelain,[39] and it has been used for this purpose in this volume of the catalogue. It should, however, be pointed out that the records can seldom be used to trace anything other than large pieces such as decorative vases, jugs and basins, punch bowls, etc.; small individual pieces such as cups and saucers, ice-cream cups, salts, etc., can rarely be identified in this way unless they form part of a large service such as those from the Rohan service catalogued below, or have some very unusual feature in their decoration that merits special

39. E.g., Eriksen, *Apollo*, January 1968, p. 38, where a vase with a bouquet of porcelain flowers sold by Duvaux to Lord Bolingbroke on September 20, 1756 (lot 2590) is identified with one in the Cholmondeley Collection.

mention in the entry in the sales register. Otherwise the descriptions of such items are too brief, and too large a number was produced in any one year, to make precise distinction possible. Furthermore, it is evident that a considerable number of objects, including some of great importance, were omitted from the sales records.

It has already been pointed out that the *marchands-merciers* were by far the most important purchasers from the factory. Names such as Lazare Duvaux, Poirier, Daguerre, Dulac, Sayde, and numerous other *marchands* like Hébert constantly appear in the factory's account books. From time to time it has proved possible to link Lazare Duvaux's purchases by means of his published *Livre-Journal* with existing pieces of Sèvres porcelain. But independently of this the *Livre-Journal* is a most valuable document for the study of Vincennes and Sèvres porcelain during the years 1748 to 1759, which it covers. Porcelain bulks very largely in the accounts, and it is a document whose pages cast a great deal of valuable light on matters of taste, price, and patronage of the factory's products.

IF THE written documents relating to Sèvres are fuller than those of almost every other porcelain manufactory in or outside France, the porcelain itself is also more informatively marked than any other known type created in the eighteenth century. For instance, seven distinct items of information can be extracted from this inscription

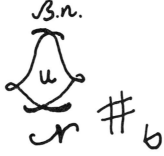

painted on the underside of a plate (Catalogue No. 110 below). The royal monogram of the interlaced L's was employed as the factory mark for Vincennes and Sèvres; the absence of a crown above the monogram shows that the material is soft-paste porcelain *(pâte tendre)*; the U within the cipher is for the year 1773, when the plate was decorated; the initials Bn and N stand for the painters Bulidon and Aloncle, specializing in flowers and birds, respectively, while the symbol # indicates the work of the gilder Chauveaux and the conjoined letters VD that of a second gilder, Vandé *père*.[40]

Such an elaborate combination of decorators' marks emphasizes the high degree of specialization among the craftsmen at Sèvres. Not all Sèvres porcelain is so richly marked as this plate; nevertheless a high proportion of eighteenth century pieces bear some cognate marks, and for a century or more it

40. The craftsmen's marks were introduced in 1753 at the same time as permission to use the royal monogram was granted. Generally they were painted over the glaze in blue but occasionally in various colors or gold. The interlaced L's are sometimes found in an elaborately floreate form, particularly on the early productions of the factory at Vincennes. The significance of this is unknown.

has been possible for students of Sèvres to decipher some or all of them with varying degrees of certainty with the aid of published charts of marks of differing reliability. It is generally believed that the painted marks are signatures put on by the worker himself out of pride in his creation, like the artist's signature on a painting. There is, however, a possibility that this is incorrect and that they do not even rank with the stamps used on furniture by the *menuisier-ébénistes* from the mid-eighteenth century onward, which were struck merely to conform with guild regulations, but were at least struck by the craftsmen themselves. It has recently been suggested[41] that certain marks were applied by the head of the atelier before the decorating was begun, as a means of assigning specific projects to individual artists. But the alternative hypothesis is being investigated at the Metropolitan Museum by comparing the handwriting of the alphabetical marks with that of the workers' signatures on the payrolls. There is sufficient similarity between the marks and the initial letters of the signatures of the artists Morin, Pierre *jeune*, and Levé *père* to encourage the point of view that the marks on porcelain are genuine signatures of the men whom they represent.

The identification of the marks of individual painters and gilders is a complicated matter that has preoccupied all students of Sèvres porcelain from Brongniart and Riocreux in 1845, through Chavagnac and Grollier who published the marks of some 335 craftsmen of one sort or another in 1906, down to the latest and most exhaustive list drawn up by Mlle Brunet in the second volume of *Porcelaine de Sèvres* in 1953.[42] Unfortunately, the almost total lack of contemporary documentation of these marks is the most serious lacuna in the archives at Sèvres. The author of this catalogue called attention in *Decorative Art from the Samuel H. Kress Collection at The Metropolitan Museum of Art* of 1964 (pp. 122 and 190) to the work records and the records of assignments allocated to individual artists. He demonstrated how the names and marks found in these previously unrecorded documents cleared up some seeming inconsistencies in the working dates of the artists named Tandart, father and son. The information was taken from folios dated 1777 and 1778–1783. More recently Svend Eriksen has drawn attention to (*Waddesdon Manor: Sèvres Porcelain*, p. 24) another manuscript book containing the names and marks of some (but not all) of the painters and gilders working at the factory in 1775. The most reliable list, the *fons et origo* from which subsequent compilations all spring, is a list that includes ninety-four eighteenth century marks drawn up by Denis-Désiré Riocreux and first printed in 1845. Riocreux worked as a flower painter at Sèvres from 1807 to 1828, when, because of failing sight, he was transferred to the ceramic museum and in 1847 succeeded Alexandre Brongniart as director. Eriksen has shown that Riocreux drew heavily on the 1775 manuscript mentioned above. But he also added other names. As, however, Riocreux had worked at the factory at a time when a number of the eighteenth century work-

41. Dauterman, Parker, and Standen, *Decorative Art from the Samuel H. Kress Collection at The Metropolitan Museum of Art*, pp. 177–179.

42. Mlle Brunet rightly emphasizes the importance, for judging the authenticity of a mark, of its position and the exact form of the marks, although as far as these last are concerned she admits that there may be understandable changes, especially in handwriting, with the passage of time (see p. 26 in her book).

[176]

men were still employed there, he can be regarded as the repository of certain verbal traditions going back to that period. These, though not impeccable, must be considered to some extent trustworthy. Eriksen has, however, recently pointed out that even Riocreux's list itself is occasionally open to doubt and that there are reasons for questioning the marks he assigns to Le Doux and Gommery, even though these have been accepted by all subsequent writers on the subject.[43] Additions to the canon laid down by Riocreux, however meticulously worked out, must necessarily be regarded as attributions of a lesser degree of soundness until more supporting documentary evidence comes to light. In any case the marks, however tentatively attributed to specific individuals, cover only just over a third of the workers known to have been employed as painters and gilders in the eighteenth century. Much research remains therefore to be undertaken in this field.[44]

Almost all the compilers of the lists of marks mentioned above concern themselves with painted marks only. Yet there exists another wholly distinct group of marks about which practically nothing is known. These are the *marques en creux*. They were incised with a stylus or similar pointed tool into the moist clay, before it was fired and coated with glaze. They may be very small and have often gone almost undetected, particularly as they can be nearly invisible if the glaze is thick. A few have been published by Chavagnac and also by Brunet, although only seven of the eighty-one illustrated by the latter concern the eighteenth century. Verlet first drew attention to the importance of these marks (*Sèvres*, p. 53) and recorded a number of them in his "Notices Descriptives des Planches" in that volume (pp. 197 ff). Perhaps the earliest attempt to record such marks consistently as one of the standard elements of catalogue description was made by the author of this catalogue in 1964 in *Decorative Art from the Samuel H. Kress Collection at The Metropolitan Museum of Art*. The same practice was followed by Svend Eriksen in his more recent catalogue of the Sèvres porcelain in the Rothschild Collection at Waddesdon. It has been adhered to in the catalogue entries below. Like the painted marks, the incised marks occur as letters, numbers, or symbols, used singly or in combination. A very few consist of names incised in full. Since they were applied before the porcelain received its first firing, they must have been incised in the workshop where the vessels were thrown or molded. From this it may perhaps be inferred that some of them, at any rate, are intended as a means of tracing the technicians responsible for carrying out some stage of their creation. Such a use seems to have been made of incised and impressed marks at Meissen after 1740, and the practice is still observed at the Nymphenburg factory. And the fact that, as Eriksen has pointed out, certain marks appear regularly on certain specific types of objects, strongly suggests that many relate to some form of specialization.

Today informed opinion is inclined to consider that many of them are the marks or "signatures" of individual *tourneurs*, *mouleurs*, and *répareurs*, especially since Eriksen has put forward one or two perceptive conjectures as to the identity of certain of them, e.g., "Bo" for the *répareur* Bono, who sometimes

43. Eriksen, *Waddesdon Manor: Sèvres Porcelain*, p. 24.

44. The absence of marks is not necessarily to be taken as a sign that a piece is not authentic. Why certain pieces are unmarked is not fully understood at present.

inscribed his name in full. This view is strengthened by the fact that somewhat similar marks were used for this purpose at Sèvres during the nineteenth century. At The Metropolitan Museum of Art over two thousand of these marks, fed with other data into a computer, have provided some enlightening correlations. The first craftsman's mark to be identified by this means was "da" for Danet *père* (see Catalogue Nos. 102, 109).[45] Others are listed in the Preface to this volume.

The value of such marks within the factory organization in enabling the work of a particular craftsman (whether skilled or faulty) to be identified, hardly needs stressing. For posterity they have the additional advantage, stressed by Dauterman and Eriksen, that they can be a particularly valuable guard against fraud, since such underglaze marks can hardly be forged on already glazed porcelain. If the incised mark of an identified *tourneur* or *répareur* conflicts with the date-letter, some irregular practice may be indicated, and a redecorated piece or an added date-letter is to be suspected. Thus, as Eriksen notes, if a piece bearing the "Bo" mark of Bono who joined the factory in 1754 appears on Sèvres bearing the date-letter for 1753, it is likely to be a redecorated piece.[46]

It is also possible that certain of these incised marks, possibly those that appear as numbers, are guiding marks *(repères)* put on to enable the workers to recognize which pieces belonged to the same set or service. When the porcelain was in the undecorated state such a relationship would not be at all obvious, and the marks would be especially helpful when large quantities of orders were being dealt with by the factory at the same time.

A further possibility which cannot be entirely ignored is that certain of the *marques en creux* may be directions to kiln workers. But at present exploration of the whole subject is in a quite early stage. As more and more such marks are published with full particulars of the pieces on which they are found,

45. Incised marks, as found on datemarked or closely datable examples of Sèvres, from twenty of the largest collections of Europe and the United States have been assembled and put through a computer (see Dauterman in *Computers and Their Potential Applications in Museums*, pp. 177–194). This has demonstrated that the computer can be employed to correlate various factors such as the handwriting of the alphabetical marks, the dates of the pieces of porcelain, and the specific types of objects. The coded descriptions of these (and other) data were fed into the machine, along with the names of all the potters and their dates. The first craftsman's name to be identified was that of a potter whose mark appears on one of the wine coolers in the Rohan service (Catalogue No. 109) and on a cup and saucer in the dinner service Catalogue No. 102. The telltale idiosyncracy of Danet's handwriting was his habit of not capitalizing the first letter of his surname. When the computer was requested to supply likely names of potters working in the 1770s, it became readily apparent that, from among several names beginning with Da, the mark "da" belonged to the *répareur* Danet *père*.

46. The chief source of Sèvres porcelain decorated outside the factory (mostly in England in the early nineteenth century) was the sales by Brongniart shortly after 1800 of the large stocks of undecorated soft-paste porcelain, when it was decided to concentrate exclusively on the manufacture of hard paste. But Verlet has, however, shown (*Sèvres*, pp. 51, 52) that there were several such sales during the eighteenth century, and some of this porcelain was also decorated outside the factory contemporaneously. The status of such "redecorated" ware, though despised today by most collectors, is quite different from the imitations and indeed forgeries of Sèvres produced in England, France, and elsewhere in the nineteenth century. Chavagnac estimated that 90 per cent of what passes for Sèvres falls into one or another of these categories. Mlle Brunet thinks this figure to be no exaggeration. Imitations of Sèvres were also made during the eighteenth century both at other porcelain factories and in different materials. They were also extensively made during the nineteenth century, particularly by the Minton factory.

it seems possible that a pattern will emerge, and eventually we shall understand them as well as (or perhaps better than) the other, painted, marks.[47]

SèVRES ENJOYS the distinction of being the only French eighteenth century factory in which the manufacture of hard-paste and soft-paste porcelain was practiced jointly over a long period. Although from an early date Sèvres pursued the secret of producing hard paste, it was always reluctant to enter the field until assured of a limitless source of the essential kaolin in France. Other French factories experimented with hard paste several decades before success finally came to Sèvres. The earliest attempt was made at Paris by René-Antoine Ferchault de Réaumur, a member of the Académie des Sciences. His experiments were begun in 1717. In 1722 he received a description of the Chinese process of porcelain-making from the Jesuit missionary Père d'Entrecolles, who also sent him samples of kaolin and petuntse, the essential ingredients. But Réaumur evidently mistook the kaolin for talc and decided to use the glass of broken bottles as a substitute for the petuntse. The resulting product, of which no surviving examples are known, was probably a modified type of glass, rather than a porcelain.

The Vincennes factory was a going concern in the early 1750s when two further developments took place. First, Jean-Étienne Guettard, a chemist employed by Louis-Philippe, Duc d'Orléans, at the Abbey of Sainte-Geneviève, claimed to have made *pâte dure* with the aid of kaolin from Alençon. Again, no examples are known, though it is curious that little attempt was made to follow up this experiment at Vincennes, although Hellot was perfectly aware of it. More important was the success of Paul-Antoine Hannong in Strasbourg. His career in France was short-lived, however. As the royal factory was given exclusive privileges from its first establishment, his manufactory was shut down by the edict of 1753 that granted exclusive rights to Vincennes for the manufacture of porcelain "dans le goût de Saxe." Hannong made overtures to Boileau, director of Vincennes, offering to exchange his secrets for certain considerations. But, to his disappointment, the plan never materialized, ostensibly because kaolin was not available in sufficient quantity. Hannong consequently entered into negotiations with Karl Theodore, Elector Palatine, which resulted in the founding of a factory at Frankenthal in 1755. In the meantime, about 1754, two little-known figures, Christian Daniel Busch, who had gained some experience at Meissen, Vienna, and elsewhere, in collaboration with a certain Stadelmayer whose background is obscure, were engaged to carry out experiments at Vincennes. But they apparently had no success either, although Busch returned to Sèvres ten years later to continue his experiments.

After the death of Paul-Antoine Hannong in 1760, Boileau tried to negotiate with his sons. But Joseph Hannong, remembering the disillusioning treatment received by his father, declined. His brother Pierre-Antoine, however, worked at Sèvres from 1761 until 1765, during which time he claimed to have divulged such secrets as were known to him, but the payment he claimed for these was not made until 1781, when a settlement at a reduced amount was arranged.

Another figure, Louis-Léon-Félicité, Duc de Brancas and Comte de Lauraguais, entered the scene

---

47. The crucial factors are the mark itself, the type of piece marked, the date when the various *répareurs*, *mouleurs*, and *tourneurs* are known to have been employed in the factory, and the date of the particular piece bearing the marks.

about 1763. He succeeded in producing a true porcelain experimentally at his Château de Lassay, also using kaolin from Alençon. The Musée National de Céramique, Sèvres, owns a bas relief of a peasant drinking after Teniers, dated 1764, coming from this source. It is regarded as the oldest surviving piece of French hard paste.

Finally, the chief Sèvres chemist Macquer was able to display some porcelain objects made with clay found at Saint-Yrieux, near Limoges, first in June 1769 to the Académie des Sciences, and then in the following December to Louis XV on the occasion of the annual sale at Versailles. The story of how the first piece demonstrated to the king burst into fragments when exposed to the flames of a spirit lamp, greatly to Louis XV's amusement, has often been told. This clay was kaolin, the indispensable ingredient of hard-paste porcelain. There were counterclaims concerning the original discovery, and once again the ceramist Guettard, the discoverer of the clay at Alençon, claimed prior knowledge. Nevertheless, it was with this clay that Sèvres embarked on the regular production of hard paste, although the new porcelain was not produced in commercial quantities until 1772, according to a *mémoire* of the director of Sèvres dated 1790 (Chavagnac, *op. cit.*, p. 164). But the future of Sèvres hard paste was not assured until about 1784 when the king purchased a factory founded eleven years earlier at Limoges, the site of an apparently inexhaustible supply of kaolin. The Limoges plant acted as a branch, turning out table ware for decoration at Sèvres.

It is a common misconception that the factory at Sèvres produced only hard-paste porcelain from that point on. The manufacture of soft paste outlived the *ancien régime* for some years, in fact until 1804.[48] The great dinner service ordered in 1783 by Louis XVI for his dining room at Versailles, but not completed until 1803 (see pp. 164–165 above) was the last major project carried out in that material until its reappearance much later in the nineteenth century. The only examples of hard-paste Sèvres porcelain catalogued below are the two vases with chinoiserie decoration on a black ground Nos. 91 A and B.

The historic organization, renamed the Manufacture Nationale de Sèvres during the Revolution, still continues to make porcelain of high quality. Supported by the state, even today it meets the challenge of supplying designs, some in a contemporary idiom and others, especially the *biscuit* figurines, repeating models that had brought such deserved fame to the factory under royal sponsoring in the last years of the *ancien régime*.

RICH AS England is in French eighteenth century furniture (on this see the Introduction to Volumes I and II of this catalogue *passim*), it is, and has been for many years, far richer in soft-paste Sèvres porcelain

48. As given in Brongniart, *Traité*, II, p. 459; Verlet, Grandjean, and Brunet, *Les Grands Services de Sèvres*, p. 16, give 1806. In an interesting letter to Brongniart, the director of the Manufacture, dated April 26, 1807, Vivant Denon, Napoleon's principal advisor on the arts, complains bitterly that the factory no longer makes soft-paste porcelain: "Je n'en conçois pas la raison, puisque cette porcelaine se tourmente moins au feu et qu'elle est suffisante pour des objets qui ne sont pas d'usage." He ends his letter with a phrase that might have provided an epigraph to this essay: "Cependant, je vous observerai toujours que, la porcelaine de Sèvres étant un objet de luxe, tout ce qui est richesse, aspect et nouveauté doit être tenté à cette Manufacture."

of the eighteenth century. All authorities on the subject are agreed that the Wallace Collection, the English Royal Collection, and, on a slightly smaller scale, the Rothschild Collection at Waddesdon Manor each contain assemblages of Sèvres that for size and range are unparalleled elsewhere in the world. It is significant that of the plates illustrating eighteenth century soft paste in *Porcelaine de Sèvres* by Verlet, Grandjean, and Brunet (the best-illustrated of the standard works on the factory), no less than forty-six out of one hundred are taken from pieces in the Wallace Collection. Illustrations of pieces in the Royal Collection are only less numerous because it is rather less accessible and less familiar to the general public. The three collections mentioned are complemented by numerous public and private collections in the British Isles, among which the collections of the Duke of Buccleuch at Drumlanrig and Boughton, the Earl of Rosebery at Mentmore, the Duke of Bedford at Woburn,[49] the Marquess of Bath at Longleat, the late Marquis of Cholmondeley in London and at Houghton,[50] the Earl of Harewood,[51] Viscount and the late Viscountess Gage at Firle[52] are only selected for mention here from a host of other owners on account of the outstanding size and quality of their Vincennes and Sèvres porcelain. Among public collections the Jones Collection in the Victoria and Albert Museum[53] and the Fitzwilliam Museum, Cambridge, also deserve particular mention.

The Englishman's love of Sèvres goes back almost to the foundation of the factory. The names of many Englishmen (and women also) appear on the factory's books, among them those of Lady Holderness in 1764, the Duke of Richmond in 1765, Lord Lincoln in 1768, Lord Kerry in 1769 and again in 1777, Lady Craven in 1773, Lords Findlater, Villiers, and Egremont in 1774, the Duke of Leinster in 1775, an unknown "General Smith" in 1778, etc., etc. Others have been mentioned in the course of this Introduction. In addition, other Englishmen are known to have placed orders through agents, such as that for a dinner service purchased in 1771 by the first Lord Melbourne through the Chevalier Lambert, who seems to have been employed as an agent by several Englishmen in their purchases of Sèvres.

Even before this list begins, the names of a number of Englishmen are listed as buyers of Sèvres in the *Livre-Journal* of Lazare Duvaux; Lord Bolingbroke's, for instance, appears several times from 1755 onward. Lords Hervey and Harcourt find mention there, too, and quite a number of pieces were bought by French clients of the *marchand-mercier* who was instructed to forward them to London. In addition, at least one important diplomatic presentation service came to England when in 1763 Louis XV gave a magnificent dinner service for sixteen persons, painted in *bleu lapis* with a *vermiculé* pattern in gold, to the

49. See Eriksen, *Apollo*, December 1965, pp. 484–491.

50. See *Great Family Collections*, ed. Cooper, p. 238, for reproductions of some of the late Lord Cholmondeley's Sèvres; also Tait, *Apollo*, June 1964, pp. 474–478.

51. See Tait, *Apollo*, January 1965, pp. 21–27; June 1966, pp. 437–443.

52. See note 22 above.

53. Victoria and Albert Museum, *Catalogue of the Jones Collection*, Part II, *Ceramics, Ormolu, etc.*, pp. 3–28. The French porcelain was catalogued by the late William King, an outstanding authority on soft-paste French porcelain who wrote only too little on the subject.

Duchess of Bedford whose husband, the fourth duke, had just negotiated the Treaty of Paris. This survives almost complete at Woburn Abbey.[49]

Whether all of the acquisitions of Sèvres mentioned above can be strictly regarded as *collecting* Sèvres porcelain is open to question. But there was undoubtedly an undercurrent of collecting in the case of some of the lesser purchases made by the English from the factory or from *marchands-merciers*. Writing in his *Journal* of a small *déjeuner quarré* that Walpole had bought at Poirier's for ten louis, Cole describes the cup and saucer and tray as "... the highest finished Things of the Kind that can be conceived: perfect Jewels that deserve to be set in gold Frames to be admired & looked at, but never to be used for Fear of breaking them."[54] He seems here to be adumbrating a collector's attitude. It was a view that Walpole seems to have shared, for it is clear from the *Description of Strawberry Hill* that most of his Sèvres was scattered about the house with other curiosities and decorative objects rather than used functionally. This applied even to such a quite undecorative piece of useful ware as "A white Sève saucepan that bears the fire: 1771," mentioned in the *Description*, which was quite evidently shown as a curiosity.[55] And when in 1782 Walpole writes to his nephew Thomas Walpole, who is leaving for Paris, asking him to bring back "one cup, or a cup and saucer of the Sève china in imitation of lapis lazuli," he is surely writing as a collector of curiosities.[56] Some confirmation of this view is to be found in London auction catalogues a little later when the phrase a "cabinet cup and saucer" appears quite frequently.

That there was some sort of collector's market for Sèvres porcelain in London in the second half of the eighteenth century is suggested by the way it began to appear in the auction rooms. The first time that it made its appearance at Christie's was in 1771, when what were described as "2 elegant vases and covers, painted from the designs of Boucher" were sold for £40. 19s., certainly no more and perhaps rather less than they would have cost at the factory. Three years later at the Dickenson sale two green urns painted with mythological scenes went for even less, £37. 16s. Thereafter Sèvres porcelain appears sporadically in the London auction rooms down to the time of the Revolution. Quite a number of pieces appeared in the Captain Carr sale in 1780, including a dessert service of seventy pieces of *bleu céleste* Sèvres painted with birds and flowers in reserves and richly gilded, which attained the price of £82. 19s., or a little over one pound a unit. On the eve of the Revolution prices seem to have been on the rise, for a *déjeuner* of rather larger size than usual, consisting of thirteen pieces (probably four cups and saucers, cream jug, covered sugar bowl, teapot, and tray) described as of "Mazarin blue and gold," reached the comparatively high price of £50. 8s.

Of individual collectors at this period we know little. That there was already Sèvres porcelain in the English Royal Collection we know from Horace Walpole, who specifically mentions it in describing Queen Charlotte's collection at Buckingham House in 1783 in his *Journal of Visits to Country Seats, etc.*

54. Cole, *op. cit.*, p. 233.

55. *Works of Lord Orford*, II, *Description of Strawberry Hill*, p. 414. Indeed, it was something of a curiosity, for it must have been one of the earliest pieces of hard-paste porcelain to have been made at Sèvres.

56. *Letters of Horace Walpole*, XII, ed. Paget Toynbee. Letter dated September 6, 1782, no. 2350.

From Marryat[57] we learn that a pair of pink Sèvres *vases à éléphants* belonged to her daughter, the Princess Sophia, though we do not know whether she acquired them before or after 1789. These may possibly be the ones now in The Metropolitan Museum of Art (*Decorative Art from the Samuel H. Kress Collection,* catalogue nos. 36 A and B). The Duke of Cumberland, brother to George III, certainly acquired his Sèvres before this, for when he died in 1790 there were a number of items of Sèvres porcelain included in Christie's posthumous sale of the contents of Cumberland House in Pall Mall in 1793. None of the splendid soft-paste Sèvres collected by George IV and now mostly at Windsor Castle can certainly be said to have been at Carlton House before the great dispersals caused by the French Revolution. But it is highly likely that some of it was there, for many of the furnishings of Carlton House at the time of its completion in 1785 were supplied by Dominique Daguerre, the Parisian *marchand-mercier* and the partner of Poirier, whose relations with the Sèvres factory we have seen to have been extremely close. The fact that Daguerre, together with his new partner, Martin-Éloi Lignereux, found it worthwhile to open a branch in Piccadilly in 1786, too, makes it pretty certain that there was a considerable demand for Sèvres at this date.

With the outbreak of the Revolution in France, however, the picture changes completely. Already by March 1790 we find a sale of china entirely from "The Royal Factory of Sèvres Porcelaine" including no less than 234 successive lots of Sèvres being held at Christie's (Lugt, *Répertoire des Catalogues de Ventes Publiques . . .,* no. 4546). This was probably organized by Daguerre, whose partner Lignereux was shortly afterward engaged to help the factory over its financial difficulties by selling off remaining stocks at absurd prices and organizing lotteries of porcelain.[58] The similar sale held in March of the following year (Lugt, no. 4698), which included forty-five lots of Sèvres and other French porcelain, was held in Daguerre's own name; and two further sales in May 1792 (Lugt, nos. 4917 and 4918) of "Porcelain consigned from Paris" were in fact brought over by "Monsieur De Guerre," as a penciled note on Christie's own copy of the catalogue tells us. The following April saw another large sale of wares "Consigned from the Porcelain Manufactory of Sèvres," brought over this time by the Comte d'Adhémar (Lugt, no. 5039). But by now such sales began coming thick and fast, and we come across auctions of "Porcelaine imported from France" (Lugt, nos. 4879, 1792); "Consigned from France" (Lugt, nos. 4981, 1793); not to mention "An Emigrant of Distinction" and "Paris Importation," both in 1797 (Lugt, nos. 5612 and 5613). Many further examples could be quoted.

After the great Revolutionary sales of 1793 and 1794, a number of sales of Sèvres porcelain and other things held in London are described on the title page of the catalogues as "Recently consigned from Hamburg" (Lugt, nos. 5472, 1796), a sale that included 248 lots of porcelain, mostly Sèvres, and another as "French Porcelaine . . . imported from Paris via Hamburg." This last sale took place at Phillips's auction rooms in 1800 (Lugt, no. 6020). These porcelains were almost certainly consigned to London by Chapeau-rouge, the agent of the Commission des Subsistances at Hamburg, and must largely have come from

57. *History of Pottery and Porcelain,* 3rd ed., p. 422.
58. See Chavagnac, *op. cit.,* p. 221.

those particularly precious works belonging either to royalty or *émigré* nobility that had been deliberately withdrawn from the Revolutionary sales on account of their particular importance or as specimens of fine eighteenth century craftsmanship[59] (see Introduction to Volumes I and II of this catalogue, p. xxiv).

The first effect of such a quantity of Sèvres porcelain flooding onto the English market was a "lowering the prices of such things here," as Sir Gilbert Eliot wrote in 1790 of the influx of French furniture and jewels brought by the *émigrés*. The price of a single plate or dish from a dinner service, which had been about one pound before 1789, dropped to an average of half that or even less by 1792 and remained so until after 1800. Most of the items in the sales mentioned above fetched well below £10; even a porcelain basket of flowers from the Sèvres factory's consignment sold in 1793 fetched only £10. 5s. It is only occasionally that a notable price is obtained. Thus at Daguerre's sale at Christie's on March 25–26, 1791, lot 62 on the second day, "An Elegant Pair of Ewers of Sèvres porcelain, mounted with Niads, goats heads, flowers" (a phrase that suggests the mounts were the work of Thomire), reached £99. 15s., and a second pair in the same sale reached the same price. Indeed decorative vases on the whole maintained their prices far better than anything else, and by 1802 the Countess of Holderness obtained £63 for a pair of Sèvres urns at Christie's (Lugt, no. 6363), and, in the same year, at Matthew Higgins's sale, the surprising price of £136. 10s. was reached by a pair of what are described as "Seve Grecian ewers."

The reason for this sudden rise is not difficult to surmise. In 1802, for the first time in well over a decade, the English were able to go to Paris. During the short-lived Peace of Amiens they flocked across the Channel. Renewed contact with the French and what they saw in the antique shops and dealers' emporiums of Paris stimulated a new interest. Marryat tells of an Englishman purchasing one of those rare pictures painted on a Sèvres plaque in Paris for 3,600 livres (about £150) at this time.[60] Others followed suit.

During the Napoleonic wars the blockade seriously interrupted the supply of French products of any sort from France, though there is no doubt that consignments of both furniture and porcelain did get through sporadically. The history of Sèvres collecting in England in the first three quarters of the nineteenth century is, in effect, much the same as the history of collecting eighteenth century French furniture during the same period. This has been discussed in the Introduction to Volumes I and II of this catalogue as well as elsewhere. These were the years when the Prince of Wales (afterward Regent, and King as George IV) was forming the magnificent collection of Sèvres now belonging to the English Crown. The role played by his pastry cook, François Benois, in advising and assisting him with this has often been described, generally with more imagination than knowledge. Although Benois seems to have had an exceptionally good "nose" for Sèvres, his influence was not so paramount as it has often been made out to be. There were others who collaborated with the prince, notably his boon companion (the cliché is

59. On Chapeaurouge, see Verlet, "Chapeaurouge et les Collections Royales Françaises" in *Festschrift für Erich Meyer zum Sechzigsten Geburtstag*, pp. 286 ff.

60. Marryat, *op. cit.*, 3rd ed., p. 426.

really justified here) Lord Yarmouth, afterward the third Marquess of Hertford, who was concurrently laying the foundations of his own collection of Sèvres, which forms an important part of the Wallace Collection today. It was, for instance, Lord Yarmouth who bought "a fine old Sève Dessert Set" for the Prince Regent at auction in 1805 for the then very high price of 390 guineas; and again in 1814 he acted for his royal friend, buying a further Sèvres service for £777. Numerous other incidents of this sort could be mentioned. In the case of the huge Tournai service painted with birds after Bouffon for the Duc d'Or-léans, the prince seems to have acted on his own behalf. The surviving bills from Robert Fogg show that he bought it for himself in two separate purchases, the first in 1803, the second and larger in 1811. For the total of 488 pieces he paid the astonishing sum of £1,448, a price not to be rivaled for half a century.[61] But there were plenty of other collectors in London, and the dealers' shops seem still to have been fairly full of eighteenth century Sèvres at this time. Miss Berry mentions in her *Journal* seeing a dessert service of pink Sèvres marked £600 in the window of Fogg, "the China Man" (as he was known).[62] His shop in Warwick Street, Golden Square near Piccadilly Circus, was much patronized by the Prince of Wales[63] and Lord Yarmouth as well as by rival collectors of Sèvres like Beckford, George Watson Taylor, Beau Brummell, Lord Gwydyr, and many others.

It was Lord Gwydyr who bought from Fogg the pink service mentioned by Mary Berry. His heirs sold it a quarter of a century later at Christie's at a considerable loss for £350. The service had meanwhile, it is true, been reduced in size. When next it appeared in the sale rooms, in J. P. G. Dering's sale, March 22, 1878, it had been further reduced to a mere fifty-seven pieces, which, even so, fetched £4,039.14s. This catena of prices—£500, £350, and over £4,000—fairly represents the economic movement of Sèvres porcelain in England in the first three quarters of the nineteenth century. Down to about 1860, when a few wealthy Parisian collectors began to buy it, there was no market for Sèvres elsewhere.

The story of collecting Sèvres porcelain during the Victorian age has been so well and so dramatically told by Reitlinger in the second volume of his *Economics of Taste* (both in his text and in his analytic lists of sale prices from which much written here has been abstracted[64]) that it is necessary only to high-

61. Although not of Sèvres, this service is mentioned here as illustrating in exemplary fashion the English taste for French porcelain at this period, and also because the correct figures have never been published previously (Reitlinger makes a particularly erroneous statement about the service in *The Economics of Taste*, p. 156). We are grateful to Miss Jane Langton, the Assistant Archivist at Windsor Castle, for bringing the surviving bills to our attention, and to H. M. the Queen for graciously permitting quotation from the Royal Archives.

62. *Extracts of the Journals and Correspondence of Miss Berry, (1783–1852)*, ed. Lady Theresa Lewis, II, p. 393. Entry for September 7, 1809. Sèvres porcelain was, of course, on sale in London shops long before the nineteenth century, e.g., Josiah Wedgwood to Bentley, letter dated November 19, 1769: "Has Mr. Crofts taken a drawing of the handles of the Seve Vases at Morgans?" (*Selected Letters of Josiah Wedgwood*, ed. Finer and Savage, p. 85).

63. An interesting list of the Prince of Wales's purchases from Fogg in the years 1812 to 1815 was published by Jones, *Burlington Magazine*, July 1908, pp. 220–221. The highest price quoted was £367 for three vases, which was paid to Fogg in 1813.

64. *The Economics of Taste*, II, pp. 155–163, and sales analysis 1748–1963, pp. 574–586.

light certain incidents. After a slight recession following George IV's death in 1830, prices rose fairly steadily in England (not so in France) to a first peak at the Bernal sale in 1855, when the fourth Marquess of Hertford paid successively £1,942.10s. for a pair of pink vases, £1,417 for a second pair, and £871 for a single vase. Other pieces sold for sums which were only slightly smaller. Having regard to the decline in the value of money, these prices are probably a good deal more than the same pieces would sell for at auction today. It is true that there were rather special reasons for these extravagant prices, for three very rich men, Lord Hertford himself, Samuel Addington, and Anthony de Rothschild were competing against one another, and a fourth, the Marquess of Bath, also played a part in sending prices rocketing. But this fact merely underlines the popularity of Sèvres porcelain in England at that period; and prices were to rise far higher in the next twenty years. It was in these mid-years of the century, too, that Charles Mills, later the first Lord Hillingdon, was declaring that he liked "to buy a bit of Sèvres" on his way home from the bank, as James Parker has told us,[65] and was thus forming the great collection of porcelain and porcelain-mounted furniture, an important part of which was presented by the Kress Foundation to The Metropolitan Museum of Art in 1958. When in 1862 the famous *Special Loan Exhibition of Works of Art* was organized at the South Kensington Museum, Section 9 of the catalogue was assigned to Sèvres porcelain and included items 1270 to 1552. To read it gives not only an excellent idea of the large number of English collectors of this porcelain at that date, but an impressive picture of the quality of their collections.

Only two significant names are missing from that catalogue, but they were of the greatest collectors of all at this period. Lord Hertford was living in Paris and was planning to lend many of his best pieces of Sèvres to the corresponding French exhibition, the *Musée Rétrospectif* held there three years later and of which he had been appointed as a Commissioner. The other is the Earl of Dudley. Although he had been buying Sèvres as early as the Stowe sale in 1848, it was only after Lord Hertford's death in 1870 that he began to dominate the Sèvres market and was to continue to do so for the next fifteen years, a period which Reitlinger has stigmatized as years of "Sèvres mania."

Lord Dudley's spectacular purchases began almost immediately after Lord Hertford's death. At the H. L. Wigram sale in 1870 he paid £1,680 for a pair of mounted *bleu-céleste* vases, and almost immediately afterward, at the San Donato sale, he created a great sensation by purchasing the 168 surviving pieces of the Rohan service (see Catalogue No. 109 below) for £10,200. Four years later at the Coventry sale, he paid almost the same sum (in fact £10,500) for a pink *vaisseau à mât* with two matching *vases hollandais*. Thereafter prices seemed to have reached a peak. Even at the Hamilton Palace sale in 1882 Sèvres did not fetch prices of quite this order, though at the Double sale in Paris the previous year two *vases Montcalm* or *vases Fontenoy* reached the astonishing figure of £6,500 the pair. When, however, in 1895 the dealer and china merchant Goode tried to sell the Coventry pink garniture, it was bought in at £8,400, well below the price Lord Dudley had paid twenty-two years earlier. It was eventually acquired in 1913

65. See the brief character sketch "Sir Charles Mills and the Hillingdon Collection," in *Decorative Art from the Samuel H. Kress Collection*, pp. 116–119.

by Pierpont Morgan for £15,500, a price that provided the culmination of another heroic decade of Sèvres collecting.

I𝚃 𝚆𝙾𝚄𝙻𝙳 be fruitless to pursue the tale of Sèvres collecting in England beyond this point. The rage for this type of porcelain, which dominated the European scene for a century, had passed its noontide, but the mention of the name of Pierpont Morgan is a reminder that Sèvres was beginning to be collected in the United States. But the early history of the collecting of Sèvres porcelain in America is considerably more difficult to trace than the collecting of French eighteenth century furniture there was found to be by the compiler of the first two volumes of this catalogue.[66] If furniture is seldom mentioned by letter writers, in memoirs and even in novels, porcelain is far more rarely touched on, and even when it is referred to obliquely the actual type of porcelain is very rarely named.

Pending the further opening up of the archives of early American collections—if indeed such exist as far as Sèvres is concerned—all that can be done is to mention a few points that have engaged the passing attention of the writers of this introduction. Gouverneur Morris's role as an early collector of fine eighteenth century French furniture has been commented on in the Introduction to the earlier volumes of this catalogue. He is known to have bought some fine Sèvres porcelain while residing in Paris during the Revolution, but none that is identifiable seems to have survived. One of his rare comments on the subject suggests that he did not particularly admire it. When he chose a *surtout de table* for Washington's use at the Presidential mansion, he bought one of porcelain of the Angoulême factory, writing "we agree that the porcelaine here [i.e., of Paris] is handsomer and cheaper than that of Sèvres." However, he appears to have given Washington at least one piece of Sèvres, for a *biscuit* group of Venus and Cupid is shown at Mount Vernon as having been presented to the first President by Morris in 1790.

James Swan, the other great importer of French furniture into the United States at the time of the Revolution, also certainly owned some Sèvres porcelain. The only pieces identifiable today that are certainly known to have been his, however, are a pair of magnificent *vases Bachelier* painted with subjects from the history of Belisarius.[67] These were delivered from the factory in January 1779 and formerly stood on the chimneypiece in the Cabinet du Conseil at Versailles. They are now in the Museum of Fine Arts, Boston. They are the only pieces of decorative Sèvres sold at the time of the Revolution that can be said to have gone to the United States immediately.

Although "Point Breeze" was elaborately furnished in the French taste, neither the few descriptions of Joseph Bonaparte's house nor the catalogue of the sale of its contents, held on June 25, 1847, after the ex-king's death, make any mention of Sèvres porcelain, even of the hard-paste productions of the Empire period. The catalogue does indeed mention part of a large dessert service of "white French and gilt China," but if it was Sèvres the fact is unspecified. The principal table service mentioned in the cata-

66. See Introduction, pp. XIX–XXXI.
67. For an account of these, see Rice, *Bulletin of the Museum of Fine Arts, Boston*, Summer 1957, pp. 31–37.

logue is, curiously enough, described as having been imported from England less than a decade earlier.[68]

The history of Sèvres collecting in the United States in the Victorian era follows an almost exactly reverse course of what happened in England. Far from there being a "Sèvres mania" in America, there seems to have been an almost total lack of interest. Even the remarkably discerning Edward Preble Deacon seems to have acquired only Louis-Philippe Sèvres, to judge by the entries in the catalogue of the sale of the contents of Deacon House, Boston, in 1871.[69] "Four chairs. Covered with fine tapestry each bearing in the back a medallion of Sèvres. Portrait of a beauty of the French Court," which fetched $38 each, must have dated from that period, and the descriptions of the considerable quantity of other porcelain-mounted furniture inspire no greater confidence, e.g., "Centre table of light wood, inlaid with forty-five medallions of Sèvres, richly gilt; gilt figures forming the pedestal," which went for $250, or "A Vase of blue Sèvres exquisitely shaped and supported between gilt jets—for six lights . . . ." One item alone might possibly have been a collector's piece. This was in the dining room and is described thus:

> Case, lined with white satin, containing an elegant Sèvres China Tea Service presented to Marie
> Antoinette by the City of Paris, and bought in Paris in 1848.

In spite, however, of the high price of one thousand dollars it fetched, making it the most costly piece in the sale, it seems likely that it was a creation of the same period as the "Six large Sèvres plates with medallion portraits" of various celebrated French beauties ranging from Agnès Sorel to Marie-Antoinette. This type of plate was a favorite product of the factory in the 1830s and 1840s. False associations with the ill-fated Queen of France were commonly put forward in a very uncritical spirit at that period (and indeed still are).

Thereafter collecting Sèvres in America follows much the same pattern as the collecting of French eighteenth century furniture.[70] It is not even known if there was any equivalent to the isolated Vanderbilt purchase of the Marie-Antoinette furniture from Hamilton Palace in 1882 or the early acquisition of some Louis XV chairs and sofas upholstered with tapestry for the Huntington Collection. Soon after 1900, however, or perhaps a little earlier, the picture changed once again. The notable collectors of porcelain are much the same as those who collected French furniture, whose names are mentioned in the Introduction to the first two volumes of this catalogue. To them, however, must be added the name of William Solomon, unmentioned in the earlier essay. The dealer René Gimpel assures us in his *Diary* that when he paid his first visit to New York in 1901 Solomon already possessed fine examples of French

68. *Catalogue of Rare, Original Paintings . . . Household Furniture etc. etc. Belonging to the Estate of the late Joseph Napoleon Bonaparte . . .* (Anthony J. Bleecher, Auctioneer) on Friday June 25, 1847, p. 20, B and C.

69. *Catalogue of the valuable Original Oil Paintings, rare Buhl and other Elegant Furniture &c . . . of the "Deacon House" . . . Feb. 1st, 2nd, and 3rd* [1871]. For a photocopy of the apparently unique surviving copy of this catalogue we are indebted to W. M. Whitehall, Librarian of the Boston Athenaeum, and Joseph Alsop.

70. Introduction to Volumes I and II of this catalogue, pp. XXIX–XXXI.

decorative art of the eighteenth century (though not paintings), and was the only New Yorker who did.[71] Pierpont Morgan, who played a comparatively minor role in the history of French furniture collecting, played a major one in the collecting of soft-paste French porcelain.

Of American collectors he was certainly the most lavish, as anyone who turns over the richly illustrated pages of his privately printed catalogue (prepared by the Comte de Chavagnac) is immediately made aware. Little is said in Chavagnac's catalogue of the *Porcelaines Françaises* in the Morgan collection about how the individual pieces were assembled. A few of the star pieces of pink porcelain are recorded as having been in the Coventry Collection or in that of Lord Dudley (sometimes both), but for the most part the source of purchase remains anonymous. But Morgan was a large-minded man with big ideas. Much of his collection was made by purchases *en bloc*. It was in this manner that he acquired the Hoentschel Collection of French woodwork now in the Metropolitan Museum. The Kress porcelain, too, was assembled in this way through the acquisition by Duveen of a major part of Lord Hillingdon's Sèvres porcelains and Sèvres-mounted furniture in a single block purchase. Other collections formed in the United States have been assembled piecemeal in the traditional European way. Notable among these were the collections of George Blumenthal, Mrs. Harvey S. Firestone, Robert Lehman, Mr. and Mrs. Jack Linsky, Mrs. Merriweather Post, Forsyth Wickes, R. Thornton Wilson, and the present collection.

As a consequence of this activity by individual collectors, certain American public collections of Sèvres are of very considerable importance, for many of them have been formed around the nucleus of the gift of a private collection. At The Metropolitan Museum of Art, New York, a balanced collection of ornamental and useful wares from the collection of R. Thornton Wilson is supplemented by vases and perhaps the world's largest collection of porcelain-mounted furniture, from the Samuel H. Kress Foundation.[72] At the Frick Collection, New York, outstanding vases and furniture mounted with Sèvres plaques are to be seen.

In New England, the Sèvres porcelain of the J. P. Morgan Collection is among the treasures of the Wadsworth Atheneum in Hartford,[73] and contains examples originally owned by Machault and inherited from him by the Comte de Chavagnac. In Boston the considerable holdings of the Museum of Fine Arts, from the collection of James Swan and Robert Treat Paine II, have recently been increased through the bequest of Forsyth Wickes.[74] At Williamstown, Massachusetts, the Clark Art Institute has a remarkable collection of cups and saucers, assembled by Sterling and Francine Clark.

At the Philadelphia Museum of Art, the French collections of Eleanor Elkins and Mrs. Morris Hawkes are rich in decorative porcelains, including rare types and a small representation of porcelain-

---

71. Gimpel, *Journal d'un Collectionneur, Marchand des Tableaux*, p. 52.

72. Dauterman, Parker, and Standen, *Decorative Art from the Samuel H. Kress Collection at The Metropolitan Museum of Art*.

73. Hood, *Apollo*, December 1968, pp. 440–445.

74. Dauterman, *Antiques*, September 1968, pp. 344–354.

inlaid furniture. In Baltimore, the Walters Art Gallery possesses a variety of pink vases and other pieces with chinoiserie decoration[75] from the Paris collection of the dealer E. M. Hodgkins, and other purchases made by the founder, Henry Walters. In Washington, D.C., Sèvres is to be found in the collection of Marjorie Merriweather Post at her residence, Hillwood (one day to become a branch of the Smithsonian Institution); a small group is at the Museum of History and Technology; and parts of a service used by George Washington are at Mount Vernon while fragments of another used by John Adams are at the White House.

In the Midwest, notable examples are to be seen at the Cleveland Museum of Art, from the collection of John L. Severance. The West Coast has an impressive collection of ornamental Sèvres and porcelain-mounted furniture at the Henry E. Huntington Library and Art Gallery in San Marino, California.[76]

But if in the United States the collecting of French porcelain lagged somewhat behind that of Europe, in cataloguing their collections American collectors have been distinctly ahead of the Europeans. The first major catalogue of collections of Sèvres porcelain to be published at all was Laking's *Sèvres Porcelain at Buckingham Palace and Windsor Castle*, which appeared in 1907. Chavagnac's catalogue of the Morgan porcelains, issued shortly afterward in 1910, was obviously modeled on this and was a good deal more scholarly. It was followed in 1930 by Volume VI of Mlle Stella Rubenstein-Bloch's catalogue of the Blumenthal Collection; the Sèvres porcelain in the Frick Collection was catalogued by W. R. Hovey and included in Volume VIII of the privately circulated catalogue of the collections printed for Miss Helen Frick. A new catalogue of the latter is understood to be actually under preparation by Mlle Brunet. In 1961 Robert Wark's catalogue of *French Decorative Art in the Huntington Collection* included all the Vincennes and Sèvres porcelains at San Marino. This was followed in 1964 by the large collection of Sèvres porcelain catalogued with the *Decorative Art from the Samuel H. Kress Collection*, now in the Metropolitan Museum, prepared by the compiler of the present catalogue. To set off against this in Europe, since Laking's catalogue of the Royal Collection appeared in 1907 there is only William King's catalogue of the French porcelain forming part of Volume II of the Jones Collection catalogue, issued by the Victoria and Albert Museum, which appeared in 1924, and Svend Eriksen's admirable catalogue of the Sèvres porcelain in the Rothschild Collection at Waddesdon Manor, which came out in 1968. This last is, without question, the most important catalogue of a collection of Sèvres porcelain to appear to date. It is hoped that the present catalogue of an American collection of porcelain formed in fairly recent years may prove a worthy follower in the tradition established by these distinguished predecessors.

CARL CHRISTIAN DAUTERMAN
F. J. B. WATSON

75. Dauterman, *Apollo*, December 1966, pp. 476–481.

76. Wark, *French Decorative Art in the Huntington Collection*.

75 A, B Pair of Plant Pots

(caisses)

H. 5½ (14.1); W. 4¼ square (10.8).

EACH is of cubical shape, in the form of a miniature orange tub, open at the top, with a gilded acorn-shaped finial surmounting each upper corner, and rests on four gilded cubical feet. The bottom of each is pierced with five small holes arranged in an x-shaped pattern.

The slightly varying turquoise-blue ground of each has a roughly heart-shaped reserve at the center of each side, framed by gilded rococo trelliswork, from which floral trails emerge. These reserves each enclose a different spray of roses, cowslip, harebell, and other flowers, together with, in most cases, fruit, among which yellow pears predominate. Sage-green leaves, occasionally tinged with yellow-green, appear on all the panels.

Each is marked on the underside with crossed L's, enclosing the date-letter A, and near one foot with the letter B (of unknown meaning), all painted in blue.

Vincennes, datemarked for 1753.

Formerly in the collection of Baroness Renée de Becker, New York.

The Sèvres sales records during the period December 20, 1753, to December 24, 1761, reveal that *caisses* were usually sold in pairs. Although size, color, and decoration are usually mentioned, there is no specific reference to the tub shape.

Other examples of this type of plant pot in the collection are Nos. 77 A and B, 78 A and B, 79 A and B, and 88.

76 A, B Two Pot-Pourri Vases

(vases pots-pourris)

76 A: H. 7⅜ (18.7); Diam. 6¼ (15.9).

76 B: H. 7⅜ (18.7); Diam. 6³⁄₁₆ (15.7).

EACH vase is of broad-shouldered baluster shape with a pierced incurving neck and four tall scrolled feet. Around the sides are four large bulbous lobes enclosed by molded leaf-scrolls springing from the feet and painted turquoise-blue with gilt enrichments. The neck is pierced with two interlacing bands of arcading, one blue and one white, having gilded edges. A white and gold ribbon is entwined through these.

The vases are not identical. On No. 76 A sprays of white and blue anemones, carnations, and other blossoms, some with buds, spring from the scroll feet, each modeled with gilded foliage in relief. The four reserves are painted with fanciful birds singly or in pairs, some in flight and some perched on delicate floral festoons. On No. 76 B the panels are painted in soft colors with detached sprigs of garden flowers together with gooseberries and grapes. The leaves have a luminous quality resulting from the use of transparent pigment with much yellow added to the green.

No. 76 A is marked on the underside with crossed L's, enclosing the date-letter A, flanked at the left by a musical note (?) or baton, the mark of the decorator, all painted in blue; incised:

No. 76 B is marked on the underside with crossed L's and a script letter N to the left, the mark of the decorator, both painted in blue. Each displays irregular "patchmarks" on the feet.

No. 76 A is Vincennes, datemarked for 1753; the decoration is by Thevenet *père* (working 1741–1777); No. 76 B is Sèvres, dating from about 1758–1760; the decoration is by François Aloncle (working 1758–1781).

Formerly in the collection of Gilbert Levi, Paris.

The difficulty of working with the soft paste of Vincennes and early Sèvres is apparent in the occasional fire cracks that appear on the underside of both these vases. In one of the reserve panels of No. 76 A the painted garland has been skillfully adjusted to conceal a defect of this kind.

Pot-pourri vases of this type were usually provided with pierced covers, e.g. a pair in the J. P. Morgan Collection at the Wadsworth Atheneum, Hartford (see Hood, *Connoisseur*, February 1965, p. 131, fig. 1).

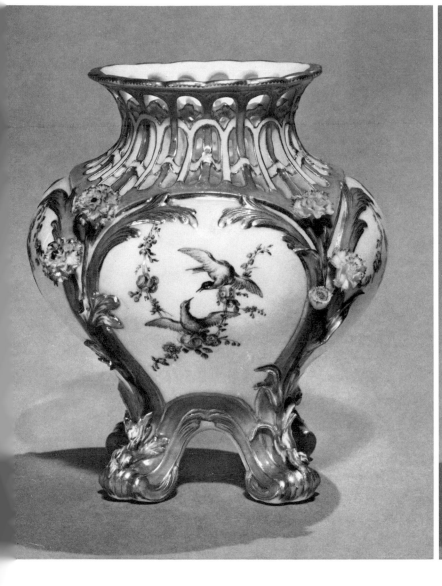

77 A, B Two Plant Pots

(caisses)

H. 3¾ (9.5); W. 2¹¹⁄₁₆ square (6.9).

OF THE same type as Nos. 75 A and B, though smaller. The reserves on the sides enclose simple nosegays of flowers without fruit, executed in a direct and assured, though somewhat sketchy manner. The gilt borders of each are similar, although they do not match completely. The bottom of each is pierced similarly to Nos. 75 A and B.

No. 77 B is marked on the underside with crossed L's, enclosing the date-letter C, and near one foot with the letter B (of unknown meaning), both painted in blue; incised:

$$8$$

No. 77 A is incised:

$$8$$

Vincennes; No. 77 B is datemarked for 1755.

For other examples of this type of plant pot in the collection, see Nos. 75 A and B, 78 A and B, 79 A and B, and 88.

78 A, B Two Plant Pots

(caisses)

H. 3⅝ (9.3); W. 2¾ square (7.0).

EACH is of cubical shape, in the form of a miniature orange tub, open at the top, with a white and gold finial at each corner. Each rests on four white cubical feet edged with gilding. The bottom is pierced with small holes.

The ground color, which varies slightly, is apple-green. On each side is a rococo-shaped reserve enclosing nosegays of flowers painted mainly in ochre-brown, blue, and puce. Each floral spray is different, and the stems are arranged in alternately ascending and descending positions. The gilded borders are composed of a variety of C- and S-scrolls, trelliswork, and strapwork; those on No. 78 A include pairs of curling scalloped leaves at either side of the reserves.

No. 78 A is marked on the underside with crossed L's, enclosing the date-letter D, and surmounted by the letter S, the mark of the decorator, all painted in blue. No. 78 B is incised: ꓭ

Each displays "patchmarks" on the underside of the feet.

Vincennes–Sèvres, datemarked for 1756; the flowers were painted by Méreaud *aîné* (working 1754–1791).

On these small flower pots Méreaud *aîné* shows a characteristic fondness for painting leaves with a harlequin effect, that is, by dividing them at the midrib into areas of blue and green or contrasting shades of green.

A similar pair of plant pots with a deep blue ground, datemarked for 1771, is in The Metropolitan Museum of Art, New York (gift of Ann Payne Blumenthal, acc. no. 43.163.4,5). They are decorated with romantic scenes, some painted by Dodin (working 1754–1803). Other examples, decorated variously with cupids, birds, and trophies, are in the Victoria and Albert Museum,

London (C 428, 429–1921; C 424, 425–1921) and elsewhere.

A pair of similar apple-green plant tubs from the collection of J. P. Morgan, New York, was sold at Parke-Bernet, New York, March 22–25, 1944, lot 629 (illustrated in catalogue). Verlet (*Sèvres*, I, pl. 36) illustrates an example in a larger size formerly in the collection of Richard Peñard y Fernandez, Paris (sold Palais Galliera, Paris, December 7, 1960, lot 143, and cites an entry in the sales records of Sèvres for the second quarter of 1760 (account of M.ʳ Tenières, folio 23):

2 caisses, 2ᵉ grandeur, oiseaux. 84 . . . 168

For other examples of this type of plant pot in the collection see Nos. 75 A and B, 77 A and B, 79 A and B, and 88.

[195]

79 A, B Pair of Plant Pots

(caisses)

H. 5¾ (14.7); w. 4⅛ square (10.5).

EACH is of cubical shape, in the form of a miniature orange tub, open at the top, with a gilded
acorn-shaped finial surmounting each upper corner. Each rests on four white cubical feet, which
are gilded with a rosette and a simple border on
each of the outer sides. The bottom of each is
pierced with five small holes arranged in an x-
shaped pattern.

The ground color is a deep apple-green with a
cartouche-shaped reserve on each side enclosing a
nosegay of flowers painted in pastel colors. The
nosegays include roses, cornflowers, poppies,
tulips, and hydrangeas, and the stems of each spray
are arranged in alternately ascending and descending positions. Flowers also emerge from the gilded
rococo scrollwork framing each reserve.

Each is marked on the underside with crossed
L's, enclosing the date-letter D and surmounting
the letter H, the mark of the decorator, all painted
in blue. No. 79 A is incised:

No. 79 B is incised:

Each displays indistinct "patchmarks" on the
underside of the feet.

Vincennes–Sèvres, datemarked for 1756.

Formerly in the collection of Baroness Leonino,
sister of Baron Henri de Rothschild, Paris.

The decorator's mark, an H, is that assigned to
Houry, although 1756 does not fall within his
generally accepted working dates (1754–1755, according to Brunet, *Les Marques de Sèvres*, p. 31; or
1747–1755, Honey, *European Ceramic Art*, p. 568;
or 1752–1755, Eriksen, *Waddesdon Manor: Sèvres
Porcelain*, p. 328).

For other examples of this type of plant pot in
the collection, see Nos. 75 A and B, 77 A and B, 78
A and B, and 88.

80 Candelabrum Vase

(vase à éléphants)

H. 13⅝ (34.6); W. 9½ (24.1); D. 5⅝ (14.4).

IN THE form of a baluster-shaped vase against the narrow neck of which two fully modeled elephant heads with prominent ears are addorsed. Their upturned trunks terminate in candle sockets pierced with vertical slits. The vase rests on a low plinth with four feet in the form of acanthus scrolls.

The elephant heads are white, touched here and there with gilding. Their trunks rest upon a pair of loop handles springing from the shoulders of the vase at each side. A complex white and gold jewel modeled in full relief hangs down the forehead of each elephant. From this a double strand of white and gold beads depends at the back of each head and passes through the loop handles.

The upper part of the body is painted turquoise-blue beneath the elephants' heads. The rest is reserved in white and is painted with six floral pendants above the shoulder. The lower part of the body of the vase is painted with eight spirally twisting panels framed with turquoise-blue ribbons heightened with gilding, each enclosing a pendant of flowers of rose-lavender intermixed with blue and yellow. The vase rests on a torus-molded foot ring diagonally striped with turquoise-blue.

Marked on the underside of the plinth with an incomplete version of the crossed L's, indecipherable traces of a date-letter and of a decorator's mark, all painted in blue. Incised:

in Li

This is apparently the mark of the *répareur* Liance *père* (working 1754–1777). A green and white paper customs label is attached within the concavity of the base and is inscribed: "K. P. R. Hauptzollamt, Charlottenburg." The feet display round "patchmarks."

Sèvres, dating from 1756–about 1760; design attributed to Jean-Claude Duplessis *père* (working 1747–1774).

REFERENCES: Falke, *Die Kunstsammlung von Pannwitz*, II, no. 422, pl. LXXIII.

Formerly in the collection of Mme Catalina von Pannwitz, Hartekamp, the Netherlands.

The survival of the original candle sockets is exceptional; other instances are two pairs of vases in the Wallace Collection, London (*Provisional Catalogue*, 1902, no. XVIII–142; illustrated in color in Verlet, *Sèvres*, I, pl. 28).

Other examples of elephant vases, varying in color and decoration, are to be found in the Samuel H. Kress Collection at The Metropolitan Museum of Art, New York (illustrated in Dauterman, Parker, and Standen, *Decorative Art from the Samuel H. Kress Collection*, no. 36 a–b); Waddesdon Manor, Buckinghamshire (illustrated in Eriksen, *Waddesdon Manor, The James A. de Rothschild Bequest to the National Trust*, pp. 19, 53); and the Wallace Collection, London (*op. cit.*, no. XVIII–143–145).

The model is generally accepted as the creation of Jean-Claude Duplessis (the original in plaster, thus attributed, is illustrated in Troude, *Choix de Modèles de la Manufacture de Porcelaines de Sèvres*, pl. 87). The attribution of the imaginative design of No. 80 to this artist is based upon his rich inventiveness, the use of boldly expanding volumes, and small details such as the undulating modeling of the mouth, accompanied by a species of shell-like rococo fluting, as seen immediately beneath the lip of No. 80. These characteristics are found singly or in combination on four vases and a round tureen known to be by him, illustrated in Troude, *op. cit.*, pls. 87, 91, 100, 101, 134.

The use of elephants' heads is a curious Oriental conceit in Sèvres porcelain, and was probably borrowed via a Meissen version. Examples of the latter are large candelabra at the Charlottenburg Schloss, Berlin, and one in the collection of Ernst Schneider, Schloss Jägerhof, Düsseldorf (illustrated in Rückert, *Meissener Porzellan 1710–1810*, pl. XXI). These candelabra, with chinoiserie motifs, were modeled by J. J. Kaendler in June 1733 and June 1735, respectively, and each stands upon three splayed elephant-head supports.

Elephant candelabra are mentioned very infrequently in the sales records of Sèvres, several entries occurring between 1757 and 1770. An entry for November 26, 1773 (folio 121 verso), referring to the sale of three *vases à éléphants*, indicates that the model, perhaps first released in 1756, was still in demand at that time.

For comparable vases in the collection, see Nos. 81, 82 A and B, and 83.

81 Candelabrum Vase

(vase à éléphants)

H. 15 (38.1); W. 10½ (26.7); D. 6½ (16.5).

OF THE same type as No. 80. It differs as follows: the neck, the twisting panels, and details on the base are a brilliant apple-green; the jeweled ornaments on the elephants' heads are gilded, but not molded in high relief; candle sockets are lacking; the ears are outlined with gilding; and handles are missing from the sides. Furthermore, the spiraling green ribbons twist in the opposite direction to those on No. 80, and they are gilded with chains of husks depending from fan-like or shell motifs. The floral decoration is more conspicuous, and takes the form of a continuous wide garland around the shoulder and an elongated pendant hanging from below the ears of the elephants. The diagonal stripings on the torus-molded foot ring are more delicate than on No. 80.

Unmarked, but decorated on the underside of the plinth with a bold diamond-shaped motif painted in green and gold, extending to the edge of all four sides (see below). Incised on one outer edge of this motif:

Lian

This is apparently the mark of the *répareur* Liance *père* (working 1754–1777).

Sèvres, dating from 1756–about 1762; the de-sign is attributed to Jean-Claude Duplessis *père* (working 1747–1774; see under No. 80).

Formerly in the collection of a member of the Rothschild family.

A companion vase, in which the green-bordered panels spiral in the opposite direction, is in the collection at Waddesdon Manor, Buckinghamshire (illustrated in Lane, "The Porcelain Collection at Waddesdon," in *Waddesdon, The Manor, The Collections, Gazette des Beaux-Arts,* fig. 2). It is of the same height, and a matching diamond figure painted green and gold appears under the plinth (see below). It is therefore possible that these two candelabra originally formed a pair, although the Waddesdon vase is not pierced at the center.

A comparable vase, painted green, was sold to Mme Lair during the period July 1760 – January 1761 (folio 36):

1 Vaze Elephant, 1.re gd.^r verd. . . . . 480.

M. and Mme Lair were prominent *marchands-merciers* under Louis XVI. Two other vases are mentioned for September 11, 1762 (folio 100):

2 [Vazes] Elephans [fond verd] . . . 528 . . . 1056.

For comparable vases in this collection, see Nos. 80, 82 A and B, and 83.

[200]

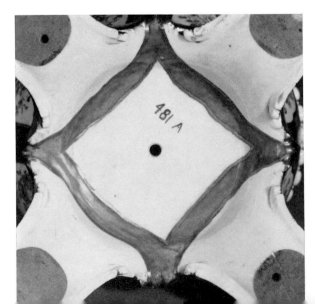

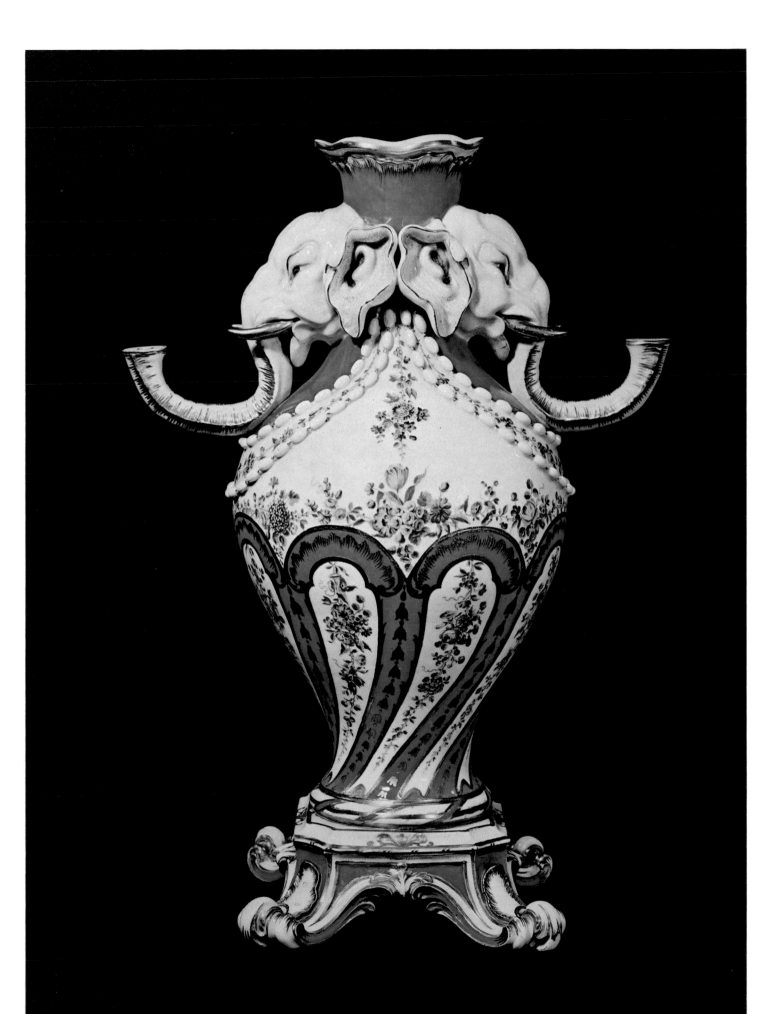

82 A, B   Pair of Candelabrum Vases

(vases à éléphants)

H. 13¾ (34.9); W. 8¼ (21.0); D. 5½ (14.1).

EACH vase is a smaller version of the two preceding candelabrum vases, Nos. 80 and 81, although closer to No. 80 in having molded jewels on the heads of the elephants, and similar handles. The ground of each is a softly varying apple-green, reserved in white in the zones between the strands of beads. Two balloon-shaped panels alternating with narrow spatulate ones are reserved on the lower half. The larger panel on the obverse of each is painted with a cupid in billowing draperies floating upon wisps of clouds, in the manner of François Boucher. The panel on the reverse (illustrated at the right) is painted with attributes of love: darts, bows, garlands, etc., also borne upon clouds. The spatulate panels enclose pendants of garden flowers. Gilding is used profusely: in particular, there are delicate garlands above the principal panels, with details tooled and burnished in a variety of textures.

No. 82 A is incised on the underside of the plinth:

$$m\mathcal{L}i$$

This is apparently the mark of the *répareur* Liance *père* (working 1754–1777). No. 82 B is painted within the concavity of the base with an effaced mark in blue resembling the bottom of the crossed L's enclosing a date-letter. On each the four feet display a circular area without glaze, somewhat discolored in the manner of indistinct "patch-marks."

Sèvres, dating from 1756–about 1760; the design attributed to Jean-Claude Duplessis *père* (working 1747–1774; see under No. 80).

Formerly in the collection of a member of the Rothschild family.

The putto on No. 82 A is a familiar Boucher type, repeated in varying poses in many paintings

[203]

and engravings. A similar figure is found in a print by H. G. Hertel, after the sanguine drawing by Boucher now in the Slatkin Collection, New York.

Several pairs of green candelabrum vases painted with cupids were sold at Sèvres between 1756 and 1760, Nos. 82 A and B undoubtedly among them. A typical entry is the following, from the factory records of the period July 1, 1757, to January 1, 1758, folio 48, verso:

> 2 Vazes a Elephant Ide [2ᵉ gd. Rubans Verds]
>   Enfans . . . 960 . . . 1920

Verlet has observed (*Sèvres*, p. 204), that this entry may be presumed to apply to one of two pairs in the Wallace Collection, London (*Provisional Catalogue*, 1902, nos. XVIII–142–145), and that they may have belonged to Mme de Pompadour, as the purchaser was Duvaux, the *marchand-mercier* who acted as agent for the marquise. One of the difficulties in tracing original ownership is illustrated by the entry for September 20, 1759, folio 95:

> 2 Vazes a Elephants Ide [Verd Enfans]
>   . . . 720 . . . 1440

in which the purchaser is not mentioned, as the sale is listed merely under *Vendu comptans*, i.e., for cash.

For comparable examples in this collection, see Nos. 80, 81, and 83.

83 Candelabrum Vase

(vase à éléphants)

H. 15½ (39.4); W. 10 (25.4); D. 6⅛ (15.6).

SIMILAR in general form and decoration to No. 81, but decorated with rose-pink. The elephants' heads have jewels molded in relief as on Nos. 80 and 82 and likewise rest upon the handles. Behind the white and gold heads, the neck is painted rose-pink. The body of the vase, largely reserved in white, is divided into six round-topped panels, spiraling in the same direction as on No. 80, their borders painted rose-pink and heavily gilded with fan or shell motifs and husk pendants. Multicolored floral garlands of great elaboration fill the spaces between the strands of beads, above the shoulder, and within the panels of the lower half of the vase. Unlike that on Nos. 80–82, the torus-molded foot ring is without ribbon decoration. One of the elephants' trunks is fitted with a serrated gilt bronze mount intended to hold a candle socket.

Marked on the underside of the plinth with crossed L's enclosing the date-letter E and with a dot above and below, all painted in blue. There is also a third dot below the monogram at the center. Each foot displays a "patchmark."

Sèvres, datemarked for 1757; the design attributed to Jean-Claude Duplessis *père* (working 1747–1774; see under No. 80), the decoration to Taillandier (working 1753–1790).

Formerly in the collection of Alfred de Rothschild, London (illustrated in Davis, *A Description of the Works of Art Forming the Collection of Alfred de Rothschild*, no. 82 [where it appears as the central object in a group of five in the photograph, pl. 82, see below]).

A candelabrum of almost identical appearance is reproduced in color (from a watercolor drawing) in Garnier, *The Soft Porcelain of Sèvres*, pl. XX (not numbered), where it is said to be in the Alfred de Rothschild Collection, London. Beneath the candelabrum Garnier reproduces a mark differing from that on No. 83 by the absence of dots and the addition of Taillandier's decorator's mark. The correspondence between the candelabrum in the illustration mentioned above and No. 83 is so close as to suggest that they were both painted by the same hand.

A pair of rose-pink elephant candelabra in The Metropolitan Museum of Art, New York (Dauterman, Parker, and Standen, *Decorative Art from the Samuel H. Kress Collection*, figs. 145, 146) were evidently cast from the same mold. They are decorated with a crisscross pattern of scalloped ribbons, and sprays of flowers in the interstices.

It is rare to find the datemark for 1757 on a piece painted rose-pink. It has never been satisfactorily explained why this color, although achieved for the first time in 1757, was not mentioned in the sales records of Sèvres for that year. Some writers have surmised that the king, for reasons of his own (possibly because he wanted to present the first example to Mme de Pompadour, whose birthday fell on December 29), chose not to disclose the new color until the annual Christmas exhibition and sale of 1758.

An entry in the account book of Sèvres for December 30, 1758, folio 75, records the sale to Monseigneur Le Prince de Condé of a pair of these vases, with a rose ground:

2 Vazes a Elephant 1.ʳᵉ [Roze Enfans] . . . 840 . . . 1680.

For comparable vases in this collection, see Nos. 80, 81, and 82 A and B.

84 A, B Pair of Flower Vases

(vases hollandais)

H. 7½ (19.0); W. 7¾ (19.7); D. 5⅝ (14.4).

EACH tapering vase, pinched around the base, is fan-shaped in profile, with irregularly curving sides interrupted at the four corners by flat tapering panels. It consists of two parts. The pierced base of the upper portion fits into a stand or container of splayed and pierced design and similar irregular shape. The stand is intended to hold water for the upper part of the vase and also for the display of short-stemmed flowers, in six cartouche-shaped openings pierced around its sloping upper edge.

Both parts are painted rose-pink. Four large oval reserves around the sides of the vase enclose flowers and fruit and are bordered with gilded scrollwork picked out with pencilings in purple. The flowers include roses, anemones, asters, and harebells; the fruits include cherries, apples, grapes, pears, and plums.

Around the stand the four pedestal-like projections at the corners are painted rose-pink with gilt-bordered panels. Between them around the base are rectangular reserves painted with trails of brightly colored flowers. The apertures are bordered with a narrow rose-pink ribbon edged with gilding.

No. 84 A is marked on the underside of the stand with crossed L's, enclosing the date-letter E, surmounting a large letter H, the mark of the decorator, all painted in blue; incised on both the underside of the vase and of the stand:

No. 84 B is incised on the underside of the vase:

×

On the underside of the stand:

Impressed on both the underside of the vase and of the stand:

C

No. 84 B displays four "patchmarks" on the underside of the stand.

At the back of each stand, where the gilding has flaked, the rose-pink glaze is suffused with orange-buff, a phenomenon not uncommon in soft-paste porcelain with this ground color.

Sèvres, datemarked for 1757. The decorator's mark, an H, is that assigned to Houry (see under Nos. 79 A and B).

Formerly in the collections of the Marchioness of Cholmondeley, London; Mrs. Edith Chester Beatty, London.

Two examples of *vases hollandais* with a rose-pink ground are to be found in the Victoria and Albert Museum, London, one in the Jones Collection (catalogue no. 121). A pair in apple-green is in the Wallace Collection, London (*Provisional Catalogue*, 1902, no. XVIII–152, 153), decorated with pastoral scenes and flowers by Thevenet *père* (working 1741–1777).

The *vase hollandais* and a newer form with curved rather than straight flaring sides (see Nos. 85 A and B) appear sporadically in the sales records of Sèvres between 1757 and 1782. The first mention of the earlier type in the Sèvres records is dated December 5–31, 1754, in an account with the *marchand-mercier* Duvaux, folio 75 verso:

> 1 Vase à l'hollandoise 1ᵉ ge Ie [bleu céleste] } 1200
>   2 Ie   2ᵉ ge Ie . . .

85 A, B Pair of Flower Vases

(vases hollandais nouveaux)

85 A: H. 8⅞ (22.6); W. 6¾ (17.2); D. 5⅝ (14.4).

85 B: H. 8⅞ (22.6); W. 6⅞ (17.5); D. 5⅝ (14.4).

EACH fan-shaped vase consists of two parts: a trumpet-shaped upper portion, flaring with a curving profile (unlike the earlier, straight-walled design, see in Nos. 84 A and B); and a tall reservoir type of stand. Both parts are cartouche-shaped in cross section, and are molded with four shallow flutings at the corners, extending from the undulating rim of the upper section to the short, scrolled supports of the stand. The upper portion, as in Nos. 84 A and B, fits into the reservoir and likewise is pierced with small holes to permit water to flow from one vessel into the other. The incurving shoulder of the stand is pierced with four apertures shaped as confronted C-scrolls flanked by ray-like piercings. The inner lip of the stand, unseen when the vase is assembled, is gilded with a chain of large and small dots bordered by narrow bands.

The gently varying turquoise-blue ground of each is reserved with four oval panels enclosing painted vignettes of picturesque rural landscapes in the manner of Pillement, with wispy foliage and various types of architecture. Several of the scenes are enlivened with minute figures, including a farmer, a hunter, and a fisherman. The panels are elaborately framed with gilding of foliated rococo scrolls and blossoms.

Each is marked on the underside of the stand with crossed L's, enclosing, on No. 85 A, the date-letter f, all painted in blue. Each stand is marked in blue on the underside with a caduceus, the mark of the decorator; incised:

æ

Each displays indistinct "patchmarks" on the undersides of the feet and of the vases.

Sèvres, datemarked for 1758; the landscape panels are by Edme Gomery (working 1756–1758), usually recorded as a painter of birds.

Formerly in the collections of the Marchioness of Cholmondeley, London; Mrs. Edith Chester Beatty, London.

Other vases of the same type are to be seen in the English Royal Collection, Buckingham Palace (Laking, *Sèvres Porcelain of Buckingham Palace and Windsor Castle*, no. 58, pl. 20); the Frick Collection, New York (Hovey, *The Frick Collection*, VIII, no. 6, pl. XXXVIII); the Henry E. Huntington Library and Art Gallery, San Marino, California (Wark, *French Decorative Art in the Huntington Collection*, figs. 111, 112); and The Metropolitan Museum of Art, New York (Dauterman, Parker, and Standen, *Decorative Art from the Samuel H. Kress Collection*, no. 41 a, b). Further examples are in the Philadelphia Museum of Art (Kimball, *Bulletin of the Philadelphia Museum of Art*, March 1944, no. 45, p. 95, pl. V); the Victoria and Albert Museum, London (Jones Collection, in green, painted with birds, *Catalogue*, II, no. 152). An example with a pink ground from the Wallace Collection, London (*Provisional Catalogue*, 1902, no. XII B–118, 119) is datemarked for 1759 and has floral decoration by Rosset (working 1753–1795). Two pairs are now at the Walters Art Gallery, Baltimore (*Catalogue of Old Sèvres Porcelain . . . belonging to E. M. Hodgkins*, nos. 4, 5; 33, 34).

A rose-pink pair, datemarked for 1763, was given by Louis XVI to Prince Henry of Prussia in 1784. This and another pair in turquoise-blue, painted with birds, datemarked for 1758, are at The Metropolitan Museum of Art, the R. Thornton Wilson Collection (acc. nos. 50.211.156, 157 and 54.147.17,18). The second pair is painted with cupids attributed to Dodin (working 1754–1802) and flowers by Dubois (working 1756–1757), who also did the flowers on the rose-pink vases.

A comparable example, from the collection of Baron Emmanuel Leonino, was sold at the Galerie Charpentier, Paris, March 18–19, 1937, lot 96 (illustrated in catalogue, pl. XIII).

In addition to the straight-walled type of *vase hollandais* represented by Nos. 84 A and B, and the curving contours of Nos. 85 A and B, a third type of *vase hollandais* is known, with walls only slightly concave. The last is to be seen in the collection of the Duke of Bedford, Woburn Abbey, in a *bleu de roi* vase decorated with birds (Wills, *Apollo*, January 1956, pp. 14–17, fig. 111).

Nos. 85 A and B are an early instance of the *vase hollandais nouveau*. The first mention of the model in the Sèvres sales records occurs during the period December 1, 1758–January 1, 1759, folio 79:

1 Vaze holandois nouvelle forme 192

Another, dated December 28–31, 1758, folio 86 verso:

1 Vaze holandois nouvelle forme Roze 300

Folio 46 for 1760 cites:

Livré pour Presentes à Monseigr. Le Contleur Gen-al,
2 Id^e [vazes] holandois Nouveaux rose et verd Tesniers.
. . . 360 720

86 Flower Vase

(cuvette à fleurs)

H. 7¼ (18.5); W. 9⅞ (25.1); D. 6¼ (15.9).

THE BODY is four-sided and rectangular in cross-section, tapering slightly toward the base. The corners are rounded, the sides gently undulating, and the top is surrounded by a flaring lip with cupid's bow edges, above a deep concave molding. The molding surrounding the base has an acanthus cartouche at the center of the long sides and is raised on four bracket feet.

The ground color is a brilliant rose-pink with an apple-green border at top and bottom and three cartouche-shaped reserves, at the front and the ends, for painted decoration. The reserve at the front is framed with green and gold scrollwork and encloses a rustic scene in the manner of David Teniers, with a peasant woman scolding her husband. The reserves on each end are violin-shaped and painted with clusters of flowers in which red, yellow, and blue predominate; the cluster at the right includes gooseberries and halved fruit. The back is decorated in green and gold with a wreath from which tangential scrolls emerge. At each angle of the vase is a pendant of bell flowers painted green, enriched with gold.

Three of the feet have been notched with a file in a manner suggesting that they were intended to fit into a stand of gilt bronze.

Marked on the underside with crossed L's (attenuated), enclosing the date-letter, seemingly a script letter g, and surmounted by the letter M, the mark of the decorator, all painted in blue; incised:

This is apparently the mark of the *répareur* Liance *père* (working 1754–1777).

Sèvres, apparently datemarked for 1759; the fig-ure painting is by Morin (working 1754–1787); the flower painting is in the manner of Pierre *aîné* (working 1759–1775); the model is attributed to Jean-Claude Duplessis *père* (working 1747–1774).

Formerly in the collections of Baroness Leonino, Paris; Baron Henri de Rothschild, Paris, brother of Baroness Leonino.

A large version, at the Wallace Collection, London (*Provisional Catalogue*, 1902, no. XII–C–146), datemarked for 1757, has a rose-pink ground with reserves enclosing cupids and trophies, by Morin. Comparable examples are to be found in the Tuck Bequest at the Petit Palais, Paris, where one in rose-pink is mounted with gilt bronze and contains a bouquet of Meissen porcelain flowers (illustrated in Giraudy, *Connoisseur*, October 1966, p. 77, fig. 1). Another is to be seen in the Victoria and Albert Museum, London, with a turquoise-blue ground and a scene of boors drinking by Vieillard (working 1752–1790). It is datemarked for 1760. Another small one in the Wallace Collection (*op. cit.*, no. XV–A–18) has a turquoise-blue ground with a peasant scene and a bunch of flowers. It is dated 1760 and bears the mark probably of Caton.

The decorative theme, presumably taken from an engraving, of a peasant woman scolding her drunken husband occurs, with some variations, on other documented examples of Sèvres painted by various artists. A *cuvette à fleurs* in apple-green, formerly in the collection of Édouard André and bearing the mark of Dodin (working 1754–1802), is illustrated in Garnier, *The Soft Porcelain of Sèvres*, pl. V. Another, in *bleu de roi*, by Morin, at the Henry E. Huntington Library and Art Gallery, San Marino, California, is illustrated in

Wark, *French Decorative Art in the Huntington Collection*, pl. 112. The motif occurs again on a deep green *cuvette à fleurs* painted by Vieillard in the Samuel H. Kress Collection at The Metropolitan Museum of Art, New York (see Dauterman, Parker, and Standen, *Decorative Art from the Samuel H. Kress Collection*, no. 40, p. 208). It was not necessarily associated with *cuvettes à fleurs*. A rosepink and green *vase vaisseau à mât* from the collection of J. P. Morgan (sold Parke-Bernet, New York, January 6–8, 1944, lot 486 [illustrated in catalogue]) had the same painting in a reserve on the front.

Two *cuvettes à fleurs* were in the collection of Baron Schroeder (sold Christie's, London, July 5, 1910, lot 36), one with a modified version of the scene on No. 86. Another was in the collection of the Earl of Harewood (sold Christie's, London, July 1, 1965, lot 17 [part of a garniture of three; illustrated in catalogue, pl. 9]). The latter is also illustrated by Tait in *Apollo*, June 1964, p. 476, pl. 5.

Le Corbeiller, in *European and American Snuff Boxes, 1730–1830*, notes that the vogue in the decoration of European snuff boxes between 1758 and 1760 shifted from floral subjects to scenes of Flemish peasants borrowed from the paintings of David Teniers the Younger. Such scenes were at the height of their popularity at Sèvres during the same period.

87 Tray for a Dressing Table

(plateau)

L. 6¹⁵⁄₁₆ (17.7); W. 5⁷⁄₁₆ (13.9).

SHALLOW tray of roughly oval shape, with a serpentine border of molded form edged with serrated gilding. The white ground is crisply painted with a continuous garland of lavender, rose, blue, and yellow flowers, suspended in swags from six bows of blue ribbon regularly disposed around the border. In the center is a simple nosegay.

Marked on the underside with crossed L's, enclosing the date-letter G and surmounting a fleur de lys, the mark of the decorator, all painted in blue; incised against the foot ring:

Sèvres, datemarked for 1759; the floral decoration is by Taillandier (working 1753–1790).

88 Plant Pot

(caisse)

H. 6¾ (17.2); W. 5 square (12.7).

A CUBICAL plant pot of the same type as Nos. 75 A and B, 77 A and B, 78 A and B, and 79 A and B, but larger. The bottom is pierced in the manner of Nos. 75 A and B. The "wetness" of the technique, the avoidance of linear detail, and the soft pastel key of the painting of the floral sprays enclosed in the reserves at each side is closely similar to the painting technique on the smaller pots mentioned. The gilt borders incorporate panels of trelliswork.

Marked on the underside at the center with crossed L's, and in one corner an elongated script letter N, the mark of the decorator, all painted in blue. Incised:

"Patchmarks" are displayed on the undersides of the feet.

Sèvres porcelain, dating from about 1760; the script N mark, notwithstanding its extraordinary distortion, seems to be that of the decorator François Aloncle (working 1758–1781), better known as a painter of birds.

89 A, B Pair of Vases, Mounted in Gilt Bronze

Overall: H. 10¼ (26.1); W. 6⅞ (17.5); D. 3⅞ (9.9).

Porcelain: H. about 7½ (19.0); Diam. 3½ (8.9).

EACH is of slender baluster shape with a short neck and gently spreading base. It is coated with a transparent and softly varying turquoise-blue glaze. Mounts of chased and gilded bronze clasping either side of the vase are in the form of bulrushes supporting two handles shaped as fret scrolls and linked by laurel garlands. At top and bottom they are held by foliated circular mounts, the latter resting upon fret scrolls.

Unmarked.

Sèvres, dating from about 1760–1765; the mounts are French, dating from about 1770–1775.

Formerly in the collection of Mrs. Henry Walters (sold Parke-Bernet, New York, April 30–May 3, 1941, lot 1359 [illustrated in catalogue]).

See also Volume II of this catalogue, Nos. 272 A and B.

90 Spyglass

(lorgnette monoculaire)

L. 2½ (6.4); Diam. 1 (2.5).

THE BODY is cylindrical, with a broad central band reserved in white and painted with miniature nosegays and individual blossoms of sapphire-blue. At the top and bottom are gilded collars of "lacework" of different design, each bordered by ring moldings of beadwork. The telescopic pull-out is of brass with roped beading around the lens holders.

Unmarked.

Sèvres, dating from about 1765.

Another slightly larger spyglass in the Louvre is painted with a trellis pattern of crossed ribbons in green and gold with flowers in the interstices. It is described and illustrated in Verlet, Grandjean, and Brunet, *Sèvres*, pl. 51 b, where the following extracts from the sales records of the Manufacture Royale de Porcelaine are reproduced:

Bachelier. 2eme semestre 1760.
1 lorgnette, fond verd . . . 12
Bachelier. 2eme semestre 1763.
1 lorgnette 12

91 A, B Pair of Vases

(vases cornet)

91 A: H. 14¹¹⁄₁₆ (37.3); W. 5¾ (14.6);
D. 5¹⁄₁₆ (12.9).

91 B: H. 14⁵⁄₁₆ (36.4); W. 5½ (14.0); D. 5 (12.8).

EACH vase has an ovoid body and tall trumpet-shaped neck, and is supported upon a high circular foot, splayed and resting upon a square plinth of gilt bronze. Each is glazed a lustrous black with chinoiserie decorations of gold and platinum, the gold in two tones and the details engraved. A pair of gilded handles in the form of fins or claws with platinum tips spring vertically from each vase, and terminate in an out-turned monster's head with platinum eyes, the jaws parted to clasp a porcelain ring (now missing). There are single bands of beading at the molded base of the neck and at the top of the spreading foot, both of platinum. The body rests in a ribbed cup of gilt bronze.

The decoration imitates Chinese lacquer work. On one side of No. 91 A, a youthful hunter is spearing a bear that has captured a large, phoenix-like bird. On the reverse, a seated woman and her standing female servant flank a table on which stands a tall vase. No. 91 B is decorated on one side with a landscape with a woman and her servant at a table. At the left, a man with a parasol ascends a stair leading to a pavilion on a high rock; a fisherman sits upon a wooded slope at the right. On the reverse, a huntsman crosses a footbridge to spear a bear partly concealed in bushes. The neck is painted with a pagoda in a landscape and figures around a potter's kiln, one of whom kneels to prepare a vase for firing. On the splayed foot of each vase are two vignettes with figures engaged in pottery-making and hunting.

Each is marked on the underside of the base with crossed L's, enclosing the date-letters OO, above the letter L, all painted in gold.

Sèvres hard-paste, datemarked for 1792; the decoration is attributed to Denis Levé (working 1754–1805).

[223]

Formerly in the collection of H. Nyberg, Aldbourne, England (sold Sotheby's, London, November 8, 1966, lot 100 [illustrated in catalogue]).

Only a very limited quantity of Sèvres porcelain with chinoiserie decoration in platinum and gold on a black ground is known. The Metropolitan Museum of Art, New York, has a set of plates (62.165.1–34), some of which bear the marks of Le Guay (working 1749–1796), Dieux (working with interruptions 1777–1811), and other artists; several carry the datemark for 1792. A few other such plates are to be found in public collections in Europe and the United States. A tea service in a traveling case in the Nationalmuseum, Stockholm, is apparently unique as a complete service. At the Musée National de Céramique, Sèvres, are a small covered tureen and a ewer and basin, the latter two datemarked for 1781. Ornamental vases are also rare; two pairs of varying shape and decoration are in the English Royal Collection, Buckingham Palace (see Laking, *Sèvres Porcelain of Buckingham Palace and Windsor Castle*, no. 286, pl. 61, and no. 299).

The original plaster model for the shape is illustrated in Troude, *Choix de Modèles*, pl. 115, where it is captioned *vase cornet à têtes de morue*.

During the last four months of 1794 a merchant named Empaytaz, with offices in Paris and Berlin, made a large purchase that included a service in black and gold chinoiserie. The Committee on Commerce for the Republic authorized the sale of porcelains from the Sèvres manufactory valued at 460,706 livres, which Empaytaz was to exchange abroad for food. Among the many services he acquired in this way was one described in Chavagnac, *Histoire des Manufactures Françaises de Porcelaine*, p. 222, as:

> un service à fond noir, paysages, figures et fabriques chinoises imitant le laque en or jaune, or vert et platine, 5,418 l.

This is an early record of the use of platinum for artistic purposes, a use that has been confirmed by spectrographic analysis of the material on these vases.

92 Sugar Bowl

(sucrier)

H. 3⅞ (9.8); Diam. 3⅝ (9.2).

THE SQUAT, tulip-shaped jar has a low domed cover with a white and gold rosebud finial. The ground color is turquoise-blue with oval reserves at each side of both jar and cover enclosing birds in flight. The single birds on the cover are dove-like and carry twigs in their beaks, while the pairs on the body are crested and resemble thrushes. The delicate tints of blue, violet, and burnt-sienna used for the birds are probably fanciful. Each reserve is surrounded by a gilded border of two crossed palms tied with a ribbon bow whose upper ends are linked by floral sprays.

Marked on the underside with crossed L's, enclosing the date-letter A and surmounted by a cross, the mark of the decorator, all painted in blue.

Vincennes, datemarked for 1753; the decoration by Xhrouet *père* (working 1750–1775), who was also known as Secroux.

93 A, B   Two Wine Coolers

(seaux à bouteille)

93 A: H. 7¾ (19.7); L. 10½ (26.7); D. 8 (20.4).
93 B: H. 7¾ (19.7); L. 10½ (26.7); D. 8⅜ (21.3).

No. 93 A is a deep cylindrical vessel with a molded rim and two foliated bracket handles, curving inward toward a low spreading foot. The ground color is a slightly varying, and in places almost *soufflé*, glaze of turquoise-blue. On either side a heart-shaped or symmetrically lobed reserve encloses loosely arranged flowers and fruit, including prominent blue convolvulus, yellow and violet tulips, and fringed iris, interspersed with plums, yellow grapes, and a pomegranate. The panels are partly framed with openwork gilded borders from which spring curling stems of gilded flowers.

No. 93 B differs chiefly in the paler color of the ground. The painted panels enclose, in addition to flowers, small flying birds with strong purple and yellow flowers. The gold borders of the reserves vary slightly in the arrangement of the surrounding sprigs and vines. Subtle differences in the modeling of the rim, handles, and foot make it clear that No. 93 B was cast from a different mold from No. 93 A.

No. 93 A is marked on the underside with crossed L's, enclosing the date-letter A and with a dot above and below, all painted in blue. No. 93 B is marked on the underside with crossed L's, enclosing a dot at the center and with dots and comma-like markings at the intersections of the L's, all painted in blue. Four additional blue dots appear inside the foot ring.

Vincennes; No. 93 A is datemarked for 1753; No. 93 B dates from about 1753–1755.

The *seau à bouteille* was used at table as a cooler for a single bottle of wine. It was made at Sèvres in several sizes.

An entry in the sales records of Sèvres, dated August 9, 1755, folio 100 verso, reads:

1 Seau à Bouteilles fleurir . . . 144

It is of interest to note that this type of vessel was held in sufficient esteem almost a century later to be included (as a cachepot) in Ingres's portrait of the Comtesse d'Haussonville (Louise de Broglie, 1818–1845) at the Frick Collection, New York (acc. no. 27.1.81). The portrait dates from the last five years of the sitter's life.

94 A, B Pair of Covered Cups

(pots à jus)

H. 3⅜ (8.6); W. 3¼ (8.3); D. 2⅜ (6.0).

EACH cup is in the form of a squat, broad-mouthed urn with a swelling body. The curving handle is bifurcated at its upper end and attached beneath the lip and at the belly. The shaped domed lid is surmounted by a stylized floral finial composed of minute petals, individually formed. The ground color is turquoise-blue. At each side of both cup and cover is a cartouche-shaped reserve with an elaborately gilded border, each enclosing a nosegay, including, on No. 94 A, a striped lily, and on No. 94 B, a pair of anemones. The flowers are boldly painted in bright colors with a conspicuous use of umber for the stems and details of the leaves.

Each is marked on the underside with crossed L's, enclosing an illegible date-letter surmounting a fleur de lys, the mark of the decorator, all painted in blue. No. 94 A is incised:

C

No. 94 B is incised:

C o

Vincennes, dating from about 1753–1756; the flower painting is by Taillandier (working 1753–1790).

Formerly in the collection of Baroness Renée de Becker, New York.

Such vessels were probably also used as custard cups.

It may be noted that the nosegays are shown as alternately ascending and descending. This device was occasionally practiced at the factory when all the reserves on a piece were decorated with floral subjects.

95 A–FF   Set of Thirty-Two Coffee Cups and Saucers

(tasses à café et ses soucoupes)

EACH deep, cylindrical cup of the type called *gobelet Bouillard* has a plain scroll handle. The saucers are correspondingly simple, with curving sides. Both are painted with small scattered nosegays and sprigs, naturalistically executed. They represent roses of various colors, anemones, asters, and a large variety of other garden flowers. The rims of both cups and saucers are decorated with toothed gilding; the foot rings and handles of the cups with narrow gilded fillets, save for four handles where additional touches of gilding simulate bellflowers and foliage, and one that terminates in scallops. Two cups have plain handles terminating in gilded leafage.

CUPS

CROSSED L'S	DATE-LETTER	DECORATOR'S MARKS	INCISED MARKS
blue	none	script h (blue), Laroche (?)	
color obliterated	none	script V, unrecorded	
blue	M (blue)	V with dot (blue), unrecorded	
blue	M (blue)	anchor (blue), Buteux *aîné*	
blue	q (blue)	V with dot (blue), unrecorded	
blue	q (blue)	6-point star with dot in center (blue), Bienfait	

CROSSED L'S	DATE-LETTER	DECORATOR'S MARKS	INCISED MARKS
blue	R (blue)	script B with dot (blue), Boulanger *père*	
puce	R (puce)	circle with rays and dot in center, with tail (blue), Fritsch (?)	
blue	R (blue)	t (blue), unrecorded	
blue	r (blue)	P q (blue), Pierre *jeune*	
puce	S (puce)	none	
blue	none	none	
none	none	none	
obliterated	none	none	
obliterated	obliterated	none	

CROSSED L'S	DATE-LETTER	DECORATOR'S MARKS	INCISED MARKS	CROSSED L'S	DATE-LETTER	DECORATOR'S MARKS	INCISED MARKS
blue	none	none		blue	V (blue)	D, C above dot (blue), unrecorded	
				gray	none	4 dots (gray), Théodore	
blue	obliterated	script L (blue), Levé		blue	none	4 dots (blue), Théodore	
none	none	none		blue	OO (blue)	reversed C, I (blue), indeterminate	
none	none	none		green	V (green)	B q (green), unrecorded 4 dots (blue), Théodore	
none	none	none		blue	A (blue) dubious	L (blue), Levé	3
none	none	none		blue	A (blue) dubious	pin, Thevenet *père*	3
none	none	none					

SAUCERS

CROSSED L'S	DATE-LETTER	DECORATOR'S MARKS	INCISED MARKS
blue	Y (blue)	none	
sepia	S (sepia)	none	
sepia	u (sepia)	V with dot (sepia), unrecorded; Y (blue), Fouré	none

CROSSED L'S	DATE-LETTER	DECORATOR'S MARKS	INCISED MARKS
none	none	none	
blue	A (blue) dubious	L (blue), Levé	3
blue	none	none	t
blue	illegible	none	
blue	none	none	none
blue	h (blue)	square with dot in center (blue), Tardy	none
blue	M (blue)	n q (blue), Nicquet	

CROSSED L'S	DATE-LETTER	DECORATOR'S MARKS	INCISED MARKS	CROSSED L'S	DATE-LETTER	DECORATOR'S MARKS	INCISED MARKS
black	M (black)	B.N. (black), Bulidon (?)		blue	R (blue)	V with dot (blue), unrecorded	
blue	N (blue)	V with dot (blue), unrecorded		blue	S (blue)	script L with dot (blue), Levé	
blue	P (blue)	script cm (blue), Commelin		puce	S (puce)	script g t (puce), Grémont *jeune* (?)	
blue	P (blue)	A (blue), unrecorded					
				blue	S (blue)	V with dot (blue), unrecorded	
blue	P (blue)	script L with dot (blue), Levé		blue	L (blue)	script G C between 2 dashes (blue), unrecorded	
blue	P (blue)	V with dot (blue), unrecorded		blue	O (blue)	V with dot (blue), unrecorded	
blue	P (blue)	circle of dots (blue), Sioux *aîné*		blue	O (blue)	PR with dot (blue), Pierre Robert	
blue	p (blue)	y (blue), Bouillat *père*		blue	O (blue)	PR with dot (blue), Pierre Robert	
sepia	q (sepia)	none	none				

CROSSED L'S	DATE-LETTER	DECORATOR'S MARKS	INCISED MARKS	CROSSED L'S	DATE-LETTER	DECORATOR'S MARKS	INCISED MARKS
blue	O (blue)	PR with dot (blue), Pierre Robert		blue	y (blue)	FB (blue), unrecorded; 4 dots (blue), Théodore	
blue	u (blue)	circle of dots (blue), Sioux *aîné*; 4 dots (blue), Théodore		blue	y (blue)	FB (blue), unrecorded; 4 dots (blue), Théodore; dot (blue), unrecorded	
gray	u (gray)	V with dot (gray), unrecorded; 4 dots (blue), Théodore					
carmine	X (carmine)	FB (carmine), unrecorded; q (blue), unrecorded	none				
blue	Y (blue)	Y (blue), Fouré; 4 dots (blue), Théodore					
blue	cc (blue)	fleur de lys (blue), Taillandier					

Vincennes and Sèvres, dating from 1753 to 1780, except for three replacements, marked PR.

The sustained demand for patterns of scattered nosegays is indicated by the large variety of decorators' marks and the range of dates represented in the set. For further information about the decorators, see Biographies.

96 Liqueur Bottle Cooler

(seau ovale à liqueurs)

H. 4⅞ (12.4); L. 12⅜ (31.5); D. 5¾ (14.7).

THE DEEP elliptical vessel is fitted with a removable openwork partition dividing it at the center. Its splayed lip is shaped as four scrolls of cupid's bow design; the body, with a handle at each end formed by a pair of acanthus scrolls, curves inward toward the oval foot ring. The ground color is a slightly varying turquoise-blue, with a reserve of roughly triangular shape at each side. These reserves enclose irregular clusters of flowers, fruit, and leaves; in one panel the leaves are decidedly gray-green, in the other somewhat more yellow and tipped with ochre. The borders of these reserves are gilded with a rich variety of motifs, including grasses, trelliswork, and palm sprays; floral swags link them to the handles.

Marked on the underside with crossed L's and with illegible characters, one of which, to the right, may be the letter C or a crescent, all painted in blue; incised:

ch   C x

Vincennes-Sèvres, dating from about 1755–1760.

97 Dinner Service

(service)

THIS is a composite service, of eighty-eight items, different parts of which, while varying somewhat, are closely related to one another by their decoration of naturalistic nosegays, scattered upon a white ground. The slight differences in other decorative details are listed below, where the service is divided into seven groups.

1

Rims decorated with a fillet of simple gilding and an inner fillet of deep blue accented with pairs of short diagonal gilded strokes.

PAIR OF FRUIT DISHES *(compotiers à coquille)*

Each is shell-shaped, with handles decorated with blue feather edging.

One is marked on the underside with crossed L's, enclosing the date-letter n and with the letters P'), for Pierre *jeune*, and R, unrecorded, all painted in blue; three dots, for Tandart *jeune*, appear on the inner wall of the foot ring; incised:

The other is marked on the underside with crossed L's, enclosing the date-letter w, surmounting a script letter L, all painted in blue; incised:

EIGHTEEN SOUP PLATES *(assiettes à potage)*

Each has a simple circular border.

CROSSED L'S	DATE-LETTER	DECORATOR'S MARKS	INCISED MARKS
blue	I (blue)	none	∪∪

CROSSED L'S	DATE-LETTER	DECORATOR'S MARKS	INCISED MARKS
puce	M (puce)	y (puce), Bouillat *père*	[incised marks]
blue	Y (blue)	Y (blue), Fouré; VD with dot (blue), Vandé *père*; pair of compasses (blue), Mutel	[incised marks]
blue	I (blue)	Y (blue), Fouré	∪∪
blue	none	script h (blue), Laroche	none
blue	L (blue)	script J with curved line (blue), unrecorded	[incised mark]
blue	L (blue)	L (blue), Levé	[incised mark]
blue	L (blue)	Y (blue), Fouré	∪∪
blue	L (blue)	script J (blue), unrecorded	[incised mark]
blue	L (blue)	Y (blue), Fouré	∪∪
blue	L (blue)	script J (blue), unrecorded	[incised mark]
blue	I (blue)	L (blue), Levé	∪∪
puce	m (puce)	y (puce), Bouillat *père*	[incised mark]
puce	m (puce)	y (puce), Bouillat *père*	LL
blue	V (blue)	none	∪∪
blue	I (blue)	L with dot (blue), Levé	∪∪
blue	Y (blue)	M (blue), Michel	[incised marks]
blue	L (blue)	L (blue), Levé	[incised mark]

PAIR OF DISHES *(compotiers ovales)*

Each is oval, with a valanced rim rising at each side.

Each is marked on the underside with crossed L's, enclosing the date-letter D, below a circle with rays, possibly for Fritsch, all painted in blue. One is incised:

The other is incised:

2

Molded with flutings descending from the border into the body (see illustration at right).

SIX DINNER PLATES *(assiettes)*

Each has a serpentine rim decorated with a fillet of gilding and with a fillet of blue at the outer and inner edges of the border.

CROSSED L'S	DATE-LETTER	DECORATOR'S MARKS	INCISED MARKS
blue	u (blue)	script Gr (blue), unrecorded; VD (blue), Vandé *père*	℮
blue	u (blue)	script Gr (blue), unrecorded; VD (blue), Vandé *père*	℮
blue	ii (blue)	script CV (blue), unrecorded	2ケ
blue	u (blue)	T with dot above (blue), Binet; X (blue), Grison	LL
sepia	V (?) (sepia)	nq (sepia), Nicquet; VD (gold), Vandé *père*; III (blue), unrecorded	႘
blue	u (blue)	script B (blue), Boulanger *père*; VD (blue), Vandé *père*	⊃⊂

PAIR OF FRUIT DISHES *(compotiers carrés)*

Each is square, with double-notched corners. The rim is decorated with one fillet of gilding and one of blue.

One is marked on the underside with crossed L's, enclosing the date-letter I, and with the letter H, to the right, for Houry, all painted in blue; incised:

The other is marked on the underside with crossed L's, enclosing an illegible date-letter, and with three dots on the wall of the foot ring, for Tandart *jeune*, all painted in blue; incised:

3

Rims decorated with toothed gilding and with

[235]

one blue fillet, accented with pairs of short diagonal gilded strokes.

PAIR OF SUGAR BOWLS (sucriers)

Each is boat-shaped, with a knobbed cover, attached to a boat-shaped stand.

Each is marked on the underside with crossed L's, one enclosing an obliterated date-letter and with a script L with a dot, for Levé, all painted in blue. This one is incised:

The other is incised:

PAIR OF TAZZE (soucoupes à pied)

Each is circular, with the rim notched to produce twelve gently rounded lobes and edged with two, rather than one, narrow blue fillets.

One is marked on the underside with crossed L's, enclosing the date-letter s, above the letters cm, for Commelin, all painted in blue; incised:

The other is marked on the underside with crossed L's, enclosing the date-letter s, below the script letters B.n., for Bulidon, all painted in green; three additional blue dots, for Tandart *jeune*, appear against the edge of the foot ring; incised:

TRAY (plateau)

Of oval shape, with two handles and a fluted, sloping border.

Marked on the underside with crossed L's, enclosing the date-letter q below the script letters Bn., for Bulidon, all painted in blue; incised:

DISH (plateau ovale)

Of oval shape, with a serpentine border.

Marked on the underside with crossed L's, painted in lavender; incised:

DISH (plateau)

Of serpentine eight-sided outline, with sloping border.

Marked on the underside with crossed L's, enclosing the date-letter n, above the letters N.q., for Nicquet, all painted in blue; incised:

STAND FOR A COVERED BOWL (plateau)

The center is outlined with toothed gilding.

Marked on the underside with crossed L's, enclosing the date-letter G, below the letter T with dot above, for Binet, all painted in blue.

4

Petal-molded, with notched rims (see illustration opposite).

PAIR OF STANDS FOR COVERED BOWLS (plateaux)

Each has a rim decorated with a fillet of gilding and one of blue accented with short diagonal gilded strokes.

One is marked on the underside with crossed L's, enclosing the date-letter n, above a square with a dot in the center, for Tardy, all painted in blue; incised:

The other is marked on the underside with crossed L's, enclosing the date-letter N, above the letters PR., all painted in blue; incised:

This stand appears to be a replacement decorated by Pierre Robert (working 1813–1832).

5

Borders molded with basketwork in the osier pattern.

TWENTY-SEVEN DINNER PLATES (assiettes)

The rim of each is decorated with a fillet of gilding and with a fillet of blue at the outer and inner edge of the border. The outer blue fillet is accented with pairs of gold dots.

CROSSED L'S	DATE-LETTER	DECORATOR'S MARKS	INCISED MARKS
sepia	y (?) (sepia)	2 dots (sepia), unrecorded	m LL
blue	cc (blue)	P7 (blue), Pierre jeune	none
gray	y (gray)	V with dot (gray), unrecorded	L L
blue	LL (blue)	script LB (blue), Le Bel jeune	34 A
sepia	X (sepia)	script LB (sepia), Le Bel jeune	LL
sepia	y (sepia)	script LB (sepia), Le Bel jeune	8 h
blue	u (blue)	FB (blue), unrecorded; VD with dot (blue), Vandé père; 4 dots (blue), Théodore	£S
blue	ii (blue)	6v(?) (blue), unrecorded	34 A
puce	X (puce)	P7 (puce), Pierre jeune	‖ dd
blue	KK (blue)	script Vt (blue), Gérard (?)	24
blue	jj (blue)	script M (blue), Michel	2H
puce	none	Vt (puce), Gérard (?)	34

CROSSED L'S	DATE-LETTER	DECORATOR'S MARKS	INCISED MARKS
sepia	y (sepia)	none	x
sepia	X (sepia)	none	gm
blue	O (?) (blue)	script B.n. (blue), Bulidon; 3 dots (blue), Tandart jeune	cT 4
blue	u (blue)	dagger (blue), Evans; VD (blue), Vandé père; 4 dots (blue), Théodore	dd
blue	KK (blue)	script M (blue), Michel	23
puce	aa (puce)	P7 (puce), Pierre jeune	5 o
blue	I (blue)	L (blue), Levé	cT
blue	hh (blue)	script M (blue), Michel	33

CROSSED L'S	DATE-LETTER	DECORATOR'S MARKS	INCISED MARKS
blue	v (blue)	none	*cT 4*
purple	X (purple)	V with dot (purple), unrecorded	*(incised mark)*
blue	ii (blue)	V with dot (blue), unrecorded	*3 I a*
brown	v (brown)	script LB (brown), Le Bel *jeune*	*sf 5*
gray	u (gray)	V with dot (gray), unrecorded; VD with dot (blue), Vandé *père*; 4 dots (blue), Théodore	LL
puce	y (puce)	V with dot (puce), unrecorded	
puce	V (puce)	V with dot (puce), unrecorded; X with 4 dots (blue), unrecorded; script BD (blue), Baudouin *père*	*ddHT*

6

With feather-edging (see illustration opposite).

THREE TUREEN STANDS *(plateaux)*

The set consists of one pair of matching stands for tureens and a third somewhat smaller. The shape of each is a modified oval, with an undulating and notched border. Each end is modeled in low relief with a pair of leaf scrolls and a large shell form, separated by a narrow perforation through the paste.

One is marked on the underside with crossed L's, enclosing the date-letter s and surmounted by a comma, for Méreaud *jeune*, all painted in blue; incised:

Jʌ

Another is marked on the underside with crossed L's, flanked by the date-letter s and a hatchet, for Rosset, all painted in blue; incised: *△*

The smaller stand is marked on the underside with crossed L's, enclosing the date-letter s, painted in blue; incised: *△*

PAIR OF FRUIT DISHES *(compotiers carrés)*

Each is square; the rim is decorated with a fillet of gilding, and the corners are rounded and fluted.

Each is marked on the underside with crossed L's, enclosing the date-letter Q, between the letters B, unrecorded, and F, possibly for Félix Levé, all painted in gray. One is incised: *C*

The other is incised: *C*

7

Borders molded with flowers and looped acanthus scrolls (see illustration on p. 186).

SIXTEEN DINNER PLATES *(assiettes)*

The rim of each is decorated with a fillet of gilding, and with a fillet of blue at the outer and inner edge of the border.

CROSSED L'S	DATE-LETTER	DECORATOR'S MARKS	INCISED MARKS
puce	bb (puce)	script LB (puce), Le Bel *jeune*	*33*

CROSSED L'S	DATE-LETTER	DECORATOR'S MARKS	INCISED MARKS	CROSSED L'S	DATE-LETTER	DECORATOR'S MARKS	INCISED MARKS
blue	dd (blue)	V with dot (blue), unrecorded		brown	y (brown)	dot (brown), unrecorded	LL
				gray	y (gray)	script LB (gray), Le Bel *jeune*	
		3LA					D
blue	dd (blue)	script LB (blue), Le Bel *jeune*		sepia	y (sepia)	dot (sepia), unrecorded	LL
				blue	Z (blue)	script B (blue), Boulanger *père*	
		35 ர					Y
blue	none	script h (blue), Laroche		blue	N (blue)	W (blue), Vavasseur *aîné*	
		S8					A
sepia	y (sepia)	script LB (sepia), Le Bel *jeune*		sepia	y (sepia)	dot (brown), unrecorded	gm
		gm					

CROSSED L'S	DATE-LETTER	DECORATOR'S MARKS	INCISED MARKS	CROSSED L'S	DATE-LETTER	DECORATOR'S MARKS	INCISED MARKS
puce	y (puce)	V with dot (puce), unrecorded	LL	brown	y (brown)	dot (brown), unrecorded	D
gray	y (gray)	V with dot (gray), unrecorded	LL				
blue	ii (blue)	V with dot (blue), unrecorded	24				
blue	ee (blue)	V with dot (blue), unrecorded	33				

Sèvres, dating from 1756–1788.

The great variety of marks appearing in this composite service attests to the extensive production of and sustained demand for this pattern. For further information on the decorators, see Biographies.

98 Dessert Plate

(assiette)

Diam. 9¾ (24.8).

THE turquoise-blue border, lightly scalloped with alternately large and small arcs, is decorated with three oval cartouche-shaped reserves enclosing vignettes of exotic birds in open meadows, one bird perching upon a low branch springing from a tree stump. The cartouches have gilded rococo borders and are linked by molded and gilded scrolls of palm leaves that form segments of the rim, their ends partly concealed by gilded festoons of flowers springing from each side of the cartouches. Six broad flutings descend into the cavetto. The plate is painted at the center with a cluster of three periwinkle-blue lobed fruits surrounded by asters, a tulip, and other flowers.

Marked on the underside with crossed L's, enclosing the date-letter F, painted in blue; incised:

Sèvres, datemarked for 1758.

A closely similar example is in the Victoria and Albert Museum, London (acc. no. C403-1921).

The sales records at Sèvres mention, for October 1, 1758 (folio 70):

72 Assiettes Fleurs . . . . 18 . . . . 1296.

For other related plates in this collection, compare Nos. 104, 106 A–C, 107, 108, 109 (in part), 110, and 111.

99 Breakfast Tray

(plateau carré)

H. 1 (2.5); W. 6 square (15.3).

THE TRAY is square, its steeply sloping outer border pierced in a pattern of apple-green wave motifs alternating with white lilies, all heightenen with gilding. Within a broad apple-green inder border a large square panel framed with floriated gilding is reserved in the center of the tray, painted with attributes of music: a hunting horn and a trumpet together with a folio of music, the whole interwoven with scrolling trails of flowers and grapes. The prevailing yellow tone of the instruments is reflected in the foliage, and contrasts with the deep rose and blue flowers and purple grapes.

Marked on the underside with crossed L's, enclosing the date-letter H and surmounting an anchor, the mark of the decorator, all painted in blue; incised:

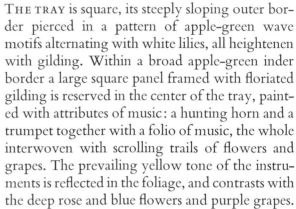

Sèvres, datemarked for 1760; decorated by Charles Buteux *aîné* (working 1756–1782).

REFERENCES: Dauterman, Parker, and Standen, *Decorative Art from the Samuel H. Kress Collection*, p. 182, fig. XIV.

Comparable examples dating from 1758 are in the Fitzwilliam Museum, Cambridge, and the Wallace Collection, London (*Provisional Catalogue*, 1902, no. XII–177). Another, datemarked for 1764, is at the Musée National de Céramique, Sèvres.

A square tray decorated with a military scene in the Meissen manner, from the collection of Oscar Dusendschön, Geneva, was sold at Sotheby's, London, December 6, 1960, lot 74 (illustrated in catalogue).

Plateaux of this type were used in breakfast services, which frequently consisted only of a tray, and a cup and saucer.

100 A, B   Two Jam Pots

(pots à confiture)

H. 3⅜ (8.6); Diam. 2⅞ (7.4).

EACH jar is of truncated and inverted pear shape, with a molded domed cover surmounted by a finial in the form of a carnation. The turquoise-blue ground of No. 100 A is decorated with a cartouche-shaped reserve at each side of the body, and with two more on the cover, all painted with flowers. The ground color of No. 100 B is slightly lighter, and the cartouches on each side of the body are painted with attributes of love (a cupid's bow, a quiver with arrows, and a flaming torch) and of royalty (a golden crown with mace and scepter). The cover of No. 100 B has a single circular reserve bordered with a floral garland.

Each is marked on the underside with crossed L's (somewhat smudged), enclosing, on No. 100 B, the date-letter H and surmounting an anchor, the mark of the decorator, all painted in blue. No.

100 A is incised: **4**

No. 100 B is incised: ⊥

Sèvres; No. 100 B datemarked for 1760; the trophies on No. 100 B were painted by Charles Buteux *aîné* (working 1756–1782). No. 100 A, decorated by another artist, is apparently contemporaneous.

Formerly in the collection of Baroness Renée de Becker, New York.

A related sugar basin with a rose-pink ground in the Jones Collection at the Victoria and Albert Museum, London (*Catalogue*, II, no. 119, pl. 9), also dates from 1760 and is decorated by Buteux.

101 Dish

(jatte)

Diam. 3⅝ (9.2).

THE turquoise-blue border of this saucer-like dish is decorated in gilding with a beaded rim and an inner border from which emerge sprays of flowers. The entire cavetto is painted with a youthful couple of Flemish peasants dancing vigorously in a rural setting, in the manner of David Teniers. The man wears an iron-red jerkin, the woman a rose-pink skirt. At the right is a plank fence, and a wine cask supporting a jug.

Marked on the underside with crossed L's, enclosing the date-letter i, and surmounted by a bar with three dots, the mark of the decorator, all painted in blue; incised: *3*

Sèvres, datemarked for 1761; the painting is by Vieillard (working 1752–1790).

The dancing couple depicted here is also included in a larger scene of carousing villagers decorating the largest of a garniture of three turquoise-blue fan-shaped vases (*vases hollandais nouveaux*) dated 1761, formerly in the collection of the Earl of Harewood (sold Christie's, London, July 1, 1965, lot 16 [illustrated in catalogue]). The subject presumably derives from an engraving.

102 Dinner Service

(service)

THIS large service, containing 115 items, is of simple white porcelain decorated only with gilding, applied almost exclusively to the rims in a toothed pattern and to the foot rings in a narrow stripe. The service comprises the following:

FORTY–TWO PLATES *(assiettes)*

The border is delicately notched to produce twelve shallow lobes, the outer edge molded with minute petal–like flutings, edged with gilding.

CROSSED L'S	DATE– LETTER	DECORATOR'S MARKS	INCISED MARKS
none	none	bold blue cross, Micaud	
none	none	bold blue cross, Micaud	
none	none	bold blue cross, Micaud	
none	none	bold blue dash, unrecorded	

The remaining 38 plates bear incised marks only, represented below.

PUNCH BOWL *(jatte à punch)*

Marked on the underside with crossed L's, floridly painted in blue.

MONTEITH *(seau crénelé)*

The gentle lobed oval body with two acanthus handles has a wavy rim notched to receive twelve wine glasses.

Marked on the underside with crossed L's, painted in blue; incised: $C\,n$

PAIR OF COVERED BOWLS *(écuelles)*

Each deep round bowl with two handles has a molded high domed cover with a loop handle ornamented with a laurel sprig. The handles are heightened with gilding.

Each is marked on the underside with crossed

L's, painted in blue; incised: O

One is also incised: GL

SALAD BOWL *(saladier)*

The circular bowl has a shaped rim and six flutings.

Marked on the underside with crossed L's, painted in blue; incised: $3P$

FIVE OVAL FRUIT DISHES *(compotiers ovales)*

The dishes have paneled sides matching the salad bowl.

Each is marked on the underside with crossed L's, painted in blue. Four are incised, respectively:

G x $G\cup$ $G\cup$

PAIR OF VEGETABLE DISHES (*jattes ovales*)

The rims of each are valanced to accentuate the paneled sides.

One is marked on the underside with crossed L's, painted in blue; incised:

The other is marked on the underside with smudged crossed L's seeming to enclose an almost obliterated letter (possibly K, the date-letter for 1763) and with other marks, largely erased; incised:

PAIR OF FRUIT DISHES (*compotiers ovales*)

Each has a valanced rim and petal-molded sides.

Each is marked on the underside with crossed L's, one enclosing the date-letter K for 1763, both painted in blue; each is incised:

THREE BUTTER DISHES (*beurriers*)

Each tub-shaped vessel has two pierced lugs as handles and a double molded band beneath the rim. The low domed cover has a bracket handle, and the attached stand is shaped as a deep soup plate.

Two are marked on the underside with crossed L's, enclosing the date-letter L for 1764, both painted in blue; all are incised:

INDIVIDUAL WINE GLASS COOLER (*seau à verre*)

The body, molded with four lobes and a spreading foot, has two scrolled and foliated handles springing from the sides. The edges are outlined with gilding, partly plain and partly toothed.

[247]

The lip is molded with shell flutings as on the dinner plates.

Marked on the underside with crossed L's, painted in blue.

FOUR FRUIT DISHES (*compotiers ronds*)

Each circular dish has a twelve-notched rim molded with shell fluting.

Each is marked on the underside with crossed L's, painted in blue.

TWO SETS OF FIVE COVERED CUPS WITH TRAY (*pots à jus et plateaux pour les servir*)

Each bellied cup has a scrolled handle and a low domed cover with a floral finial; each six-sided tray is molded with shell flutings and rococo scrolls.

Eight of the cups are incised on the underside, respectively:

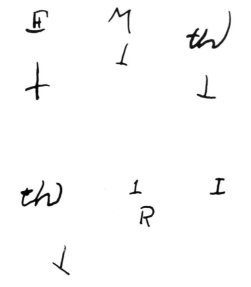

One cup, a replacement, is of hard-paste porcelain, the handle gilded with dots and crosses, marked faintly on the underside with crossed L's, and an unidentified sword mark below, painted in pale violet; incised:

The cover is of soft-paste porcelain.

Each tray is marked on the underside with crossed L's, painted in blue; one is incised:

The other is incised:

PAIR OF TWIN JAM POTS WITH STANDS
(plateaux à deux pots à confiture)

Each vessel has a disk-shaped cover with an acorn-shaped finial. Each pair rests on an oval attached stand with a valanced molded border. The rims and finials are decorated with toothed gilding.

[248]

Each is marked on the underside with crossed L's, enclosing the date-letter L for 1764, both painted in blue; each is incised:

TEAPOT (théière)

The plain ovoid pot has a matching cover with a fruit-shaped finial and an ear-shaped handle.

Marked on the underside with crossed L's, painted in blue; incised:

SUGAR BOWL (sucrier)

The cylindrical body curves inward toward the foot ring; the low domed cover is molded at the lip and has a white and gold finial in the form of a stylized flower.

Marked on the underside with crossed L's, surmounted by the letter B, the mark of an unidentified decorator (not Boulanger), both painted in blue; incised:

MILK JUG (pot à lait)

The baluster-shaped pot has a handle formed by two entwined twigs; the lid is surmounted by a finial in the form of a peach.

Marked on the underside with crossed L's, surmounted by a dot, both painted in blue; incised:

CREAM PITCHER (pot à crème)

The body is bulbous with a broad lip, a foliated twig handle, and three splayed feet.

Unmarked.

TEN COFFEE CUPS AND SAUCERS *(tasses à café et ses soucoupes)*

Each deep cylindrical cup curves inward toward the foot and has a simple scroll handle. The saucer is deep with curving sides.

Nine of the cups are marked on the underside with crossed L's, eight painted in blue, one in pale green. Incised, respectively:

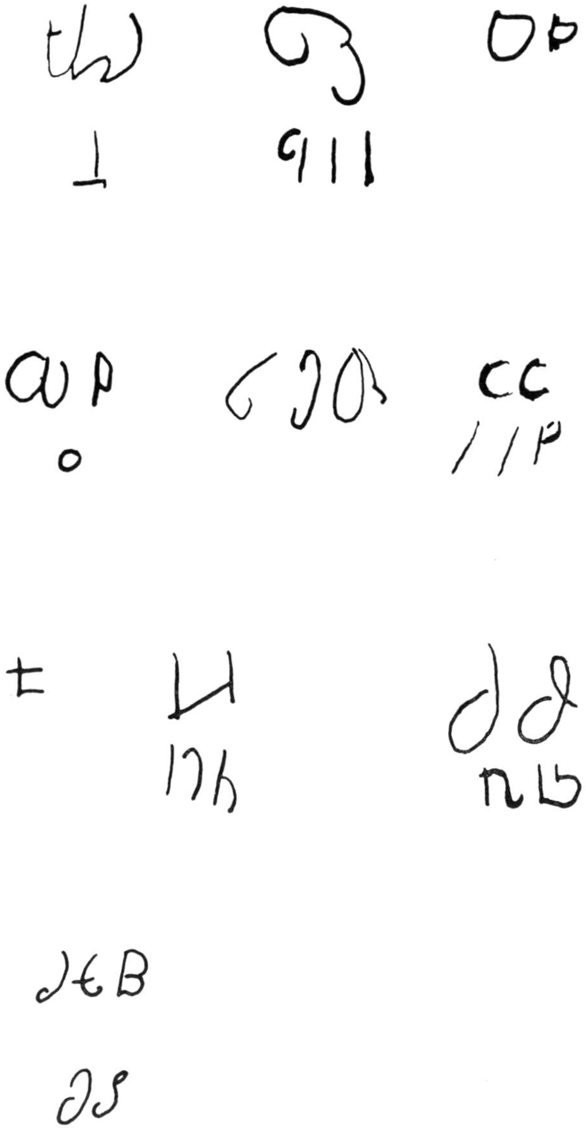

Each of the saucers is marked on the underside with crossed L's, painted in blue. One encloses the date-letter L for 1764; the other nine are incised, respectively:

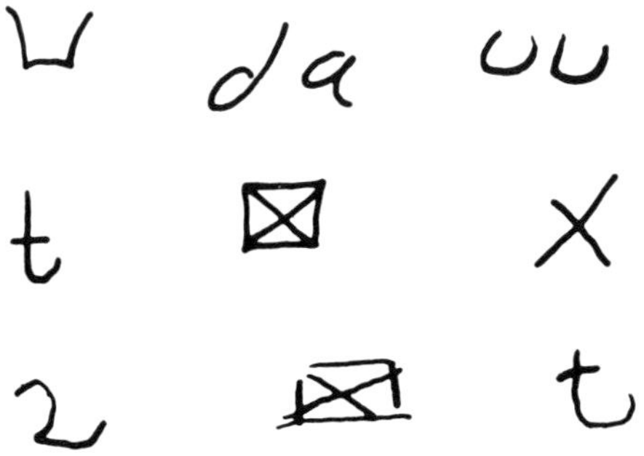

The "da" is the mark of the thrower Danet *père*.

SIX TEACUPS AND SAUCERS *(tasses à thé et ses soucoupes)*

Each cup is tulip-shaped, and without handles. The saucers are deep with curving sides.

Each cup is marked on the underside with crossed L's, two enclosing the date-letter K for 1763, all painted in blue. Two cups are incised:

Four are impressed:

Four of the saucers are marked on the underside with crossed L's, painted in blue; all six are incised:

FOURTEEN CHOCOLATE CUPS AND SAUCERS
(tasses à chocolat et ses soucoupes)

Each cylindrical cup has an ear-shaped handle. The saucers have broad sloping borders.

The cups are unmarked. Two of the saucers are marked on the underside with crossed L's, painted in blue. A third has a smudged blue mark resembling a shoe with suggestions of the initials xs and xx, very small; the remainder are without paint-ed marks. Three are incised:

Nine are impressed:

Sèvres, datemarked for 1763–1764. For further information about the decorators, see Biographies.

103 Breakfast Cup and Tray

(coupe et plateau)

Cup: H. 1⅞ (4.8).

Tray: W. 4¼ square (10.8).

THE CUP is of cylindrical shape, with a scrolled handle. The square tray has a steeply sloping border pierced with wave scrolls alternating with lilies, both outlined with gilding. Both cup and tray are painted in green and sepia with pendent floral garlands, touched with gilding. The rim of the cup is decorated with a series of gold dots, both inside and outside.

Each is marked on the underside with crossed L's, enclosing the date-letter N and surmounting a musical note, the mark of the decorator, all painted in purplish brown. The cup is incised on the underside: C 3

The tray is incised on the underside:

Sèvres, datemarked for 1766; decorated by Antoine-Toussaint Cornailles (working 1755–1800).

The square trays of breakfast services have rarely survived with their matching cups.

104 Dessert Plate

(assiette)

Diam. 9¾ (24.8).

THE turquoise-blue border, lightly scalloped with alternately large and small arcs, is decorated with three oval reserves enclosing floral sprays and linked by foliated C-scrolls in low relief and husk festoons, both gilded. The plate is painted at the center with a vignette of a purple flycatcher, perched on a branch in a wooded landscape.

Inscribed on the underside in black: "Moucherole du Cap françois." Marked on the underside with crossed L's, enclosing the date-letter P and surmounting an elongated script letter N, the mark of the decorator, all painted in blue; incised:

ᒷ ᒷ

Sèvres, datemarked for 1768; decorated by François Aloncle (working 1758–1781), painter of birds and animals.

See also Nos. 98, 106 A–C, 107, 108, 109 (in part), 110, and 111.

(déjeuner)

THIS service consists of fifteen pieces. Each is decorated with a turquoise-blue *oeil-de-perdrix* ground with oval reserves enclosing an unidentified monogram consisting of the initials s, c, and r, executed in flowers. These oval reserves are linked by garlands of laurel dotted with berries within ribbon-like reserves. The "partridge eyes" consist of tiny hexagonal reserves bordered with deep blue dots and produce a fine overall honeycomb texture. In the monogram, the letter s is made up principally of heart-shaped yellow-green leaves with occasional violet blossoms; the c, of cornflowers; and the r, of pink roses. The several medallions and festoons are bordered with gilded fillets as are the rims. Each cover is fitted with a stylized floral finial. The service consists of the following:

TWO PLATES *(assiettes)*

Each has a gently notched circular border, and a broad reserve surrounding the monogrammed medallion in the center.

Each is marked on the underside with crossed L's, painted in blue. One is incised: **LL**

The other is incised: **LL**

BUTTER DISH WITH COVER *(beurrier)*

This is a straight-walled circular tub-shaped vessel with two pierced lug handles. It is attached to a deep basin-like dish and fitted with a low dome cover having a bracket finial.

Marked on the underside of the stand with crossed L's, painted in blue; incised: **X**

PAIR OF CUPS AND SAUCERS *(tasses et ses soucoupes)*

Each cup of the *litron* type is cylindrical, with a notched scroll handle. Each saucer is deep and circular with flaring sides.

Each is marked on the underside with crossed L's, painted in blue. One includes a Maltese cross, the mark of Xhrouet. The cups are incised:

The saucers are incised:

TWO CREAM PITCHERS *(pots à crème)*

Each is of squat pear shape, with a scalloped rim, a sturdy scroll handle, and three splayed rustic feet.

One is marked on the underside with crossed L's, painted in blue. The other is marked on the underside with the letter r followed by a dot, unrecorded, painted in blue.

SUGAR BOWL WITH COVER AND STAND *(sucrier et plateau)*

The round bowl rests upon a low retracted foot; its two handles are molded with internal C-scrolls. The domed cover, recurved at the rim, sports a yellow carnation finial.

Marked on the underside of the stand with crossed L's, painted in blue; incised: ⊠

THREE COVERED CONSERVE JARS *(pots à confiture)*

These consist of a pair of taller cylindrical jars and one shorter jar; each has a low domed cover with a yellow carnation finial.

Each is marked on the underside with crossed

L's, painted in blue. The two taller jars are incised:

$\int$

The other is incised:

$\mathcal{IR}$

TWO EGG CUPS (*coquetiers sans pied*)

Each is in the form of a half ovoid, and rests on a low round base.

Each is marked on the underside with crossed L's, painted in blue. One is incised:

$\mathcal{J}a$

This is the mark of the thrower Danet *père*.

TRENCHER SALT (*salière*)

It is in the form of an oval with molded spreading sides.

Marked on the underside with crossed L's, painted in blue; incised:

$\mathcal{J}$

CHAMBER CANDLESTICK (*bougeoir*)

The base is shell-shaped, bordered with blue feather edging. This piece is not part of the original service, as it lacks the *oeil-de-perdrix* decoration.

Unmarked.

Sèvres, dating from about 1770–1772; the monograms and laurel festoons attributed to Jean-Baptiste Tandart (working 1754–1803).

The monograms and festoons are attributed to Tandart by comparison with a signed cup and saucer of 1767 in the R. Thornton Wilson Collection at The Metropolitan Museum of Art, New York (acc. nos. 50.211.141, 142).

This extraordinary service illustrates the nature and extent of the porcelain furnishings of an exceptionally well-equipped Louis XVI traveling table. Another Sèvres service, in a fitted marquetry case of the Louis XVI period, in the collection of James Hasson, was sold at Christie's, London, May 19, 1966, lot 73 (illustrated in catalogue, pl. 9), and several others are known.

This service is one of the fittings of a traveling table, described in Volume I of this catalogue as No. 124. For a description of the silver, see Volume III, No. 68.

[257]

106 A–C   Three Dessert Plates

(assiettes)

Diam. 10⅛₆ (25.6).

THE BORDER of each is similar to that of No. 98, except that the oval reserves enclosing birds are linked by C-scrolls in bolder relief and more conspicuously gilded. Sprays of gilded roses fill the sprandrel-shaped areas between the scrolls. The turquoise-blue glaze of the border descends over the inner edge to form a series of pointed scallops. Each plate is painted in soft colors at the center with a loose floral cluster, principally of roses.

Each is marked on the underside with crossed L's, painted in blue. Nos. 106 A and B are incised:

[258]

No. 106 C is incised:

Sèvres, dating from about 1770–1775.

See also Nos. 98, 104, 107, 108, 109 (in part), 110, and 111.

107 Dessert Plate

(assiette)

Diam. 9⅝ (24.5).

OF SIMILAR design to No. 98, except that the rim of the turquoise-blue border is decorated with toothed gilding, and there are sprays of gilded flowers at the ends of each reserve. The plate is painted at the center with an elaborate floral cluster incorporating berries and a striped brown gourd.

Marked on the underside with crossed L's, and with four dots, the mark of the decorator, all painted in blue; incised: ⌐ ⌐

Sèvres, dating from about 1770–1775; decorated by Théodore (working 1765–1779/1780), a painter and gilder.

See also Nos. 98, 104, 106 A–C, 108, 109 (in part), 110, and 111.

[259]

108 Dessert Plate

(assiette)

Diam. 9¾ (24.8).

THE turquoise-blue border, lightly scalloped with alternately large and small arcs, is decorated with three kidney-shaped reserves each painted with highly colored birds, one of them a pheasant, the other two unidentifiable. The reserves, which alternate with gilded wreaths, are decorated with gilded rims and pairs of laurel sprays. The cavetto is painted with a garland of green laurel leaves entwining a gilded circle with a cluster of three pink roses at its center. Six flutings occur at the edge of the cavetto.

Marked on the underside with crossed L's, enclosing the date-letter s and surmounting a script N, the mark of the decorator, all painted in blue.

Painted over the glaze in gold: IN; incised:

Sèvres, datemarked for 1771; decorated by François Aloncle (working 1758–1781). The meaning of the letters IN is unknown.

Formerly in the collection of Richard Peñard y Fernandez, Paris (sold Palais Galliera, Paris, December 7, 1960, lot 154).

See also Nos. 98, 104, 106 A–C, 107, 109 (in part), 110, and 111.

THE fifty-four items described below form a major portion of an ambassadorial service, each piece of which is decorated with reserves enclosing exotic birds in varied landscape settings, within gilded borders. On the plates and a pair of small wine coolers, the borders of the reserves are plain and linked by festoons of oak leaves; on the remaining pieces they are in the form of wreaths of oak leaves. Among the birds depicted, some species, such as magpies, doves, pheasants, ducks, and thrushes, are represented literally, while others are purely fanciful. The monogram LPR, for Louis, Prince de Rohan, in two tones of gold appears on many though not all of the pieces of the service, the L being darker than the flanking letters.

The service consists of the following items:

TWENTY-EIGHT PLATES *(assiettes)*

The wavy-edged borders painted in a slightly varying turquoise-blue are molded in low relief with alternating C-scrolls and three kidney-shaped cartouches, each enclosing a bird in a landscape. The cartouches are linked together by gilded oak-leaf swags suspended from rings. The owner's monogram, framed within a wreath of oak leaves and acorns springing from the branches of a log, is painted at the center of each plate.

CROSSED L'S	DATE-LETTER	DECORATOR'S MARKS	INCISED MARKS
none	none	none	L (script)
none	none	none	x
none	none	none	x
none	none	none	x
none	none	none	L L
gray	S (gray)	cp. (gray), Chappuis *aîné*	x
gray	illegible	cp (pale green), Chappuis *aîné*	L (script)
none	none	none	L L
none	none	none	x
none	none	none	x
pale blue	S (blue)	dagger (blue), Evans	x
sepia	S (lavender)	F between 2 dots (lavender), Fallot	L (script)
black	T (gray)	F between 2 dots (gray), Fallot	x
black	S (sepia)	F between 2 dots (sepia), Fallot	none

CROSSED L'S	DATE-LETTER	DECORATOR'S MARKS	INCISED MARKS
gray (defaced)	none	F between 2 dots (gray), Fallot	CT
none	none	none	L L

CROSSED L'S	DATE-LETTER	DECORATOR'S MARKS	INCISED MARKS
black	T (sepia)	F between 2 dots (sepia), Fallot	
pale lavender	T (pale lavender)	F between 2 dots (pale lavender), Fallot	
pale lavender	S (pale lavender)	cp. (pale lavender), Chappuis *aîné*	
none	none	none	
lavender	S (pale lavender)	F between 2 dots (pale lavender), Fallot	
black	S (sepia)	F between 2 dots (sepia), Fallot	
deep blue	KK (blue)	bar and 3 dots (blue), Vieillard; Y (blue), Fouré	
blue	S (blue)	script N (blue), Aloncle	none
blue	S (blue)	script N (blue), Aloncle	
gray	T (gray)	F between 2 dots (gray), Fallot	

Two plates are unmarked.

TWO FRUIT DISHES (*compotiers à coquille*)

Each is in the form of an oval shell with an undulating border, and, in the center, a circular reserve painted with birds in a landscape.

One is marked on the underside with crossed L's, enclosing the date-letter s for 1771 and surmounting a script letter N, for Aloncle, all painted in chalky blue; incised:

The other is incised:

[262]

FOUR TRAYS FOR ICE CUPS
(*plateaux bourets*)

The deep sloping border with six petal-shaped lobes is molded with shellwork in low relief and gilded with a fillet along its outer and inner edge. The center of each tray is painted with birds in a landscape within a triangular reserve with sinuous edges; one contains a rose in relief.

Each is marked on the underside with crossed L's (three painted in black, one in blue), three enclosing the date-letter s for 1771 and surmounting a letter F between two dots, for Fallot. On the fourth, two dots appear below the crossed L's, and may be an incomplete mark of the decorator. Incised, respectively:

TWO PAIRS OF CONSERVE POTS (*plateaux à deux pots de confiture*)

Each truncated ovoid jar has a flat projecting lid surmounted by an acorn finial. The jars are attached in pairs to shallow oval stands with cusped borders, having an inner molding parallel to the rim. All parts are decorated with bird scenes enclosed within reserves. Two of the covers, though generally matching the others, are painted with larger wreaths of flowers.

One stand is marked on the underside with crossed L's, enclosing the date-letter T for 1772 and

surmounting a letter F with two dots, for Fallot, all painted in green-gray; incised:

The other stand is marked with largely obliterated crossed L's, probably enclosing the date-letter s for 1771, painted in black; incised:

FOUR FOOTED SALVERS *(soucoupes à pied)*

The scalloped rim is divided into twelve lobes, and the low foot with vertical sides is similarly lobed. Within a reserve at the center of each is a circular medallion enclosing a landscape with birds.

One is marked on the underside with crossed L's, enclosing the date-letter T for 1772 and surmounting a script letter N, for Aloncle, all painted in blue. Incised, respectively:

TWO ICE CUPS *(tasses à glace)*

Tulip-shaped, with a scrolling handle and spreading stem foot. A circular reserve at the front of each is painted with a crested bird perched on a branch.

Each is marked on the underside with crossed L's, one painted in blue, the other in gray. One bears a letter F between two dots, for Fallot; incised:

The other carries the script letters cp, for Chappuis; incised:

TWO SUGAR BOWLS WITH COVERS *(sucriers)*

Each boat-shaped vessel with *bombé* sides is attached to an oval stand. The cover, bowl, and stand are decorated with six cartouche-shaped reserves painted with birds in landscapes. At either end of the vessel are two further reserves enclosing a gilded monogram.

One is marked on the underside with crossed L's, enclosing the date-letter T for 1772 and surmounting a dagger, for Evans, all painted in blue.

TWO PUNCH BOWLS *(jattes à punch)*

Each deep circular bowl with a ring foot is

[265]

decorated around the sides with three kidney-shaped reserves bordered with gilded oak leaves. These enclose brilliantly colored birds perched on branches. Between each of the reserves is a gilded monogram.

One is marked on the underside with large crossed and foliated L's, enclosing the date-letter T for 1772, painted in blue; its foot ring is pierced on the inside with four tapering holes; it was probably decorated by Evans.

TWO WINE COOLERS *(seaux à bouteille)*

Each is of deep cylindrical shape, curving inward toward the low spreading foot and molded with bracket handles formed by scrolling acanthus leaves. Large reserves at each side bordered with gilded oak leaves enclose pairs of birds in a wooded landscape. There is a gilded monogram beneath each handle.

One is incised on the inside of the foot ring:

This is the mark of the thrower Danet *père*.

Any marks on the other have been obscured by plaster fill in the base. Both probably decorated by Evans.

PAIR OF WINE COOLERS *(seaux à demi-bouteille)*

Of the same shape as the preceding wine coolers, though smaller and differing slightly in details of decoration. The reserves are painted with pairs of birds in vignettes. The blue ground color does not cover the molded foot, and the gilding differs in the following respects: the borders of the reserves are simple bands joined by festoons of oak suspended from rings; sprays of oak leaves spring from the bottoms of the reserves; several scattered sprays of gilded flowers and leaves ornament the interior.

Each is marked on the underside with crossed L's, painted in blue, and carries a sticker inscribed FOR LEOPOLD DE ROTHSCHILD ESQ.

THREE OVAL LIQUEUR BOTTLE COOLERS *(seaux ovales à liqueurs)*

Each is of deep boat shape, with an undulating rim and a bracket handle formed by acanthus leaves at either end. Each is decorated with gilded monograms at the ends and cartouche-shaped reserves at the sides. These enclose pairs of birds perched on branches. Two are fitted with the usual reticulated and removable barrier, missing in the third.

Each is marked on the underside with crossed L's, surmounting a script letter N, for Aloncle, painted in blue. Of the two furnished with removable barriers, one is marked with the date-letter s for 1771; incised:

The other has the date-letter T for 1772; incised:

The remaining piece bears the date-letter s for 1771.

TRIPLE SALT *(salière en corbeille)*

In the form of three circular baskets joined together, their arched handles tied to one another with gilded ribbons terminating in a knot forming a finial. On the sides of each of the three lobes is an oval reserve enclosing a bird in a woodland setting, and framed by a plain gilt border flanked by descending sprays of oak.

Marked on the underside with crossed L's, painted in blue.

Sèvres, datemarked for 1771–1772, except for one plate, a replacement datemarked for 1788.

Formerly in the collection of Louis, Prince de Rohan; portions subsequently belonged to Prince Demidoff, Palazzo San Donato, Florence; Earl of Dudley, Himly Hall, Dudley, Staffordshire; Leopold de Rothschild, Exbury; Anthony de Rothschild, Ascott Wing, England; Thelma Chrysler Foy, New York (sold Parke-Bernet, New York, May 22–23, 1959, lot 431 [illustrated in catalogue]).

The service originally consisted of 368 pieces, almost half of which came to this country during World War II and was dispersed among the following collections: Mrs. James P. Donahue, New York; Woolworth Donahue, New York; Charles E. Dunlap, Newport, Rhode Island; Mrs. Harvey S. Firestone, Jr., Akron, Ohio; Thelma Chrysler Foy, New York; Mrs. Barbara Hutton, New York; Marjorie Merriweather Post, Washington, D.C.; Louis Quarles, Milwaukee; the late Mrs. Arthur J. Riebs; the late Edith Wetwore; Mrs. Forsyth Wickes, Newport, Rhode Island; City Art Museum of St. Louis; Minneapolis Institute

of Arts; Museum of Fine Arts, Boston; Toledo Museum of Art; William Rockhill Nelson Gallery of Art, Kansas City, Missouri.

Other parts of the service are in the Louvre, in the Musée National de Céramique, Sèvres, and in the English Royal Collection at Windsor Castle. A single plate from the collection of J. P. Morgan, New York, was sold at Parke-Bernet, New York, March 22–25, 1944, lot 651 (illustrated in catalogue).

Louis-René-Édouard, Prince (later Cardinal Prince) de Rohan (1734–1803), for whom this service was made, descended in the Soubise branch of one of the most illustrious feudal families of France. He is remembered by posterity chiefly for his part in the celebrated affair of the diamond necklace of Marie-Antoinette, which earned him the nickname of *le cardinal Collier*. Under Louis XV, in 1771, he was appointed *ambassador extraordinaire* to the court at Vienna, and it may be assumed that the ambassadorial service was ordered in the same year or the following, when he took up his post (he arrived in Vienna on January 6, 1772). Émile Tilmans, in his *Porcelaines de France* (p. 281), says that "he took with him a service

	D'autres pieces		1511	6	2712			45	
3	Pots a Sucre	10		30					
1	Id.º			12					
1	Id.º			36					
1	Pot a lait			12					
1	Gobelet sans soucoupe			5					
1	Couvercle de Pot a Sucre	12		15					
2	Tasses a toilette et soucoupes			24					
48	Assiettes	1	10	72					
6	Id.º	3		18					
1	Pot au eau et tasse			24					
1	Gobelet et soucoupe			5					
2	Id.º et Id.º	4		8					
5	Id.º et Id.º	3		15					
1	Pot a sucre			4					
1	Ecuelle et plateau			12					
1	Pot a pommade			1	10				
1	Pot de Chambre			6					
1	Id.º			8					
				1818	16	1818	16			

Livré à Mg.r le Prince Louis De Rohan
Du 7. Septembre 1772.

8	Pots à Oilles et Terrines avec plateaux	288		2304					
36	Assiettes a potage	12		432					
22	Coquetiers	6		132					
2	Plats d'entrées ou plateaux pour pot à jus	36		72					
6	Saucieres	36		216					
6	Saladiers Oisonniés 1.re	48		288					
6	Id.º Id.º 2.º	33		198					
4	Seaux a Bouteille	120		480					
6	Id.º a ½ Bouteille	84		504					
	Dessert Bleu Fleste oiseaux et Chiffres								
120	Assiettes	36		4320					
24	Compotiers Differents	48		1152					
8	Plateaux Bouret	42		336					
6	Id.º a 2 pots a Confitures	126		756					
10	Soucoupes a pieds	48		480					
96	Tasses a glacer	21		2016					
8	Sucriers de M.r Le Premier	126		1008					
4	Fromagers et plateaux	144		576					
2	Jattes a punche et Mortier	600		1200					
4	Seaux a Glacer	252		1008					
6	Id.º Crennelés	204		1224					
6	Id.º a Bouteille	204		1224					
6	Id.º a ½ Bouteille	156		936					
				20862		4630	16		45	

of Sèvres porcelain of exceptional importance and of a particularly regal appearance, well calculated to convey to a foreign court the artistic richness of France." In actuality, this timing is impossible, as demonstrated by the date of the entry in the sales records of Sèvres, i.e., September 7, 1772, where (folios 33 verso, 34) the service is itemized (see illustrations). The total cost of the 368 pieces of the dessert service (the listing of which commences with the tenth Rohan item in the illustration to the left) amounted to 20,772 livres.

During Rohan's career as a diplomat his lavish fêtes and scandalous behavior displeased Maria Theresa, who desired to have him recalled to France. Two months after the death of Louis XV, Rohan was ordered to return to France by the new king and queen, who received him coldly. Marie Antoinette in particular was antagonistic toward him, and this prejudice militated against his ambition to become prime minister. Nevertheless, he did become grand almoner, then cardinal, and also succeeded to the family office of the bishopric of Strasbourg in 1779. Throughout the years, however, he sought to gain the favor of Marie Antoinette. Thus he fell into the trap of the diamond necklace affair, from which he was acquitted in 1786 in a trial before the parliament. However, the king exiled him to his abbey at La Chaise-Dieu and stripped him of his grand almonry. During the period of the Revolution the partisans attempted to espouse him as a victim of despotism, but he remained loyal to the Crown. As a Prince of the Church he refused to take the oath of the constitution in 1791, and took refuge in Ettenheim, in the German portion of his diocese, where he remained for the rest of his life.

(assiettes)

Diam. 9⅞ (25.1).

THE turquoise-blue border of each, lightly scalloped with alternately large and small arcs, is decorated with three kidney-shaped reserves painted with sprays of flowers and framed with foliate gilding. C-scrolls in relief alternate with the reserves and are linked to them by festoons of flowers. Beneath each reserve, a few gilded leaves spill onto the cavetto. Six shallow flutings descend from the border into the cavetto of each plate, in the center of which is painted a vignette of a bird perched in shrubbery. The central motif of each plate is of a different design.

The plates are marked on the underside as follows:

CROSSED L'S	DATE-LETTER	DECORATOR'S MARKS	INCISED MARKS
blue	u (blue)	dagger (blue), Evans; B (blue), Boulanger *père*; #(gold), Chauveaux *aîné*; VD. (blue), Vandé *père*	*lldd*
blue	u (blue)	dagger (blue), Evans; VD. (blue), Vandé *père*	*HLL*
blue	y (blue)	dagger (blue), Evans; VD. (gold), Vandé *père*	*9*
sepia	u (sepia)	cps (sepia), Chappuis *aîné* (?); script B (blue), Boulanger *père*	*Y*
gray	u (gray)	script B.n (gray), Bulidon; script N (gray), Aloncle; #(blue), Chauveaux *aîné*; VD (blue), Vandé *père*	*H X*
sepia	u (sepia)	script B.n. (sepia), Bulidon; script N (sepia), Aloncle; #(blue), Chauveaux *aîné*; VD. (blue), Vandé *père*	*lldd*
blue	u (blue)	script L.G. (blue), Le Guay *père*; script N (blue), Aloncle; VD. (blue), Vandé *père*	*H X*
blue	u (blue)	script L.G. (blue), Le Guay *père*; script N (blue), Aloncle; VD., Vandé *père*; 2 dots (blue), unrecorded	*X / W*
blue (incomplete)	none	dagger (blue), Evans; # (pale blue), Chauveaux *aîné*	*LS*
gray	none	cp (sepia), Chappuis *aîné*; B (blue), Boulanger *père*; # (gold), Chauveaux *aîné*; VD. (blue), Vandé *père*	*X*
gray	u (gray)	cps (sepia), Chappuis *aîné* (?); script L.G. (blue), Le Guay *père*; B (blue), Boulanger *père*; VD. (blue), Vandé *père*	*LS*
lavender	u (lavender)	cp (lavender), Chappuis *aîné*; script L.G. (blue), Le Guay *père*; VD. (blue), Vandé *père*	*H X*
lavender	illegible	script L.G. (blue), Le Guay *père*; VD. (blue), Vandé *père*	*H X*
gray	u (sepia)	cp (sepia), Chappuis *aîné*; # (gold), Chauveaux *aîné*; VD. (blue), Vandé *père*	*L L*

CROSSED L'S	DATE-LETTER	DECORATOR'S MARKS	INCISED MARKS	CROSSED L'S	DATE-LETTER	DECORATOR'S MARKS	INCISED MARKS
blue	none	ch (blue), Chabry *fils*; # (blue), Chauveaux *aîné*; VD (blue), Vandé *père*		pale blue	Y (blue)	# (pale blue), Chauveaux *aîné*; x (?) (blue), Grison; dagger (blue), Evans; VD. (blue), Vandé *père*	L L
lavender	u (lavender)	cp (lavender), Chappuis *aîné*; # (blue), Chauveaux *aîné*; VD. (blue), Vandé *père*	H d c′ · H	blue	u (blue)	script B.n. (gray), Bulidon; script N (blue), Aloncle; # (blue), Chauveaux *aîné*; VD. (faint blue), Vandé *père*	
lavender	u (lavender)	cp (lavender), Chappuis *aîné*; # (blue), Chauveaux *aîné*; VD. (blue), Vandé *père*	ℒ · H				) / ⅃ ⅃
blue	u (blue)	dagger (blue), Evans; B (blue), Boulanger *père*; # (gold), Chauveaux *aîné*; VD. (blue), Vandé *père*	H L L				
gray	none	cp comma (sepia), Chappuis *aîné*; illegible mark (blue)	H))				

Sèvres, dating from about 1773–1776.

For further information about the decorators, see Biographies.

An entry in the Sèvres sales records for April 28, 1774, folio 148 verso, mentions plates that may be similar:

20 Assiettes bleu celeste guirlandes, bleu et or ... 42 ... 840

See also Nos. 98, 104, 106 A–C, 107, 108, 109 (in part), and 111.

111 A–D Four Dessert Plates

(assiettes)

Diam. 9⅝ (24.5).

THE turquoise-blue border of each is gently undulating and is decorated with three kidney-shaped reserves painted with pheasants and other wild fowl in open landscapes. The reserves, surrounded by a plain gilt border, are linked by gilded festoons of oak leaves. Each plate is painted at the center with a garland of green laurel leaves entwining a gilded circle, enclosing the letters LJDM in a monogram, for Louise-Jeanne de Durfort, Duchesse de Mazarin (1735–1781).

Each is marked on the underside with crossed L's, enclosing the date-letter X and surmounting a letter B, presumably the mark of the gilder, all painted in blue. Nos. 111 A and D are marked with a script letter N, the mark of the decorator; Nos. 111 B and C are marked with a dagger, the mark of the decorator. No. 111 A is incised on the underside:

No. 111 B:

No. 111 C:

No. 111 D:

Sèvres, datemarked for 1775; Nos. 111 A and D decorated by François Aloncle (working 1758–1781); Nos. 111 B and C decorated by Étienne Evans (working 1752–1806); each probably gilded by Boulanger *père* (working 1754–1784).

Formerly in the collection of Richard Peñard y Fernandez, Paris (three sold Palais Galliera, Paris, December 7, 1960, lot 161 [illustrated in catalogue, pl. LXV]).

According to the sales record of Sèvres for 1775 and 1776, the Duchesse de Mazarin purchased a number of plates at various prices, none, however, corresponding in description to Nos. 111 A–D. Plates of this type might be expected to cost about thirty livres apiece. Objects sold through the *marchands-merciers* were not always itemized in the factory's accounts; it therefore seems likely that Nos. 111 A–D were supplied in this way rather than as the result of a direct sale to the duchesse by the factory.

See also Nos. 98, 104, 106 A–C, 107, 108, 109 (in part), and 110.

112 A, B Pair of Monteiths

(seaux crénelés)

H. 5 (12.7); L. 7½ (19.0); D. 8 (20.4).

EACH is of oval shape, with an undulating rim deeply notched to receive the stems of glasses. At either end is a handle of curling acanthus form. The sides are broadly ribbed and curve inward at the base toward the serpentine foot ring. Brightly colored sprays of flowers and fruits are scattered over the sides. The rim and handles are heightened with deep blue feather edging and gilding.

Each is marked on the underside with crossed L's, enclosing the date-letter EE, painted in blue. Below the crossed L's, on No. 112 A, is a script letter L, and at the right are indecipherable letters and a stemmed circle, all representing decorators; No. 112 B is marked with the script letter L at some dis-

tance to the left of the crossed L's, with indecipherable marks and a stemmed circle to the right. No. 112 A is incised on the underside close to the rim:

1811

No. 112 B is incised on the underside close to the rim: 8

Sèvres, datemarked for 1782; decorated by Denis Levé (working 1754–1805) and others, including probably Cardin (working 1749–1786).

THE SERVICE consists of eighteen knives and eighteen four-tined forks. Each turquoise-blue porcelain handle is straight-sided, octagonal in cross section, and is decorated with gilding of a lacelike trellis pattern minutely spangled with small dots. There is a rectangular reserve with rounded ends enclosing a spray of flowers at the center of the two principal sides of each piece. The modern metal fittings are of silver gilt.

The porcelain is unmarked. The silver is marked as follows, the knives on one side of the blade near the ferrule end, and the forks on the underside, near the base of the tines:

RC over a pellet, in a shaped shield, an unrecorded marker's mark.

A lion passant and an uncrowned leopard's head, each in a rectangle, London hallmarks used from 1821 onward.

The letter B in a rectangle, the London date-letter for 1937.

A crab in a rectangle, a French customs mark found on silver imported from 1893 onward.

Sèvres, dating from about 1765.

Two contemporary sales records at Sèvres are of interest in connection with this service. One is dated September 1765 (folio 56):

5 Manches de couteaux . . . . 12 . . . . 60.

The other, May 1766 (folio 73 verso):

2 Manches de Couteaux . . . . 24 . . . . 48.

114 A,B Pair of Statuettes: La Petite Fille au Tablier, and Le Jeune Suppliant

114 A: H. 8½ (21.6); W. 5⅛ (13.0);
D. 4¼ (10.8).

114 B: H. 8¼ (21.0); W. 4½ (11.4);
D. 3½ (8.9).

EACH is a standing figure of a barefooted child: a girl, and her bowing admirer. The girl (No. 114 A) has a kerchief tied under her chin and wears a sleeveless jacket over a laced bodice and a full skirt. With outstretched arms she holds an assortment of fruit gathered in her apron. Her companion (No. 114 B), a small boy with tousled hair, beribboned jacket and breeches, bends his right knee and holds his clasped hands to his chin. The base of each, simulating rock ledges, supports baskets heaped with flowers and fruit, partly concealed by the figures. The basket of flowers on No. 114 A rests on a low pedestal.

No. 114 A is incised on the underside:

$$CR$$

No. 114 B:

$$Bu$$

Biscuit of Vincennes-Sèvres; models created in 1752 by Blondeau (working 1752–1753), after a drawing by François Boucher.

An example of La Petite Fille au Tablier is at the State Hermitage Museum, Leningrad (illustrated in Birioukova, *Figurines et Groupes en Porcelaine des manufactures françaises du XVIIIᵉ siècle*, pl. 29). One of Le Jeune Suppliant, thought to date from about 1775, is in the Victoria and Albert Museum, London (acc. no. c608–1909). Slight variants of both, until recently in the collection of Wilfred J. Sainsbury, London, were described and illustrat-

ed in *Antiques*, December 1965, p. 824, figs. 2, 4. Versions dating between the years 1750 and 1756 are represented at the Musée National de Céramique, Sèvres.

According to Bourgeois and Lechevallier-Chevignard (*Le Biscuit de Sèvres*, nos. 494 and 362, respectively), this pair was part of a series of eight "Enfants d'après Boucher" modeled by Blondeau in 1752.

The sculptor Blondeau is mentioned only briefly by Chavagnac and Grollier, who quote (*Histoire des Manufactures Françaises de Porcelaine*, p. 261) a record of payment from the archives of the factory for 1753:

A Blondeau, sculpteur, pour 8 modèles d'enfants d'après Boucher, 384 l.

The reference apparently alludes to Pierre Blondeau, a Paris sculptor and professor at the Academy of St. Luke. Although the earliest figures created at Vincennes were coated with glaze, the practice of omitting the glaze was introduced about 1750 or shortly thereafter. Glazed and colored figures become the exception after that time.

The abundance of entries in the Sèvres sales records referring to "Enfans de Boucher" attests the popularity of these models during the 1750s and '60s. They were apparently available in a range of sizes, as indicated by differences in prices. The price most frequently found (probably for figures by Blondeau) is 42 livres apiece; figures at this price were often sold in groups of eight. Other models, sometimes referred to as "Grandes Enfans de Boucher," sold for 48 livres, while

Le Souper Fin from the Monument du Costume, plate dated 1781. The Metropolitan Museum of Art, acc. no. 34.22.2

smaller ones, "Moyens Enfans de Boucher," went for 30 livres. There were also two even smaller sizes, some called "Plus petits Enfans de Boucher," priced at 18 livres, and others called simply "Petits enfans de Boucher," at 15 livres.

It seems reasonably certain that in France, as in Germany, small ceramic sculptures were used to ornament the table. In the contemporary engraving Le Souper Fin (see above), published by Moreau *le jeune* in the *Monument du Costume*, a small sculptural group of The Three Graces appears as a centerpiece on a table used by four diners. Its similarity to the Sèvres biscuit composition created by Louis-Simon Boizot (1743–1809) in 1772 suggests the possibility that a Sèvres sculpture was used as a model.

115 Statuette: Le Joueur de Cornemuse

H. 7½ (19.0); W. 3⅞ (9.8); D. 2⁵⁄₁₆ (5.9).

THE FIGURE is a handsome young boy leaning against a slanting tree stump and fingering a musette (see below); his left leg is flexed at the knee, and his left foot rests upon the right. Beside him, on the oval base of rockwork, is an overturned basket, almost concealed by grapes and radishes.

Unmarked.

Biscuit of Vincennes-Sèvres; the model created in 1752, attributed to Blondeau (working 1752–1753), after a drawing by François Boucher. No. 115 probably was cast about 1770–1775.

An earlier example coated with white glaze was in the collection of the Comte de Chavagnac, Paris.

A slightly larger variant of this figure until recently in the collection of Wilfred J. Sainsbury, London, is illustrated in *Antiques*, January 1956, p. 47.

The accepted name "Le Joueur de Cornemuse" evidences the loose usage of the word *cornemuse* among the French. In actuality the instrument held by the figure is a musette. This, as well as the *cornemuse*, is a specialized form of bagpipe. It was developed during the seventeenth century from the peasant bagpipe by reducing the latter in size and replacing the blowpipe with a bellows that fitted under the arm. An illuminating account of the musette and related instruments by E. Winternitz appeared in *The Metropolitan Museum of Art Bulletin*, Summer 1943, pp. 56–83.

[283]

116 A, B Pair of Statuettes: La Bergère Assise, and Le Porteur de Mouton

116 A: H. 8¼ (21.0); W. 5¾ (14.7);
D. 4½ (11.4).

116 B: H. 8¼ (21.0); W. 7⅜ (18.7);
D. 4¼ (10.8).

EACH is a youthful figure seated upon an irregular base of rockwork. The shepherdess (No. 116 B), whose slender torso is emphasized by a low-cut bodice, supports her right arm upon a basket of flowers. She wears flowers in her hair, which is tied by a ribbon bow. Her left arm hangs at her side, the palm of her loosely clenched hand turned outward. Slippers with ribbon bows show below her voluminous skirt.

The youth (No. 116 A) wears an open jacket and knee breeches. Half kneeling, he proffers a basket containing a lamb and massed flowers. Beside his right foot lies a broad-brimmed felt hat.

No. 116 A is incised on top of the base:

No. 116 B is incised on the underside with a letter F.

Biscuit of Vincennes-Sèvres, dating from the third quarter of the eighteenth century.

Wilfred J. Sainsbury in *Antiques*, January 1956, affirms that La Bergère Assise represents Mme Marie-Justine-Benoîte Favart (1727–1772), a leading comedienne, in a scene from a popular play. The Rue Favart beside the Comédie Française is named after her playwright husband. Models for this statuette and Le Porteur de Mouton were made for Mme de Pompadour's dairy at the Château de Crécy, a predecessor of the more famous one associated with Marie-Antoinette at Versailles.

The authorship of these figures remains to be established. According to Bourgeois and Lechevallier-Chevignard (*Le Biscuit de Sèvres*, nos. 111

and 510), both models were created by Jean-Baptiste de Fernex (working at Vincennes about 1753–1756), after drawings by Boucher.

The incised letter F of the shepherdess would seem to confirm this view, as Chavagnac and Grollier (*Histoire des Manufactures Françaises de Porcelaine*, p. 323) indicate the use of an incised letter F as the probable mark of this artist. There is also the possibility that the F is the mark of Falconet.

Little is recorded concerning Fernex; even the correct orthography of his name is uncertain. He signed himself, or was referred to, variously as De Fernex, Defernex, or simply Fernex (see Réau, *Gazette des Beaux-Arts*, LXXIII, 1931, pp. 349–365). In the few years just before Falconet's appointment to Sèvres, Fernex preceded him as head of the sculpture workshop. In 1754 and 1755, he was responsible for figures executed "d'après les dessins de Boucher." After the advent of Falconet in 1757, his name is no longer found among the modelers working at the factory.

No. 116 A, however, carries a florid letter B. This mark is a disputed one, sometimes given to Bachelier (working 1751–1793), Bourdois (working 1773–1774), or one of the three Brachards (Nicolas, working 1754–1809; Jean-Charles-Nicolas, working 1782–1824; and Jean-Nicolas-Alexandre, working 1784–1827). The character of the writing, however, corresponds more closely to that of one of the two Bougons whose signatures appear in the payroll records of Sèvres during the period 1763–1767.

Stylistically, Nos. 116 A and B do not appear to be the work of the same hand. The marks support

[285]

the impression that the shepherdess is from the early series by Fernex, while the shepherd is later.

Yet another sculptor of shepherdess figures is Depierreux, whose work during 1746–1748 is reflected in the sales record of Vincennes for August 27, 1754, folio 54:

1 Bergére de Depiéreux. . . . 9.

117 A, B Pair of Groups: La Lanterne Magique, and La Marchande de Plaisirs

117 A: H. 6⅛ (15.6); W. 6½ (16.5); D. 5 (12.7).

117 B: H. 6 (15.3); W. 5½ (12.8); D. 5 (12.7).

In La Lanterne Magique (No. 117 A), also known as La Curiosité, a young girl is stooping over a basket of food to peer into a box operated by a small boy whose right arm rests on the top of the apparatus. Beside the girl stands an infant boy eagerly awaiting his turn. The figures stand on a low plinth simulating ledges of rock.

The companion group (No. 117 B), known alternatively as Le Tourniquet, consists of three children (a girl and two boys) gathered about a drum-shaped wheel of chance. The girl seems to be spinning the pointer, while the boys look on eagerly with raised hands. The rockwork plinth is enlivened with a seated dog, a staff, and a basket of fruit.

No. 117 B is incised, behind the foot of the boy at rear: **F**

presumably for the sculptor. No. 117 A is unmarked.

Biscuit of Sèvres; models created in 1757 by Étienne-Maurice Falconet (working at Sèvres 1757–1766).

Both groups are represented at The Metro-politan Museum of Art, New York (acc. no. 58.60.10–11); the Schreiber Collection in the Victoria and Albert Museum, London (Rackham, *Catalogue of the Schreiber Collection*, I, no. 822); also at the Musée National de Céramique, Sèvres, where alternate names, apparently used in the archives of the factory (see below), are employed on the labels. An example of No. 117 B is in the State Hermitage Museum, Leningrad (illustrated in Birioukova, *Figurines et Groupes en Porcelaine des manufactures françaises du XVIIIᵉ siècle*, pl. 36).

The following entries appear in the sales records of the factory: for December 24, 1757, folio 45:

Groupe de la Curiosité — Biscuit. . . . 120.

for July 1–January 1, 1758, folio 53:

3 Groupes de la Curiosité . . . Ide [Biscuit]. . . . 120. . . . 360.

for January 1–July 1, 1758, folio 66:

5 Ide [Groupes] de Curiosité et Lotterie Ide [Biscuit]. . . . 120 . . . . 600.

for December 26, 1758, folio 75 verso:

3 Groupes de Lotterie Et Curiositée Biscuit. . . . 120 . . . 360.

118 Statuette: L'Amour Menaçant

Figure: H. 9¼ (23.5); W. 7½ (19.0); D. 4⅜ (11.1).

Stand: H. 3 (7.7); Diam. 6⅝ (16.8).

THE NUDE winged figure is seated upon a cloud, with a spray of flowers at his feet to the left. He raises his right forefinger to his chin, and with his left hand extracts an arrow from a quiver, partially concealed within the cloud. His short wings appear poised for flight. The disc base fits into a molded circular stand resting on three paneled supports.

Both figure and stand are unmarked.

Biscuit of Sèvres; model created in 1758 after the marble version of Cupid by Étienne-Maurice Falconet (working at Sèvres 1757–1766).

The plaster original is in the Musée National de Céramique, Sèvres. For examples of both Cupid and Psyche in other collections, see under Nos. 119 A and B.

A *biscuit* figure of Cupid on a *bleu de roi* plinth from the collection of Mrs. Henry Walters was sold at Parke-Bernet, New York, April 30–May 3, 1941, lot 1352 (illustrated in catalogue).

The Sèvres sales records indicate that such a figure was sold to Mme de Pompadour on December 30, 1758 (folio 78):

1 Amour.... Biscuit.... 144.

Two others appear for April 1761 (folios 48 and 49):

1 Amor *Biscuit*.... 96
4 Amor.... 96.... 384.

In a letter to the Direction des Bâtiments, dated October 15, 1755, the sculptor Falconet requested a block of marble from which to carve the figure L'Amour, which had been commissioned by Mme de Pompadour. Two years later the finished work was exhibited at the Salon.

The original marble was installed by Mme de Pompadour at her Paris residence, the Hôtel d'Évreux, today the Élysée Palace; it is now at the Louvre. A terracotta version, presumed to have belonged to her, appeared among the effects of her brother and heir, the Marquis de Ménars. Item no. 206 of his sale of 1785 was "L'Amour assis sur un nuage, portant le doigt sur sa bouche pour imposer le silence, en terre cuite, par M. Falconet; de 8 pouces de haut. . . ."

So great was the success of L'Amour that the figure soon became available in other media. A surprising number of reproductions appeared in marble, bronze, lead, glazed pottery, and biscuit porcelain, only a few of which can have been by Falconet himself. It appears in several contemporary paintings, most notably in Fragonard's well-known Hazards Heureux de l'Escarpolette (Wallace Collection, *Catalogue of Oil Paintings and Water Colours*, no. P 430).

Louis Réau in his *Étienne-Maurice Falconet* (I, pp. 183–191), from which the above notes are taken, calls attention to the provocative ambiguity in the pose of this Amour, which, unlike earlier ones by Bouchardon and Saly, is a seated figure. The viewer may well ask which theme is uppermost—Silence, as indicated by the fingers to the lips, or Mistrust, as suggested by the hand reaching for a quiver. The dual interpretation has led to a variety of alternate names for the sculpture, including Soyez Discret and Garde à Vous.

119 A, B Pair of Statuettes, Mounted in Gilt Bronze:
L'Amour Menaçant and La Nymphe Falconet

119 A: (overall) H. 15¼ (38.7).
 (porcelain) H. 9¼ (23.5); W. 5 (12.7);
 D. 5⅝ (14.4).

119 B: (overall) H. 15⅛ (38.4).
 (porcelain) H. 9⅛ (23.2); W. 5 (12.7);
 D. 8 (20.4).

LA Nymphe Falconet (No. 119 A), usually called Psyche, is a smiling nude figure seated upon a rock with her legs crossed at the ankles. Her hair is tied in a bun. At her right side she conceals a bow, which she clasps with both hands. A few tufts of grass spring from the circular plinth. Each figure is fixed to a chased and gilt-bronze pedestal of drum shape, modeled with four panels of single rosettes in relief, and four inverted consoles linked by crossed laurel branches, all supported by a plain cruciform plinth.

For a description of L'Amour Menaçant (No. 119 B), also known as Cupid, see No. 118, which is an identical figure.

The mounts may conceal marks.

Biscuit of Sèvres; models created in 1758 (No. 119 B) and 1761 (No. 119 A) by Étienne-Maurice Falconet (working at Sèvres 1757–1766). The mounts date from about 1775.

The plaster originals are in the Musée National de Céramique, Sèvres.

The figures are also represented at the British Museum, The Metropolitan Museum of Art, New York (acc. no. 45.60.1–2), the State Hermitage Museum, Leningrad (illustrated in Birioukova, *Figurines et Groupes en Porcelaine des manufactures françaises du XVIIIe siècle*, pls. 41, 42), the Jones Collection in the Victoria and Albert Museum (*Catalogue*, II, no. 139, 139 A, pl. 17), and the

Wallace Collection, London (*Provisional Catalogue*, 1902, nos. XIX-2, 10, 18). In each instance, they are fitted with plinths of glazed and decorated Sèvres porcelain.

A pair in bronze with mounts in the form of candelabra from the collection of Grigoril Stroganov, Leningrad, was sold at R. Lepke, Berlin, May 12–13, 1931, lots 156, 157 (illustrated in catalogue). Another pair mounted on porcelain stands, from the collection of Grace Rainey Rogers, was sold at Parke-Bernet, New York, November 18–20, 1943, lot 346 (illustrated in catalogue). Others were sold from the collections of Mrs. H. Dupuy, Parke-Bernet, New York, April 2–3, 1948, lots 389, 390 (illustrated in catalogue); Chester Beatty, Sotheby's, London, November 15, 1955, lot 123 (illustrated in catalogue), and René Fribourg, Sotheby's, London, June 25, 1963, lot 64 (illustrated in catalogue).

For further comments on the Cupid, see under No. 118. The figure of Psyche was made later to complement it, and appears to be first documented as a plaster cast in the catalogue of the Salon of 1761. Possibly the porcelain version was not exhibited there, at least not until later, for Gabriel de Saint-Aubin refers to it in a copy of the Salon catalogue with notes and marginal drawings preserved at the Bibliothèque Nationale as "non veue au Sallon mais executée a Seve."

See also Volume II of this catalogue, Nos. 274 A and B.

120 A, B Pair of Statuettes: Les Petits Vendangeurs

120 A: H. 6 (15.3); W. 4 (10.2); D. 2¾ (7.0).

120 B: H. 5⅝ (14.4); W. 4⅜ (11.1); D. 3 (7.7).

No. 120 A is a standing figure of a barefooted girl wearing a fringed kerchief on her head and a tucked-up overskirt. She clasps a basket of grapes with both hands, as she leans, her left foot thrust forward, against a tree stump. Her companion (No. 120 B) is a well-dressed boy with broad-brimmed felt hat and a *jabot*. In his right hand he holds a tilted cup and in his left a wine flask. He rests his right elbow upon a basket of grapes sup-ported upon a tree stump. The rockwork base of each is flat and of irregular shape.

No. 120 A is incised on the underside: *F*

apparently for the sculptor. No. 120 B is unmarked.

Biscuit of Sèvres; models created in 1757 by Étienne-Maurice Falconet (working at Sèvres 1757–1766) after a drawing by François Boucher. Nos. 120 A and B were probably cast about 1760.

121 Group: Enfants Buvant du Lait

H. 7⅛ (18.1); W. 5½ (14.1); D. 3⅞ (9.8).

THE GROUP consists of two small boys, one raising a bowl to his lips, the other striving to gain his attention. The larger boy, with slashed jacket, is seated upon a rock flanked by a basket of fruit and a game basket, containing a rabbit. The younger child, on tiptoe, leans on the arm of the other, causing the milk to spill. The rockwork base is flat and of irregular shape.

Incised on the top of the base:

Biscuit of Sèvres; the model created in 1759 by Étienne-Maurice Falconet (working at Sèvres 1757–1766). It was inspired by a Boucher drawing or an engraving by Jean Daullé (1703–1763) after Boucher.

For a note on this mark, see under Nos. 116 A and B.

The model was represented until recently in the collection of Wilfred J. Sainsbury, London. It is described and illustrated in *Antiques*, December 1965, p. 824, fig. 11.

122 Statuette

H. 11½ (29.1); Diam. of base. 4⅝ (11.7).

THE STANDING figure of a young woman is clothed in Grecian draperies, which have slipped from her right shoulder. In her arms she holds a bouquet of flowers and two billing doves, upon which she fixes her gaze. At the right, a draped tree stump with a cluster of cut flowers at its base supports the figure.

Incised at the back of the tree trunk:

Biscuit of Sèvres.

For a note on this mark, see under Nos. 116 A and B.

The stance of No. 122 is similar to that of the figures of Flora and Hebe modeled by Falconet between 1761 and 1767.

123 A, B Pair of Jars

(pots à pommade)

H. 5⅛ (13.0); Diam. 3¾ (9.5).

EACH jar has cylindrical walls and low domed lids, ornamented in relief with sprays of plum blossoms, in the manner of the Fukien *blanc de chine*. The porcelain is creamy white, with a delicate green translucency. It is coated with a transparent lead glaze.

Unmarked.

Saint-Cloud, dating from about 1725.

Similar jars were made, apparently for toilet use, at Mennecy at about the middle of the century. A pair from the collection of Wright E. Post and Edward C. Post is at The Metropolitan Museum of Art, New York (acc. no. 30.58.10–11).

124 Pomegranate, Mounted in Gilt Bronze as a Perfume Burner

(brûle-parfum)

Overall: H. 5⅞ (15.0); L. 10⅝₆ (26.2); D. 7⅛ (18.1).

Porcelain: H. 5 (12.7); W. 7 (17.8); D. 4 (10.2).

THE PERFUME burner is in the form of a pomegranate leaning against two gnarled, bent, and foliated tree stumps of aubergine color. The fruit is partially peeled to reveal a cluster of iron-red seeds within the yellow rind mottled with blue and green. It springs from a turquoise-blue stem with matching leaves. The truncated shoulder is pierced with four round openings, lined with metal ferrules and surmounted by a bronze mount in the form of a basin containing porcelain blossoms. The rustic plinth is roughly rectangular, and is tinted with variegated green, yellow, and blue glaze. The porcelain rests upon an elevated platform of tooled and gilded bronze, forming a narrow frame of curling foliage supported on a series of rococo scrolls.

Unmarked.

Chantilly, dating from about 1735; the mounts date from about 1740–1750, except for the collar, which appears to date from the early nineteenth century.

EXHIBITED: Antique Porcelain Company, London, *English and Continental Porcelain of the 18th Century*, 1951.

Formerly in the collection of Louis-Philippe-Robert, Duc d'Orléans.

Pomegranates and melons on rockwork bases exist in other contemporary French soft pastes. Examples of Chantilly are represented at the Musée Condé, Chantilly, and of Mennecy in the collection of Mrs. Morris Hawkes at the Philadelphia Museum of Art. Others, from St. Cloud, are at The Metropolitan Museum of Art, New York (acc. nos. 94.4.152–153); the Musée des Arts Décoratifs, Paris; and the Victoria and Albert Museum, London (acc. nos. c348–1909 and c456–1909).

A comparable model in Chantilly porcelain from the collection of Frédéric Halinbourg, Paris, was sold at the Hôtel Drouot, Paris, May 22–23, 1913, lot 128 (illustrated in catalogue, p. 50 *bis*). It was described as a "brûle-parfum, en forme de grenade."

See also Volume II of this catalogue, No. 265.

125 A, B Pair of Warblers, Mounted in Gilt Bronze as Candelabra

(girandoles)

Overall: H. 6¼ (15.9); W. 7⅝ (19.4);
D. 4⅝ (11.7).

Porcelain: H. 4⅛ (11.0); W. 3¾ (9.5);
D. 1½ (3.8).

EACH bird is modeled with the head sharply turned, its plumage delicately patterned brown and black, and the pale green and yellow head sharply marked with a black streak behind the eye. The legs straddle a low gnarled tree stump painted with irregular patches of pale green. Behind each bird rise two gilt-bronze branches with oak leaves of painted metal interspersed with delicate porcelain flowers, harmonizing in color with the corolla of porcelain petals at the base of each candle socket. These porcelain accessories are in the same colors as the plumage of the birds, but with additional touches of red and blue. Each porcelain figure is supported upon an arched stand of chased and gilded bronze in a design of tumbled rococo scrolls interspersed with floral sprays.

Marks not visible.

Mennecy, dating from about 1740–1745; the mounts date from about 1750.

See also Volume II of this catalogue, Nos. 262 A and B.

[301]

126   Chinese Figure, Mounted in Gilt Bronze as a Candelabrum

(girandole)

Overall: H. 8%₁₆ (21.7); W. 8½ (21.6); D. 6¼ (15.9).

Porcelain: H. 3½ (8.9); W. 2⅝ (6.7); D. 3⅛ (8.0).

THE FIGURE is a smiling, stocky boy *magot*, seated in a relaxed pose with his head thrown back, his arms in a conversational attitude, and his knees parted. The thumbs and forefingers are flexed to permit the figure to grasp a small object (now missing) in each hand. The boy wears a white jacket patterned with blue cornucopias from which emerge yellow and blue asters. His turquoise-blue pantaloons are dotted with maroon "snowflake" motifs. Iron-red slippers complete the costume. Behind the figure a low shrub of gilt bronze, supporting delicately tinted porcelain anemones and peonies, springs from an arched support composed of rococo scrolls and foliations forming a tripod.

Unmarked.

An imitation of indeterminate date of Mennecy of 1740–1750; the mounts date in part from about 1750.

See also Volume II of this catalogue, No. 259. The change of attribution was made subsequent to the publication of Volume II.

127 A, B Pair of Chinese Figures, Mounted in Gilt Bronze as Candelabra

(girandoles)

127 A: (overall) H. 6¼ (15.9); W. 7¼ (18.4);
      D. 4⅞ (12.3).
      (porcelain) H. 4¼ (10.8); W. 3⅛ (8.0);
      D. 3 (7.8).

127 B: (overall) H. 6¼ (15.9); W. 7¼ (18.4);
      D. 4⅞ (12.3).
      (porcelain) H. 4¼ (10.8); W. 3 (7.6);
      D. 3⅜ (8.6).

EACH Chinese boy has an upturned, smiling face, the lips parted as if in song, and long ear lobes. Nos. 127 A and B are seated in almost identical poses, their knees flexed and wide apart. Each wears a close-fitting garment with rolled collar, long sleeves, and long pantaloons, the upper portion painted with maroon dragons, the knees with yellow roundels bordered with turquoise and enclosing dragon heads. Over this costume is a poncho-like cape of mottled pea-green, penciled in black with foliage and fruit. The hands of one of the figures have been replaced. Rising in front of each figure are the twin arms of the gilt-bronze candelabra, ornamented with porcelain blossoms, and springing from a gilt-bronze platform of irregular shape, elevated upon several scrolling and branching supports of rococo design.

Marks not visible.

Mennecy, dating from about 1740–1750; the mounts date from about 1750.

The figures derive from prototypes of Chinese blue and white porcelain, examples of which are in the collections of the Bayerisches Nationalmuseum and the Residenz, both in Munich.

A rather similar pair of candelabra, in which one of the figures is female, was in the collection of J. Pierpont Morgan, New York (see *Catalogue des Porcelaines Françaises de M. J. Pierpont Morgan*, ed. Chavagnac, no. 33, pl. VIII, for one illustrated in color). This pair was sold at Parke-Bernet, New York, January 6–8, 1944, lot 491 (illustrated in catalogue).

For comparable examples in this collection, see Nos. 128 A and B.

See also Volume II of this catalogue, Nos. 260 A and B.

128 A, B Pair of Chinese Figures, Mounted in Gilt Bronze as Candelabra

(girandoles)

128 A: (overall) H. 9 (22.9); W. 10 (25.4);
   D. 5⅝ (14.3).
   (porcelain) H. 4½ (11.4); W. 2¹⁵⁄₁₆ (7.5);
   D. 2⅝ (6.6).

128 B: (overall) H. 9 (22.9); W. 10 (25.4);
   D. 5⅝ (14.3).
   (porcelain) H. 4⁷⁄₁₆ (11.2); W. 2¹³⁄₁₆ (7.2);
   D. 2⅞ (7.4).

OF THE same type as Nos. 127 A and B, each seated figure of a *magot* is dressed in a close-fitting white costume painted with scattered floral motifs of blue, turquoise, yellow, and iron-red. No. 128 A differs from its companion in wearing an imperial yellow surplice painted with foliage, while No. 128 B wears an oval "bib" of clay yellow with a red floral design. In addition, No. 128 A smiles broadly and holds a small round object (a peach?) in his right hand. Behind each figure is a branching shrub of painted metal, bearing tinted porcelain blossoms and iridescent wine-red fruit; the side branches support candle sockets and drip pans of gilt bronze. Each figure rests upon a spreading elevated base of chased and gilded bronze formed of rococo scrolls and foliage.

Marks not visible.

Mennecy, dating from about 1740–1750; the mounts date from about 1750.

A Mennecy figure of similar though not identical type and pose (height 4½ inches) from the collection of Mrs. Basil Ionides, Buxted Park, was sold at Sotheby's, London, April 21, 1964, lot 13 (illustrated in catalogue).

For comparable examples in this collection, see Nos. 127 A and B. See also Volume II of this catalogue, Nos. 261 A and B.

129 Three Porcelains, Mounted in Gilt Bronze as an Inkstand

(encrier)

Overall: H. 6¹¹⁄₁₆ (17.0); W. 13¹¹⁄₁₆ (34.7); D. 6¾ (17.2).

Figure: H. 3⅜ (8.6); W. 2⅜ (6.0); D. 2½ (6.4).

Inkwells: H. 1⅝ (4.2); Diam. 3 (7.7).

A CENTRAL figure of an acolyte is flanked by a pair of apple-shaped inkwells, all three being raised prominently upon a gilt-bronze stand of *rocaille* design. The figure is seated upon a mound of mottled turquoise-blue rockwork, and wears a white robe decorated with bold enamel colors with clusters of iron-red and yellow blossoms and turquoise-blue foliage emerging from cobalt-blue cornucopias. He clasps with both hands a double strand of cord attached to a pair of slippers and slung over his right shoulder.

The inkwells are encrusted with sprigs of small red and yellow blossoms resembling convolvulus and trumpet blossoms on scrolling umber stems with pale green curling leaves. The elaborate mount of chased and gilded bronze is of rococo outline, and molded to form three pedestals, the highest of which encloses the inkwell. The surface is ornamented with scrolling acanthus and shell forms framing an asymmetrical panel of scale pattern at either end.

Marks not visible.

Mennecy, the figure dating from about 1740–1750, the bowls from about 1745–1750; the mounts date from about 1750.

Formerly in the collection of Baroness Renée de Becker, New York.

The male figure here corresponds closely in pose to the female of a pair of Mennecy figures in the collection of Margaret Gould, illustrated in Alfassa and Guérin, *Porcelaine Française*, pl. 74 a. The latter figure shows variations in the painting of the hair and costume, and carries a rabbit slung over her right shoulder.

Two Mennecy figures of a slightly variant form and pose (heights 3½ and 3⅝ inches) from the collection of Mrs. Basil Ionides, Buxted Park, were sold at Sotheby's, London, April 21, 1964, lots 11 and 12 (illustrated in catalogue).

See also Volume II of this catalogue, No. 264.

CHELSEA AND OTHER
ENGLISH PORCELAIN

INTRODUCTION

Unlike Germany and France, England had ready access to porcelain on so large a scale that the urge to manufacture her own developed only relatively late. For everyday use, the East India Company imported about a quarter of a million pieces of Chinese hard-paste tablewares a season, and in the mid-century years, just as the English factories were getting on their feet, the average was close to 500,000.[1] The attraction of this trade was that individual decoration could be commissioned and that the prices were astonishingly low, the Company paying only £1,145, for example, for over 108,000 pieces in 1755.[2] The disadvantages of the system were the occasionally inferior quality of the ware, the lapse of time (sometimes two years) between order and delivery, and the all-too-real danger of loss in transit. For its luxury trade England began importing Meissen porcelain in quantity in the 1740s. Displaying, in its accomplished variety, a whole new approach to porcelain, Meissen was held in something of the same awe Chinese porcelain had inspired a century earlier. The Duchess of Dorset, attending the Princess Mary on her marriage in 1740 to the Landgrave Frederick of Hesse Cassel, received "a set of Dresden china . . . a set of Dresden teacups, and a service of Dresden China"[3] as gifts clearly equivalent in value to the more obvious gold plate and jewelry received on the same occasion.

With these two resources at hand, England delayed rather longer than her Continental neighbors in developing a domestic porcelain manufacture. Some attempts, to be sure, had been made as early as the seventeenth century: John Dwight of Fulham (about 1637–1703) obtained a patent in 1671 for his discovery of "the misterie and invencon of making transparent earthen ware," a process that resulted in a kind of near-white stoneware of some transparency. More elusive is the claim in 1699 of a Mr. Pattenden of Bristol who "hath found out a most curious Art of making Artificial China-Ware, which comes so near the real China that there can be no Distinction between them . . . it being both Beautiful and Serviceable, and far beyond anything of white Japan."[4] The results of these tentative efforts were so

1. These figures represent only the official trade, the captains of the Company ships being permitted to import porcelain on their own account. This was not an inconsiderable addition to the volume: in 1759, for example, two captains brought home an estimated 55,000 pieces over and above the Company's 250,000 (Morse, *Chronicles of the East India Company Trading to China 1635–1834*, I, pp. 229, 282, 292).

2. These figures have been extrapolated from the descriptive inventory in Morse, *op. cit.*, V, pp. 34–35.

3. Undated letter of Mrs. Elizabeth Montagu (*Correspondence*, ed. Climenson, I, p. 53).

4. Advertisement in *The Post Boy*, April 25, 1699, transcribed by Scott, *Extracts* [from the Burney Collection in the British Museum] *from notices which appeared in London newspapers referring to objects of fine and decorative art 17th & 18th centuries*, vol. I.

inadequate that without energetic support it was impossible that they should succeed. And this support was lacking. The royal patronage that encouraged and established the Meissen and Sèvres factories and imbued them with their aristocratic style was not matched in England, where porcelain manufacture had to wait for the private businessman. It was not until the middle of the eighteenth century that a number of competitive factories sprang up more or less simultaneously. The earliest of these to be recorded is that at Bow. In 1744 a patent was granted to Edward Heylyn (1695–after 1758) and Thomas Frye (1710–1762), an Irish portrait painter, for the purpose of "manufacturing a certain material whereby a ware might be made of some nature or kind, and equal to, if not exceeding in goodness and beauty, China or Porcelain ware imported from abroad." One ingredient of this material was a china clay, "unaker," found in "the back of Virginia" and brought to London in 1743 by one Andrew Duché (1710–1778), who subsequently bought the land where it had been discovered.[5] The availability at low cost of this clay unquestionably provided the clue to Bow's early economic stability. While 1750 marks the year of the earliest dated pieces from the factory, "large quantities of Tea-cups, saucers, etc." were, according to Daniel Defoe,[6] being made there by June 1748. Under the energetic direction of Alderman George Arnold (1691–1751) and Frye the factory continued successfully until Frye's death in 1762, when it began to decline, being finally acquired in 1776 by the enameler-turned-proprietor William Duesbury (1725–1786).

About the time of the founding of Bow, the Huguenot émigré Nicholas Sprimont (1716–1771) was turning from a career as a silversmith[7] to porcelain manufacture at Chelsea. The origin of his involvement in the Chelsea China Works remains obscure; it appears, however, that he obtained the financial support of Charles Gouyn (before 1737–1782)—a Huguenot refugee like himself and a jeweler by profession— on the strength of a soft-paste porcelain developed by one Thomas Briand. "Mr. Bryand, a Stranger," exhibited "a sort of fine Ware made by himself from native materials of our own Country" to members of the Royal Society on February 10, 1742/43, and from the sequence of events there is some reason to identify Briand with Sprimont's "casual acquaintance . . . a chymist who had some knowledge this way."[8] The earliest dated wares of the factory are three "goat-and-bee" jugs dated 1745, but as Sprimont's connection with Chelsea before 1747 is not certain, his influence on the silver-oriented pieces can

5. Duché began as a potter from Savannah and died a rich gentleman in Philadelphia. His wealth is presumed to have come from his dealings with the Bow factory. The "unaker" which he discovered—and the name of which has never been satisfactorily explained—was to figure again in English ceramics, some quantities being imported about 1768 for Josiah Wedgwood's use in developing his jasper ware. The site of the pit where the clay was found, near what is now Franklin, North Carolina, was honored by an historic marker in 1950.

6. Defoe, *A Tour thro' the Whole Island of Great Britain*, 4th ed., I, p. 2.

7. He registered his mark at Goldsmiths' Hall on January 25, 1742; his recorded work in English silver spans the years 1743–1746.

8. "The Case of the Undertaker of the Chelsea Manufacture of Porcelain Ware," written by Sprimont between 1752 and 1759. Reprinted in Jewitt, *The Ceramic Art of Great Britain*, I, pp. 171–172.

only be surmised.[9] With the exception of an interlude of two years (1757–1759) owing to Sprimont's ill health, the factory was productive under his direct management until 1762, when he moved to Richmond. He finally sold the factory in 1769. After a brief ownership by the jeweler and entrepreneur James Cox (before 1747–1791/92) it was acquired in 1770 by William Duesbury and in 1784 subsumed in the latter's factory at Derby.

In March 1749 Benjamin Lund received a license to quarry in Cornwall for soapstone with which to make porcelain at his factory at Bristol. His enterprise was short-lived, being bought out only three years later by the Worcester Porcelain Company (formed June 4, 1751) under the direction of Richard Holdship, with such democratic financial backing as that of John Wall (1708–1776), a Worcester physician; Edward Cave, the London publisher of the *Gentleman's Magazine*; William Davis, an apothecary; and Samuel Bradley, a goldsmith. The most durable of the English porcelain factories, Worcester remains—after a sequence of corporate recastings—in active production today, but its most creative period may be said to have ended in 1783 with the death of William Davis and the sale of the original company to Thomas Flight.

Dating from about the same year as the Bristol factory was an establishment at Longton Hall in Staffordshire, founded by William Jenkinson (died 1771), who "had obtained the art secret or mystery of making a certain porcelain ware in imitation of china ware." Withdrawing from the venture in 1753, Jenkinson left it in the hands of William Nicklin (born 1742), William Littler (1724–1784), and Nathaniel Firmin. Firmin's shares in the partnership were, upon his death the following year, transferred to his son Samuel (died 1796). Despite considerable financial support from a Yorkshire clergyman, the Rev. Robert Charlesworth (about 1717–1786), the proprietors were never able to get on a solid footing, and their partnership was abruptly dissolved by their exasperated patron on June 9, 1760.

The last factory to be set up in this extraordinarily creative burst of only seven years from 1744 to 1751—the very years that Sèvres was coming into existence—was that at Derby, where porcelain was being made at least by 1750, although it was not until January 1, 1756, that John Heath, a local potter and banker, the jeweler Andrew Planché (1728–after 1751), and William Duesbury agreed to establish the factory on a formal basis. It flourished independently until Duesbury's purchase of the Chelsea works in 1770, and survived until 1848. In view of the focus of the present collection, however, there is no need to carry its history further than the onset of the Chelsea-Derby period. Indeed, it is in the first twenty years of England's venture in the manufacture of porcelain—the years that saw the birth of the examples catalogued in the following pages—that one may observe her most vigorous and characteristic achievement in this vein.

9. A goat-and-bee jug dated 1743 has been recorded by Mackenna (*Apollo*, XL, 1944, pp. 136–137). In considering the early date of these jugs in relation to their considerable technical competence, Lord Fisher (*Apollo*, XL, 1944, pp. 138–139) raises the intriguing possibility that they were not made at the fledgling Chelsea factory but elsewhere in Chelsea by Thomas Briand. The model for the jugs has been inconclusively ascribed both to a silver version of 1737 by Edward Wood (working 1735?–1752) and to an alleged one by Sprimont himself.

Since these factories were commercial enterprises unsupported by state or royal patronage, it was their necessary—and in most cases explicit—intention to capitalize on the existing market for porcelains imported from Canton and Meissen. Bow deliberately set out to make "a more ordinary sort of ware for common uses" with which to draw off the China-trade competition; it was certainly no coincidence that three enameled inkwells dated 1750 were also inscribed "Made at New Canton," or that the plan of the factory building itself, according to later testimony by one of the factory painters, was "taken from that at Canton in China." Bow's early success is indicated clearly enough in Mrs. Elizabeth Montagu's suggestion in 1750 that a friend of limited means might furnish a house "in the present fashion, of some cheap paper and ornaments of Chelsea China or the manufacture of Bow."[10] But with little hope of matching this competition in either price or volume most factories chose to cater to the Meissen-oriented luxury trade. The proprietors of Derby repeatedly declared their wares to be "after the finest Dresden Models" and proudly advertised (*Public Advertiser*, May 17, 1757) "the great Perfection the Derby Figures . . . are arrived to, that many good Judges could not distinguish them from the real Dresden." And in 1762 the then bankrupt Richard Holdship asserted that his factory at Worcester had been "set up and established . . . in Imitation of Dresden Ware." The principal result of this orientation was an emphasis on ornamental and figural wares in which Chelsea was predominant, producing a wealth of decorative tablewares and figures that were freely imitated by the other factories. By January 9, 1750, Sprimont was advertising "a Variety of Services for Tea, Coffee, Chocolate, Porringers, Sauce-Boats, Basons, and Ewers, Ice-Pails, Terreens, Dishes and Plates, of different Forms and Patterns, and . . . a great Variety of Pieces for Ornament in a Taste entirely new." Possibly included in this last phrase were figures that were being made at Chelsea by this year and that, like many of the tablewares, were chiefly inspired by German prototypes. The indebtedness of the English factories to Meissen in the early years of their existence was profound, involving not merely imitation but a thoroughgoing absorption of the Meissen style of painting and modeling. Of straightforward copying there was a good deal, especially of figures, which were Meissen's most influential contribution to the art of porcelain. Chelsea raised anchor and red anchor versions of Italian Comedy characters, of the well-known Monkey Orchestra, of the Continents, of the Tyrolean Dancers—to mention a few—were direct copies of Meissen models.[11] One historian[12] has gone so far as to assert that direct copying was so widespread that "without definite proof it would be unsafe" to describe any English figures dating after the middle of the century as composed without reference to a Meissen original. Just the same, Chelsea is known to have drawn on the plates of George Edwards (born 1694), published in 1743 in his *Natural History of Uncommon Birds*, for some twenty models of exotic birds, while other subjects were copied from such varied sources as Francis

10. Letter to her sister Sarah, January 3, 1750 (*Correspondence, op. cit.*, I, p. 271). Mrs. Montagu's implication that the cost of Chelsea and Bow porcelains was comparable is surprising, since from the evidence it would appear rather that they were at opposite ends of the price scale.

11. A comprehensive survey of the subject is Arthur Lane's *English Porcelain Figures of the Eighteenth Century*.

12. Lane, *op. cit.*, p. 44.

Barlow's engraved illustrations for Aesop's *Fables*, and engravings after Boucher by Simon-François Ravenet (1706–1774). Several of the figures modeled at Chelsea by Joseph Willems (working about 1749–1763, died 1766) are also considered to have been original compositions.

In the Meissen tradition, but unexpectedly independent of Meissen designs, were the scent bottles and etuis once familiarly grouped together under the name of "Chelsea toys." It is now apparent that these were first made in England not by Sprimont but at an independent factory at Chelsea. The existence —long suspected on the strength of stylistic and chemical analysis—of this rival establishment has since 1960 been unequivocally established by the researches of R. J. Charleston and the late Arthur Lane.[13] Named for a figural group in the Victoria and Albert Museum, the "Girl-in-a-Swing" factory apparently came into being through a group of dissident workmen whom Sprimont had brought down from Staffordshire. Alert to the new demand for porcelain and supported, according to the evidence, by Gouyn (who in 1751 was described as "late Proprietor and Chief Manager" of Sprimont's works), they set themselves up at a still unidentified site in Chelsea. The decision to produce so sophisticated a line of wares as *galanteriewaren* was presumably not made by the group of locally trained Midlands potters, but by someone at ease in the Continental tradition of their manufacture and use. Such a person was Gouyn who, as Messrs Lane and Charleston pointed out, was a jeweler and would therefore have been attracted to this type of ware requiring metal mounts (and it has been observed[14] that the quality of the gold mounts of the Girl-in-a-Swing scent bottles is very good). The "Girl-in-a-Swing" factory was in operation from some time in 1751 until the autumn of 1754. Thirty models, considered by the authors to be the work of a single modeler, have been attributed by Lane and Charleston to this factory; others, like Nos. 130, 131 in this catalogue, are added from time to time. More problematical is the attribution of other examples (e.g., Catalogue Nos. 132, 133), which, although versions of models considered by Lane and Charleston to have originated at the "Girl-in-a-Swing" factory, are rather different in treatment and coloring. In a recent opinion by Kate Foster[15] this second group of toys, which Miss Foster designates Category II, represents still another manufacture, independent of both Gouyn and Sprimont. At the time of writing, the question of identification of the Girl-in-a-Swing modeler and the possibility of yet other rival factories are being actively explored.

The dissolution of the "Girl-in-a-Swing" factory had a considerable effect on the course of the Chelsea manufacture. In November 1754 Sprimont unexpectedly advertised the sale of "Snuff-boxes, Smelling Bottles, Etwees and Trinkets for Watches." Remarking that "Nothing of the above kind was in their former Sale," he appears to have bought up the stock and, upon discovering how profitable the market was, added the production of "toys" to his repertoire. A few of Sprimont's models, for example Catalogue No. 134 below, were variants of Girl-in-a-Swing examples, but a comparison of the master molds with Chelsea figures has revealed no use of the former by Sprimont.

13. Lane and Charleston, *The English Ceramic Circle, Transactions*, V, part 3, 1962, pp.111–144.
14. Foster, *Scent Bottles*, p. 63.
15. *Ibid.*, p. 67.

IN A PETITION to the government protesting the untaxed "introduction of immense quantities of Dresden porcelain," which he considered damaging to the prosperity of his own factory, Nicholas Sprimont complained that "a certain foreign minister's house has been, for a course of years, a warehouse for this commerce, and the large parcel, advertised for public sale on the seventh of next month, is come, or is to come, from thence."[16] This was, however true, rather ungrateful of Sprimont. The minister was Sir Charles Hanbury Williams, England's ambassador to Dresden, whose collection of Meissen was stored for the time being in the basement of Holland House. In 1751 Everard Fawkener, secretary to the Duke of Cumberland who was "a great encourager of the Chelsea China," approached Hanbury Williams who wrote that "He desired me to send over models for different Pieces from hence [Dresden]in order to furnish the undertakers with good designs. . . . But I thought it better and cheaper for the manufacturers to give them leave to take any of my China from Holland House and to copy what they like."[17] The precise extent to which Sprimont made use of this offer is not known, but a glance at the catalogue of Chelsea's sixteen-day sale of March 10–27, 1755, provides ample testimony—petition notwithstanding—of his dependence on Meissen, and probably on Hanbury Williams himself, for his designs. Directly traceable to Meissen originals are such items as "Two artichoaks FIRST SIZE for desart," "A most beautiful tureen, in the figure of a HEN and CHICKENS," and the numerous leaf and flower dishes that were copied both at Chelsea and elsewhere (cf. Catalogue Nos. 72, 146, 168). The same origin can probably be assumed for the "Two fine EELS as big as the life" of which Chelsea variations are Catalogue Nos. 157 and 158 below. It was in this type of work that the English factories were most successful in their transmutation of an alien style, adapting and enlarging the Meissen repertoire until it became their own. The bird figures, the fruit and vegetable forms, the leaf dishes exhibit an easy naturalism quite unlike the detached spirit of their German prototypes. This is in no small measure due to the material itself. Until 1768, when a hard-paste porcelain was patented by William Cookworthy,[18] all the factories were using one or more substitute formulae. Whether of the glassy frit (Chelsea), bone ash (Bow), or soapstone (Worcester) type, the resulting pastes were less stable and the glazes less white than the German and Oriental hard paste. It is precisely a slight creaminess of tone, a thicker potting and less edgy modeling, that give this genre of English porcelain its peculiar charm.

IN DECORATION as in modeling the English were responsive to outside influence. The impact on the Meissen and Sèvres factories of Oriental styles has already been touched on (pp. 10, 11, 160). It was no less profound in England, where they were disseminated both directly by the Oriental originals and indirectly

16. "The Case of the Undertaker . . ." (see note 8).

17. Letter of June 9, 1751, to Henry Fox. Printed in King, *Chelsea Porcelain*, p. 37.

18. Cookworthy (1705–1780), a Plymouth apothecary, had been on the track of hard-paste at least since 1745 when he wrote of having spoken with Duché. His patent for the "discovery of materials of the same nature as those of which Asiatic and Dresden porcelain are made" was granted March 17, 1768, but the cost of manufacture was prohibitive, and the attempt was abandoned in 1781.

by Continental transcriptions. An entry for 1756 in the memorandum book of John Bowcocke, manager of Bow's London warehouse, leaves no doubt as to the use of collectors' pieces:

> May 28. Patterns received from Lady Cavendish: a Japan octogon cup and saucer, lady pattern; a Japan bread and butter plate.[19]

It is probable, however, that the greater number of Oriental-inspired patterns were borrowed at second hand from European sources. In view of the similarities in composition between the English and French soft-paste formulae, it may be supposed that Chantilly and Saint-Cloud porcelains were known and imitated in England; such an influence is apparent particularly in the Chelsea pieces decorated in the manner of Fukien *blanc de chine*, with prunus branches in relief, in a style that seems more closely akin to the early French variations than to the more formal Meissen ones. But it was the Kakiemon style of painting as filtered through the Meissen workshops that was to figure so prominently in the early decoration of English porcelains. Examples of the "Fine old Partridge pattern" (two quail and a flowering prunus), the "Hob in the Well," and the "twisted dragon" and "tyger and rock" patterns described in the Chelsea catalogue of 1755 are closer to Meissen than to the Japanese originals of the same subjects from which Meissen took them. Popularized by Chelsea, they were widely copied by the painters at Bow, Derby, and Worcester. Kakiemon influence is apparent, too, in the polygonal vases and dishes of Chelsea and Bow whose decoration featured the crane or phoenix, peonies, prunus, and the like in the traditional palette of iron-red, turquoise, green, and gold. Little use was made in England of the chinoiserie subjects so favored at Meissen by J. G. Herold (e.g., Catalogue Nos. 57 A–D above); such scenes as that on Catalogue No. 175 below occur infrequently.

More original to English porcelain was the naturalistic bird and flower painting that evolved in part from similar work practiced at Meissen. Closely related to that factory's *Deutsche Blumen* were the botanical renderings on Chelsea tablewares of "India plants" (see Catalogue No. 152 below) and other plants, many of them copied from illustrations by Georg Dionysius Ehret (1708–1770). These appeared from 1755–1760 in *Figures of Plants* published by Philip Miller, gardener of the Chelsea Physic Garden which had been presented to the Apothecaries' Company by Sir Hans Sloane (a connection that led to the long-standing and erroneous identification of Ehret's work as "Sir Hans Sloane's plants").[20] Ehret also published, from 1748 to 1750, fifteen plates of *Plantae et Papiliones Rariories*, which were copied, both literally and with variations, by the Chelsea painters. Some botanical illustration was practiced at Bow and Derby, but the style was gradually modified and softened into the plump, unpretentious bouquets and sprays influenced as much, one suspects, by the Englishman's traditionally affectionate approach to gardening as by any other more formal stylistic source.[21]

---

19. Jewitt, *op. cit.*, I, p. 210.

20. For an elucidation of the problem see Synge-Hutchinson, *Connoisseur*, CXLII, 1958, pp. 88–94.

21. Nothing has been said in these pages of the influence of Sèvres, which was to supplant that of Meissen after that factory's eclipse by the Seven Years' War, but which is scarcely in evidence in the present collection.

THE MARKED affinities among the English porcelain factories—the freely exchanged models, the closely related decorative schemes—were not a result only of competitive practices. A certain number of pieces were decorated outside the factories by a few independent enamelers. Such a one was William Duesbury who, born in Staffordshire in 1725, was established in London as a china painter by 1751. In his account book for 1751–1753 are entries for such items as "1 pr of Chellsea Drooping B[ird]," "A Chellsea Nurs," "6 Bogh figars," "1 sett of Bogh sesons inhamilld," and "2 pr of Dansers Darby figars." Many other pieces, although unattributed in the entries, have been shown[22] to have come from these factories, as well as from Staffordshire and even Meissen ("Drisdon"). Part of Duesbury's success was due to the fact that few of the factories started out with complete staffs of skilled decorators. A consistency of style points to a resident painter at the elusive "Girl-in-a-Swing" factory, but as late as November 1753 Bow was still looking for painters to satisfy its needs, and the factory is thought to have depended rather heavily on Duesbury in its early years. The London workshop of James Giles (1718–1780) was the source of several genres of painting found on porcelains of the late 1760s and 1770s. Several of the artists in his atelier remain unidentified, being known by their specialties: "The Master of the Dishevelled Birds," "The Sliced Fruit Painter," the "Landscape Painter." Besides Giles, only Jeffryes Hamett O'Neale is known by name; his fable and animal subjects occur on Chelsea pieces of the red-anchor period (1752–1758), as well as on later pieces from Worcester and Bow. Sprimont's reliance on outside decorators is also apparent from the advertisement of the London enameler Thomas Hughes (1705–1763), who from 1755 to 1757 announced "Great choice of Chelsea china" for sale and "Superfine Chelsea flowers enamelled."[23] Of the decorators resident at the factories in the first twenty years of their existence, only a few names are recorded.[24] The ubiquitous William Duesbury gave up his London shop and moved to Longton Hall, where he worked from 1754 to 1756. Mentioned at the same factory in 1755 is a John Hyfield whose name is associated with romantic views of castles and ruins. At Worcester, James Rogers was responsible for some bird painting, and the name of the Bow painter Thomas Craft is known from a short account he wrote of that factory in 1790. But if the size of the Bow factory was representative—Craft stated there were three hundred workmen (not all painters, of course) employed during his service—it is likely that the names of the decorators are forever lost, and that such local characteristics and mannerisms as appear in their work will continue to be enjoyed for their own merit.

CARL CHRISTIAN DAUTERMAN
CLARE LE CORBEILLER

22. MacAlister, ed., *William Duesbury's London Account Book 1751–1753*, pp. XVI, XXI, 10, 11, 40, 41, 47.

23. Tapp, *English Ceramics Circle, Transactions*, II, no. 6, 1939, p. 57.

24. Wedgwood provides a glimpse of the Chelsea factory in 1765, in a letter to his brother John written in late July: "there is one Jinks who was a gilder in enamel at the Chelsea works, now is at Bow China works; if it would not be too tedious I wish you would buy a creamcolour enamelled cream Ewer and get Jinks to gild all the spaces but the flowers &c and burn the gold in . . . I believe it is neither a secret or very curious art for Women only are employed in it at Chelsea. . . ." (*The Selected Letters of Josiah Wedgwood*, ed. Finer and Savage, p. 36).

130 Scent Bottle: Fountain

H. 3 (7.7); W. 2⅞ (7.4); D. 1¼ (3.2).

THE BOTTLE is modeled as a dolphin fountain with a white and gold basin formed as a shell. The neck of the bottle consists of entwined dolphins, one ascending, the other descending, flanked by green aquatic plants. A foliated gilded metal mount encircles the lip. The dolphins are tinted with pastel tones of blue, yellow, and rose. A short stem of coral held in the mouth of the uppermost dolphin forms the stopper (a replacement), and blue water gushes from the mouth of the lower. Painted within the irregularly shaped hollow base is a spray of pale blue and iron-red flowers.

Unmarked.

"Girl-in-a-Swing" factory at Chelsea, dating from about 1751–1754.

A case for distinguishing between the products of Sprimont's Chelsea factory and the so-called "Girl-in-a-Swing" porcelains was presented in a paper by Arthur Lane and Robert Charleston, delivered before the English Ceramic Circle on November 19, 1960, and published in 1962 in the *Transactions* of that organization. Since 1961, the probable existence of two separate factories at Chelsea has been generally recognized. The dates 1751–1754 are based on the opinion of Lane and Charleston that a rival factory, although established in 1749, was not in full production until 1751. With respect to scent bottles, the possibility of other, still unnamed factories is being explored as this goes to press (see Introduction).

The model is in the collection of Irwin Untermyer, New York (Hackenbroch, *Chelsea and Other English Porcelain in the Irwin Untermyer Collection*, pl. 64, fig. 81). Another, from the collection of Otto and Magdalena Blohm, Hamburg and Caracas, was sold at Sotheby's, London, April 24–25, 1961, lot 268 (illustrated in catalogue, listed as Chelsea).

A related model, substituting fish for dolphins, from the collection of R. W. M. Walker, was sold at Christie's, London, July 19, 1945, lot 269. Another, from the collection of Stewart Granger, was sold at Christie's, London, May 20, 1963, lot 100 (illustrated in catalogue, listed as Chelsea).

131 Double Scent Bottle: Doves

H. 2⅝ (6.7); w. 2¼ (5.7); Diam. of base 1 1/16 (2.7).

THE DOUBLE bottle is modeled as two billing doves, the right wing shoulder of each surmounted by a chained stopper shaped as a butterfly and mounted in gold. The birds are colored pale blue, flecked with russet-brown, their wings barred with yellow, white, violet, brown, and green. Sprigs of mottled green and yellow leaves supporting a single rose at the rear are applied to the tree stump. The base is painted with sprigs of yellow and deep pink roses, which are repeated inside the foot, together with small garnet-red blossoms.

Unmarked.

"Girl-in-a-Swing" factory at Chelsea, dating from about 1751–1754.

Formerly in the collection of Baroness C. G. von Seidlitz, Paris.

A similar scent bottle is in the Joicey Bequest at the London Museum (see Bryant, *The Chelsea Porcelain Toys*, pl. 3, no. 6; others in the collections of F. T. Galsworthy and Mrs. A. E. Marlow are also mentioned). The model is also found in the Rous Lench Collection (Mackenna, *Chelsea Porcelain, the Red Anchor Wares*, pl. 76, fig. 151); and in the collections of Irwin Untermyer, New York (Hackenbroch, *Chelsea and Other English Porcelain in the Irwin Untermyer Collection*, pl. 63, fig. 83); and R. W. M. Walker (King, *Chelsea Porcelain*, pl. 43, fig. 3).

A comparable example from the collection of Mrs. K. Marlow was sold at Christie's, London, June 29, 1937, lot 37, while one from the collection of J. P. Morgan, New York, was sold at Parke-Bernet, New York, January 6–8, 1944, lot 456 (illustrated in catalogue). Another example, from the collection of Sir Bernard Eckstein, was sold at

Sotheby's, London, March 29, 1949, lot 108 (illustrated in catalogue, pl. XXIV). One from the collection of Oscar Dusendschön, Geneva, was sold at Sotheby's, London, December 6, 1960, lot 12 (illustrated in catalogue). Two examples owned by Otto and Magdalena Blohm, Hamburg and Caracas, were sold at Sotheby's, London, April 24–25, 1961, lot 266 (illustrated in catalogue, pl. V, listed as Chelsea), and October 9–10, 1961, lot 514 (illustrated in catalogue, pl. V, listed as Chelsea). A bottle from the Stewart Granger Collection was sold at Christie's, London, May 20, 1963, lot 84 (illustrated in catalogue, pl. VIII, listed as Chelsea). Another, formerly in the collection of Mrs. Meyer Sassoon, was sold from the collection of Mrs. Derek Fitzgerald at Sotheby's, London, October 12, 1965, lot 49 (illustrated in catalogue). One from the collection of Mrs. Gay Claude Leigh was sold at Sotheby's, London, April 4, 1966, lot 45 (illustrated in catalogue).

For a note on Chelsea vs. Girl-in-a-Swing porcelain, see under No. 130.

132 Scent Bottle: Venus and Cupid

H. 3⅛₆ (7.9); W. 1½ (3.8).

THE BOTTLE is modeled as a flower-encrusted clock, flanked at the left by a standing figure of Venus in a loose yellow robe and at the right by Cupid pointing to the dial, on which the hands point to the hour of twelve. Between the figures is a seated Dalmation puppy. All rest upon a low, square platform, the arched sides of which are inscribed in black: L'HEURE DU BERGER FIDELLE. A single rose, set in a gold mount with chain, forms the stopper. The underside of the base is painted with green pebblework.

Unmarked.

"Girl-in-a-Swing" factory at Chelsea, dating from about 1751–1754.

Formerly in the collection of Baroness C. G. von Seidlitz, Paris.

The model is found in the Franks Collection in the British Museum, and in the Schreiber Collection in the Victoria and Albert Museum, London (Rackham, *Catalogue of the Schreiber Collection*, I, pl. 23, fig. 242; it is also illustrated in Bryant, *The Chelsea Porcelain Toys*, pl. 19, fig. 2). Other examples are in the collection of Frau Cahn-Speyer, Vienna (see Braun in *Kunst und Kunsthandwerk*, XVIII, 1915, p. 67, fig. 36), and in the Irwin Untermyer Collection, New York (Hackenbroch, *Chelsea and Other English Porcelain in the Irwin Untermyer Collection*, pl. 66, fig. 137).

Bryant (*op. cit.*, p. 24) refers to a Mennecy bottle of similar design as having appeared in the Christie's catalogue for March 17, 1892, lot 371. The reference, however, is erroneous, as the item does not appear in the catalogue cited. A Chelsea example, from the collection of Francis Ayerst, was sold at Christie's, London, on August 1, 1916, lot 144, and another on April 18, 1923, lot 27. Another, from the collection of Lady Binning (formerly belonging to Mrs. W. S. Salting), was sold at Christie's, London, May 6, 1930, lot 3. A simi-lar scent bottle from the collection of Otto and Magdalena Blohm, Hamburg and Caracas, was sold at Sotheby's, London, July 4–5, 1960, lot 9 (illustrated in catalogue, pl. 1). A comparable example, formerly in the collection of Mrs. Meyer Sassoon, was sold from the collection of Mrs. Derek Fitzgerald at Sotheby's, London, October 12, 1965, lot 20 (illustrated in catalogue), and another, from the collection of Mrs. Gay Claude Leigh was sold at Sotheby's, London, April 4, 1966, lot 42 (illustrated in catalogue).

The example in the British Museum has a rococo pedestal about as high as the bottle itself; the arched base suggests that No. 132 must have originally been supplied with such a pedestal.

The model is among those ascribed to the "Girl-in-a-Swing" factory by Lane and Charleston in their definitive study of this group of porcelains (*English Ceramic Circle Transactions*, V, Part 3, 1962, pl. 136, a).

The presence of an inscription in French, and pale yellow in the costume are features that may associate No. 132 with a group newly defined by Kate Foster, tentatively called "Category II" (see Introduction).

133 Scent Bottle: Masked Figure

H. 3⅜ (8.6); W. 1³⁄₁₆ (3.0); D. 1⅛ (2.9).

THE BOTTLE is modeled as a seated maiden wearing a black harlequin mask, a low-cut pale yellow bodice, pink skirt, and flowered white underskirt. With her right hand, she plucks at a bunch of grapes above her head, while, with her left, she holds a yellow basket filled with grapes in her lap. The low round base is inscribed in orange-red: POUR MON AMOUR. The gold-mounted finial is in the form of a multicolored bird pecking at grapes cupped in leaves. A yellow-green pebble-work pattern surrounding a single rose is painted within the base.

Unmarked.

"Girl-in-a-Swing" factory at Chelsea, dating from about 1751–1754.

Similar scent bottles are in the Hamburg Museum; the Joicey Bequest at the London Museum; and the Schreiber Collection in the Victoria and Albert Museum, London (Bryant, *The Chelsea Porcelain Toys*, pl. 23, fig. 1; also Rackham, *Catalogue of the Schreiber Collection*, I, pl. 24, fig. 244). Other examples are in the collection of Frau Cahn-Speyer, Vienna (see Braun in *Kunst und Kunsthandwerk*, XVIII, 1915, p. 74, fig. 64), and Irwin Untermyer, New York (Hackenbroch, *Chelsea and Other English Porcelain in the Irwin Untermyer Collection*, pl. 71, fig. 167).

"A Chelsea scent-bottle formed as a lady with a basket of grapes, with a bird and grape stopper" was sold at Christie's, London, June 26, 1906, lot 41. An example from the collection of Lady Binning (formerly in the collection of Mrs. W. S. Salting) was sold at Christie's, London, May 6, 1930, lot 6; another in the same sale, lot 7, is similar to No. 133 in that the figure wears a mask. A comparable scent bottle from the collection of J. P. Morgan, New York, was sold at Parke-Bernet, New York, January 6–8, 1944, lot 458 (illustrated in catalogue). One from the collection of

Sir Bernard Eckstein was sold at Sotheby's, London, March 29, 1949, lot 107 (illustrated in catalogue, pl. XXIV). Another, from the collection of Otto and Magdalena Blohm, Hamburg and Caracas, was sold at Sotheby's, London, July 4–5, 1960, lot 14 (illustrated in catalogue, pl. 11). Similar examples from the collections of Mrs. Derek Fitzgerald (formerly in the collection of Mrs. Meyer Sassoon) and Mrs. Gay Claude Leigh were sold at Sotheby's, London, October 12, 1965, lot 8 (illustrated in catalogue), and April 4, 1966, lot 41 (illustrated in catalogue).

The model is among those ascribed to the "Girl-in-a-Swing" factory by Lane and Charleston in their pioneering study of this group of porcelains (*English Ceramic Circle Transactions*, V, Part 3, 1962, pl. 136, a).

The presence of a single rose under the base, an inscription in French, and pale yellow in the costume are features which No. 133 shares with a group newly defined by Kate Foster, tentatively called "Category II" (see No. 132 and Introduction).

134 Double Scent Bottle: Monkeys

H. 2¼ (5.7); W. 1¾ (4.5); D. 1¼ (3.2).

THE LARGER bottle is modeled as a seated brown monkey holding a rose in its right forepaw and with its head forming the stopper. Attached to its back by means of black straps over the shoulders is a pale yellow basket, containing an infant monkey; this is a second bottle, the head forming the stopper. The rim of the basket is studded with miniature flowers. The translucent domed base is painted with violet, orange, and pale blue sprigs, repeated in part inside the base, where they are accompanied by blue harebells and a yellow rose. The base is edged with serrated gilding. A small chain and foliated gold mounts join the stoppers to the bodies.

Unmarked.

Chelsea, dating from the red anchor period, 1752–1758.

A similar model is in the Franks Collection in the British Museum (see Bryant, *The Chelsea Porcelain Toys*, pl. 5, no. 4; an example in the collection of F. T. Galsworthy is also mentioned). Others are in the collection of Frau Cahn-Speyer, Vienna (see Braun in *Kunst und Kunsthandwerk*, XVIII, 1915, p. 75, fig. 65), and Irwin Untermyer, New York (Hackenbroch, *Chelsea and Other English Porcelain in the Irwin Untermyer Collection*, pl. 62, fig. 92).

A scent bottle of closely corresponding description, presented by Adolph Weil, was sold at the British Red Cross sale at Christie's, London, April 12, 1915, lot 19. A comparable model from the collection of John Henry Taylor, Newstead, Birstall, Leicester, was sold at Sotheby's, London, November 11, 1930, lot 97 (illustrated in catalogue, pl. III). One from an anonymous collection was sold at Sotheby's, London, February 17, 1948, lot 89 (illustrated in catalogue), and another, also from an anonymous collection, was sold at Christie's, London, April 13, 1959, lot 98 (illustrated in catalogue). A similar example, from the collection of Otto and Magdalena Blohm, Hamburg and Caracas, was sold at Sotheby's, London, July 4–5, 1960, lot 30 (illustrated in catalogue, frontispiece). Two others, formerly in the collection of Mrs. Meyer Sassoon, were sold from the collection of Mrs. Derek Fitzgerald at Sotheby's, London, May 4, 1965, lot 47, and October 12, 1965, lot 52 (both illustrated in the catalogues).

In a letter to the writer, dated June 19, 1967, Robert J. Charleston pointed out the existence of a variant form of this model, apparently representing the "Girl-in-a-Swing" factory version (illustrated in Hackenbroch, *op. cit.*, pl. 62, fig. 93, as Chelsea).

135 Double Scent Bottle: Cupid

H. 2¾ (7.0); W. 1⁷⁄₁₆ (3.7); D. 1⁷⁄₁₆ (3.7).

THE DOUBLE bottle is modeled as Cupid, seated with a pair of billing gray doves in his lap and a white and gold bow under his left arm. He is colored white, touched with pale flesh tints. The head serves as the stopper for the principal bottle. A marbleized brown quiver hanging upon his back serves as the second bottle, its porcelain stopper tinted to represent the multicolored feathers of arrows. The domed base is translucent, edged with serrated gilding and painted inside and out with blossoms in rose, powder-blue, yellow, and iron-red. The foliated neck mounts are of gold.

Unmarked.

Chelsea, dating from the red anchor period, 1752–1758.

Formerly in the collection of Baroness C. G. von Seidlitz, Paris.

Comparable examples are recorded in the Franks Collection in the British Museum (Bryant, *The Chelsea Porcelain Toys*, pl. 10, no. 1), and in the collection of Irwin Untermyer, New York (Hackenbroch, *Chelsea and Other English Porcelain in the Irwin Untermyer Collection*, pl. 66, fig. 130).

A comparable bottle from the collection of Emma Budge, Hamburg, was sold at P. Graupe, Berlin, September 27–29, 1937, lot 697. Another in the collection of Otto and Magdalena Blohm, Hamburg and Caracas, was sold at Sotheby's, London, October 9–10, 1961, lot 507 (illustrated in catalogue, pl. IV). It passed into the Stewart Granger Collection, London, and was sold at Christie's, London, May 20, 1963, lot 58 (illustrated in catalogue, pl. V). Another, from the collection of Mrs. Meyer Sassoon, was later sold from the collection of Mrs. Derek Fitzgerald at Sotheby's, London, October 12, 1965, lot 35 (illustrated in catalogue).

H. 2⅝ (6.7); W. 2 (5.1); D. 1⁵⁄₁₆ (3.4).

THE BOTTLE is modeled as a seated pug dog, wearing a high collar, the body delicately penciled in gray, the face masked in black. The oval domed base with a gilded rim is painted with three floral sprays in bright blue, iron-red, and garnet, repeated on the underside where they surround a yellow marguerite. Mounts of gilt metal form a collar around the dog's neck.

Unmarked.

Chelsea, dating from the red anchor period, 1752–1758.

Similar examples are in the Franks Collection in the British Museum, London, the Schreiber Collection in the Victoria and Albert Museum, London (Rackham, *Catalogue of the Schreiber Collection*, I, pl. 24, fig. 241), and in the Irwin Untermyer Collection, New York (Hackenbroch, *Chelsea and Other English Porcelain in the Irwin Untermyer Collection*, pl. 64, fig. 80). Three "Chelsea porcelain scent-bottles, modelled as pug-dogs" from the Lady Dorothy Nevill Collection were sold at Christie's, London, July 1, 1913, lot 11. Two examples from the collection of Otto and Magdalena Blohm, Hamburg and Caracas, were sold at Sotheby's, London, July 4–5, 1960, lot 27 (illustrated in catalogue, pl. III) and October 9–10, 1961, lot 519 (illustrated in catalogue, pl. V). A comparable scent bottle from the collection of Oscar Dusendschön, Geneva, was sold at Sotheby's, London, December 6, 1960, lot 13 (illustrated in catalogue). Another, from the collection of Mr. and Mrs. James MacHarg was sold at Sotheby's, London, May 22, 1962, lot 158 (illustrated in catalogue). A pug dog, formerly in the collection of Mrs. Meyer Sassoon, was sold from the collection of Mrs. Derek Fitzgerald at Sotheby's, London, October 12, 1965, lot 51 (illustrated in catalogue). Another, from the collection of Mrs. Gay Claude Leigh was sold at Sotheby's, London, April 4, 1966, lot 49 (illustrated in catalogue, listed as Girl-in-a-Swing).

For a note on Chelsea vs. Girl-in-a-Swing porcelain, see under No. 130, and Introduction.

137 Scent Bottle: Cluster of Plums

H. 2⁹⁄₁₆ (6.5); W. 1⅜ (3.5); D. 1⅜ (3.5).

THE BOTTLE is modeled as a leafy cluster of five damson plums hanging from a single stem, the fruit delicately tinted with areas of rose-violet and milky blue, and interspersed with yellow-green pointed leaves. A russet-brown stem forms the neck of the bottle, which is fitted with a foliated gold mount and, around the lip, a chained stopper in the form of a twig.

Unmarked.

Chelsea, dating from the red anchor period, 1752–1758.

Formerly in the collection of Thelma Chrysler Foy, New York (sold at Parke-Bernet, New York, May 15, 1959, lot 108).

An identical model is in the Franks Collection at the British Museum (see Bryant, *The Chelsea Porcelain Toys*, pl. 12, no. 6). Bryant (*op. cit.*, p. 66), writing in 1925, commented that "the same model is found in Battersea Enamel."

A similar bottle from the collection of Stewart Granger was sold at Christie's, London, May 20, 1963, lot 104 (illustrated in catalogue).

For other bottles in the form of fruit, see Nos. 138 A–C and 139.

138 A–C   Three Scent Bottles: Peaches

138 A: H. 2½ (6.3); D. 1⁹⁄₁₆ (4.0).

138 B: H. 2⁷⁄₁₆ (6.2); D. 1⅝ (4.2).

138 C: H. 2³⁄₁₆ (5.6); D. 1⁹⁄₁₆ (4.0).

THE BOTTLES appear to have been formed in a common mold, and each is shaped as a firm, round fruit surmounted by a cluster of leaves issuing from a thick stem that serves as the neck and is fitted with a serrated gold mount. Minor details formed by hand and attached with slip consist of smaller fruits of variable size and shape resting upon the shoulder of each, and a bent tendril descending from stem to shoulder. No. 138 A is delicately colored with areas of lavender and cream, with yellowish-green leaves and a miniature fruit of the same color. It is fitted with a serrated gold rim mount, chained to a stopper in the form of a short leafy twig. No. 138 B is of a golden plum-like color with broad areas vertically penciled in mauve partially revealing the light ground. The miniature fruit and leaves are green and the foliated gold mount at the lip is fitted with a porcelain stopper formed as two billing birds. No. 138 C is pale greenish white, delicately tinted with patches of puce and fitted with a gold rim mount and a gold stopper of ribbed dome shape. As on No. 138 A, the small fruit and leaves are yellowish green.

Unmarked.

Chelsea, dating from the red anchor period, 1752–1758.

The model is found in The Metropolitan Museum of Art, New York (gift of J. Pierpont Morgan, acc. no. 17.190.1732).
"A Chelsea scent-bottle from an unidentified collection, formed as a peach, with a bird stopper" was sold at Christie's, London, June 26, 1906, lot 29. Another, also from an unidentified collection, was sold at Christie's, London, May 30, 1960, lot 129 (illustrated in catalogue). An example from the collection of Stewart Granger was sold at Christie's, London, May 20, 1963, lot 103 (illustrated in catalogue). An additional bottle from the collection of Mrs. Derek Fitzgerald (formerly in the collection of Mrs. Meyer Sassoon) was sold at Sotheby's, London, October 12, 1965, lot 27 (illustrated in catalogue).

For other bottles in the form of fruit in this collection, see Nos. 137 and 139.

139 Scent Bottle: Apple

H. 3 ⅛ (8.0); w. 1¾ (4.5).

THE BOTTLE is shaped as an apple, with a cluster of small leaves and fruit around the neck, and a green twig forming a stopper. It is painted pale greenish white, mottled with puce and red. The stopper is attached by a chain to a foliated gold mount.

Unmarked.

Chelsea, dating from the red anchor period, 1752–1758.

Formerly in the collection of Mrs. K. Marlow (sold at Christie's, London, May 6, 1930, lot 62).

The apple, a form infrequently found in Chelsea porcelain, is represented in the collections of Mrs. Meyer Sassoon (Blunt, *The Cheyne Book of Chelsea China and Pottery*, pl. 27, fig. 42), and Irwin Untermyer, New York (Hackenbroch, *Chelsea and Other English Porcelain in the Irwin Untermyer Collection*, pl. 64, figs. 147, 148).

In addition to its use for scent bottles, the apple shape was also employed at Chelsea for sweetmeat boxes. An example is illustrated in Savage, *18th-Century English Porcelain*, pl. 11, a.

For other bottles in the form of fruit in this collection, see Nos. 137 and 138 A–C.

H. 3 1/16 (7.8); W. 2 (5.1).

THE DOUBLE bottle is modeled as a recumbent greyhound (whose head serves as a stopper) beside an ovoid vase. The latter is painted with a nosegay of roses and buttercups between a gilded stripe around the shoulder and gilded gadroons above the flaring foot. Its stopper is a songbird perched upon a crown. Each stopper is attached by a fine chain to a gold mount of foliate design. The vessels stand upon a domed base painted with sprigs, with dentate gilding around the rim. The hollow underside is painted with a bouquet of roses.

Unmarked.

Chelsea, dating from the late red anchor period, 1755–1758.

A comparable example is in the Franks Collection at the British Museum (see Bryant, *The Chelsea Porcelain Toys*, pl. 5, no. 3; others in the collections of Mrs. A. E. Marlow and Dr. and Mrs. H. Bellamy Gardner are also mentioned). Still others are in the collections of Frau Cahn-Speyer, Vienna (see Braun in *Kunst und Kunsthandwerk*, XVIII, 1915, p. 74, fig. 64), and Irwin Untermyer, New York (Hackenbroch, *Chelsea and Other English Porcelain in the Irwin Untermyer Collection*, pl. 63, fig. 88).

"A scent-bottle, with a greyhound and a vase" was sold at Christie's, London, March 24, 1881, lot 16. Another, from the collection of Sir Julian Goldsmid, was sold at Christie's, London, June 9, 1896, lot 640, and one from an unidentified collection was sold at Christie's, London, on March 29, 1911, lot 71. An example from the Alfred Trapnell sale was sold at Christie's, London, March 16, 1914, lot 129. A scent bottle from the collection of Mrs. K. Marlow was sold at Christie's, London,

June 29, 1937, lot 36. Another, from the collection of J. P. Morgan, New York, was sold at Parke-Bernet, New York, January 6–8, 1944, lot 452 (illustrated in catalogue). A comparable model from the collection of Stewart Granger was sold at Christie's, London, May 20, 1963, lot 65 (illustrated in catalogue, pl. v). Another, from the collection of Mrs. Derek Fitzgerald (formerly in the collection of Mrs. Meyer Sassoon) was sold at Sotheby's, London, October 12, 1965, lot 36 (illustrated in catalogue).

H. 2⅞ (7.4); W. 1⅞ (4.8); D. 1 (2.5).

THE DOUBLE bottle is modeled as a pear-shaped flask molded with gilded rococo scrolls. One mouth is fitted with a stopper in the form of a monkey's head wearing a conical yellow hat. The head and shoulders of a gray-brown monkey project at one side, the head again serving as a stopper. Three cartouches of pale blue, puce, and iron-red blossoms are painted on the rococo-molded exterior, which is heightened with gilding. Within the hollow foot is a painted nosegay of chalky blue asters and yellow roses. The foliated neck mounts are of gold.

Unmarked.

Chelsea, dating from the late red anchor period, 1755–1758.

A comparable model is in the Franks Collection at the British Museum (Bryant, *The Chelsea Porcelain Toys*, pl. 5, no. 2). Another was in the collection of Mrs. Meyer Sassoon, London (Blunt, *The Cheyne Book of Chelsea China and Pottery*, pl. 28, fig. 23, no. 4). A similar example is in the collection of Irwin Untermyer, New York (Hackenbroch, *Chelsea and Other English Porcelain in the Irwin Untermyer Collection*, pl. 63, fig. 91; formerly in the collection of Frau Cahn-Speyer, Vienna).

A comparable double scent bottle from an anonymous collection was sold at Sotheby's, London, February 17, 1948, lot 75 (illustrated in catalogue).

H. 3¼ (8.3); W. 1⅝ (4.1); D. 1¼ (3.2).

THE BOTTLE is modeled as Cupid, seated, wearing a soft turquoise-green hat with upturned brim, and a loose drapery across his loins. He works at a female portrait bust in white with mallet and chisel in his right and left hands, respectively. Over his left shoulder is slung a quiver of arrows, the strap inscribed in deep red TOUTES LES PARTIES SONT CHARMANTES. Behind the figure rises a truncated tree stump, encrusted with small flowers, and fitted with a chained stopper in the form of a small bouquet. Hanging at the back of the stump is a portfolio with an iron-red cover. On the underside of the hollow base is a gilded floral spray. A small chain and foliated metal mount join the stopper to the body.

Unmarked.

Chelsea, dating from the gold anchor period, 1758–1765.

An example of this figure is in the collection of Irwin Untermyer, New York (Hackenbroch, *Chelsea and Other English Porcelain in the Irwin Untermyer Collection*, pl. 66, fig. 141). Another, from the collection of Mrs. Derek Fitzgerald (formerly in the collection of Mrs. Meyer Sassoon) was sold at Sotheby's, London, May 4, 1965, lot 13 (illustrated in catalogue).

The subject of this scent bottle was apparently suggested by a contemporary engraving, which in turn derived from one of eight panels depicting children as allegories of the Arts and Sciences, painted by Boucher. The originals were commissioned by Mme de Pompadour for a small octagonal boudoir in the Château de Crécy about 1751–1753, now in the Frick Collection, New York (see *The Frick Collection*, III, pl. LXXII). It is probable that engravings from these Boucher subjects were available in England at about the time these bottles were made. Cartoons were prepared for five of the panels, reproduced as oval tapestries for chair backs, made at the Gobelins factory in the mid-eighteenth century. A set is now at the Henry E. Huntington Library and Art Gallery, San Marino, California (Wark, *French Decorative Art in the Huntington Collection*, figs. 16 and 17). Similar subjects, though not so close in spirit as the Boucher scenes, were engraved by Gravelot during his period of residence in England about 1734–1754 (see Guérinet, *Vignettes de Gravelot*, pl. 4).

143 A, B   Two Scent Bottles: Cupid at an Altar

143 A: H. 3¼ (8.3); W. 1¼ (3.2).

143 B: H. 3⅜ (8.6); W. 1⅜ (3.5).

EACH bottle is modeled as a cherub at an altar, placing a wreath upon a heart. The figure wears a light drapery around his waist, and across one shoulder a banderole enameled white. On No. 143 A this is inscribed: IL A SA RECOMPENSE. The altar is gilded with strygils and stylized rosettes. A tree stump (which forms the bottle proper) blends into the figure, and tinted miniature blossoms are applied to it as they are to the flat circular base. A floral stopper is chained to the plain gold rim mount.

No. 143 B differs in that the banderole is inscribed: VOUS LE MERITEZ. The altar is covered with yellow and rose drapery, and the pattern of the gilding at its base is a floral trellis. A cluster of orange-red fruit surmounts the stopper, which is mounted with gilded metal.

Unmarked.

Chelsea, dating from the gold anchor period, 1758–1765.

A similar bottle was in the collection of Frau Cahn-Speyer, Vienna (see Braun in *Kunst und Kunsthandwerk*, XVIII, 1915, p. 72, fig. 55). Another is in the collection of Irwin Untermyer, New York (Hackenbroch, *Chelsea and Other English Porcelain in the Irwin Untermyer Collection*, pl. 66, fig. 122).

A comparable example was sold from an unidentified collection at Christie's, London, December 18, 1922, lot 35. Another was sold from the collection of Mrs. Derek Fitzgerald (formerly in the collection of Mrs. Meyer Sassoon) at Sotheby's, London, May 4, 1965, lot 9 (illustrated in catalogue).

H. 3⅝ (9.2); W. 1⅜ (3.5); D. 1¼ (3.2).

THE BOTTLE is modeled as a dovecote of three stories, the yellow roofs suggesting a pagoda. From the various arched and grilled doors emerge the heads and foreparts of small pale blue and yellow-breasted songbirds. At the base are a recumbent white lamb and a speckled beige hen with three yellow chicks, one under her wing. There are twelve birds in all including a blue-gray one perched upon the stopper. A pale lavender ramp rises at one side of the structure, forming a balcony at the second story. The underside is gilded with a floral sprig and serrated border. The stopper, neck, and base are gold-mounted.

Unmarked.

Chelsea, dating from the gold anchor period, 1758–1765.

Comparable examples are in the Bloomfield Moore Collection in the Philadelphia Museum of Art (see Barber, *Artificial Soft Paste Porcelain*, p. 24, fig. 36), and in the Victoria and Albert Museum, London.

Other examples are in the collections of A. H. S. Bunford (Honey, *Old English Porcelain*, pl. 23, h); Frau Cahn-Speyer, Vienna (Braun in *Kunst und Kunsthandwerk*, XVIII, 1915, p. 74, no. 61); Mrs. Meyer Sassoon, London (Blunt, *The Cheyne Book of Chelsea China and Pottery*, pl. 27, no. 4, fig. 37; also illustrated in Bryant, *The Chelsea Porcelain Toys*, pl. 19, no. 4); and Irwin Untermyer, New York (Hackenbroch, *Chelsea and Other English Porcelain in the Irwin Untermyer Collection*, pl. 63, fig. 82; formerly in the Bellamy Gardner Collection).

According to Bryant, *op. cit.*, p. 19, a comparable example was sold at Christie's, London, March 24, 1881, lot 17. Another, from the Lady Dorothy Nevill Collection, was sold at Christie's, London, July 1, 1913, lot 12. A similar bottle, from the collection of Mrs. K. Marlow, was sold at Christie's, London, June 29, 1937, lot 39. Another was sold from the J. P. Morgan Collection, New York, at Parke-Bernet, New York, March 22–25, 1944, lot 456 (illustrated in catalogue). A scent bottle from the Stewart Granger Collection was sold at Christie's, London, May 20, 1963, lot 62 (illustrated in catalogue, pl. v); another, mentioned above as formerly in the collection of Mrs. Meyer Sassoon, was sold from the collection of Mrs. Derek Fitzgerald at Sotheby's, London, October 12, 1965, lot 10 (illustrated in catalogue).

145 Scent Bottle: Apollo and Daphne

H. 3¹¹⁄₁₆ (9.4); W. 1³⁄₁₆ (3.0); D. 1¼ (3.2).

THE BOTTLE is modeled as Apollo and Daphne, the red-berried foliage into which Daphne is being metamorphosed forming the neck and stopper. Daphne wears a loose flowered robe lined with yellow, and Apollo a cloak of turquoise and rose, edged with gold. A banderole supporting Apollo's copper-red quiver is inscribed in iron-red: EVITEZ SON SORT. The base is strewn with molded and applied flowers, and on the underside displays an etched gold floral spray with dentate turquoise border.

Unmarked.

Chelsea, dating from the gold anchor period, 1758–1765.

Formerly in the collection of Baron Max von Goldschmidt-Rothschild, Frankfurt am Main.

The model is represented in the Franks Collection at the British Museum (Hobson, *Catalogue of the Collection of English Porcelain*, no. 133). Other examples are in the collections of Lt.-Col. G. B. Croft Lyons; R. von Hirsch (Bryant, *The Chelsea Porcelain Toys*, pl. 28, no. 6); and Irwin Untermyer, New York (Hackenbroch, *Chelsea and Other English Porcelain in the Irwin Untermyer Collection*, pl. 67, fig. 188).

An example formerly in the collection of Mrs. Meyer Sassoon was sold from the collection of Mrs. Derek Fitzgerald at Sotheby's, London, October 12, 1965, lot 31 (illustrated in catalogue).

146 A, B Pair of Sunflower Dishes

H. 2³⁄₁₆ (5.6); W. 6 (15.3); D. 5 (12.7).

EACH is modeled in the form of a cluster of flowers, with a gnarled green twig serving as a handle. The principal blossom is a large white and yellow sunflower with a pebbled aubergine-colored center; along one side appear multicolored blossoms and notched leaves in two shades of green. The rustic handle is entwined with a spiral ribbon. Although produced from the same mold, Nos. 146 A and B vary slightly in their painted detail.

No. 146 A is marked on the underside with an anchor painted in red over the glaze; No. 146 B is unmarked.

Chelsea, dating from 1752–1758.

Formerly in the collection of Mrs. de Trafford.
Similar dishes were sold from the collections of A. H. Harris (Sotheby's, London, April 17, 1951,

lot 139 [illustrated in catalogue]); Mrs. Dudley Cory-Wright (Christie's, London, December 3, 1962, lot 83 [illustrated in catalogue]); and Selwyn Parkinson (Sotheby's, London, June 21, 1966, lot 155 [illustrated in catalogue]).

Very similar sunflower dishes were made at Longton Hall, examples of which are a pair from the collection of the Marquess of Exeter (sold Christie's, London, July 13, 1959, lot 73 [illustrated in catalogue]).

The function of this type of dish is made clear by an entry in the catalogue of the auction held at the Ford salesroom, London, March 10–27, 1755, for the Chelsea Porcelain Manufactory:

Third Day's Sale, March 12, 1755, no. 31: Four large sun flower leaves, and 4 sun flowers to ditto [for desart].

147 Sunflower Dish

H. 1¾ (4.5); W. 4¼ (10.8); D. 3⅞ (9.8).

THE DISH is almost identical to Nos. 146 A and B, but is smaller and differs in minor elements of modeling and color, as, for instance, in the heart of the main blossom, which is brown and aubergine.

Unmarked.

Chelsea, dating from 1752–1758.

A comparable dish from the collection of Mr. and Mrs. Sigmund J. Katz is illustrated in Savage, *18th-Century English Porcelain*, pl. 26 a. It bears a red anchor mark and is dated about 1755. The same model appears in the Lady Ludlow Collection at Luton Hoo as the stand for a sweetmeat dish (see Hayden, *Old English Porcelain, the Lady Ludlow Collection*, no. 144, pl. 61).

Sunflower dishes were used for dessert.

148 A, B Pair of Fig-Leaf Dishes

148 A: H. 2³⁄₁₆ (5.6); W. 8¹⁄₁₆ (20.5);
D. 6¾ (17.2).

148 B: H. 2³⁄₁₆ (5.6); W. 7⅞ (20.0);
D. 6¾ (17.2).

EACH is modeled in the form of a five-lobed leaf with a bowed handle in the form of a bent twig painted deep green. The interior is veined with pale puce, overlaid at the center by a small nosegay, and the edges of the leaf are bordered with straw-yellow, grading to yellow-green. A leaf painted deep green appears under one of the lobes of No. 148 A.

Each is marked on the underside with an anchor, painted in red over the glaze.

Chelsea, dating from 1752–1758.

A comparable pair is in the Allen Collection at the Victoria and Albert Museum, London (catalogue no. 79).

The following appears in the catalogue of the auction held at the Ford salesroom, London, March 10–27, 1755, for the Chelsea Porcelain Manufactory:

Third Day's Sale, March 12, no. 88: A compleat service for desart, consisting of a large double leaf compotier, 2 vine leaf dishes, 2 large fine fig leaves, 4 small fig leaves, and 4 cabbage lettices.

See also Nos. 149 A and B.

149 A, B   Pair of Fig-Leaf Dishes

149 A: H. 2¼ (5.7); W. 8 (20.4); D. 6⅜ (16.2).

149 B: H. 2¼ (5.7); W. 8 (20.4); D. 6½ (16.5).

EACH is of the same type as Nos. 148 A and B, but differs in that the ribs and veins are molded and painted yellow-green, while the borders are painted with graded tones of blue-green.

Each is marked on the underside with a small anchor, painted in red over the glaze. The glaze within the foot ring of No. 149 A shows the so-called "dry edge effect," or shrinkage, more characteristic of Worcester porcelain.

Chelsea, dating from 1752–1758.

A similar type of dish was made at Worcester (see a pair of leaf dishes from the collection of Selwyn Parkinson, sold at Sotheby's, London, June 21, 1966, lot 196 [illustrated in catalogue]).

The following appears in the catalogue of an auction held at the Ford salesroom, London, March 10–27, 1755, for the Chelsea Porcelain Manufactory:

Second Day's Sale, March 11, no. 41: Two small fig-leaves, and two fine cabbage lettices, for desart.

See also Nos. 148 A and B.

150 Cabbage-Leaf Bowl

H. 3¾ (9.5); D. 6½ (16.5).

THE DEEP circular bowl has curved sides molded as overlapping cabbage leaves. Each leaf has a graduated green border fading to cream, and has a central rib, violet-rose in color, which extends to the foot ring where the same color appears in delicate streaks. The interior is painted with two sprigs and a nosegay including a pale lavender tulip and a russet-brown anemone.

Marked on the underside with an anchor, painted in red over the glaze, accompanied by three spur marks resulting from the firing of the glaze.

Chelsea, dating from 1752–1758.

This is an example of the "leaf-basons" mentioned from time to time in the various eighteenth century sale catalogues of Chelsea porcelain. The type was also made at Longton Hall. An example in the collection of H. M. the Queen Mother is illustrated in Tilley, *Teapots & Tea*, pl. LIV, no. 162, 4 a. Another is in the collection of J. J. Tupnell (illustrated in Mackenna, *Chelsea Porcelain, the Red Anchor Wares*, pl. 33, fig. 66).

A comparable pair from the collection of the Marquess of Exeter was sold at Christie's, London, July 13, 1959, lot 55 (illustrated in catalogue). A second pair from the collection of Robert O'Brien was sold at Sotheby's, London, April 7, 1964, lot 85 (illustrated in catalogue). A third pair, from an unidentified collection, was sold at Christie's, London, July 6, 1964, lot 25 (illustrated in catalogue).

The apparent prototype for such cabbage-leaf bowls existed in Meissen porcelain of 1745–1750

(see Rückert, *Meissener Porzellan, 1710–1810*, no. 693, pl. 161).

The following appears in the catalogue of the auction held at the Ford salesroom, London, March 10–27, 1755, for the Chelsea Porcelain Manufactory:

Third Day's Sale, March 12, no. 6: Four small cabbage leaves and a large cabbage leaf and bason.

151 Ivy-Leaf Dish

Diam. 8¼ (21.0).

THE MOLDED border of this dish is formed by six heart-shaped jade-green leaves, with beet-red stems and veinings. The center is painted with strawberries, gooseberries, and a pear.

Marked on the underside with an anchor, painted in red over the glaze, accompanied by three spur marks resulting from the firing of the glaze.

Chelsea, dating from 1752–1758.

For a similar example, differently painted, in the collection of William Bemrose, see Bemrose, *Bow,*

Chelsea and Derby Porcelain, pl. x. There is also one in the Glaisher Collection at the Fitzwilliam Museum, Cambridge, dated about 1752.

A very similar model, with coarser stems and leaves of rougher texture, was made at Longton Hall. An example from the collection of W. A. Evill is illustrated in the catalogue of the exhibition *English Pottery and Porcelain,* held at the Victoria and Albert Museum, London, 1948, pl. 74, fig. 338. A pair from the collection of W. H. Poole was sold at Sotheby's, London, October 16, 1956, lot 32 (illustrated in catalogue).

[342]

152 A–D   Set of Four Cups and Saucers

Cup: H. 2½ (6.4).

Saucer: Diam. 5¼ (13.4).

EACH has petal-fluted walls with scalloped and gilded rims; the cups are without handles. Each cup is painted on the exterior with two sprigs of flowers, and each saucer with a single sprig. Among the species represented are purple hare-bells, mignonettes, petunias, orange-red convolvulus, and yellow jonquils. The foliage is executed in variegated tones of soft green and yellow. Inside each cup is painted a single rose.

Each is marked on the underside with an anchor, painted in red over the glaze.

Chelsea, dating from 1752–1758.

The painted floral decoration is an English adaption of German (i.e., Meissen) floral subjects taken from illustrated botanical books. The result is naturalistic and highly decorative.

[343]

H. %6 (1.5); W. 3¹¹⁄₁₆ (9.4); D. 1¹¹⁄₁₆ (4.3).

THE GROUP consists of three pea pods, each burst open to reveal a row of close-set peas. The color is a dappled green, inclining to yellow within the pods.

Marked on the underside of one of the stems with an anchor, painted in red over the glaze.

Chelsea, dating from 1752–1758.

Individual pods are illustrated in Mackenna, *Chelsea Porcelain, the Red Anchor Wares*, pl. 77, fig. 155, where they are described as uncommon.

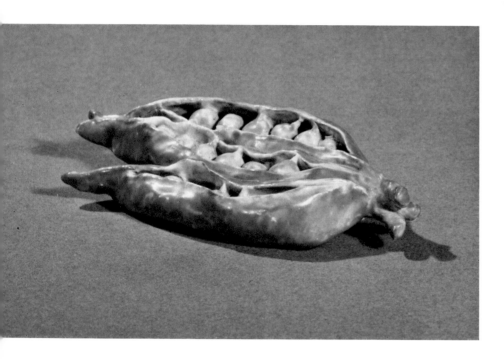

154   Fruit Dish

Diam. 8½ (21.6).

THIS circular dish with an indented turquoise rim is painted with cherries, peaches, and two brightly colored butterflies, these motifs running over from the cavetto onto the border.

Marked on the underside with an anchor, painted in red over the glaze.

Chelsea, dating from 1752–1758.

The type is represented at the Victoria and Albert Museum, London, by an example dated about 1745 (acc. no. C45-1944).

Decoration of this character is allied to the designs of "Sir Hans Sloane's Plants," after the owner of the Apothecaries' Herb Garden in Chelsea, but the effect here is not so botanically detailed. The term is slightly anachronistic since Sloane died in 1753, and botanical decoration derived from garden plants became popular chiefly after 1756, the date of the completion of two folio volumes of colored illustrations, *Figures of Plants*, by Philip Miller, the Apothecaries' gardener. (The folios were not actually published until 1760.) While Chelsea painters often worked from the plants themselves, it is also possible to find exact counterparts for their decoration in Miller's illustrations. There was a scientific correctness about the designs by Miller, in that the insects represented were the actual species responsible for cross-pollenating the plants and fruit. By Sloane's will of July 20, 1749, his collection of books, manuscripts, coins, gems, other antiquities, and natural history specimens was bequeathed to the nation and became the nucleus of the British Museum.

155 A–C   Set of Three Dessert Baskets

155 A and B: H. 3 (7.7); Diam. 6¼ (15.9).

155 C: L. 9 (22.9); W. 7¼ (18.5).

THE SET consists of one larger oval dish and a pair of smaller circular dishes, all with openwork sides of pierced latticework. Pairs of rustic handles in the form of double loops painted green and studded with small flowers are attached to the rims, and the exterior of each has turquoise and yellow blossoms applied at the intersections of the lattice pattern. A pair of purple cherries is painted inside the large dish, and orange-red fruit inside each of the smaller. Flying moths and other insects fill the remaining space.

Unmarked.

Chelsea, dating from about 1755–1760.

A basket similar to Nos. 155 A and B, though with different handles and decoration, in the collection of F. Severne Mackenna, Droitwich, Worcestershire, is illustrated in his *Chelsea Porcelain, the Red Anchor Wares*, pl. 13, fig. 25.

The following appears in the catalogue of the auction held at the Ford salesroom, London, March 10–27, 1755, for the Chelsea Porcelain Manufactory:

Third Day's Sale, March 12, no. 47: A BEAUTIFUL SERVICE FOR A DESART, consisting of an oval pierced basket with handles, 2 fine pierced plates, and 2 melons, 2 vine leaf dishes, and 4 small cabbage leaves.

156   Dessert Dish

H. 3⅞ (9.8); W. 10⅞ (27.7); D. 9¼ (23.5).

THE SCALLOPED oval dish has a low handle of spirally twisted green stems at each end, studded with pink flowers. The exterior is molded with a bold basketwork pattern, with turquoise blossoms applied at the intersections of the weave; the foot is painted pale lemon-yellow. The interior is painted with a spray of orange-red cherries, surmounted by flying butterflies, moths, and other insects, chiefly in tones of yellow, brown, aubergine, and green. The rim is edged with chestnut-brown.
Unmarked.

Chelsea, dating from about 1755–1760.

The following appears in the catalogue of the auction held at the Ford salesroom, London, March 10–27, 1755, for the Chelsea Porcelain Manufactory:

> Third Day's Sale, March 12, no. 33: Two fine basket workt dishes ornamented with green leaves, and 2 fine deep vine leaved dishes enamelled with flowers.

H. 9⅝ (24.5); W. 6⅛ (15.6); D. 5 (12.7).

EACH is in the form of a baluster-shaped eel pot molded of reeds, with a pinched openwork neck and flaring mouth. The vertically ribbed body is painted with colorful butterflies and other small insects, encircled by four crossbandings diagonally flecked with gilding. The stems and leaves of bulrushes and other water plants, painted a delicate yellow green, surround the base and ascend to the shoulder to form an elongated loop handle at either side. In front of each vase are two ducks, violet-rose in color, with much of the white body color showing through their plumage. The drake, with turquoise neck and topknot, preens its right wing.

Each is marked among the vegetation at the base with an anchor, painted in gold over the glaze.

Chelsea, dating from 1758–1765.

A pair from the collection of Alfred Hutton is illustrated in Blunt, *The Cheyne Book of Chelsea China and Pottery*, pl. 24, fig. 83 A. Another pair was formerly in the collection of the late Sir Philip Sassoon, Trent Park, Herefordshire.

The model is represented at The Metropolitan Museum of Art, New York (acc. no. 40.177), and also at the Museum of Fine Arts, Boston (illustrated in *Antiques*, June 1939, p. 281).

A similar vase of Derby porcelain, dated about 1790, is at the Fitzwilliam Museum, Cambridge, and a pair, also of Derby porcelain, from the collection of F. A. Reeves, was sold at Christie's, London, March 11, 1954, lot 15 (illustrated in catalogue).

The idea of adapting the eel-pot shape for a porcelain vase is first found at Meissen about 1735–1740 (see Charles, *Continental Porcelain of the Eighteenth Century*, pl. 12). Some Chelsea examples bear the red anchor mark of the period 1752–1758.

See also Nos. 158 A and B.

158 A, B   Pair of Vases

H. 9¾ (24.8); W. 6 (15.3); D. 4¾ (12.1).

OF THE same type as Nos. 157 A–D except that they are without the painted insects.

Marks, if present, are concealed by the wooden plinths.

Chelsea, dating from 1758–1765.

No. 158 B was formerly in the collection of Sir Charles Hardinge, Ketton Hall, Durham.

H. 7 (17.8); Diam. of base 4⅝ (11.7).

EACH has a ribbed socket resting upon a baluster-shaped stem of medium height, modeled with swirling rococo motifs in relief, including prominent C-scrolls. An applied floral garland twines around the shaft, and clusters of blossoms in relief are scattered upon the base. The socket, shaft, and base are painted with nosegays, flowers, and touches of turquoise and gold, except on No. 159 B, where puce replaces the turquoise, and on No. 159 D, where grass-green appears in place of turquoise.

Each is marked on the underside with an anchor, painted in gold over the glaze. No. 159 C bears a label marked in black: C 68.

Chelsea, dating from 1758–1765.

Three of the four pairs were formerly in the collection of William George Bradley, 5th Earl of Craven, Five Ashes, East Sussex; the remaining pair was formerly in the collection of R. W. M. Walker, London (sold Christie's, London, July 18, 19, 1945, lot 72).

A comparable set of six candlesticks from the collection of Lt. Col. G. B. Croft Lyons is illustrated in King, *Chelsea Porcelain*, pl. 23, fig. 1.

The asymmetrical modeling of Nos. 159 A–H is closely similar to examples made in silver by Jean-Claude Duplessis *père*, *orfèvre du Roi* under Louis XV, and may have been suggested by earlier engraved designs by Juste-Aurèle Meissonnier in his *Oeuvre* (published between 1734 and 1750).

160 A, B Pair of Perfume and Pot-Pourri Vases

160 A: H. 18⅟₁₆ (46.0); W. 9½ (24.1); D. 9½ (24.1).

160 B: H. 18¼ (46.4); W. 9 (22.9); D. 8⅟₁₆ (22.7).

EACH is in the form of a turreted dovecote tower surmounting a flower-studded mound, which rests upon a circular base composed of rococo scrolls. The exterior of each hollow cylindrical vessel simulates stone masonry of terracotta color (No. 160 A is somewhat paler). Three yellow turrets emerge from the arcaded cornice. At the top is a lantern-like structure rising in two stages, pierced with round-headed arches outlined with white stones, to mark the principal doorway, which has a pale yellow door. A row of white-bordered circular windows with yellow centers appears beneath the cornice.

A flock of twelve pigeons painted puce and white with touches of black, supplemented on No. 160 A by patches of turquoise-blue, swarms over each superstructure. A single male bird stands on the steps before the closed central door. The high, spreading base is dappled with pale green and molded with branches and shrubs bearing multi-colored blossoms. On No. 160 A a fox clambers up the steep mound, his muzzle pointed significantly at the birds overhead. The swirling cluster of scrolls of the base is raised upon four splayed shell-like feet, all parts being outlined in gilding and penciled with turquoise-blue.

The undersides of all the supporting scrolls show patches bare of glaze. The interior of the base of No. 160 A is shaped as a stepped dome with a flat top, pierced by a small vent hole at the center; the companion piece shows an irregularly formed central depression, but is not pierced.

Each is marked with an anchor, painted in gold

over the glaze: No. 160 A along the upper edge of the front scrollwork; No. 160 B halfway up the mound base, about three-quarters of an inch to the left of the larger tree stump.

Chelsea, dating from 1758–1765.

EXHIBITED: The Metropolitan Museum of Art, New York, since 1955.

A similar perfume vase at the Victoria and Albert Museum, London (acc. no. C135–1926) has a base of rockery only, lacking the rococo scrollwork. A fox is present, as on No. 160 A. Another example, slightly smaller, is in the collection of the Duke of Bedford, Woburn Abbey, Bedfordshire (see Wills, in *Apollo*, January 1956, pp. 14–17, fig. VII). A similar perfume vase dating from the red anchor period (about 1752–1758) is illustrated in Mackenna, *Chelsea Porcelain, the Red Anchor Wares*, pl. 46, fig. 92.

In the catalogue of the 1755 sale of Chelsea porcelain at public auction, Nicholas Sprimont, then proprietor of the factory, listed several ornaments appearing to correspond to these. The descriptions vary slightly; for example: "A most beautiful perfume pot, in the form of a PIGEON-HOUSE, with pigeons, a fox, &c" and "A large and curious PERFUME POT in the form of a PIGEON HOUSE richly ornamented with PIGEONS, A FOX, &c" (see King, *Chelsea Porcelain*, appendix, p. 78, no. 73; p. 94, no. 90; and p. 112, no. 92).

Essence vases and perfume "pots" appear in successive sales of Chelsea ware in 1760 and 1761, as

well as in the announcement of a sale in 1763—a sale that seems not to have taken place. The presence of the gold anchor mark thus suggests a date for these dovecote vases between 1758, when that mark first became general, and 1765, after which the factory's activities seem to have been limited largely to the decoration of wares made previously.

As the internal construction of these "perfume pots" does not permit the use of a candle or spirit burner to generate a fragrance by vaporizing liquid perfume, it may be assumed that the large central cavity was used as a container for pot-pourri. It is possible that the three smaller receptacles in the form of turrets may have served for burning incense pastilles.

The uncommonly large size of these pieces bespeaks consummate skill in the handling of a difficult medium.

161 A, B   Two Candlesticks

H. 9 (22.9); Diam. of base 4 (10.2).

EACH stem is formed as an infant Bacchus enveloped in a spiraling vine of purple and yellow grapes, his right hand supporting the candle socket, his left holding a cup. The socket is of floral form with a broad corolla veined with purple and bordered with green and yellow. The spreading circular base is painted with insects, and molded with scrolls heightened with turquoise and gold.

Unmarked. Each displays "patchmarks" on the underside; No. 161 B has a large round opening on the underside.

Derby, dating from about 1755–1760.

Two comparable candlesticks are in the Schreiber Collection at the Victoria and Albert Museum, London (Rackham, *Catalogue*, I, no. 293), although the figures are posed in a reversed position to those on Nos. 161 A and B. Two others are in the Allen Collection of the same museum (catalogue no. 29, as Bow); for an illustration see Gilhespy, *Derby Porcelain*, no. 22.

Two other similar candlesticks, from the collection of Lt. Col. and Mrs. L. F. Smeathmam, are illustrated in a Victoria and Albert Museum exhibition catalogue, *English Pottery and Porcelain*, marking the twenty-first anniversary of the English Ceramic Circle, 1948 (figs. 308, 309).

Although this particular model does not appear in a list of Derby figures and their prices made in the early nineteenth century, pairs of candlesticks of about the same height were valued at £1.10 (Haslem, *The Old Derby China Factory: The Workmen and Their Productions*, p. 176, nos. 284, 287).

162 Butter Tub

H. 4½ (11.4); W. 5 (12.7); D. 4 (10.2).

THE OCTAGONAL vessel has flaring sides and domed cover with a strawberry sprig finial. The front and back walls are painted with vignettes of exotic birds, including a pheasant and a species resembling a secretary bird; the end walls are decorated with butterflies and other flying insects, a theme repeated upon the cover, where they surround the molded leaves of the strawberry finial. The rims of the cover and box are finished with a narrow fillet of chestnut-brown. The birds and insects are painted in tones of aubergine, iron-red, pale yellow, and green.

Unmarked. On the underside are three irregular "patchmarks."

Derby, dating from about 1755–1760.

Formerly in the collection of E. Gillespie, Edgbaston, Birmingham.

163 Woodpecker

H. 6¼ (15.9); w. 3¾ (9.5); D. 4⅛ (10.5).

THE BIRD, perched on a tree stump, is looking sharply over its left shoulder. The almost white body is painted with a prominent patch of purple that encircles the eye and forms a triangular zone at the throat, then continues across the shoulders and onto the lower wing feathers, where it is mixed with white. The tail is sepia. The figure stands on a spirally modeled tree stump studded with flowers and leaves.

Unmarked. On the underside are three irregular "patchmarks."

Derby, dating from about 1755–1770.

The woodpecker model is rarely seen, and is not named among the species of birds mentioned in Haslem's *The Old Derby China Factory: The Workmen and Their Productions* (p. 178), where the only reference to birds is "Canary Birds, Tomtit, Linnet, Birds on Branches, two sizes."

[359]

164 A–D   Two Pairs of Fig-Leaf Dishes

164 A, B: H. 2 (5.1); W. 8½ (21.6);
D. 8⅛ (20.6).

164 C, D: H. 2 (5.1); W. 8¼ (21.0);
D. 8 (20.4).

EACH DISH is of conventionalized fig-leaf design, with a handle in the form of a forked twig, one branch of which extends halfway to the center of the dish. The interior is painted with nosegays of roses and anemones, principally pink and purple, interspersed with single blossoms and a central butterfly, colored yellow, pink, and blue. The rims of one pair are edged with brown, those of the other with claret.

Unmarked.

Longton Hall, dating from about 1755–1760.

Similar dishes have been published in *English Pottery and Porcelain*, catalogue of an exhibition at the Victoria and Albert Museum marking the twenty-first anniversary of the English Ceramic Circle, 1948 (pl. 74, no. 340); and in Watney, *Longton Hall Porcelain* (fig. 58 A). One in the collection of Mrs. Sigmund J. Katz is illustrated in Savage, *18th-Century English Porcelain*, pl. 74 a. The type is also found painted with harbor scenes; an example was in the collection of Marcel Steele (sold Sotheby's, London, June 26, 1962, lot 85 [illustrated in catalogue]).

Dishes of this type appear to have been used as stands for leaf-shaped basins. An announcement in the *London Public Advertiser*, for April 12–25, 1757, mentions "leaf Basons and Plates" among the varied wares offered at public sale (Watney, *op. cit.*, p. 66).

165 A, B Two Fig-Leaf Dishes

165 A: H. 1⅝ (4.2); W. 8¹⁵⁄₁₆ (22.7);
D. 8³⁄₁₆ (20.9).

165 B. H. 1¾ (4.5), W. 8⅞ (22.6);
D. 7¹⁵⁄₁₆ (20.1).

EACH is of conventionalized fig-leaf shape, with a handle in the form of a stout green stem, following the line of the rim. The end of the cavetto to which the handle is attached is molded in relief with three purple and yellow pansies and a spray of leaves, and at the opposite end are three molded ginkgo leaves, their violet stems extending as branching tendrils to form the molded rim of the dish. Nosegays and single blossoms (and on No. 165 A, flying insects) are painted in brilliant colors at the center.

Unmarked.

Longton Hall, dating from about 1755–1760.

Although the dishes may be regarded as a pair, there is some difference in the color of the ginkgo leaves, which on No. 165 A are blue-green and on No. 165 B, grass-green.

A similar dish, part of a sauceboat and stand, from the collection of Dr. and Mrs. Statham, was sold at Sotheby's, London, October 16, 1956, lot 122 (illustrated in catalogue). Another, from the collection of Mrs. Peggy Ann Hawkins, Lexington, Virginia, was sold at Sotheby's, London, June 2, 1959, lot 66 (illustrated in catalogue). A dish, one of a pair, from the collection of Marcel Steele, was sold at Sotheby's, London, June 26, 1962, lot 83 (illustrated in catalogue), and another pair of comparable shape and decoration from the collection of Mrs. Rudolph de Trafford was sold at Christie's, London, October 28, 1963, lot 43 (illustrated in catalogue).

[361]

166 A, B Two Leaf Dishes

166 A: H. 7⅛ (18.1); W. 5¾ (14.7);
D. 5¼ (13.4).

166 B: H. 7¼ (18.5); W. 5½ (14.1);
D. 5¼ (13.4).

EACH is heart-shaped with scalloped edges and with a handle in the form of a green twisted stem. The walls are sloping and of petal-form, molded in relief to represent three overlapping leaves. The interior of No. 166 A is painted with four sprigs of flowers in purple, copper-red, starch-blue, and yellow, and the rim is edged with deep reddish purple, in imitation of the rims of Meissen. On No. 166 B the border is tinted yellow-green, grading softly to straw-yellow; each leaf-shaped division is painted with a cluster of naturalistically colored flowers near the end of each puce-colored central rib.

Unmarked.

Longton Hall, dating from about 1755–1760.

A dish of the type of No. 166 A in the collection of Mr. and Mrs. Donald A. MacAlister is illustrated in a Victoria and Albert Museum exhibition catalogue, *English Pottery and Porcelain*, marking the twenty-first anniversary of the English Ceramic Circle, 1948 (pl. 74, fig. 339). A pair similar to No. 166 A from the collection of the Earl of Buckinghamshire was sold at Sotheby's, London, June 18, 1963, lot 94 (illustrated in catalogue).

167 A, B Pair of Leaf Dishes

H. 1⅜ (3.5); W. 8⅜ (21.3); D. 6⁷⁄₁₆ (16.4).

EACH is modeled in relief to represent a large three-lobed leaf lying within a scalloped oval basket-work tray, edged with chestnut-brown. The leaf is bordered with green and yellow. The interior of each dish is painted with a three-branched rib in pinkish lavender, upon which are disposed a large rose, an amber anemone, an amber carnation, and a stem with purple blossoms. Smaller flowers fill the interstices.

Unmarked. The glaze within the foot ring of No. 167 B shows the "dry edge" effect of shrinkage, more frequently found on Worcester porcelain.

Longton Hall, dating from about 1755–1760.

[363]

168 A, B Pair of Leaf and Flower Dishes

H. 2½ (6.4); W. 8⅛ (20.6); D. 7½ (19.0).

EACH is molded in the form of a cupped leaf of modified triangular form, with a handle in the form of a twig, terminating in a bud at one end and a broad green leaf that descends into the dish at the other. The interior is molded in relief with the petals of a white and yellow peony surrounded by a double corolla brushed with puce.

Unmarked.

Longton Hall, dating from about 1755–1760.

A very similar dish from the collection of Mrs. Rudolph de Trafford was sold at Christie's, London, October 28, 1963, lot 44 (illustrated in catalogue). A pair from the collection of Mrs. D. Vernon Harcourt was sold at Sotheby's, London, October 12, 1965, lot 130 (illustrated in catalogue).

The design of these dishes is closely related to that of the contempory *Paönenschalen* made at Meissen. Compare No. 72 in this catalogue.

169 Leaf Dish

H. 1¾ (4.5); Diam. 7⅞ (20.0).

THE CIRCULAR dish has an elaborately serrated
border molded in relief with two pairs of confronted pin-oak leaves, elaborately pierced, painted yellow-green at the edges, and molded with
pale lavender ribs and veins.
    Unmarked.

Longton Hall, dating from about 1755–1760.

170 A, B Pair of Miniature Canaries

170 A: H. 2⁷⁄₁₆ (6.2); W. 2¼ (5.7); D. 1¾ (4.5).

170 B: H. 2³⁄₁₆ (5.6); W. 2⁹⁄₁₆ (6.6); D. 2 (5.1).

EACH yellow canary is penciled delicately with sepia, the male (No. 170 A) with touches of purplish brown upon the head. Each is perched on a tree stump, the branches of which support broadpetaled flowers and leaves.

Unmarked.

Bow, dating from about 1758.

The canaries are early examples of bird sculptures in bone-ash paste.

A similar model is in the Museum of the Rhode Island School of Design, Providence; three others are in the collection of Irwin Untermyer, New York (Hackenbroch, *Chelsea and Other English Porcelain in the Irwin Untermyer Collection*, pl. 87, fig. 258).

171 Miniature Finch

H. 3¾ (9.5); W. 4¼ (10.8); D. 3½ (8.9).

THE SMALL bird, perched on a tree stump, is preening the under surface of its extended right wing. The plumage is multicolored, with areas of streaky blue at the head and tail, puce on the back, breast, and wing primaries, and yellow at the shoulders and tail. All of these areas are sparsely stippled with black hatchings. The tree stump is studded with yellow and blue-green leaves and small flowers.

Unmarked. The bird is inscribed "Cecil No. 113," Cecil being the family name of Lord Rockley.

Bow, dating from about 1760.

Formerly in the collection of Lord Rockley.

The model exists in the Schreiber Collection in the Victoria and Albert Museum, London (Rackham, *Catalogue*, I, no. 63). An example, mounted on the lid of a vase, was in the collection of Lady Ludlow (Hayden, *Old English Porcelain, the Lady Ludlow Collection*, pl. 53), and another is in the collection of Irwin Untermyer, New York (Hackenbroch, *Chelsea and Other English Porcelain in the Irwin Untermyer Collection*, pl. 87, fig. 257, where it is called a bunting).

A comparable model from the collection of Sir Bernard Eckstein was sold at Sotheby's, London, March 29, 1949, lot 79 (illustrated in catalogue, pl. XVI). Another, from the collection of Mrs. Edward Hutton, was sold at Sotheby's, London, November 23, 1965, lot 22 (illustrated in catalogue).

H. 3⅛ (8.0); Diam. 2¾ (7.0).

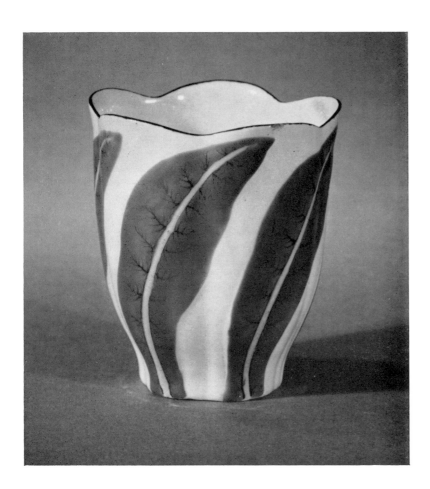

THE DEEP, tulip-shaped cup is delicately lobed, its undulating rim edged with umber. Around its sides are five slightly raised *scolopendrium* leaves, painted rich green, each leaf inclining to the right and having a yellow central rib that stops just short of the pointed tip.

Unmarked.

Worcester, dating from about 1755.

A closely similar cup, with its saucer, is in the collection of F. Severne Mackenna, Droitwich, Worcestershire (see Mackenna, *Worcester Porcelain, the Wall Period and Its Antecedents*, pl. 40, fig. 81). Vessels with this type of decoration are commonly called "scolopendrium cups."

The design was copied from Chelsea. For an example from that factory, with its saucer, see Mackenna, *Chelsea Porcelain, the Red Anchor Wares*, pl. 9, fig. 18.

173 A, B   Pair of Leaf Dishes

173 A: H. 6¼ (15.9); W. 6 (15.3).

173 B: H. 6¼ (15.9); W. 5¾ (14.7).

EACH shallow circular dish is of the so-called "Blind Earl" type, with a scalloped border. From either end of the green rustic handle springs a scrolling stem with paired blue-green leaves of almond shape, molded in low relief and filling a large area of the cavetto and the border. From the forked end of the handle a further stem emerges, terminating in two pink rosebuds in high relief, one resting upon the border, the other on the curve of the chute. The stems are painted with short brown spicules.

Unmarked.

Worcester, dating from about 1765–1770.

A variant form dating from about 1770 in the Humphrey Collection (catalogue no. C29–1915) at the Fitzwilliam Museum, Cambridge, has a border molded and gilded with C-scrolls. Because some of the details are molded in relief and therefore easily recognizable by a blind man, this type of dish has been popularly called "Blind Earl." The term is anachronistic, if, as is believed, it refers to George William, 6th Earl of Coventry, who did not become blind until 1780; a similar model was produced at Chelsea during the red anchor period (1752–1758).

See Nos. 174 and 175.

174 Leaf Dish

H. 1¼ (3.2); w. 6⅜ (16.2); d. 5¾ (14.7).

THE CIRCULAR dish has a scalloped border and a handle in the form of a twig. It is of the same type as Nos. 173 A and B, but differs in that the molded relief is left uncolored. The cavetto is painted with garlands and nosegays of multicolored flowers, and the rim is gilded with a toothed pattern.

Unmarked.

Worcester, dating from about 1765–1770.

Comparable examples with varying painted decoration are in the collections of The Metropolitan Museum of Art, New York (acc. no. 39.181.4), and the Victoria and Albert Museum, London (Allen Collection, catalogue no. 219). Others are illustrated in Barrett, *Worcester Porcelain*, fig. 31 B; Hannover, *Pottery and Porcelain*, III, *European Porcelain*, fig. 819; Honey, *Old English Porcelain*, pl. 64; and Marshall, *Coloured Worcester Porcelain of the First Period*, pl. 53, no. 1083. See also No. 175.

175 Leaf Dish

H. 1¼ (3.2); W. 6¼ (15.9); D. 5¾ (14.7).

THE DISH is of the same type as No. 174, but differs in that the center is painted with three seated Oriental figures: at right, a sage (probably Putai) with a fan, leaning against a mound of rock; at center, a boy acolyte holding a lotus stem; and at left, a youth holding a brocade ball. The wavy rim is gilded with a dotted and serrated narrow band.

Unmarked.

Worcester, dating from about 1765–1770.

A dish decorated in the same manner is illustrated in Hobson, *Worcester Porcelain*, pl. XXIV.

[371]

ORIENTAL PORCELAIN

INTRODUCTION

The Mounting of Oriental Porcelain

Tʜᴇ ᴘʀᴀᴄᴛɪᴄᴇ of mounting highly prized and exotic objects of various sorts in precious or semi-precious metals is of very considerable antiquity. A visit to any of the great ecclesiastical treasuries of Europe quickly makes this evident. Perhaps the most notable place where numerous examples of such works are to be found is the Treasury of St. Mark's at Venice. Here, displayed today in vitrines but formerly in regular liturgical use, are cups dating from classical antiquity carved from precious or semi-precious stones mounted in metal (generally silver gilt but occasionally of other and more precious materials) at Byzantium in the early Middle Ages or further west in the later, Gothic period. The intention was obviously to pay tribute to the rarity of the prized object rather than to enhance its appearance by the contrast with the setting.

During the Renaissance the practice was not confined to ecclesiastical treasuries only. Among the precious objects to be seen in the Argenteria in the Palazzo Pitti at Florence are many ancient cups and vases of sardonyx, amethyst, and even petrified wood, mounted in silver gilt for the Medici in Renaissance times. On a number of them, Lorenzo de' Medici, il Magnifico (1449–1492), had his name cut (generally in the form ʟᴀᴜʀ ᴍᴇᴅ) as a sort of collector's mark and as an indication of the esteem in which he held such things.[1] As evidence that the practice was not confined to southern Europe and had begun even before this, there is at the Musée Jacques Coeur at Bourges a yellow agate cup coming from the former Sainte-Chapelle of the palace there. This was almost certainly once mounted in gold as a chalice for Jean, Duc de Berry (1340–1416).[2] At a later time it was deemed to have been a relic of the Marriage at Cana, but, in fact, it is probably of Fatimid origin. Rare as it is today, such pieces appear fairly regularly in inventories of the late Middle Ages and Renaissance.

Lorenzo de' Medici, too, had among his treasures cups of Arabic work dating from the Fatimid period and carved probably in Cairo, mounted in silver gilt like the antique vessels already mentioned. With such objects as these we approach more closely to the subject of this essay: the mounting of Oriental porcelain in settings of a Western character. Closer still is the so-called *scodella* [bowl] *di Usan*

---

1. The most accessible corpus of illustrations is to be found in Morassi, *Art Treasures of the Medici*.

2. Illustrated in Meiss, *French Painting of the Time of Jean de Berry*, II, fig. 472.

Figure 1. Glass bowl of Persian manufacture, with Byzantine silver-gilt mounts of the XI century. Treasury of St. Mark's, Venice

OPPOSITE

Figure 2. Watercolor drawing of the Fonthill-Gaignières vase. Bibliothèque Nationale

Figure 3. Detail of frontispiece from Britton's Graphical and Literary Illustrations of Fonthill Abbey, Wiltshire, showing the same vase illustrated in Figure 2. The Metropolitan Museum of Art Library

Hassan, Shah of Persia, in the Treasury of St. Mark's.[3] This is a bluish-green glass bowl (Figure 1), decorated with running hares in relief. It is mounted with a deep rim of silver gilt, partially enameled and set with imitation precious stones, of Byzantine workmanship of the eleventh century, and therefore antedating Usan Hassan's reign by some three centuries. An inscription on the base of the bowl indicates that it was made at Khorasan in Persia.

More cognate still to our subject matter (for it is a purely secular work) is an object that appeared in Western Europe in the fourteenth century. This is a bottle of white Chinese porcelain, now in the National Museum of Ireland, Dublin, which is known sometimes as the Gaignières-Fonthill vase from the drawings of it made for the archaeologist Gaignières in 1713 (Figure 2) and the records of its appearance when it was in the collection of William Beckford of Fonthill (Figure 3). Although most unhappily it has lost the original mounts today, the late Arthur Lane was able to show[4] that this bottle, made in or near Ching-tê-chên around 1300, was mounted in silver gilt with elaborate armorial decoration in enamel on the occasion, in or shortly after 1381, of the succession of Charles III of Durazzo to the throne of Naples. The mounts were almost certainly of Hungarian workmanship and created at the court of Louis the Great of Hungary (1326–1382) for presentation to Charles III.

The subsequent history of this remarkable piece need not detain us here; Lane worked it out in impressive detail. The tragic feature of its history is that this, the earliest example of mounted Chinese porcelain to have survived into the modern period, should have been stripped of its mounts some time between its appearance at the Fonthill sale in 1823 and William Beckford's death in 1844, at a period

3. See Gallo, *Il Tesoro di S. Marco e la Sua Storia*, pp. 206–212, pl. 64, figs. 108, 109.

4. Lane, *Burlington Magazine*, April 1961, pp. 124–132.

when its great historical importance was already well understood. It is certain that Beckford himself would never have deprived it of its precious European setting. Possibly the damage was done by a thief who believed the mounts to be of gold.

In its day this mounted porcelain object was not so exceedingly rare as we are inclined to suppose today. In the 1416 inventory of Jean, Duc de Berry, for instance, the following item appears:

Item. une aiguière de pourcellaine ouvrée, le pié, couvercle et biberon de laquelle sont d'argent doré

This piece had been presented to the duke by the Avignon Pope John XXIII in November 1410 and has sometimes been confused with the Gaignières-Fonthill vase.

Arthur Lane also drew attention to an entry in the *Inventaire des Joyaux de la Couronne de France* drawn up in 1560, which describes as existing at Fontainebleau:

Un petit vase de pourcelaine avec son couvercle, l'once, le pied et le biberon d'argent doré,
    estimé XX

which was evidently an object of considerable antiquity at that date. It may indeed even have been the

Figure 4. Two from a group of Wan Li porcelain vessels (1573–1619), mounted by an unidentified London silver-smith about 1585. The Metropolitan Museum of Art, Rogers Fund, 44.14.2, 4

piece mentioned earlier in the Duc de Berry's inventory. Other examples of such things could be quoted from early inventories.

The earliest piece of Oriental porcelain to survive still complete with its mounts seems to be a celadon bowl of the Sung period (980–1279) mounted in silver gilt as a covered cup. It is to be found today in the Landesmuseum at Cassel.[5] This object is known to have been brought back from a voyage in the Orient undertaken by Count Philip of Catzenelnbogen between 1433 and 1444. The mounts were added soon after the count's return, and in any case before 1453, as the armorial bearings on the cup's mounts bear witness. Doubtless, a few other examples of mounted Oriental porcelain were to be found in Europe before the sixteenth century, but if so they have been destroyed or have lost their mounts. Nevertheless, it is evident that the practice of mounting Oriental porcelain is of considerable antiquity even if it is rare before the seventeenth century.

IN THE SIXTEENTH and seventeenth centuries, communications with the Far East grew gradually easier, and quite a number of pieces of Chinese porcelain, particularly the blue-and-white porcelain of the Ming Dynasty (1368–1644), survive complete with their contemporary European mounts, usually of silver or silver gilt. The arrival of the first piece of this blue-and-white porcelain in England can be documented with precision to 1506. In that year the King of Castile, Philip of Austria, and his wife,

5. Illustrated by Hackenbroch, *Connoisseur*, June 1955, p. 22, fig. 3.

Joanna, were driven off course by a storm and forced to land at Weymouth in Dorset where Sir Thomas Trenchard entertained them at Wolverton House. In gratitude their guests presented them with two Chinese bowls of the Hsüan-Tê period (1426–1435) decorated in blue and white. Later in the sixteenth century one of these bowls was provided with silver-gilt mounts.[6] It survives in an English private collection.

Better known, though not reaching England quite so early, is a celadon cup dating from the early Ming period with silver-gilt mounts, known as the Warham cup.[7] This was presented to New College, Oxford, by Archbishop Warham in 1530, a date that provides a *terminus ante quem* for the mounting. What appears to be the earliest example of Chinese porcelain with dated mounts is a blue-and-white Ming bowl in the Museo Civico at Bologna, whose silver-gilt mounts of unknown (perhaps Portuguese) provenance are dated 1554. A little later than this is a Chinese porcelain bowl of gray-blue color with silver-gilt mounts bearing the London date-letter for 1569/1570 and the mark, FR, of an unidentified goldsmith. This object, known as the Lennard cup from the name of its former owner, is now in the collection of the David Foundation at London University. In fact, quite a number of examples of blue-and-white Chinese porcelain, with silver-gilt mounts dating from the Elizabethan period, survive. Clearly they were popular. A particularly notable group of them once in the possession of William Cecil, Queen Elizabeth's Lord Treasurer, is presumed to have remained at Burghley House until acquired by J. P. Morgan early in this century. It is now in The Metropolitan Museum of Art, New York (Figure 4).[8] An important covered cup of Ming porcelain with English silver-gilt mounts from the second half of the sixteenth century is in the collection of Irwin Untermyer, New York.[9] More spectacular than these must have been a bowl of white Chinese porcelain mounted in gold, which Lord Burghley presented to Queen Elizabeth on New Year's Day, 1587, and which he followed up with the present of a similarly mounted cup of the same material a year later. But these have long since vanished. No doubt the gold mounts were melted down.

The English love of mounted Oriental porcelain seems to have waned somewhat toward the end of the sixteenth century, and thereafter, for a time, Dutch silversmiths seem to have become the principal practitioners of the technique. This was certainly a consequence of the foundation of the highly successful Dutch East India Company in 1602. The mounts used by Dutch silversmiths on Oriental porcelain were generally a good deal more conventionalized and less imaginative than those used earlier in Elizabethan England. A bowl would be surrounded with a fairly simply decorated rim and provided with a molded foot, the two mounts being often linked along the sides by bands of strapwork or some other simple pierced motif. Such bowls are often to be seen in Dutch still lifes of the period, and they created a pattern that was frequently adopted in France in the latter part of the century. It is, however, hardly

6. *Ibid.*, p. 24.
7. *Ibid.*, fig. 4.
8. *Ibid.*, figs. 10, 11.
9. Hackenbroch, *English and Other Silver in the Irwin Untermyer Collection*, rev. ed., no. 4.

necessary to discuss Dutch practice here in detail. Sufficient evidence has been produced to show that the mounting of Oriental porcelain was a widely established practice in Europe by the early seventeenth century.

A great change occurred in the commerce in Oriental porcelain during the course of that century. Since the end of the Middle Ages, the carrying trade with the East had been almost entirely in the hands of the Portuguese and the Spaniards, except for a few pieces that continued to reach Europe by the overland route from Asia, generally through Venice. Perhaps the first occasion on which any great quantity of Oriental porcelain reached England was when the *Madre de Dios*, returning from Goa, was captured off the Azores in 1592 with a rich cargo of Eastern treasures, including, according to Hakluyt, "porcellan vessels of China." But with the opening of the seventeenth century, other European countries determined to capture at least a part of this important Hispanic trade. The first English East India Company was granted a charter by Queen Elizabeth on the last day of the sixteenth century. Two years later the Dutch East India Company was founded, and in 1604 a similar though short-lived French company was formed under the protection of Henry IV. It was to be revived several times in the course of the century. The Danes followed in 1616. The result of this activity was that by the latter part of the century Oriental china had ceased to be a rarity in Europe. Paradoxically, the consequence of this was not to make Chinese porcelain less highly prized. Instead, it became even more fashionable, and every sovereign or great nobleman wished to have a "China cabinet," the walls of which were almost entirely covered with Oriental porcelain on wall brackets, on shelves, on chimneypieces, and in niches (see Introduction to Meissen porcelain, pp. 5, 10). That the large quantities of specie leaving Europe for the East to pay for this "China mania" provided a great stimulus to the invention of European porcelain is also commented on in the Introduction to Meissen porcelain (see p. 3).

It was characteristic of Louis XIV's urge to outdo all rivals that his first important essay in this new taste for Oriental porcelain should have been to build the Trianon de Porcelaine as a garden pavilion for Mme de Montespan in 1670–1671,[10] even though it was only made of European faïence tiles decorated in a vaguely Chinese fashion. The taste for Oriental exoticism in France was given a great fillip shortly afterward, in 1683, by the arrival of the so-called Siamese embassy (in fact it was a privately organized trade delegation), which brought a rich consignment of materials of various sorts, including a quantity of porcelain, from the Far East as presents to the king, his family, and the leading courtiers at Versailles.[11] Although a good deal is known about this embassy and its consequences for France's Eastern trade, it is unfortunate that the section of the *Inventaire Générale des Meubles de la Couronne* dealing with the presents for the king has disappeared altogether, for it certainly included much Chinese porcelain. What few descriptions of Oriental porcelains survive in the inventory today are regrettably

10. See Danes, *La Première Maison Royale de Trianon, 1670–1687*.

11. The most useful account of the consequences of the visit of this embassy to Paris is to be found in Belevitch-Stankevitch, *Le Goût Chinois en France au Temps de Louis XIV*, an altogether most valuable study of the early development of the taste for Chinese works of art in France.

brief. As Fontanieu, the *intendant-général*, was to remark later in 1718 of these vanished entries in the inventory, "presque toutes le porcelaines de ce chapître ne sont pas designées d'une façon convenable à les faire reconnoistre." A few items of mounted porcelain appear among the *Vase d'Agathes*, etc., for instance:

> 123 Une couppe de porcelaine, avec son couvercle sur lequel est un anneau tortillé de vermeil, le pied rond et plat avec un bord de fueüilages de vermeil, haulte de 7 pouces, et 4 ½ de diamètre.[12]

but there are only three or four of them.

A manuscript inventory of the *Agates, Cristaux, Porcelaines, Bronzes et autres Curiositiez qui sont dans le cabinet de Monseigneur le Dauphin à Versailles*, drawn up in 1689, is, however, a good deal more informative.[13] It contains an entire section for *Porcelaines Données par les Siamois*, listing sixty-four pieces and describing them in considerable detail, and, in addition, has a separate section for Oriental porcelains acquired from other sources that includes no less than 304 items with full descriptions.

The Grand Dauphin, Louis XIV's eldest son (1666–1711), though a political nonentity, was a passionate collector. We know from contemporary descriptions that his apartments at Versailles, Choisy, Saint-Germain, and especially at Meudon were filled to overflowing with precious objects, especially mounted cups and vases of rock crystal, lapis, agate, and other semi-precious stones, many of them displayed in cases designed by André-Charles Boulle himself. At his death they were dispersed. The finest rock-crystal objects went to his son the King of Spain, his jewels to his younger son, the Duc de Berry, but the greater part of the mounted objects from Meudon, including most of his Oriental porcelains, were sold "avec une indécence qui n'a peut-être eu d'example," according to Saint-Simon, to pay the Dauphin's debts.

The manuscript inventory mentioned above has enabled Pierre Verlet to trace a few of the vases of agate and other semi-precious stones surviving in museums today,[14] but with one solitary exception, the mounted porcelains the Dauphin possessed have baffled identification. The exception is the Gaignières-Fonthill vase already described. This appears as item 111 in the inventory and was in his apartments at Choisy. The Dauphin, who was a careful collector, recorded in the margin that it had cost him the relatively small sum of thirty pistoles, a good deal less than many of his unmounted Oriental porcelains.

THE GREATER part of the Grand Dauphin's mounted Oriental china was set in silver gilt. The opening item of the section of the inventory dealing with *Porcelaines* may serve as an example:

> 1 Une grande Urne de Porcelaine bleüe garnie au pied d'un grand cercle à feuillages, de son couvercle de mesme terminé par deux pommes une grosse & une petite avec deux anses en festons, deux oiseaux dessus passées dans les musles de Lions; Le tout de vermeil doré, haute d'un pied & large de cinq pouces une ligne.

12. Guiffrey, *Inventaire Général du Mobilier de la Couronne sous Louis XIV*, I, p. 190.

13. The manuscript was formerly in the Chardin and Philips collections and reappeared in the London sale rooms of Messrs Knight, Frank, and Rutley on May 18, 1960, lot 304.

14. *Art de France*, III (1963), pp. 135–151.

This had cost the prince 150 pistoles and is indicated also in the margin as being at Meudon.

Intermixed among the numerous pieces mounted in silver gilt that the Dauphin possessed are listed a small number mounted in gilt bronze. One of these few appears as item 307 in the inventory:

> Une grande Urne bleue & blanche ornée au corps d'une grande campagne en broderie & d'une moyenne au bas, sur un pied en cul de lampe de cuivre doré à godrons, soutenu de trois consoles entre lesquels sont trois masques d'appliques, avec son couvercle orné d'une campagne en broderie & d'autres petits ornemens, enrichi de deux cercles à moulure de cuivre doré & terminé par une pomme de pin dans une espèce de vase à feuillages. Haute de seize pouces deux lignes & de diamètre au corps deux pieds trois lignes.

This had cost the Dauphin the considerable sum of two hundred pistoles, but most of the ormolu-mounted porcelain was valued at far less than this.

None of the Dauphin's porcelains, except the Gaignières-Fonthill vase already noted, can be traced today. Many were still identifiable in the eighteenth century and considered important enough to have attention drawn to them in contemporary sale catalogues when they came up at auction. In the catalogue of the Duc de Tallard's sale in 1756, for example, several pieces are indicated as having come from the collections of Monseigneur. "Tout le monde sait que ce Prince avoit formé dans ce genre le plus rare assemblage qu'il soit possible d'imaginer," a note on p. 258 of the catalogue asserts, and continues, "après sa mort, son Cabinet fut vendu, suivant ses dernières volontés; c'est de cette manière que toutes les belles Porcelaines qu'il contenoit furent dispersées dans plusieurs Cabinets." One of these cabinets was eventually the celebrated collection of Oriental porcelain belonging to the Duc d'Aumont. The catalogue of the sale held in 1782 after the duke's death includes a section headed *Porcelaines d'Ancien Bleu et Blanc de la Chine*. In this, Julliot and Paillet, the auctioneers, write: "Les Porcelaines de ce Cabinet en cette espèce, ont originairement appartenu pour la plupart à Monseigneur le Dauphin; fils de Louis XIV, qui aimoit ce beau genre, & s'en étoit fait une Collection recommandable." They suggest (the phraseology is not perfectly clear) that the twelve succeeding items came, in fact, from the Dauphin's collection. Evidently they had undergone some modification in the course of the eighteenth century, for the compilers of the catalogue note of "Une précieuse Garniture de trois grandes Bouteilles . . ." mounted in gilt bronze (lot 199), "C'est bien à juste titre, que les morceaux de premier genre en cette sorte ont été estimés, & il faut qu'on en ait toujours fait un grand cas, puisqu'il y a environ 30 ans qu'on a vu ces bouteilles garnies de vermeil relevé de fleurons d'or, ce qui constate bien le mérite qui leur avoit été reconnu."

The substitution of the less costly gilt bronze for the original silver-gilt mounts is likely to have been a matter of taste rather than due to any damage that the original Louis XIV mounts may have suffered with the passage of time. The relative scarcity of ormolu-mounted porcelains in the Grand Dauphin's inventory as compared with silver-gilt mounts is likewise a reflection of the taste of his period rather than of any special leaning toward fastuous display by a member of Louis XIV's own family. Oriental vases with gilt-bronze mounts dating from the Louis XIV period are rare today compared with those of the Louis XV and Louis XVI periods, and probably always were. One of the few surviving pieces of Chinese porcelain mounted with gilt bronze that can be dated to the Louis XIV period with some certainty is a large dark blue vase mounted with a severely chased lid and base and having twisted handles springing from female masks attached to the shoulders at each side. The base of this is engraved *Cabinet du Roi V. G. No. 17*.[15] To write thus is not to assert that ormolu-mounted porcelain of the Louis XIV period does not survive, nor that it cannot be identified on stylistic grounds. Generally, the mounts follow a more or less similar design to those in silver gilt of the same period. They usually consist of handles springing from masks or winged half-figures, moldings of a relatively simple pattern, finials in the form of pineapples or bowls of fruit, and a general enhancing of the architectural character of the porcelain, in contrast to the fantastic character of the mounts devised in the following reign. But almost certainly ormolu-mounted Oriental porcelain of the Louis XVI period was always fairly rare. Most of it probably dates from the second half of the reign, when the king's disastrous foreign policy had made silver-gilt mounts difficult to create on economic grounds.

But if indeed the reorientation of taste in mounted porcelain that characterized the eighteenth century had some of its roots in such materialistic factors as this, the change had come to stay. It is unusual to find records of Oriental porcelain set in mounts of silver gilt later in the eighteenth century, when economy was certainly no longer a conditioning factor, and when they appear they are likely to be rare survivors from an earlier period. Such was probably the "Théiere de pareille [i.e., white] Porcelaine montée en Vermeil & endommagée," which was part of lot 68 of the sale of the famous collection of Oriental porcelain formed by M. Angran, Vicomte de Fonspertuis, dispersed in 1747. In the case of an even rarer item in the same sale, lot 52, "Un magnifique Pot-Pourri à double couvercle, d'ancienne Porcelaine truitée, à fleurs de couleur, & monté en or," we know this to have been the case, for Gersaint, the compiler of the catalogue, tells us that it had formerly belonged to that famous collector Mme de Verruë, a mistress of the Regent, who had been given it by "Monsieur de Duc, Prince de Condé, qui avoit beaucoup d'amour pour l'ancienne Porcelaine, & qui la connoissoit parfaitement." This was in fact the founder of the Chantilly factory, the potent influence of whose collection of Oriental porcelain on the invention of porcelain in France has been stressed in the Introduction to Sèvres porcelain in this volume.

But a good deal more than half the 320 lots of porcelain included in the Fonspertuis sale in 1747 were mounted in gilt bronze. There can be little doubt that, at this period, Oriental porcelain was quite as greatly admired, even by connoisseurs, when set in mounts of gilt bronze as in its unadorned state. Possibly even more so. In other words, the taste was not, in fact, a purely decorative one. The late Seymour de Ricci noted more than half a century ago that the earliest French sale catalogue in which mounted porcelain was included was that of the collection of the polymath *fermier-général* Bonnier de La Mosson, held in Paris in January 1744.[16] Certainly the writer has been unable to find any earlier instance, and indeed Paris sales in which porcelain of any sort was included at all seem to have been very rare before about 1745. The 1744 sale did not comprise many pieces of mounted Chinese porcelain,

15. Illustrated in Guérin, *La Chinoiserie en l'Europe au XVIIIe Siècle*, pl. 34. Its present whereabouts is unknown to the writer.

16. De Ricci, *Catalogue of a Collection of Mounted Porcelain Belonging to E. M. Hodgkins*, pp. 5–6.

for Bonnier de La Mosson was a great deal more interested in science than in art. Nevertheless, toward the end of the long sale there is a section of the catalogue devoted to porcelains, and a number of them, both Oriental and European, were mounted in gilt bronze. From that time onward, mounted porcelain began to be included in Parisian sales in considerable quantities.

Sale catalogues are, as has been stressed throughout the Introductions to the various volumes of the Wrightsman catalogue, one of the most valuable barometers of public taste that have come down to us, and from such evidence it is perfectly clear that a very marked fashion for Oriental porcelain mounted in gilt bronze must have sprung into existence in France some time around 1740.

In 1741 we find in the *Journal du Garde Meuble de la Couronne* a few mounted porcelains listed as being purchased from the *marchand-mercier* Julliot for the Château de Choisy, either for the apartments of Mme de Mailly or for the king himself. These seem to be the first records of mounted Oriental porcelain being bought for the Crown since the scanty references to it in the Louis XIV period mentioned above. The earliest of these entries, dated April 22, 1741, merely concerns "Un petit Lion de porcelaine bleu céleste, garni en chandelier de bronze doré, avec petites fleurs de porcelaine" (these last items were probably of Meissen porcelain, for the famous Vincennes flowers were yet to come), purchased from Julliot. More important were "Deux pots pourris de porcelaine du Japon fond blanc, à fleurs de couleurs, garnis de bronze doré d'or moulu," which were supplied by the same *marchand-mercier* on December 16, 1741, with two porcelain and ormolu candlesticks "pour servir dans la Garderobe du Roi au château de Choisy." From this time onward, mounted porcelain is fairly frequently mentioned in the *Journal*. In June of the following year, for instance, "le Sr Hébert marchand" furnished a considerable number of important pieces "pour servir dans l'appartement de Mad^e la comtesse de Mailly" in the same château. Thenceforward for a time this famous *marchand suivant la Cour* seems to have shared almost equally with Julliot the honor of furnishing mounted porcelains to the Crown.

That these purchases suddenly begin to appear in the *Journal* in 1741 suggests that the reawakened taste for mounted Oriental porcelain (it seems to have remained more or less dormant during the 1720s) was a fairly new one, though even in this early part of Louis XV's reign the court was never quite in the forefront of fashion. This confirms the evidence of sale catalogues that the climacteric moment for the widespread change of taste in this field occurred in the late 1730s.

To UNDERSTAND why this change should have occurred at this particular moment in time it is necessary to consider, very briefly, the special position that China occupied in French thought in the eighteenth century.[17] The first European reaction to the arrival of large quantities of Chinese objects (textiles, porcelains, lacquers, etc.) toward the end of the seventeenth century was a romantic one. The Chinese were seen as a strange, exotic people living amid quaint surroundings, in a remote never-never land, a sort of arcadian dream world where the laws of morals, science, and religion hardly operated.

17. On this subject see Reichwein, *China and Europe: Intellectual and Artistic Contacts in the Eighteenth Century*, 2nd ed., and Besterman, ed., *Studies on Voltaire and the Eighteenth Century*, XXI, both *passim*.

This is very evident, for instance, in Watteau's chinoiserie decorations at the Château de La Muette, dating from the second decade of the eighteenth century, or in the tapestries of the Tenture des Chinois woven by the Filleul brothers at the Beauvais factory a little earlier. Neither bears any close relationship to China as it really was or indeed attempts to do so.

But if "the men of commerce" who brought Chinese artifacts back from the East to Europe were, as Voltaire wrote, "in search only of wealth," there were others who visited China with much more academic intentions. The Jesuit missionaries, especially, went to China in the most zealous spirit. They wished to study and understand this great nation in order to convert it to European Christianity. But their studies of the history, religion, and customs of this ancient civilization had a paradoxical consequence. As a result of what they learned and reported home about Chinese society from these sources, a considerable number of French thinkers were very nearly converted from Christianity (with which they were, in any case, ceasing to be in sympathy) to an overweening admiration for Confucianism. In 1769, Nicolas-Gabriel Clerc assigned the beginning of this revolution in thought (it was no less than that) to the opening years of the eighteenth century. "From this moment onward," he declared, when writing about the nature of Chinese civilization in *Yu le Grand, Histoire Chinoise*, "a clear conviction banished all uncertainty. . . . Everyone was forced to admire a people as old as it is wise, and as pre-eminent in religion as it is in wisdom." The Jesuit *Lettres Édifiantes et Curieuses*, which began to be published in 1702 and continued for many years, was one of the most influential sources for this reorientation. So was Du Halde's *Description Geographique, Historique . . . de l'Empire de Chine . . .*, which appeared in 1735. But these are mere isolated examples. The bibliography of books and writings on China or related to Chinese thought published in eighteenth century France is immense.[18] It not only includes scientific, philosophical, and religious works of the type already mentioned, but embraces numerous books like *L'Espion Chinois*, which purported to be translated from the Chinese and criticized French habits and morals from a supposedly Oriental point of view, as well as the many satirical or merely erotic fairy tales set in a Chinese framework that were published in France during the eighteenth century. These generally contrasted French and Chinese manners and society to the detriment of the former.

Voltaire was one of the chief propagandists of this curiously excessive admiration for all things Chinese. His play *L'Orphelin de la Chine* (1755) is subtitled *Les Morales de Confucius en Cinq Actes*, and, earlier on, in the *Lettres Philosophiques* (1734), he had written of the Chinese as having "perfected moral science, and that is the first of the sciences." Elsewhere he declares, "what should European princes do when they hear of such examples [of Chinese morality]? Admire and blush, but above all imitate." In 1756, at the suggestion of the physiocrat François Quesnay and urged on by Mme de Pompadour, Louis XV solemnly guided a plough at the opening of the spring tilling in deliberate imitation of the age old fertility ritual performed by the emperors of China at the spring equinox.[19] Admiration could

18. See Cordier, *Bibliotheca Sinica*, 2nd ed.

19. In 1761 the queen, Marie Leszczinska, played an active part as an amateur painter in decorating one of her rooms at Versailles with paintings in the Chinese style (see *Gazette des Beaux-Arts*, May-June 1969, pp. 305 ff.).

[385]

hardly be carried further. By the time the *Encyclopédie* appeared, its principal editor Diderot, a man of great common sense, could declare that the Chinese "dispute the palm with the most enlightened peoples of Europe." A recent writer has declared, ". . . as an example of cultural misunderstanding on a wide scale, the Chinese vogue in seventeenth and eighteenth century France is almost unique in the history of Western thought."[20] But it was more than a vogue. Mistaken or not, it was a real revolution in thought and feeling.

Artistically chinoiserie was the expression of this revolution.[21] Chinoiserie has often been regarded merely as one aspect of the rococo, indeed even (by a writer like Reichwein) as one of the principal causes of the rococo movement. But this is not so. Chinoiseries appeared in France long before the rise of the true rococo, created primarily by Meissonnier, Pineau, and a few others in the 1720s and 1730s. Indeed, chinoiseries have little or nothing in common with Meissonnier's designs for silver or Pineau's architectural decorations, in which the full rococo first appears. These actually made their first appearance at a time when trade restrictions on imports from the Far East were certainly limiting the arrival of Chinese textiles in France and when the influx of porcelain, lacquer, and other Oriental artifacts may also have been reduced below the level at which it had been running at the beginning of the century.

Nevertheless, there was a certain sympathy, almost a consanguinity, between Chinese art and the rococo. It cannot be doubted that familiarity with the strangely distorted perspectives, arbitrary distribution of motifs, and anti-classical compositions of Chinese art, especially as it was known from the decorations on porcelain, lacquer, and textiles, made the use of asymmetry, one of the most prominent features of the full rococo, more readily acceptable to French eyes. The new and strange character of chinoiseries and of the rococo had a good deal in common. Each was anti-classical and nonrealistic.

Whether the French ever believed that their chinoiserie actually resembled Chinese art at all closely is doubtful. Certainly such a belief would have had no basis in fact. Western motifs constantly intrude. In Le Trône, for example, from the series of Beauvais tapestries known as the Tenture des Chinois, a Chinese prince is shown seated beneath a fantastic canopy of almost neo-Gothic form, while a courtier is being wheeled in a garden chair of purely European design. It is the same with the Chinese tapestries designed by Boucher in 1742, nearly half a century later, also for weaving at the Beauvais factory. Here Oriental princesses admire themselves in toilet mirrors of the normal French pattern or take tea while seated on chairs of purely Western design. This intermixing of the familiar and the exotic was not merely the result of insufficiently detailed knowledge of how the Chinese lived. It must have made the Chinese elements in chinoiserie more acceptable to Europeans. It may well be that this was one of the aesthetic motifs behind the vogue for mounting Oriental porcelain in gilt-bronze mounts of a purely Western character. The mounts not only softened the strange character of the Eastern material and made it more readily assimilated by the European eye; they also made it fit more easily into the French interiors where such pieces had inevitably to be displayed.

20. Guy, "The French Image of China before and after Voltaire," in *Studies on Voltaire and the Eighteenth Century*, ed. Besterman, XXI, p. 11.

21. Honour, *Chinoiserie: the Vision of Cathay*, is an admirable discussion of the subject.

WE HAVE already seen that the first recorded examples of mounted porcelain purchased for Louis XV's court came from the *marchand-mercier* Julliot, and that soon afterward Hébert, the only *marchand-mercier* to have an establishment within the confines of the palace of Versailles itself, was also supplying mounted Oriental porcelain to the Crown. The *marchands-merciers* provided the chief retail outlet for imports of porcelain and other Oriental materials onto the French market. For evidence of this it is only necessary to glance at the trade card of the famous *marchand-mercier* Gersaint, the friend of Watteau (Figure 5). Here Chinese objects of every sort are piled up in front of a large cabinet of Chinese lacquer, on the summit of which a bowing *magot* is seated holding a smaller *pagode* in one hand. These things were his principal stock in trade, and the very name of his shop, À la Pagode, gave indication of the wares he retailed.[22] Besides, the *marchands-merciers* were, we know, in regular contact with Amsterdam, the leading port in Europe for the importation of Eastern goods, and were among the principal buyers of Chinese and Japanese goods there.

Figure 5. Trade card of the marchand-mercier Edmé-François Gersaint, engraved after a drawing by Boucher

The role of the *marchands-merciers* as innovators in the sphere of taste needs no stressing here. It has already been emphasized in the Introduction to Volumes I and II of this catalogue (pp. LII–LXI), particularly in relation to the use of Sèvres porcelain plaques for the decoration of furniture. It is impossible to doubt that even if these energetic middlemen were not the first to devise the idea of mounting Oriental porcelains in gilt bronze, they fostered and developed the taste. The evidence provided by the *Livre-Journal* of Lazare Duvaux alone is conclusive on this subject. It is almost impossible to open to any page of this *marchand-mercier's* daybook without encountering one or more items of mounted porcelain, either Oriental or Occidental. Nothing could bear more forceful witness to the persistence throughout the decade 1749 to 1759 of the mania (it was no less) for mounted porcelains, which had arisen rather more than ten years before Duvaux's account book opens. Any selection of entries to illustrate this point must necessarily be arbitrary, so a single, particularly costly, item is chosen here to exemplify the taste and give some idea of the high prices mounted Oriental porcelain commanded by the middle of the century.

> Du 6 décembre [1751]
> Mme la Marq. de Pompadour: Un vase d'ancienne porcelaine bleue imitant le lapis, garni en bronze doré d'or moulu, 1,320 l.—Deux autres vases en hauteur de porcelaine céladon ancienne, montés en forme de buire, en bronze ciselé & dorés d'or moulu, 1,680 l.—Un autre morceau en hauteur à six pans de porcelaine bleu-clair, monté en bronze doré d'or moulu, 1,080 l.—Quatre vases céladon gauffrés, garnis en bronze doré d'or moulu, 1,200 l.
>
> (*Livre-Journal*, no. 967)

Hundreds of other entries would have been equally appropriate for quotation. Some are quoted in the catalogue below under the individual pieces of mounted porcelain to which they appear to bear some more or less tenuous relationship (for example, Catalogue Nos. 187, 191 A and B, and 197 A and B).

Lazare Duvaux certainly commissioned *bronziers* to prepare mounts for porcelain. On August 18, 1751, we find him providing Mme de Pompadour with:

---

22. Juillot's establishment bore the sign Aux Curieux des Indes, and another *marchand's*, Aux Curieux de la Chine.

> Une garniture de porcelaine, bleu-céleste uni, composée de deux chats, & trois bouteilles à dragons garnies en bronze doré d'or moulu, dont les modèles ont esté faits esprès, 1,480 l.
>
> *(Livre-Journal, no. 886)*

On December 30 of the same year, M. de Julienne, the great collector of paintings, purchased porcelain vases from Duvaux and had them mounted:

> Quatre grands vases de porcelaine bleue à cartouches, de 24 louis, 576 l.—Avoir coupé les vases & fait des pieds & gorges à moulures & godrons dorés d'or moulu, 216 l.
>
> *(Livre-Journal, no. 997)*

This throws some light on the methods of mounting vases. Occasionally Duvaux would even have porcelain mounted in some unusual technique. Thus, on October 10, 1751, he supplied Mme de Pompadour with:

> Deux vases de porcelaine bleu-céleste, forme de cruche, montés en cuivre argenté & ciselé, 750 l.
>
> *(Livre-Journal, no. 921)*

On one occasion, on May 1, 1758, he actually reverted to the practice of the previous century and mounted porcelain in silver gilt:

> M. de Dauphin: La garniture en argent ceselé & doré d'or moulu pour un huilier de porcelaine, avec ses caraffes de cristal doré, 156 l.
>
> *(Livre-Journal, no. 3116)*

though in this instance there is no positive evidence that the material was Oriental and not Western porcelain.

Frequently *marchands-merciers* would create elaborately complex compositions such as standishes, perfume burners, scent fountains, etc. For a change, let us take an example of the elaboration of some of these creations from the *Journal du Garde Meuble*. On May 18, 1744, we find the following:

> Livré par le Sr Hébert
> Pour servir dans la Garderobe du Roy, à coté de la nouvelle chambre à coucher de sa Majesté à Versailles.
> Une fontaine de Porcelaine ancienne, truitée gris, de 22 pouces de haut et 16 pouces de large par le bas, montée sur deux gros chiens de porcelaine ancienne fond blanc et couleurs, ornée de bronze d'or moulu, avec une écrivisse bronze sur le couvercle, Le Robinet représentant un signe, Le vase de la fontaine cerclé dans la porcelaine même d'une dentelle brune avec deux anneaux mobiles de pareille porcelaine.
>
> (Archives Nationales, 0¹3313, fol. 113ᵛᵒ)

Often, too, they would combine Oriental and Western porcelain in a single composition:

> Du 20 fevrier 1745 . . . Par le Sr. fayolle. Pour servir sur la cheminée du cabinet de Madame la Dauphine au milieu des deux Girandolles cidessus [which were of Meissen porcelain]. Un pot pouri d'ancienne porcelaine truitée avec son couvercle. Le tout garni de guirlandes de fleurs et d'un bouquet monté en bronze doré d'or moulu, haut de 10 pouces 1/2.
>
> (Archives Nationales, 0¹3313, fol. 173)

where the body was clearly of Chinese porcelain and the bouquet of Meissen flowers.

Duvaux's *Livre-Journal* is also one of the rare sources of information about the craftsmen who made porcelain mounts. Jean-Claude Duplessis (died 1774) seems to have been his principal chosen instrument for this purpose (see the Introduction to Sèvres porcelain in this volume, pp. 161–162, for a lengthier discussion of this craftsman). Duplessis's name appears against a number of entries in the *marchand-mercier*'s daybook. On one occasion (May 15, 1752, no. 1124), Duvaux seems to have even paid his coach fare to Asnières, the country house of the Marquis Voyer d'Argenson, possibly in order that he might discuss the designs of mounts with that fervent collector, for fifteen months later we find the following entry:

> Du 21 [August 1753]: La monture en cuivre ciselé d'un vase de porcelaine bleue, payée à M.
> Duplessis, 720 l.—La dorure d'or molu dudit vase, 192 l.   (*Livre-Journal*, no. 1493)

Duplessis certainly mounted a great deal of porcelain, both European and Oriental. We even get a little light on the style of his mounts from an entry for June 15, 1754:

> Mme la Marq. de Pompadour: La garniture en bronze doré d'or moulu de deux urnes de porcelaine
> céladon, modèles faits exprès par Duplessis, 960 l.—La garniture en bronze doré d'or moulu d'un
> vase en hauteur de porcelaine céladon, à tête de belier, nouveau modèle de Duplessis, 320 l. Le
> port à Bellevue, 3 l. 12 s.   (*Livre-Journal*, no. 1810)

But for the most part we are as much in the dark about the styles in which the various Chinese porcelains were mounted for Duvaux as we are about the names of most of those making the mounts for him or for other clients.

In the entries below one or two attempts have been made, though very tentatively, to identify the makers of mounts and likewise to group together a few pieces whose mounts seem, on stylistic grounds, to be the work of a single *bronzier* or to have come from a single workshop (see, for instance, under Catalogue Nos. 186 A and B). Thus, in the *Wallace Collection Catalogues: Furniture* (see under Nos. F 115 and 116) I have suggested that certain types of mount commonly found on Chinese porcelain in the mid-eighteenth century (many are struck with the crowned C) are in the manner of the goldsmith Thomas Germain *(maître* 1720–1748), who may have provided models for the mounts or even have made them in his workshop. Mounts of a closely related type are to be found here on the pot-pourri bowl Catalogue No. 178. Those on the pair of pot-pourri bowls Catalogue Nos. 176 A and B are of closely related character. In the catalogue below I have tentatively suggested that the mounts on the pair of vases Nos. 189 A and B may perhaps have been designed by Jean-Claude Duplessis. But such suggestions are put forward very hesitantly and must be recognized for what they are—no more than attributions. Positive and certain knowledge in this field is very difficult to obtain. The d'Aumont sale catalogue of 1782, for example, describes in some detail a number of Oriental porcelains mounted by Pierre Gouthière *(maître* 1758–1813/14), but one pair only has been identified with certainty (Dreyfus, *Catalogue Sommaire du Mobilier et des Objets d'Art*, no. 438, pl. XVIII). We are, however, sufficiently familiar with Gouthière's style in other contexts to make certain attributions to him of the mounts of a few Chinese porcelains highly plausible, e.g., a pair of *brûle-parfums* of turquoise-blue porcelain in the form of swans in the Louvre (Dreyfus, *op. cit.*, no. 432, pl. XXXIII).

But for the most part, the creators of these mounts are anonymous and likely to remain so. Thus we learn from the *Almanach Dauphin* of 1777 that a certain Ase was "renommé pour les garnitures de porcelaines et autres vases précieux," but we know absolutely nothing more about him, and the possibility of identifying any of his work is exceedingly remote. The mounts of certain porcelains are sometimes traditionally ascribed to one of the Caffiéris (e.g., *Wallace Collection Catalogues: Furniture*, nos. F 103, 104), but there is no positive evidence that any of the family ever made mounts for porcelain at all.

We learn from Hébert's *Dictionnaire Pittoresque et Historique* that in 1766 Blondel de Gagny possessed a number of vases, etc., mounted by the goldsmith Simon Gallien (*maître* 1714–1757). Among them were "deux Dauphins de porcelaine céladon," mounted by him apparently as ewers.[23] Were these the celadon fish of a type not infrequently met with, mounted with base, handle, and lip incorporating reeds, shells, and scrolls? We do not know, but we have evidence from elsewhere that Gallien provided models for furniture mounts, and a pair of celadon ewers mounted in just this way are in the Wallace Collection (*Wallace Collection Catalogues: Furniture*, nos. F 105, 106). The refinement of their mounts strongly suggests that they are the work of a goldsmith.

Blondel de Gagny also employed a certain Vassou ("dont les talens sont connus," according to the sale catalogue of 1776) to mount vases of porcelain and other materials for him. But the chances of identifying the work of either craftsman with any certainty is exceedingly remote today. The same may be said of the Varins, *père et fils*, who worked for the French Crown in the middle of the eighteenth century and received payments for "ouvrages de bronze en bas relief, vases, figures et autres." Indeed, it is by no means certain that they even made mounts for vases of Oriental porcelain, though it seems highly probable. And for every name of this sort that has come down to us we may be sure that dozens have been forgotten.

If we know little of the craftsmen responsible for the creation of the mounts for Oriental porcelain, we know even less of the artists responsible for designing them insofar as this was done outside the *bronzier*'s workshop. There is some evidence that this did happen from time to time. Lazare Duvaux quite frequently mentions mounts for porcelain "dont on a fait les modèles" (e.g., no. 884) or as being "modèles fait exprès" (e.g., no. 1628). The phrases are admittedly ambiguous, but it would have been consistent with the general practice of *marchands-merciers* if Duvaux had provided the designs himself. More positive evidence that mounts were sometimes specially designed by someone other than their maker is to be found in the sale catalogue of François Boucher's collection, held on February 18 ff., 1771 (Lugt, *Répertoire des Catalogues de Ventes Publiques*, no. 1895). Two items under the heading *Porcelaine Truitée* are described thus:

> 817 Deux vases d'ancienne porcelaine, ornés de deux têtes de belier, dont les cornes servent d'anses, avec guirlande de laurier, piedouche à gorge ornée de bronze doré, très-bien exécutés d'après les desseins de M. Boucher. Chacun porte 7 pouces de haut, sur 5 de large.

23. Hébert, *Dictionnaire Pittoresque et Historique . . .*, 1766, I, pp. 54–55.

The next item but one was

> 819 Deux autres vases, couleur ventre de biche, ornés d'anses composées de serpents qui s'entrelacent
> & d'un masque de satyres avec guirlandes, en bronze doré, de la composition de M. Boucher.

Neither fetched particularly outstanding prices (144 livres and 101.1 livres, respectively), but the descriptions are sufficiently detailed to make identification of examples of the original mounts possible should they appear.

The architect F.-J. Belanger (1744–1818) is on record as designing some of the mounts executed by Pierre Gouthière for the Château de Bagatelle, and may also have done so for the comparatively rare number of Oriental porcelains known to have been mounted by this craftsman for the Duc d'Aumont, for Belanger was patronized by the duke and was closely associated with the marble-cutting atelier he had created (see Volume III of this catalogue, under No. 306), where Gouthière certainly worked. But at almost every point we are balked by lack of positive evidence, and on the whole we know very little about the branch of eighteenth century French craftsmanship concerned with mount-making.

Even to discuss the history of the collecting of mounted Oriental porcelain is impossible, our sources of information are so scanty. In the eighteenth century, it seems that almost all the great collectors of Oriental porcelain from Julienne to the Duc d'Aumont admired it equally whether it was mounted or not. Mme de Pompadour purchased so much mounted porcelain from Lazare Duvaux that she might perhaps be regarded as a collector. Possibly, too, the Duchesse de Mazarin, daughter of the Duc d'Aumont, might qualify. Of the ninety-eight lots of Oriental porcelain in her posthumous sale in 1781, no less than sixty were mounted. An analysis of contemporary sale prices suggests there was a slight plus value for mounted porcelains, but the difference is marginal, and essentially the technique is a subordinate if charming genre. There is, however, little doubt that the taste for mounted porcelains was on the decrease in the Louis XVI period. Of nineteenth and twentieth century collectors, only the Maréchale de Lannes, Duchesse de Montebello, seems in mid-century to have had an exceptionally large collection. This was dispersed by auction after her death at a sale that included eighty-nine lots of mounted porcelain, totaling 132 vases (February 2 ff., 1857, Lugt, *Répertoire des Catalogues de Ventes Publiques*, no. 23338). The prices fetched for none were excessive, the highest being £170 for a pair of celadon bottles with Louis XV mounts. The duchesse is a more or less solitary figure in her period. Early in the present century E. M. Hodgkins published the well-known *Catalogue of a Collection of Mounted Porcelain* prepared by Seymour de Ricci, but as Hodgkins was a dealer his collection was inevitably assembled primarily with an eye on the market. Nineteenth century and early twentieth century collectors of Oriental porcelains, unlike their eighteenth century predecessors, usually despised the mounts on Eastern porcelains and often discarded them. I myself well remember as a boy to have been told with delight by that great collector of Chinese porcelain, the late Leonard Gow, how often he had ruthlessly torn the mounts from some of his finest Ming porcelains and cast them on the rubbish heap. But that was half a century ago. Such vandalism, one hopes, must be rare today.

F. J. B. Watson

Oriental Ceramics in the Wrightsman Collection

IT IS A CURIOUS circumstance that many of the types of Chinese porcelain collected so enthusiastically in Europe in the eighteenth century should be known to us by names that are not Chinese. Today one hears French terms more often than Chinese, and this in spite of the fact that the English, the Germans, and others were very active collectors. Thus one talks of certain polychromes as being of the *famille verte, rose, noire,* or *jaune,* and of the monochromes *blanc de chine, café au lait, clair de lune,* and the various *sangs (de boeuf, de pigéon, de poulet).* This is not to say, however, that Chinese equivalents do not exist, but, rather, that they have only recently begun to gain some currency.

In this catalogue we are primarily concerned with porcelain of a muted gray-green or blue-green color, called celadon. Several explanations have been offered for the origin of the name. The one most frequently heard is that it was the name of a shepherd in a play adapted from the novel *L'Astrée,* by Honoré d'Urfé, published in 1610. Those who hold this belief assume that Celadon's muted green costume suggested a name for a certain shade of green. Robert Schmidt[1] asserts that these porcelains had already been coming into Paris in large numbers at that time. Another explanation of the name associates it with Saladin, Sultan of Egypt, who in 1171 presented forty pieces of celadon to Nur-ad-din, Sultan of Damascus. Those who subscribe to this theory regard the term celadon as a corruption of the name of the donor of this magnificent gift.

Western admirers of celadon have other names for it, designating it by the place of origin, such as Yüeh, Lung-ch'üan, or Northern Celadon. To the Chinese, however, the celadons that Westerners so greatly esteem are included in the broad group called *ch'ing tz'u,* which roughly translated, means green (or blue) porcelain.

Technically, celadon as we recognize it is a ceramic characterized by a sometimes thick, waxy-looking glaze made of feldspar and silica, to which a small amount of iron is added to contribute the gray-green or blue-green color.

It has been customary to think of celadons as a class that does not quite manage to conform to the Western definition of porcelain. We hold that whiteness, translucency, and resonance are three basic attributes of true porcelain. By these standards, celadon is a refined type of stoneware, approaching porcelain in its resonance but lacking the other two essentials. Its high-fired body is usually designated as a "porcellanous material." Sherman Lee[2] has taken a more generous view, in saying that "Modern science and Chinese ceramic tradition agree in defining porcelain *(Tz'u)* to include any high-fired ceram-

---

1. *Porcelain as an Art and a Mirror of Fashion,* p. 31.

2. *Bulletin of the Cleveland Museum of Art,* March 1956, pp. 46–52.

ic of a homogeneous nature where the separation of glaze from the body has been obliterated, regardless of the color or degree of translucency of the result. Accordingly the term 'porcelain' definitely includes celadons of the Sung Dynasty (960–1279) or even earlier, and the term 'proto-porcelain' has been coined to indicate the early ancestors of this green-glazed family." This definition of porcelain, taken in the light of fairly recent archaeological discoveries in China, gives the art of porcelain-making a perspective of over two thousand years.

The celadon vases in this collection, all of which are mounted in gilt bronze, illustrate the major techniques employed in the decoration of the later celadons. On Nos. 186 A and B the clambering lizards represent motifs in high relief of the sort often molded separately and applied upon the surface. A modification of this technique occurs on Nos. 182 A and B, with their mystic trigram and *yin-yang* symbols molded directly on the surface. No. 180 shows a design formed by piercing the walls with symmetrical arrangements of circles, scrolls, and petal shapes. On Nos. 181 A and B symbols of longevity, reserved in the blue-gray glaze, are painted thickly in white and outlined with pencilings of cobalt-blue. No. 179 illustrates a design created by incising the unfired clay with a beveled wooden tool.

Another decorative refinement is the crazing or fissuring of the glaze. While this may seem to the layman to be the result of chance, it is actually a deliberate effect achieved through exquisite mastery of the kiln. Usually the crackle develops as an irregular network of straight and curving lines extending over the entire surface, with the infinite variety of cracks in the thawing ice on a pond. At times it is made to produce patterns running in principally vertical or horizontal directions, or even spiraling around the neck of a vase. It may be dark and assertive or so subtle as to be invisible until the piece is within arm's reach; again, it may be so small and regular as to deserve the allusion to fish scales in the term *truité*.

The use of forms taken from bronze ritual vessels is a characteristic of celadons, as illustrated by Nos. 182 A and B, 186 A and B, 189 A and B, and 190 A and B. This imitation of bronzes has persisted for more than two thousand years, and there exists a group of proto-celadon vessels that, because of their strong resemblance to bronzes of the Warring States period (about 480–222 B.C.), are believed to date from the third century B.C.; indeed, there is feldspathic glazed pottery, in the shape of bronzes, taken from recently excavated tombs in Anhui Province, which archaeologists date to 800 B.C.[3]

THE REPUTATION of Japanese porcelain in the mind of the European collector rests basically on the enameled porcelain made in the vicinity of Arita, on the island of Kyushu. At the aesthetic pinnacle is a class called Kakiemon, after a family of potters and porcelain painters who came to the fore in the seventeenth century. Their particular contribution was the development of enameling, or painting in colors on the surface of the glaze.

No one can say precisely when or how the Japanese first learned how to prepare and successfully paint in enamels, but the fact that their earliest efforts employed red and blue is taken to indicate that

---

3. *Kaogu Xuebao (Chinese Journal of Archaeology)*, no. 4, 1959, pp. 59–91, pls. I–XVIII.

they must have been familiar with similar effects in pottery issuing from private Chinese factories in Ching-tê-chên and Fukien.[4] Traditionally, an Arita pottery merchant, Toshima Tokuyemon, succeeded in mastering the technique, with the help of his foreman, Sakaido Kakiemon (1598–1666), after a long series of experiments. From this collaboration there evolved in the Kakiemon family a distinct style of painting in enamels that extended into a school bearing that name. From the Kakiemon circle the highly stylized representations of floral and animal subjects emanated during the last years of the seventeenth and the early years of the eighteenth century.

The two bowls Nos. 176 A and B are of outstanding importance as examples of the Kakiemon style. In addition, they corroborate early descriptions of this style, which, according to records uncovered by T. Volker,[5] can be traced to 1659, when fifty flasks with red and green painting were ordered by the Dutch. This type of decoration is not known to have been in existence before that date; when executed in a palette extended to include yellow and overglaze blue, as in these bowls, it is safer to assume a date closer to 1780.

Kakiemon porcelain was exported to Europe as part of the China trade and exerted a profound influence upon European ceramic producers for many decades. The style was strongly reflected in the faïence of Delft as well as in the porcelain of Meissen, Chantilly, and the principal English factories. European examples of the Kakiemon style are represented in this catalogue by Nos. 63–66.

A second category of porcelain for which Arita is acclaimed is that of sculptural ornaments in the form of birds and fish. These often bear such a close resemblance to ones made at the same time in China as to make attribution difficult. However, the motif of the leaping carp, as seen in the magnificent pair Nos. 197 A and B with French mounts of gilt bronze, seems peculiarly Japanese; so, too, do the bold splashes of color with which the bases are decorated. Another indication of their provenance is that similar carp were classified as Japanese in the sale catalogue of 1769 of the Gaignat Collection (see under Nos. 197 A and B), since it is exceptional that they should have been thus described at a period when geographical distinctions among Oriental porcelains were not generally observed.

The dating of these ornaments is open to conjecture. Jeffrey S. Story, in a letter to the writer, commented, ". . . in the present state of our knowledge I think circa 1700 is about the best we can do. The Gaignat catalogue provides one terminus for our period and the date when enamelled Japanese porcelain was first imported into Europe (about 1685) provides the other terminus." There is no definite documentation, from European collections known to have been in existence between these dates, as to when such pieces were first available to Western collectors, so for the present we may regard the Genroku period (1688–1703) as the earliest date for them.

C. C. D.

4. Jenyns, *Japanese Porcelain*, p. 108.

5. *Porcelain and the Dutch East India Company*, pp. 129, 130.

176 A, B   Pair of Bowls, Mounted
in Gilt Bronze
as Pots-Pourris

Overall: H. 15⅛ (38.4); W. 16¼ (41.3);
D. 10¼ (26.0).

Porcelain: H. including 1-inch (2.5) bronze
neck ring 9½ (24.2); Diam. 9½ (24.2).

EACH deep, round bowl with low domed cover
has sides that taper, then curve abruptly to meet
the recessed ring foot. They are painted boldly
over the glaze in blue, iron-red, green, and yellow
with clusters of chrysanthemums, peonies, and
other flowers, interspersed with fences and other
garden structures, and accented by cloud scrolls at
the borders. Each is richly ornamented with chased
and gilded bronze mounts surmounted by a spirally twisting spray of flowers and berries on the
cover. Separating the lid from the bowl is a wide
collar edged with bulrushes and scrolls and pierced
with cartouche-shaped openings of varying design. At either side an upswept handle of scrolled
and entwined bulrushes springs from the four
blown acanthus leaves, which form the feet, and
links up with the collar.

Japanese, dating from the second half of the
seventeenth century, perhaps 1660–1680; the
mounts are French, about 1745–1750, and are in
the manner of Thomas Germain (maître orfèvre
1720–1748).

Formerly in the collection of Baroness Renée
de Becker, New York.

These bowls are early examples of the Japanese
porcelains from Arita associated with the enamel

painting of the Kakiemon family of potters and porcelain painters. It is believed that Sakaida Kakiemon (1596–1666) was the first artist to have decorated Japanese porcelains with enamels (or overglaze) colors. The date of his first success is placed at about 1660 or slightly earlier. It is from the Kakiemon circle that the highly stylized representations of floral and animal subjects emanated during the last years of the seventeenth and the early years of the eighteenth century. Kakiemon porcelain was exported to Europe as part of the "China trade" and exerted a profound influence upon European ceramic producers for many decades. The style was strongly reflected in the faïence of Delft as well as in the porcelains of Meissen, Chantilly, and the principal English factories. European examples in the Kakiemon vein are represented in this catalogue by Nos. 45 A and B, 63, 64, 65, and 73 A-JJ.

The glaze of Nos. 176 A and B is bluish white and is characteristic of Arita porcelains produced before the last decade or two of the seventeenth century, when it was superseded by a clear white glaze, upon which was painted a delicate and more formal decoration. A clue to the dating of this newer type is suggested by its presence in the English Royal Collection at Hampton Court Palace, where some of the porcelains were reported by Lane (*Transactions of the Oriental Ceramic Society*, 1949/1950, pp. 29–31) as having "under the base a small circular seal of red wax stamped with the arms of William and Mary. . . . " Lane believed from this evidence it could safely be assured that the entire collection had been formed before Queen Mary II's death in 1694.

See also Volume II of this catalogue, Nos. 249 A and B.

177 Table Fountain, Mounted in Gilt Bronze

Overall: H. 15¼ (38.7); W. 10½ (26.8); D. 7⁷⁄₁₆ (18.8).

Birds: H. 4⅞ (12.4); W. 4 (10.2); D. 2½ (6.4).

Jar: H. 6 (15.2); Diam. 3¾ (9.5).

THE MAIN body of the fountain consists of a cylindrical canister of white Chinese porcelain *(blanc de chine)* with its sides pierced in a diagonal fret pattern and lined with copper. It is flanked by a pair of Meissen swans, seated among bulrushes of naturalistically painted tin *(tôle peinte)* and supported on a flat circular platform of burnished gilt bronze resting on an elaborately scrolled base ornamented with acanthus leaves and floral sprays. In the front is stalactitic work suggesting dripping water. Three groups of scrolls form the feet.

The top of the canister is surrounded by a broad collar of engraved gilt bronze with a border of pendent stalactitic rockwork, and at the bottom, above the rim surrounding the base, is a tap, also of gilt bronze in the form of a frog crouching among bulrushes of *tôle peinte*. A tube in its mouth permits scented water to flow from the interior of the cylinder when the tap is turned. The cylinder is surmounted by a domed lid of white porcelain (a modern replacement) surmounted by a knob in the form of a circular rimmed platform of gilt bronze from which springs a group of metal bulrushes painted naturalistically. The body is flanked at each side by a large scrolling gilt-bronze handle from which bulrushes and leaves emerge.

The canister rests on a tree stump of gilt bronze, on either side of which is a small swan, its brown- and black-marked head held high and slightly turned toward the front. Each bird rests on an oval dome-shaped base colored yellow-green, that beneath the bird at the right being penciled in sepia.

Marks on the birds, if they exist, are concealed by the mounts. Stamped on the mounts four times (on the base in front of the right-hand swan,

on each handle, and on the lid) with the crowned C (for a note on the crowned C, see under Nos. 16 A and B).

The *blanc de chine* vessel dates from the late Ming or early Ch'ing Dynasty of the seventeenth century; models of the Meissen swans probably created about 1747, attributed to Johann Joachim Kaendler (working 1731–1775). The mounts are French, dating from 1745–1749.

The species of swan represented is the mute swan (*Cygnus olor*), native to Europe and Asia.

The pierced porcelain cylinders may have been made originally as brush pots or cricket cages.

A pair of identical cylindrical canisters of Chinese porcelain, which were sold as lot 4 in the Christie's sale of February 24, 1966, were inscribed inside the base in Chinese characters "made by Lin in the T'ien Ch'i period (1620–1627) of the great Ming Dynasty."

Such small composite table fountains are rare. One or two are mentioned by Lazare Duvaux and in eighteenth century sale catalogues. One of turquoise-blue Chinese porcelain supported by two lions of the same material is in the Louvre (catalogue no. 449) and formerly belonged to Marie-Antoinette. An earlier example combining Meissen swans, bulrushes in *tôle peinte*, and a vase of powder-blue Chinese porcelain, also formerly in the French Royal Collection, was on the Paris art market in 1956 (illustrated in color in *Le XVIIIᵉ Siècle Français*, Collection Connaissance des Arts, p. 110). This latter, although apparently incomplete, perhaps came from the same workshop as No. 177.

Two composite objects very similar to No. 177 were lot 348 in the sale of the collection of the historian of French porcelain, Comte X. de Chavagnac (sold Paris, Hôtel Drouot, June 19–21, 1911 [illustrated in catalogue]). They were composed of the bodies of two upright cylindrical teapots of white *blanc de chine* porcelain flanked by a pair of Meissen swans, above a cluster of painted metal bulrushes and a scrolling base of gilt bronze. They were not mounted as perfume fountains. They were clearly produced in the same French workshop as No. 177 and are described as coming from the *ancienne collection de Machault*, i.e. Jean-Baptiste de Machault d'Arnouville, controller of finances and administrator of the Vincennes factory from 1745 to 1754.

A jug at the Munich Residenz affords another interesting comparison. Originally a brush holder of reticulated *blanc de chine* porcelain, it was converted into a pouring vessel by means of a liner and mounts of gold and silver-gilt, the latter bearing the Paris datemark for 1729/1730. It has also been fitted with a cover, presumably of white French porcelain. For a description and illustration, see the 1958 catalogue of the Schatzkammer, no. 971, pl. 47.

Small fountains were originally made for rinsing the hands before or after eating, and often hung on the wall near the dining room door or, later, formed part of the architectural decoration of the room. Such miniscule fountains as No. 177 were, however, almost certainly intended merely to dispense scent to perfume the hands, etc. They are sometimes referred to as *fontaines à parfum*, but there seems no contemporary justification for this name.

The swans appear to be the same model as those illustrated in Savage, *18th-Century German Porcelain*, pl. 19 b (end figure, right), where they are attributed to the Swan Service made for Count Brühl. For a discussion of this point, see under Nos. 9 A and B.

A slightly larger pair of swans, dated about 1740–1750, in the collection of C. H. Fischer, Dresden, was sold at J. M. Heberle, Cologne, October 24, 1906, lots 660 and 670 (illustrated in catalogue, pl. 5). A pair mounted in gilt bronze with Chinese powder-blue jars, from the collection of Thelma Chrysler Foy, New York, was sold at Parke-Bernet, New York, May 23, 1959, lot 643 (illustrated in catalogue). Another pair, mounted in a Louis XV gilt-bronze fountain group, from the collection of Mrs. Derek Fitzgerald, London, was sold at Sotheby's, London, November 26, 1963, lot 158 (illustrated in catalogue). A pair identified as "c. 1737," was sold anonymously at Christie's, London, November 2, 1964, lot 120 (illustrated in catalogue).

A pair of identical Meissen swans is to be found on the mounted pot-pourri bowl No. 35. For others, see Nos. 33 A–C, 34, 36 A and B, 37 A and B. and 38 A and B.

178 Bowl, Mounted in Gilt Bronze as a Pot-Pourri

Overall: H. 16½ (41.9); W. 14½ (36.8).

Porcelain: H. including 1½-inch (3.8) bronze neck ring and 1¼-inch (3.2) ring on cover 12 (30.5); Diam. 12 (30.5).

THE GRAY-green bowl of pumpkin shape is richly mounted in gilded and chased bronze as a pot-pourri bowl. The stepped lid has a flat top with peach finial, almost concealed by the bronze. The mounts, of rococo design, include a shell and coral finial, a pair of bulrush handles springing from the base at each side, a pierced band separating the cover from the vessel, and a circular base, irregularly ribbed, supported on four feet in the form of blown acanthus scrolls.

Stamped on the mounts on the base, and in the center of the front and back, with the crowned C (for a note on the crowned C see under Nos. 16 A and B).

European imitation of Chinese celadon of the seventeenth century; the mounts are French, in the manner of Thomas Germain (*maitre orfèvre* 1720–1748), and possibly by J. C. Duplessis *père* (working 1747–1774), and date from 1745–1749.

See also Volume II of this catalogue, No. 246. The change of attribution was made subsequent to the publication of Volume II.

179　Jar, Mounted in Gilt Bronze

Overall: H. 15⅛ (38.5); W. of base 10⅜ (26.4).

Porcelain: H. 7⅞ (20.0); Diam. 8⅝ (21.9).

THE CONTOURS of this pear-shaped jar with broad, rounded shoulders are subtly interrupted by the line of a narrow collar, and of an almost imperceptible furrow surrounding the body midway and caused by pressure of the potter's fingers in fitting the upper and lower parts together. The decoration, as seen through the sea-green glaze, is executed in two registers: the broad upper zone displays scrolling foliated motifs tooled with intaglio outlines; in the narrower band above the foot, erect plantain leaves have been incised with a fine stylus.

The gilt-bronze mounts consist of a lid of swirling leaves, flowers, and berries rising from foliated scrolls, interspersed with flowers, berries, and ribbed shell motifs; and a base supported on four feet formed of scrolled acanthus leaves over which flowers and berries are trailed.

Chinese celadon, dating from the seventeenth century, during the late Ming or early Ch'ing Dynasty; the mounts are French, dating from about 1750, in the manner of Thomas Germain (*maître orfèvre* 1720–1748).

See also Volume II of this catalogue, No. 251.

180 Vase, Mounted in Gilt Bronze as a Pot-Pourri

Overall: H. 10¾ (27.2); W. 10⅜ (26.4).

Porcelain: H. 7¾ (19.7); Diam. 6¼ (15.9).

THE BODY is formed of two deep, circular bowls coated with transparent sea-green glaze, mounted one upon the other lip to lip to form a pot-pourri vase. The lower bowl has a ring-molded flaring foot. Cover, body, and foot are pierced with a repeating design of star-shaped and fleur de lys motifs alternating with diamond-shaped groupings of small circular apertures.

The whole is richly mounted in chased and gilded bronze, the cover surmounted by a finial of flowers, leaves, and berries, the sides of the cover fitted with two short scroll handles. A broad central band molded with acanthus scrolls serves to anchor two substantial, scrolled handles chased with leaves and berries that spring from the scrolling gilt-bronze base, which rests on six asymmetrically shaped rococo feet.

Stamped on the rim mounts of the lower bowl with the crowned C (for a note on the crowned C, see under Nos. 16 A and B).

Chinese celadon, dating from the eighteenth century; the mounts are French, dating from 1745–1749.

Formerly in the collections of Jacques Doucet (sold Galerie Georges Petit, Paris, June 7–8, 1912, lot 213 [illustrated in catalogue]); Mme Menthe, Paris.

See also Volume II of this catalogue, No. 247.

181 A, B Pair of Vases, Mounted in Gilt Bronze as Pots-Pourris

Overall: H. 10 (25.4); W. 8½ (21.6); Diam. 6⅜ (16.2).

Porcelain: H. approx. 8¾ (22.3); Diam. 6½ (16.5).

EACH ovoid jar, with a disk-shaped lid, is coated with a blue-gray glaze. Upon the slightly convex upper surface of the cover, and again upon opposite sides of the jar, motifs thickly painted in white are outlined and accented with pencilings of cobalt-blue. The cover of each is decorated with a low flowering shrub. On one side of the body of No. 181 A appears a gnarled pine flanked by fungus and a cluster of bamboo, and on the reverse a flying crane and a spotted deer, symbols of longevity. On one side of No. 181 B is a straggling prunus shrub, in flower, and on the reverse a long-tailed bird hovers above a cluster of leaves. The cover of each is separated from the jar by a wide scrolled and foliated band of pierced, chased, and gilded bronze, thus converting it to a pot-pourri vase. Sprays of leaves forming handles spring from the spreading openwork stand of acanthus leafage of rococo design and clasp the sides of the vessel.

Chinese celadon, dating from the early eighteenth century; the mounts are French, about 1750–1755.

Because of the infrequent mention of the type in the account books of the *marchands-merciers*, it may be assumed that such ovoid jars were scarce in eighteenth century France.

See also Volume II of this catalogue, Nos. 248 A and B.

182 A, B Pair of Vases, Mounted in Gilt Bronze

Overall: H. 9½ (24.2); w. of handles 6¼ (15.9).

Porcelain: H. 6¾ (17.2); w. 2½ square (6.4).

EACH straight-walled vase coated with sea-green glaze is square in section with sides decorated in relief in imitation of a jade ritual object (*ts'ung*). A *yin-yang* motif is molded at the center of each side, with a unit of the Eight Mystic Trigrams above and below it. A richly scrolling and pierced lip of gilt bronze, chased with flutings and accented with a pair of openwork rococo cartouches, is fitted to the circular neck; it is joined by two scrolling handles that clasp opposite angles of the vase and link the lip to the pierced and foliated base supported on four scrolling feet.

Chinese celadon, dating from the Ch'ing Dynasty during the eighteenth century; the mounts are French, also eighteenth century, in the style of Louis XV.

Such vases became fashionable in Europe, but perhaps reached the West in any quantity only after 1758. The daybooks of Lazare Duvaux, which end in that year, mention only a single example.

See also Volume II of this catalogue, Nos. 253 A and B.

183 A, B Pair of Vases, Mounted in Gilt Bronze

Overall: H. 11¼ (28.6); W. 7½ (19.0).

Porcelain: H. 7¼ (18.5); Diam. 5⅜ (13.7).

EACH baluster-shaped vase is coated with a transparent sky-blue glaze revealing lightly incised double bands of decoration both at the neck and at the base. This decoration consists in each instance of an outer band of opposed triangles with diagonal hatchings, and an inner band of leafage in which long and short leaves appear in alternation. Each is fitted at the neck with a scrolled and foliated gilt-bronze collar. Two upswept handles of acanthus leaves and scrolls, from which sprays of berries spring, link this collar with the gilt-bronze stand resting on two double-scrolled and two single-scrolled acanthus feet.

Chinese, dating from the Ch'ing Dynasty during the eighteenth century; the mounts are French, eighteenth century, in the style of Louis XV.

Formerly in the collection of Mrs. Jacques Balsan, Lantana, Florida.

A pair of comparable baluster vases from the collection of Louis-Jean Gaignat (1697–1768), secretary to the king and Receveur des Consignations, was sold by Pierre Rémy, Paris, February 14–22, 1769, lot 104. One was sketched by Gabriel de Saint-Aubin in the margin of the catalogue of that sale, which was reproduced in 1921 under the title *Catalogues des Ventes et Livrets de Salons Illustrés par Gabriel de Saint-Aubin*, XI, with a foreword by Émile Dacier.

See also Volume II of this catalogue, Nos. 252 A and B.

184 Bowl, Mounted in Gilt Bronze

Overall: H. 8 (20.3).

Porcelain: H. 6⅝ (16.9); Diam. 9½ (24.1).

THIS thick-walled bowl is coated with a pale gray-blue celadon glaze displaying an allover large-scale crackle. Immediately below the swelling lip, the sides bulge slightly and then contract in an even curve as they descend to the base. The bowl rests upon a chased and gilded bronze stand, supported on four scrolled and foliated feet, between each pair of which a small leaf motif depends.

Stamped on the mount on the side of one of the scrolls with the crowned C (for a note on the crowned C, see under Nos. 16 A and B).

Chinese celadon, dating from the Ch'ing Dynasty, during the Ch'ien Lung period (1736–1795); the mounts are French, dating from 1745–1749.

Formerly in the collection of Baroness Renée de Becker, New York.

See also Volume II of this catalogue, No. 240.

185 A, B Pair of Bottles, Mounted in Gilt Bronze

Overall: H. 10¼ (26.1); W. of base 5⁷⁄₁₆ (13.9).

Porcelain: H. 8¾ (22.3); Diam. 4¾ (12.0).

EACH bottle, with a spherical body and slender flaring neck, is coated with a blue-green celadon glaze. At either side of the neck is an angular ear-shaped handle, pierced with fretwork in the upper part and terminating in a pendent scroll. Encircling the neck and shoulder are thread-like molded fillets, with a cluster of three at the broadest circumference of the body. The flaring foot is mounted on a fasciated circular base of chased and gilded bronze and supported on four pierced and scrolled acanthus leaf feet. The lip is mounted with a ring of gilt bronze.

Chinese celadon, dating from the Ch'ing Dynasty, during the Ch'ien Lung period (1736–1795); the mounts are French and probably date from about 1765–1775.

See also Volume II of this catalogue, Nos. 239 A and B.

186 A,B   Pair of Vases, Mounted in Gilt Bronze as Ewers

Overall: H. 19¾ (50.2).

Porcelain: H. 13¼ (33.7); Diam. of vase 8¾ (22.3).

EACH swelling pear-shaped vase on a tall flaring foot is coated with a boldly crackled glaze, which on No. 186 A is gray, and on No. 186 B blue-gray. Upon the neck of each, two climbing lizards are molded in high relief. Each vase is mounted as a ewer with a spout formed by two interlocking shells of chased and gilded bronze, beneath which depend shells and leaves. At one side of each vase is a large scrolled and foliate handle of gilt bronze on which rests a winged dragon, its tail entwined around the handle.

Chinese celadon, dating from the Ch'ing Dynasty during the eighteenth century; the mounts are French, about 1750, except for the fluted foot surrounding the base, which may be of a later date, perhaps about 1770–1780.

A celadon vase with incised underglaze decoration and similarly mounted as a ewer was illustrated in *Connaissance des Arts*, April 1959, p. 52. The mounts of this vase are certainly by the same hand as those of Nos. 186 A and B. Certain technical features, e.g., the method of joining the two halves of the mount surrounding the neck, are identical on each.

Lot 92 in the Gaignat sale (Pierre Rémy, Paris, February 14–22, 1769) comprised:

> Deux Vases d'ancienne porcelaine-céladon, gauffrée, craquelée, d'environ 20 pouces de haut: montés en buire avec un dragon sur les anses en bronze doré.

A marginal drawing by Gabriel de Saint-Aubin in a copy of the catalogue in the collection of the Baron du Teil (illustrated in Dacier, *Catalogue des Ventes et Livrets de Salons Illustrés par Gabriel de Saint-Aubin*, XI, p. 63) shows that the mounts were of exactly the same form as those on Nos. 186 A and B, though the shape of the porcelain vases was slightly different. They were sold for 515 livres to "Pliurer, hôtel de Moras" according to the artist's annotation. Such mounts are in all probability the production of a single *fondeur-ciseleur*'s workshop.

See also Volume II of this catalogue, Nos. 242 A and B.

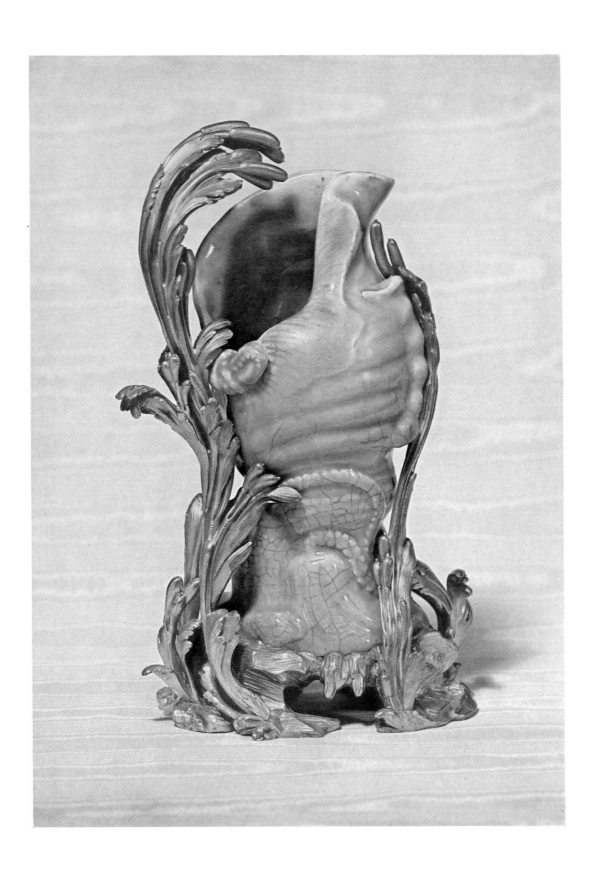

187 Vase, Mounted in Gilt Bronze as a Ewer

Overall: H. 11¾ (29.8); w. of base 6⅛ (15.6);
D. 5⅝ (14.3).

Porcelain: H. 9⅜ (23.8); w. 4½ (11.4); D. 4¼ (10.8).

THE VASE is modeled in the form of a spirally ribbed conch shell, up-ended so that its open end serves as a spout. The pointed lower end rests on a base of rockwork, and is clasped in the scrolling tentacles of an octopus molded in high relief. The whole is coated with a transparent gray-green glaze with a broad crackle on the lower half and a series of fine incised hatchings along one edge of the mouth. The vase is richly mounted and caged in chased and gilded bronze as a ewer. Four sprays of acanthus leaves and bulrushes rise from the base in the form of pierced rockwork. One of these, of scrolling shape, forms the handle, and a second is shaped to the silhouette of the opposite side of the shell. The two other shorter sprays clasp the base of the vase.

An inventory number, 50010, is painted on the bottom of the vase. (It is modern, perhaps a dealer's stock mark.)

Chinese celadon, dating from the Ch'ing Dynasty during the eighteenth century; the mounts are French, dating from about 1775.

Formerly in the collection of Mrs. D. Kilvert, New York.

The model is an unusual one. On September 4, 1756, the *marchand-mercier* Lazare Duvaux sold to Mme la Marquise de Pompadour:

> Un grand vase de porcelain céladon, à coquille, monté en bronze doré d'or moulu. . . , 1,440 l.
> (*Livre-Journal*, no. 2581).

This is the only mounted porcelain of shell shape mentioned in the *marchand-mercier*'s daybook, and it is not impossible that No. 187 is, in fact, the one once belonging to Mme de Pompadour.

See also Volume II of this catalogue, No. 243.

188 A, B Pair of Vases, Mounted in Gilt Bronze as Ewers

Overall: H. 14¾ (37.5); W. 7¾ (19.7); D. 6⁵⁄₁₆ (16.0).

Porcelain: H. 9⅝ (24.5); Diam. 5⅜ (13.6).

EACH baluster-shaped vase with vertical ribs is coated with a transparent pale sea-green glaze, and has been converted into a ewer by chased and gilded bronze mounts. The neck of each is mounted with a collar of molded gilt bronze with a spout and a pendent leaf spray at back and front. Springing from the pierced base, composed of scrolls, is a slender handle in the form of bulrushes, which is attached to the rim by split scrolls. A spray of berries follows the curve of the upper part of the handle.

Chinese celadon, dating from the Ch'ing Dynasty during the Ch'ien Lung period (1736–1795); the mounts are French, about 1750.

A similar ewer (one of a pair) in the Jones Collection at the Victoria and Albert Museum, London, is illustrated by Melton, *Apollo*, February 1957, p. 63.

A comparable but slightly larger pair of mounted ewers in the collection of Mme Alexandrine de Rothschild was sold at Sotheby's, London, May 18, 19, 1967, lot 137 (illustrated in catalogue).

A pair of similar ewers from the collection of Louis-Jean Gaignat (1697–1768), secretary to the king and Receveur des Consignations, was sold by Pierre Rémy, Paris, February 14–22, 1769, lot 87. Gabriel de Saint-Aubin sketched one in the margin of his catalogue of that sale (see under Nos. 197 A and B).

It has been suggested by Levallet (*La Renaissance de l'Art Français*, February 1922, pp. 60–67) that mounts of this type were made by Jean-Claude Duplessis *père* (working 1747–1774).

See also Volume II of this catalogue, Nos. 244 A and B.

189 A, B   Pair of Vases, Mounted in Gilt Bronze

Overall: H. 15¹⁵⁄₁₆ (38.2); W. 10½ (26.7); D. 6¼ (15.8).

Porcelain: H. 10⅝ (27.0); W. 4¼ (10.8); D. 2¼ (5.7).

EACH blue-green vase, rectangular in section and shaped as a traditional ritual vessel, is richly mounted in chased and gilded bronze. The tall trumpet-shaped neck of each rises from a drum-shaped body resting upon a splayed podium molded on either face with a medallion incised with a Chinese character, that on the obverse being *fu* (signifying good luck in the sense of riches), and the reverse *shou* (signifying long life). Bordering the medallions and the angles of the neck are foliated serpentine scrolls, partly incised and partly in low relief. The vases have been cut down at the base. The mouth of each is surrounded by a pierced and foliated lip of gilt bronze, from which spring two boldly sweeping handles formed of acanthus leaves and berries tied by ribbon bows to a spray of bulrushes at the lower end of the neck. Each rests on a square base of pierced and foliated gilt bronze supported on four scrolling feet.

Chinese celadon, dating from the Ch'ing Dynasty during the eighteenth century; the mounts are French, about 1740–1750, in the manner of Jean-Claude Duplessis *père* (working 1747–1774).

Formerly in the collection of Edith Chester Beatty, London.

See also Volume II of this catalogue, Nos. 250 A and B.

190 A, B   Pair of Vases, Mounted in Gilt Bronze

Overall: H. 11⅜ (28.9); W. 5⅝ (14.3); D. 4⅜ (11.1).

Porcelain: H. 9½ (24.1); W. 4½ (11.4); D. 3⅛ (8.0).

EACH vase of baluster shape, rectangular in section with a translucent deep green glaze, derives from a traditional bronze ritual vessel, having a pair of handles molded as rampant lions flanking the incurving neck. The body is spade-shaped in contour, and rests on a slightly splayed rectangular foot. The mouth of each vase is surrounded with an interlacing ribbon of chased and gilded bronze. A floral garland of gilt bronze is looped through the lion handles and depends across each side, hanging in a pendant below each handle. The base is surrounded by a mount chased with a guilloche pattern.

Chinese celadon, dating from the Ch'ing Dynasty during the Ch'ien Lung period (1736–1795); the mounts are French, dating from about 1765–1775.

A pair of similar vases mounted in the rococo style in the collection of Jacques Doucet, Paris, was sold at the Galerie Georges Petit, Paris, June 7–8, 1912, lot 211 (illustrated in catalogue).

See also Volume II of this catalogue, Nos. 254 A and B.

191 A, B Pair of Vases, Mounted in Gilt Bronze

Overall: H. 14½ (36.8); W. 8½ (21.6); Diam. 8 (20.3).

Porcelain: H. 13½ (34.3).

THE FORM of each vase is that of a calabash or gourd with a deep central constriction dividing the smaller upper section from the broad bulbous base. A uniform coating of pale gray-green glaze envelops each vessel, which terminates in a narrow, cylindrical neck. Encircling the lip is a simulated cord in chased and gilded bronze, its double strands crossing as they descend, and making a turn about the waist, where one becomes looped and tasseled. The other end clings to the rounded surface of the porcelain and continues to the base, where it forms a double-stranded support resting upon four simple knots.

Chinese celadon, dating from the Ch'ing Dynasty during the Ch'ien Lung period (1736–1795); the mounts are French, also eighteenth century.

Formerly in the collection of Princesse Murat and Prince Joachim Murat (sold Palais Galliera, Paris, March 2, 1961, lot 73 [illustrated in catalogue, pl. XVII]).

The vase is in all likelihood of the type referred to by Lazare Duvaux as "vases céladon en forme de calebasse." An example of a similar type is recorded in his *Livre-Journal*, where entry 2259, dated October 18, 1755, describes the purchase by M. d'Azincourt:

Deux vases céladon en forme de calebasse, à relief, montés avec des branchages dorés, 960 l.

A gourd of this shape is a principal attribute of one of the Eight Immortals, Li K'ung Mu, "Li Hollow Eyes," popularly known as Li T'ieh-kuai, or "Li with the Iron Crutch." He is always depicted with his crutch and a gourd full of magic medicines. He is the friend of the sick, devoting himself to their care and to the study of Taoist lore. It is believed that he jumps into his gourd at night for rest, to re-emerge in the morning. Hence the popularity of this type of vase.

[417]

192 A, B Pair of Vases, Mounted in Gilt Bronze

Overall: H. 12⅛ (30.8); Diam. of lip 5½ (14.0).

Porcelain: H. 10⅞ (27.6); Diam. of lip 4¾ (12.0).

EACH vase is tall and trumpet-shaped, flaring toward the base and lip, with a wide band in relief encircling the waist. Its shape derives from an early bronze ritual vessel known as a *ku*. The exterior and much of the interior are coated with a variegated jasper-red glaze. Each is mounted around the central band with chased and gilded bronze in the neoclassical style, with a pair of rams' heads in high relief, linked by a spirally twisted ring from which depend swags of tasseled drapery caught up by a flower. A leaf-and-dart molding runs around the lip, and a guilloche band encircles the foot.

Chinese, dating from the Ch'ing Dynasty during the Ch'ien Lung period (1736–1795); the mounts are French, dating from about 1775–1785.

See also Volume II of this catalogue, Nos. 255 A and B.

193 Four Porcelains, Mounted in Gilt Bronze as an Inkstand

Overall: H. 6¼ (15.9); W. 11¼ (28.6); D. 10½ (26.7).

Porcelain: Cups: H. 2½ (6.4); W. 4 (10.2); D. 3 (7.6).
Joss-stick holder: H. 3 (7.6); W. 1¾ (4.5); D. 2¾ (7.0).

THREE *blanc de chine* porcelain libation cups of the traditional "rhinoceros-horn" shape molded with floral sprigs in relief stand upon a trilobate platform of red and gold lacquer decorated with a basket of flowers. At the rear is a seated *fu*-lion, its head turned sharply to the left, an incense holder before him. A pair of foliated gilt-bronze candle arms springing from a central stem flank the lion. Foliated mounts surround the base of each cup; a simple gilt-bronze molding encircles the lip. The lacquer panel is surrounded by a narrow border of chased and gilt bronze accented with three foliated cabochon cartouches upon three feet of shell form.

Chinese (Fukien), the *fu*-lion dating from the Ming Dynasty during the seventeenth century, and the cups from the Ch'ing Dynasty during the eighteenth century; the mounts are French, about 1740–1750.

See also Volume II of this catalogue, No. 245.

194 A–C   Clock and Two Candelabra, Mounted in Gilt Bronze

Overall: Clock: H. 11⅜ (28.8);
Diam. 6³⁄₁₆ (15.7).

Candelabra: H. 7 (17.8); W. 6⅞ (17.5);
D. 3⅞ (9.8).

THE CLOCK rests on a circular podium, with two handles in the form of miniature dragons, supporting two Chinese warriors behind whom are two giant rats climbing joss-stick holders in the form of bushes. The whole is of deep starch-blue porcelain of the K'ang Hsi type (1662–1722). From behind there spring gilt-bronze branches with flowers of cast metal painted blue, on which the circular clock case of gilt bronze is supported. This in turn is surmounted by an eagle of deep starch-blue porcelain from whose shoulders floral sprays of gilt bronze and blue-painted metal depend at either side of the clock. The base is mounted above and below with borders of tooled gilt bronze and floral sprays of the same material. Lizards of gilt bronze run around the lower border. The white enamel clock face is inscribed: *Thiout L'ainé/A Paris*.

The movement of the clock, originally by Antoine Thiout *l'aíné* (1692–1767), has been replaced in modern times by an eighteenth century watch movement.

Each candelabrum consists of a pair of figures of a Chinese man and woman standing in front of a low wall behind which is a stele, the whole of deep starch-blue porcelain of the K'ang Hsi type. Behind this porcelain group rise branches of gilt bronze with flowers of blue-painted metal, supporting, on each side, a drip pan and a candle-holder, both of turquoise-blue Sèvres porcelain, decorated with sprays of gilt foliage in relief and flowers. The base of each group rests on a stand of tooled gilt bronze supported at the corners on four feet in the form of sprays of leaves of gilt bronze, with running lizards applied to the sides.

Chinese porcelain dating from the Ch'ing Dynasty during the seventeenth or eighteenth century; Sèvres dating from the eighteenth century; the mounts are French, dating from about 1750, with later additions.

Formerly in the collection of Baron Eugène Fould-Springer, Paris.

See also Volume II of this catalogue, Nos. 241 A–C.

195 A, B Pair of Pheasants

195 A: H. 26 (66.0); W. 7¼ (18.5);
D. 10⅛ (25.8).

195 B: H. 25⅝ (65.2); W. 8⅜ (21.3);
D. 10½ (26.7).

EACH large bird stands erect with one foot flexed against its breast, the other supported on a tall pillar of rock pierced with small irregular openings. The plumage is painted in a wide range of overglaze colors. The pointed crest of each bird is iron-red, dotted with gold, and descends to the gilded beak. The gold-rimmed eyes are set far forward in a field hatched with pale iron-red. At some distance behind each is an oval patch of pale turquoise-blue. The neck is dappled in black with rows of arched markings against a bone-white ground delicately tinted with yellow, green, and rose. The breast and under parts are painted in a variegated iron-red, with vertical pencilings, paling toward the yellow, scaly legs. A border of bright turquoise-blue separates the breast and rump from the outer edges of the wings. Cobalt- and turquoise-blue, rose-pink, leaf-green, and iron-red, all heightened with gilding, are the principal colors of the wings and the long,

straight tail. The wing coverts, matching the pale tones of the neck, are patterned with imbrications, and the primaries and secondaries are accented with long quill-like markings in white. The base has a lava-like surface, splashed with aubergine, turquoise, deep blue, and gray, the colors mingling in a running pattern. Each base is molded in relief with three fungus motifs (*ling-chih*), of which two are rendered indistinct by the multicolored glaze, while the third stands out in a contrasting color.

Chinese, dating from the Ch'ing Dynasty during the Ch'ien Lung period (1736–1795).

A somewhat smaller pair of pheasants (height 42.0 cm., though otherwise comparable) in the collection of Jacques Doucet, Paris, was sold at the Galerie Georges Petit, Paris, June 7–8, 1912, lot 205 (illustrated in catalogue). A comparable pair was sold anonymously at Christie's, London, April 1, 1968, lot 86 (illustrated as frontispiece).

196 A, B   Pair of Cranes

H. 17⅝ (44.7); W. 5⅞ (14.9); D. 4¾ (12.1).

EACH erect white bird with a long pointed beak and slender curving neck stands astride a mound of weathered brown rockwork, upon the top of which it rests one foot. Upon the crown of each bird's head is a round, unglazed topknot of spongy appearance, which on one bird almost overhangs the brown eyes. A long stripe descending behind the neck and broadening at the wing shoulders is coated very thinly, as is the beak. These areas display a semi-*biscuit* surface in pale buff color.

Chinese, dating from the Ch'ing Dynasty during the Ch'ien Lung period (1736–1795).

A pair of similar though not identical cranes from an anonymous collection was sold at Christie's, London, October 26, 1964, lot 50 (illustrated in catalogue).

[425]

197 A, B Two Vases, Mounted in Gilt Bronze

197 A: (overall) H. 12⅞ (32.7); W. 6⅜ (16.2);
D. 7 (17.8).
(porcelain) H. about 11⅞ (about 30.1);
W. 4 (10.2); D. 5⅝ (14.4).

197 B: (overall) H. 13 (33.0); W. 6½ (16.5);
D. 6½ (16.5).
(porcelain) H. about 11⅞ (about 30.1);
W. 5⅛ (13.0); D. 6 (15.2).

EACH is molded in the form of a carp, its mouth open, leaping vertically from the water, its tail curved in the air to the left to provide a spring from a base of turbulent wave motifs. The fish are identical in pose and detail except for the presence of flipper-like fins on the underside of No. 197A. The body of each fish is painted in natural colors, predominantly gray mottled with pale aubergine on the scaly back. The belly grades from flesh-pink to oyster-white, and is patterned with flame-like patches of iron-red, especially on the extremities of the fins and gills. The white eyes with black pupils are surrounded by gilding and outlined with iron-red. Each carp springs from a roughly cylindrical base modeled with a swirling pattern of breaking waves traced in yellow-green, which wash over the body. The rest of the base is decorated with bold splashes of iron-red, black on green, and gray. The fish are almost identical; they are not mirror pairs. On No. 197 A, however, two porcelain fins extend from the belly. On No. 197 B two low projections on the ventral surface, touched up with red pigment, appear to represent vestiges of similar fins. The open mouth of each fish is outlined with a narrow rim of gilt bronze from which shreds of seaweed hang at the corners. The base fits into a support of scrolled and foliate gilt bronze from which spring three irregularly spaced groups of bulrushes clinging to its sides. This support rests on five foliate scrolls forming the feet, which are entwined with leaves, berries, and flowers.

Japanese Arita ware, dating from about 1700; the mounts are French, dating from about 1750–1755.

A pair without mounts was in the Gaignat Collection, sold by Pierre Rémy, Paris, February 14–22, 1769, lot 122:

> Deux Carpes de porcelaine du Japon, sur leurs rochers vernissés en partie.

They formed the subject of a marginal drawing by Gabriel de Saint-Aubin in the copy of the catalogue belong to the Baron du Teil (reprinted as *Catalogues des Ventes et Livrets de Salons Illustrés par Gabriel de Saint-Aubin*, XI, p. 70 of the facsimile catalogue edited by Dacier; see under Nos. 1 A and B). Mounted examples of the model are rare. The model is mentioned only four times in the *Livre-Journal* of Lazare Duvaux, and all the examples were unmounted, e.g., on March 20, 1756, the *marchand-mercier* sold to the Duc d'Orléans:

> Deux carpes de porcelaine ancienne sur des rochers rustiques, de 14 louis, 336 l.

(no. 2436)

The price is exceptionally high.

A mounted pair from the collection of the Marchioness of Cholmondeley was sold at Sotheby's, London, April 17, 1964, lot 6 (illustrated in catalogue). The rockwork was squarer and more conventionally marked, while the mount consisted of a band of rockwork only around the foot. A

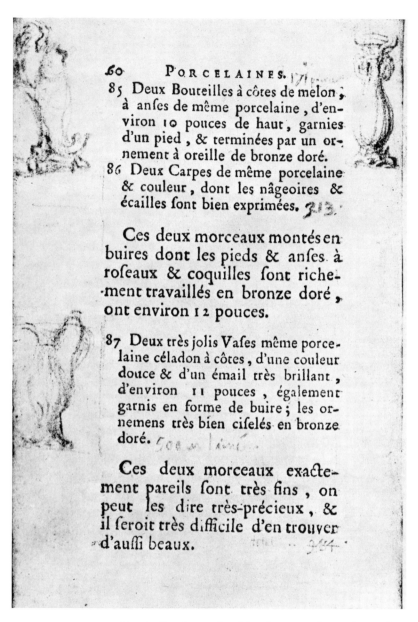

Facsimile of page 60 of the Gaignat sale catalogue from Catalogue des Ventes et Livrets de Salons Illustrés par Gabriel de Saint-Aubin. The Metropolitan Museum of Art Library

simiiar pair without mounts was bequeathed to the Fitzwilliam Museum, Cambridge, by Lady Ward in 1962, one of them being reproduced in the *Annual Report* for that year (pl. III, lower left). Two further pairs are in the collection of Mr. and Mrs. William Wilberforce Winkworth, London, and of Mr. and Mrs. Soame Jenyns (illustrated in Jenyns, *Japanese Porcelain*, fig. 35A), all without mounts. Variants of the model in Chinese K'ang Hsi porcelain are known. A pair of turquoise-blue carp with French mounts similar to but much simpler than those of Nos. 197 A and B, were advertised by a New York dealer in *Connoisseur*, June 1964, p. CXXIX. In these the carp were springing from waves, not from rocks, and the figure of the deity Chung K'uei (deity of scholars) was crouched in the curved tail.

Carp are common in Chinese celadon porcelain, and examples were quite often mounted. A pair mounted as ewers was likewise in the Gaignat sale (*op. cit.*, lot 86). They lacked the rocky base and waves, but were mounted with a base of gilt bronze and a handle converting them into ewers. Gaignat had purchased them from Lazare Duvaux on September 2, 1751, for 1200 livres (no. 896); at his sale they sold for 213 livres. They too were the subject of a marginal drawing by Gabriel de Saint-Aubin (left). A pair similarly mounted is depicted on the chimneypiece behind the Baron de Besenval (1722–1791) in his portrait by H.-P. Danloux (1753–1809) belonging to the Princesse Amadée de Broglie (exhibited in *Marie-Antoinette, Archiduchesse, Dauphine et Reine*, Versailles, 1955, catalogue no. 281).

BIOGRAPHIES OF CRAFTSMEN

THE FOLLOWING biographies include artists and artisans whose work is represented in this catalogue. At the end of each entry, the relevant catalogue numbers are listed, the marked or documented examples in Roman type, the attributed ones in italic. Other craftsmen mentioned in the text of catalogue entries or introductions can be traced through the Index of Craftsmen.

Information concerning Meissen employees has been drawn chiefly from Honey, *Dresden China*, and Rückert, *Meissener Porzellan 1710–1810*. The standard works of Berling, Carolsfeld, Doenges, Ducret, and Zimmermann, as listed in the Bibliography, have been indispensable. For the workers at Sèvres, extensive use has been made of Chavagnac and Grollier, *Histoire des Manufactures Françaises de Porcelaine*, and Brunet, *Les Marques de Sèvres*, supplemented by research through the personnel records and listings of special projects in the archives of the Manufacture Nationale de Sèvres. Some names and dates have been revised to conform with information from parish registers recently published in Eriksen, *The James A. de Rothschild Collection at Waddesdon Manor: Sèvres Porcelain*. The alternate dates obtained from this publication are indicated by asterisks in the entries.

Among those named below, a few were prominent as artists and also as administrators whose personal styles, transmitted to subordinates, lent a distinctive stamp to the products of their factories. Examples of such figures are the art director J. G. Herold and the model master J. J. Kaendler, both of Meissen.

François-Joseph Aloncle (born 1734) was employed at Sèvres from 1758 to 1781. He entered the factory as a professional painter and was entrusted mainly with the painting of scenes featuring birds and animals. His mark is a florid script letter N.

76 A and B, *88*, 104, 108, 109, 110, 111 A to D

Baudouin père (born 1724) was employed at Vincennes-Sèvres as a gilder from 1750 to 1800. His mark consists of the script letters BD.

97

Jean-Baptiste Bienfait (born 1735 or about 1738*) was employed as a painter at Sèvres from 1756 until after 1770.* His mark is a six-pointed star.

95 A to FF

Binet (born 1731) was employed at Vincennes-Sèvres as a painter of flowers from 1750 to 1775. His mark is a Roman letter T with three dots.

97

Pierre Blondeau, a sculptor who taught at the Académie de Saint-Luc, Paris, modeled children after Boucher and animals after Oudry for Vincennes-Sèvres. He is chiefly recorded in Bourgeois and Lechevallier-Chevignard, *Le Biscuit de Sèvres*, where thirteen works attributed to him are illustrated, dating from 1752, 1753, and 1776.

114 A and B, *115*

Bougon was the name of a family of potters, six of whom were employed at Sèvres between 1753 and 1812. Four were *répareurs*, one a *répareur et sculpteur*, and one a *sculpteur*. Their marks are not known, although one may have used the florid script letter B found on sculptures and sometimes assigned to Jean-Jacques Bachelier (1724–1806) or Bourdois (working 1773–1774), or to Jean-Charles-Nicolas Brachard (working 1782–1824). Among all the signatures on the Sèvres pay sheets for 1763 to 1767, the only one written with such a florid letter B and assignable to a sculptor is that of Bougon, apparently the *répareur et sculpteur* Martin Bougon (working 1759–1780, 1788–1795, and 1806–1812).

116 A and B, 121, 122

Bouillat père (born before 1743*) was employed at Sèvres as a flower painter from 1758 to 1793. Among the objects decorated by him are plaques for furniture, notably a large panel installed on a *secrétaire* in The Metropolitan Museum of Art, New York (acc. no. 58.75.57). For further information, see Dauterman, Parker, and Standen, *Decorative Art from the Samuel H. Kress Collection at The Metropolitan Museum of Art*, pp. 158–159, 180. His mark, which he shared with his son, is a script letter Y.

95 A to FF, 97

Jean-Pierre Boulanger, known as **Boulanger père** (born 1725), was employed at Vincennes-Sèvres from 1754 to 1784. He had worked earlier at Saint-Cloud. Boulanger is usually regarded as a gilder, although Garnier in *The Soft Porcelain of Sèvres*, p. 26, describes him as a painter of "detached bouquets." Among the objects he painted are plaques for furniture. His mark, a script letter B, is sometimes followed by a dot.

95 A to FF, 97, 110, *111 A to D*

Bulidon was employed at Sèvres from 1763 to 1792. He was a painter of flowers, especially *bouquets détachés*, and some of his work was for furniture plaques. His mark consists of the script letters *Bn* or *B.n.*

95 A to FF, 97, 110

[430]

Charles Buteux, known as **Buteux aîné** (born 1719* or 1721), was employed at Sèvres as a painter from 1756 to 1782, and is noted chiefly for trophies of military, nautical, and gardening implements, although figure painting is also ascribed to him. His mark is an anchor.

95 A to FF, 99, 100 A and B

Cardin was employed as a flower painter at Sèvres from 1749 to 1786. He was appointed second in authority in the painting atelier in 1759, associate in the school of design in 1780, and chief of the painters in 1793. His mark is a circle with a dot and a stem.

112 A and B

Étienne-Jean Chabry, known as **Chabry fils** (born before 1749*), was employed at Sèvres from 1765 to 1787 (Chavagnac gives his starting date as 1763). He is known as a sculptor and, in his later years, as a painter of pastoral scenes and mythological figures in landscapes. His mark consists of the script letters *ch*.

110

Antoine-Joseph Chappuis, known as **Chappuis aîné**, was employed at Sèvres from 1761 to 1787 or later (Chavagnac gives his starting date as 1756). He painted birds, landscapes, and animals, and is described in the parish registers for 1786 and 1787* as *chef des fours*. His mark consists of the script letters *cp*.

109, 110

Michel-Barnabé Chauveaux, or **Chauvaux**, known as **Chauveaux aîné** (born about 1729* or 1731), was employed at Sèvres from 1752/1753 to 1788. Chavagnac records him as a gilder and states that he was raised to the first class in 1780; other sources, however, identify him as a gilder and painter. His mark, a #, usually in gold, is frequently found on porcelain painted with birds.

110

Michel-Gabriel Commelin (born about 1753*) was employed at Sèvres as a flower painter from 1768 to 1802 (Chavagnac gives his starting date as 1765). Among the objects he painted were furniture plaques. His mark consists of the script letters *cm*.

95 A to FF, 97

Antoine-Toussaint Cornailles, or **Cornaille**, was employed at Sèvres from 1755 to 1800 as a painter of flowers. He had worked earlier at the Chantilly manufactory. Among the objects he decorated were plaques for furniture. His mark is a musical note.

103

Danet père, a *tourneur*, was employed at Sèvres. His mark, the script letters *da*, appears on table articles at least as early as 1764. His signature, written with a small letter d, is found in the pay records for 1775 and 1776. Brunet (p. 52) gives three listings under Danet, all, however, for *répareurs* who began their careers at Sèvres in 1773 or 1774. The script mark *da* on a *déjeuner* datemarked for 1779 in the Wallace Collection, London, may be attributed to Danet *père*.

102, 105 A–O, 109

Jean-Claude Duplessis père (died 1774) was of Italian origin; his real name was Ciamberlano. He was attached to the Vincennes-Sèvres factory from 1745 or 1747 to 1774 and provided designs for both porcelains and their gilt-bronze mounts. It should be noted that Chavagnac lists him as Claude-Thomas Chambelan and describes him as being in charge of molders, throwers, and assemblers from 1745 to 1748, when he became responsible for bronze mounts and, additionally, in 1753 for the overall design of models for Vincennes and Sèvres. Some of his ideas appear to be related to those of Pierre Germain as engraved in the latter's *Modèles et Élémens d'Orfèvrerie*, published in 1748. Duplessis was appointed goldsmith to the king in 1758. For an account of his activities as a *fondeur-ciseleur*, see Volume II of this catalogue, pp. 565–566.

80, 81, 82 A and B, 83, 86, 178, 189 A and B

Johann Friedrich Eberlein (1696–1749) was the principal assistant of J. J. Kaendler (*q.v.*) from the date of his arrival at the Meissen factory, on April 18, 1735, until his death on July 7, 1749. Before appearing at Meissen, he had worked with the Saxon court sculptor Jean-Joseph Vinache (or Vinage; 1696–1754), and had spent some time in England. Although older than the talented Kaendler, and a thoroughly competent modeler, Eberlein was clearly a subordinate, and his projects were often worked over or finished by the *Modellmeister*. As an independent artist, Eberlein employed the swan motif in 1735, and modeled a large number of figures, including mythological groups, personifications, court figures, and animals, all strongly related to the style of Kaendler. His important position as second sculptor, however, is shown by his participation in major works, such as the reproduction of the monumental Neptune fountain, newly created for the park of Count Brühl's Marcolini Palace in Dresden by Lorenzo Mattielli (about 1695–1748). Made in collaboration with Kaendler, this porcelain tour de force was executed in 1745 for installation inside the palace. It consisted of 104 pieces, but unfortunately was not preserved. He also assisted Ehder (*q.v.*) with the great figure of Augustus III in Polish dress, statuettes of the Twelve Apostles for the Empress Wilhelmina Amalia, the Swan Service, a porcelain fireplace for Schloss Pförten (the last two commissioned by Count Brühl), and many other smaller works, such as vases personifying the Elements.

7 A and B, 8, 9 A and B

Johann Gottlieb Ehder (1717–1750), the son of a Leipzig stonecutter, worked at Meissen from 1739 until his death. He worked with J. J. Kaendler and J. F. Eberlein (*qq.v.*) on decorations for a figure of Augustus III in Polish dress and two years later on the Neptune fountain for Count Brühl. Less gifted than Eberlein, he created independently table decorations such as farmhouses and barns, a type of work more suited to his abilities than figure modeling. Nevertheless, he did create some figure groups, as well as small works such as pipe heads and cane handles, and a few animals and birds, including parrots, waxwings, and hoopoes.

11, 14, 15 A and B, 29 A and B

Étienne Evans (born 1733) was employed at Sèvres from 1752 to 1806. He is known chiefly as a painter of birds "in habitat," although landscapes and animal subjects by him are also recorded. He also decorated plaques for furniture. His mark is a dagger.

                                97, 109, 110, 111 A to D

Étienne-Maurice Falconet (December 1, 1716–January 24, 1791) was a noted sculptor in the employ of Sèvres as *chef de l'atelier de sculpture* from 1757 to 1766. Bourgeois and Lechevallier-Chevignard in *Le Biscuit de Sèvres* illustrate about fifty figures and groups from his hand. The most famous pair of figures in porcelain is his L'Amour Menaçant and La Nymphe Falconet (Cupid and Psyche), which are Nos. 118 and 119 A and B in this catalogue. Most of his figures express rococo qualities, but in contrast La Baigneuse (Bather) of 1758 is regarded as an important foretaste of the oncoming wave of neoclassicism. Chavagnac states that he worked for Sèvres as early as 1754. An incised Roman letter F, believed to be his mark, may be confused with that of Fernex (*q.v.*).

      116 A and B, 117 A and B, 118, 119 A and B, 120 A and B, 121

Fallot, or **Falot**, was a painter and gilder at Sèvres, where he was employed from 1773 to 1790 (Chavagnac gives his date of entry as 1764). He painted birds and chinoiserie. His mark is a Roman letter F.

                                                        109

Jean-Baptiste de Fernex, or **Defernex** (about 1729–1783) was employed as a sculptor at Vincennes, where he worked in the sculpture workshop from about 1753 to 1756. During this period he executed figures in *biscuit*, mainly after drawings by Boucher. After the advent of Falconet in 1757, his name is not found among those of the modelers working at the factory. He was inscribed in the École Académique on October 1, 1758, but with no mention of his master. Fernex was admitted to the Academy of St. Luke in 1760, and exhibited sculpture in the Salons of 1762

and 1774. He also conducted a private school of sculpture and design. By 1777, and probably before, he had become sculptor to the Duc d'Orléans, but he died poor and alone in 1783. For further information, see Réau, *Gazette des Beaux-Arts*, LXXIII, 1931, pp. 349–365. His mark is an incised Roman letter F.

                                            116 A and B

Mathieu Fouré, or **Fourée**, was employed as a flower painter at Vincennes-Sèvres in 1749 and again from 1754 to 1762 (Chavagnac gives his starting date as before 1748). His mark is a Roman letter Y.

Y.   95 A to FF, 97, 109

Fritsch was employed at Sèvres from 1763 to 1764 as a figure painter (Chavagnac gives his terminal date as 1765). His mark is a symbol of the sun.

                                                95 A to FF, 97

Mme Gérard, *née* **Vautrin**, was employed as a flower painter at Sèvres from 1781 to 1802. Her mark consists of the script letters *Vt*.

   97

Thomas Germain (1673–1748) was a goldsmith of Paris. His influence on the development of the rococo style in metalwork, including gilt-bronze mounts for porcelain, was enormous. While resident in Italy, he apprenticed himself to a native goldsmith, and as a result he received many commissions for ecclesiastical silver. He was back in Paris in 1706, working mainly, if not entirely, in gilt bronze. In 1720, he became a *maître orfèvre* with quarters in the Rue de la Monnaie. Subsequently, he became goldsmith to the king, with quarters at the Louvre.

Germain ranks among the most prolific and brilliant goldsmiths of France. His works include commissions for Louis XV and other crowned heads of Europe, as well as for the French nobility. For a more detailed account, see Volume II of this catalogue, p. 567.

176 A and B, 178, 179

Edme Gomery, or **Gommery** (born 1736) was employed at Sèvres as a painter of birds from 1756 to 1758. His mark is a caduceus.

85 A and B

Étienne-Jean Grémont, known as **Grémont jeune** (born 1754*), was employed at Sèvres as a flower painter from 1769 to 1775 and again from 1778 to 1781. His parents were in the same employ, the mother making flowers, the father as a thrower and *répareur*. His mark consists of the conjoined script letters *Gt*.

95 A to FF

Grison 2ᵉ fils was employed as a painter at Sèvres from 1772 to 1773. A florid script letter x, associated with the gilder Grison *fils aîné* (working 1750–1751), may also have been used by him, but this usage has not been established.

97, 110

Grund Junior, presumably the younger Johann Elias Grund, is mentioned in the Meissen factory records, along with his father, as a *Former* (molder or modeler) in 1739. His mark consists of three impressed dots forming a triangle, easily mistaken for those of Seidel and Müller (*qq.v.*).

64

Johann Georg Heintze, or **Heinze, Heintz** (born about 1707), a native of Dresden, seems to have been one of the most popular painters at Meissen. He was engaged as the first apprentice of J. G. Herold (*q.v.*) at Meissen in 1720, became a journeyman in 1725, and in 1731 was called "perhaps his best painter" by Herold. From 1733 on, he was paid a fixed monthly salary, and from 1739 or 1740, he served as a foreman in the painting studio, a post he was forced to resign on account of illness in 1745. Despite receipt of a pension, he was again working in 1747. In January 1748 he was imprisoned in the Königstein because muffle kilns and porcelain found in his house were regarded as evidence that he was surreptitiously practicing as a *Hausmaler*, i.e., a craftsman who decorated porcelain outside factory control. He was required to decorate porcelain for Meissen while imprisoned. With a fellow prisoner, Johann Gottlieb Mehlhorn, he escaped in 1749 and was captured in Prague, but managed to flee to Vienna and eventually to Breslau. In September 1749, he asked for permission to return to Meissen; it was apparently denied, and he went instead to Berlin. Records of his career there are lacking.

Heintze was chiefly a painter of figures and landscapes, including views of cities and harbor scenes, some in purple monochrome, one dated 1734. A number of pieces have been attributed to him because of their similarity to a signed enamel plaque in the Landesgewerbemuseum, Stuttgart, which bears a view of the Albrechtsburg at Meissen, and also because of the Heintze mannerism of writing the date on a milestone or similar object in the scene.

62

Christian Friedrich Herold (about 1700–1779), perhaps a cousin of the more famous Johann Gregor Herold (*q.v.*), was born in Berlin. Until 1725 he worked for a maker of enamel boxes, Alexander Fromery, in Berlin. In that year he came to Meissen, and in 1731 was engaged as a painter of "fine Japanese figures and landscapes," and apparently was responsible for the chinoiserie style with figures painted in black or red outlines and washed with colors. During his long stay at Meissen, Herold made many experiments in colors and with gold decoration and in 1740 received compensation for experiments in gilding porcelain. In 1750, it was said that he could attach figures of beaten gold to porcelain and glass permanently. He is now known chiefly for his harbor scenes, many on boxes of enamel on copper. In 1737, he was accused of appropriating undecorated porcelain to decorate outside the factory, to which he replied that his outside work was in enamel on copper. He died at Meissen in 1779.

Several signed pieces are recorded in Zimmermann, *Meissner Porzellan*, pp. 81, 82, and Honey, *European Ceramic Art*, p. 304: an enamel box painted with chinoiserie in the Royal Saxon Collection, Dresden (*C. F. Heroldt Fecit*); a brown tankard with Chinese scenes in the Goldschmidt-Rothschild Collection, Berlin, said to be dated Meissen, April 8, 1732; and a cup and saucer in the British Museum, dated September 12, 1750. Pazaurek (*Meissner Porzellan-malerei des 18. Jahrhunderts*, pp. 123, 125, fig. 66) also calls attention to a second tobacco box of enamel, painted with harbor scenes, in the Königsberg Museum, Prussia (now Kaliningrad). A sugar bowl and tea caddy with the arms of Clement Augustus, Archbishop of Cologne, in The Metropolitan Museum of Art, New York (acc. nos. 50.211.232ab, 233ab) are thought to be by him.

51

Johann Gregor Herold, or **Höroldt, Hoeroldt** (August 6, 1696–January 26, 1775), was born in Jena and died in Meissen. Nothing is known of his youth except that he was the son of a tailor, and he appears first in 1718 in Strasbourg, and then, at the beginning of 1719, in Vienna, working at the porcelain factory as a painter under C. C. Hunger. A year later he was taken to Meissen by Samuel Stöltzel, a former Meissen employee who was returning after a period of employment at the Du Paquier factory in Vienna. On the basis of trial pieces shown to the factory commission on May 22, 1720, Herold was hired immediately. Special praise was given to his ability to produce blue, red, and other colors that acquired a faultless surface texture during the high-temperature firing. In 1723, he was named court painter, and in 1725 he married. From 1731, he was arcanist and director of painters, with the title *Hofkommissar* and a fixed salary. He had control over all the painters, the preparation of the gold and colors, and, so far as he was able, the actual

painting of the especially fine services. It is known from the records, however, that Herold furnished certain pieces to serve as "models and curious pieces." According to a contract of February 25, 1732, he was required only to design and oversee the painting.

It was during this period of Herold's supervision that important developments in color and glazes took place, as well as the flowering of chinoiserie decoration. With the growing influence of J. J. Kaendler (*q.v.*), however, Herold's authority declined, and in 1756, at the beginning of the Seven Years' War, he went to Frankfurt am Main. On his return to Meissen in 1763, he had control only over the technical aspects of the painting and occupied a position subordinate to Christian Wilhelm Ernst Dietrich (working 1728–1779). This led to his retirement with a pension in September 1765.

The attribution of pieces to Herold himself is difficult. A vase formerly in the Dresden Schloss but destroyed during World War II, decorated with chinoiseries and a yellow ground, carried the signature *Johann Gregorius Höroldt inven. Meissen den 22. Jann Anno 1727*, but this inscription does not include the usual *fecit* (Honey, *European Ceramic Art*, I, p. 305). Another signature, *J. G. Höroldt fec. Meissen 17 Augusti 1726*, is found on a baluster vase in the Meissen Stadtmuseum, also decorated with chinoiseries, but with a powder-blue ground and gold silhouettes. Drawings and engravings of chinoiseries, such as one in the Graphische Sammlung in Munich signed *J. G. Höroldt inv. et fecit 1726*, derived in part from Augsburg prints such as those by Martin Engelbrecht (1684–1756), are stylistically close to those on the porcelains of this group, and may have served as models for other painters.

In addition, a number of pieces have been found that apparently bear a cryptic signature, either in initials or pseudo-Chinese characters. Examples include a cylindrical pitcher in the Schlossmuseum, Arnstadt, signed in a cryptic manner (attributed to Herold by Menzhausen, *Keramik-Freunde der Schweiz*, May 1965, pp. 3, 4, fig. 2) and two cylindrical pitchers in the Kunstgewerbemuseum, Budapest, one with a letter H, the other with a hidden signature (see Marik, *Keramik-Freunde der Schweiz*, May 1965, pp. 5–7, figs. 6, 8).

It is also known, from entries in the factory records from March to June 1725, that he painted a tea and chocolate service for the King of Sardinia, Victor

Amadeus II. A cup and saucer from this service are in The Metropolitan Museum of Art, New York (acc. nos. 54. 147. 75, 76).

A detailed analysis of Herold's use of prints was made by Ducret, *Keramik-Freunde der Schweiz*, July 1957, pp. 38–40. See also Schönberger, *Meissener Porzellan mit Höroldt-Malerei* for a discussion of Herold's style.

46, 49 A and B, 57 A to D, 58 A to D, 59

Pierre Houry (born about 1724*) was employed at Sèvres as a flower painter from about 1752 to 1755. (Chavagnac gives his starting date as 1747, which appears to be that of the *mouleur* Oury). His mark is a Roman letter H.

H

79 A and B, 84 A and B, 97

Johann Joachim Kaendler, or **Kändler** (June 15, 1706–May 18, 1775), was the son of a minister and became the chief sculptor of the Meissen factory. Not much is known of his early experience and training. In 1723, he became a pupil of Benjamin Thomae, the court sculptor at Dresden and pupil of Balthasar Permoser (1651–1732), and in this capacity he participated in the decoration of the royal treasure house, the Grünes Gewölbe (Green Vaults). Here he apparently attracted the attention of Augustus the Strong, who summoned him to Meissen in June 1731 and supplied him with a small room in the palace where he could work alone. Such partiality, coupled with Kaendler's superior talent and imagination, contributed to strained relations with the Meissen *Modellmeister* Kirchner (*q.v.*). During his first weeks at the factory, the new modeler created several pieces, among them a large eagle with wings outspread, which overcame technical problems that had restricted the scale and posing of figures up to that time. When Kirchner resigned in 1733, the young Kaendler was immediately appointed model master, in which role he was responsible for creating new models and supervising as well as instructing other modelers and their apprentices.

In the early years of his Meissen career he created a wide variety of bird and animal models for the Japanese Palace. Their unprecedented naturalism and

sense of movement attest to Kaendler's genius in interpreting the drawings he made from life in the Moritzburg animal garden, and from stuffed examples in the Elector's collection. They also demonstrate his ability to translate from other pictorial sources, such as the studies of exotic animals by his contemporary, Christian Keinovius.

Kaendler's sculptural projects, thought to number over a thousand, were often modeled with the help of his assistants, Eberlein, Ehder, or Reinicke (*qq.v.*). Harlequins, Chinese figures, shepherds, shepherdesses, and Italian comedy figures were his favorite themes. Other important categories include half-size busts of saints, Popes, and Hapsburg emperors. His confidence in the porcelain material was shown by his desire to create an equestrian statue of heroic size of Augustus III, of which a small preparatory model became part of the Royal Saxon Collection, Dresden.

Kaendler's conversion from the vigorous plastic style of the baroque to the greater delicacy of the rococo is marked by the famous Swan Service made for Count Brühl in 1737–1741, in which the design of the candlesticks was influenced by the factory's collection of engravings after the designer Juste-Aurèle Meissonnier (about 1693–1750), one of the early masters of the French rococo.

By 1764, however, Kaendler had lost prestige and was made a subordinate to the director of Meissen's new art academy, Christian Wilhelm Ernst Dietrich. The nature of his last project, a set of mythological groups for Catherine II of Russia, dating from 1772–1774, shows his attempt to adjust himself to the new taste of classicism.

2 A and B, 3 A and B, 4 A and B, 5, 6 A and B, 9 A and B, 10 A and B, 11, 12, 13 A and B, 16 A and B, 17 A and B, 18, 19, 20, 21 A and B, 22 A and B, 23 A and B, 24, 25, 26, 27, 28, 29 A and B, 30, 31 A and B, 32, 33 A to C, 34, 35, 36 A and B, 37 A and B, 38 A and B, 39 A and B, 40 A and B, 41 A and B, 177

Johann Gottlob Kirchner (born about 1706) was a sculptor at Meissen, though his employment there was not continuous. During his earliest stay, from April 1727 to February 1729, he produced a Temple of Venus, with many figures (which appears not to have survived); a sculptural table fountain for rose water with a basin in the form of a shell (represented

[435]

at The Metropolitan Museum of Art, New York, acc. no. 54.147.65); and a series of large bird and animal sculptures, mainly fashioned after Oriental originals. Following his dismissal for misconduct or illness, he worked as a sculptor at Schloss Belvedere in Weimar, but was recalled to Meissen in June 1730, and was appointed model master in the following year. His duties included supervision of the modeling shop and the training of apprentices. He was responsible for designing not only figural works but also ornamental pieces and tablewares. During this second period of employment, his work included a lifesize bristling Bolognese dog, to be found in The Metropolitan Museum of Art (acc. no. 54.147.69). Among his other important sculptures were a St. Peter for the chapel of the Japanese Palace in Dresden, and a series of large animals in the white, among them, in collaboration with Kaendler, a rhinoceros after the 1515 engraving by Dürer.

Shortly after the arrival at Meissen of J. J. Kaendler (*q.v.*) in 1731, Kirchner applied for an increase in salary, which was refused. As a result, he offered his resignation, which was not accepted until March 31, 1733. He is known to have received a subsequent commission from the factory for the creation of two figures in 1737; one of these was the statuette of Augustus III in the Royal Saxon Collection, signed with the initials G. K. Little is known of his later life, except that he lived for some time in Berlin, as a sculptor and painter.

1 A and B

Laroche, or **De la Roche**, was employed by Sèvres in 1758 or 1759. He practiced flower painting and other forms of decoration, including the application of *bleu-céleste* grounds and gilding, until 1802. His mark consists either of the script letter LR or of a script letter *h* ending in a loop.

95 A to FF, 97

Le Bel jeune was employed at Sèvres as a flower painter from 1773 (Chavagnac gives his starting date

as 1765) to 1793, when he became gilder. His mark consists of the script letters LB, conjoined or separated.

97

Étienne-Henri Le Guay, known as **Le Guay père** (born 1721), was born in Saint-Cloud and was employed at Vincennes in 1749 as a painter in blue. In the same year he went to Sarreguemines, but re-entered Vincennes in 1751 as a gilder, in which capacity he served until 1796. His mark consists of the script letters L.G.

110

Denis Levé (born 1731) was employed at Sèvres as a painter of flowers and ornaments from 1754 to 1805. Among the objects decorated by him were plaques for furniture. His mark is usually a letter L, either Roman or script, although at times his name is written out in full.

91 A and B, 95 A to FF, 97, 112 A and B

Félix-Clément Levé (born 1761*) was employed at Sèvres as a flower painter from 1777 to 1779; his father, Denis (*q.v.*), was also a flower painter there. His mark is a Roman letter F.

97

Antoine-Mathieu Liance (born 1732), a native of Paris, was a *répareur en ornements* at Sèvres from about 1754 to 1777.* He worked on elaborate pieces such as elephant vases, refining and perfecting the molded detail. Three of his sons were also employed at Sèvres as *répareurs* or *sculpteurs*. His mark is an incised script letter L, sometimes accompanied by other letters of his name, such as M Li or Lian.

80, 81, 82, 86

Charles-Louis Méreaud, or **Méraud, Mérault**, known as **Méreaud jeune**, was employed at Sèvres as a painter of flowers and ornaments from 1756 to 1779.* His mark is a comma or the number 9.

97

Pierre-Antoine Méreaud, or **Méreau, Mérault**, known as **Méreaud aîné** (born about 1735*), was employed at Sèvres as a painter of flowers and as a gilder from 1754 to 1791. His mark is a letter s.

78 A and B

Jacques-François Micaud (born about 1735*) was born at Villeneuve and employed at Sèvres from 1757 to 1810 as a painter of flowers and ornaments. His mark is a St. Andrew's cross.

102

Ambroise Michel was a flower painter at Sèvres from 1772 until 1780. His mark is a Roman letter M.

97

Jean-Louis Morin (born 1732* or 1733) was employed at Sèvres from 1754 to 1787. He is best known for harbor scenes in the manner of Claude-Joseph Vernet (1714–1789), and for vignettes of military life. It is a curious fact that his mark, a letter M, either Roman or script, is found in conjunction with figure painting of greatly varying quality: sketchy dock hands, awkwardly posed, and sometimes ill-proportioned, in contrast to soldiers, who are meticulously drawn and finished. This situation suggests that Morin

may have preferred to do military subjects, or that there may have been an unidentified second painter using a letter M as his mark.

86

Gottfried Müller was a sculptor who is associated with the early history of Meissen. He may have worked with Böttger as early as 1708 in the Venus-bastei, Dresden. From the mid-1720s through the 1730s he was at Meissen, creating figures, vases, birds of large size, and accessories for services. His mark consists of three impressed dots forming a triangle, easily mistaken for those of Grund Junior and Seidel (*qq.v.*).

64

Mutel (born about 1736*) was born in Paris and employed at Vincennes-Sèvres as a painter of birds and landscapes from 1754 to 1759, 1765 to 1766, and again from 1771 to 1773. He is known also to have been a fan painter. His mark is a pair of compasses.

97

Nicquet, or **Niquet, Niguet**, a flower painter and gilder, was employed at Sèvres from 1764 until 1793 or later, according to Chavagnac. His mark consists of the script letters *nq*.

95 A to FF, 97

Jean Pierre, known as **Pierre aîné**, was employed at Sèvres from 1759 to 1775 as a gilder, according to Brunet (p. 33) and Honey (*European Ceramic Art*, II, p. 569). However, Chavagnac and Grollier (p. 347), citing a visitors' guide to the Sèvres Museum and Manufactory, identify Pierre *aîné* as a painter of flowers and bouquets "avant 1800." Brunet illustrates his mark as  ; Honey gives it as ; while Chavagnac shows it as and . Pierre *aîné*'s career at Sèvres overlapped that of his son Jean-Jacques (*q.v.*) from 1763 onward.

86

Jean-Jacques Pierre, known as **Pierre jeune**, was employed as a flower painter at Sèvres from 1763 to 1800. He is known especially for bouquets that are frequently tied with bowknotted ribbons. His mark consists of the letter P followed by what may be an apostrophe, the number 7, the letter q, or an imperfect letter j.

For a discussion of other marks found on furniture plaques painted in the style of Pierre *jeune*, see Dauterman, Parker, and Standen, *Decorative Art from the Samuel H. Kress Collection at The Metropolitan Museum of Art*, pp. 189, 190.

P J.　　　　　95 A to FF, 97

Christian Heinrich Petzsch, an arcanist, was employed by the Meissen factory in 1732. His mark is a crescent.

)　　　　　*63*

Peter Reinicke (1715–1768) was born in Danzig and became a modeler at Meissen on April 1, 1743. He seems to have been a capable and industrious worker and assisted Kaendler (*q.v.*), whose style he imitated, in many important series of sculptures, including the busts of Popes and Hapsburg emperors; the figures of national types (after de Ferriol's *Différentes Nations du Lévant*, published in Paris in 1714); the Paris street vendors after drawings by Huet; English genre figures after engravings by Tempesta; and the famous Monkey Orchestra, traditionally a caricature of the orchestra of Count Brühl. Other works include figures after Callot engravings, Chinese groups, Italian comedy figures, and some animals. In his last years, beginning in 1765, Reinicke restored old models.

31 A and B, 33 A to C, 34

Pierre-Remi Robert (1782–1832) was employed at Sèvres as a painter of landscapes and ornaments from

1813 until his death. His mark consists of the Roman letters PR.

PR　　　　　95 A to FF, 97

Pierre-Joseph Rosset (born about 1735) was employed at Vincennes-Sèvres from 1753 to 1795 as a painter, originally of flowers and later of landscapes and animals. His mark is an ax or hatchet.

　　　　　97

Schiefer was employed at Meissen. Doenges, in *Meissner Porzellan*, p. 89, mentions him among the *Former* (modelers and, presumably, moldmakers) Fritsche, Albrecht, Müller (*q.v.*), and other associates of Böttger during the first decade or so of that factory. His mark is a dotted, incised cross.

✛　　　　　*63*

Seidel was employed at the processing shops at Meissen (dates unpublished). His mark consists of three impressed dots forming a triangle, easily mistaken for those of Müller or Grund Junior (*qq.v.*).

∴　　　　　*64*

Bartholomäus Seuter, or **Seutter**, **Seite** (1678–1754), an Augsburg *Hausmaler* (*q.v.*) on faïence and Meissen porcelain, was also an enameler, engraver, dealer, chemist, and silk dyer. On porcelain, he and other members of his family were apparently responsible for a kind of chinoiserie in gold, characterized by C-scrolls in the border ornament, as appears on a teapot signed by his brother Abraham (1690–1747) *A. Seite 1736 Augusta* (recorded in Honey, *European Ceramic Art*, I, p. 555, illustrated II, pl. 150 B.). Abraham's signature also appears as that of a gilder on a Meissen chinoiserie cup at the Victoria and Albert Museum, London, and also on a teapot and bowl, part of a matching traveling service, in a private collection in Zürich (see Ducret, *Keramos*, XXXVII, figs. 3, 13). Bartholomäus's faïence decoration consisted chiefly of European flowers, in connection with which he provided drawings for a volume of plates entitled *Eigentliche Vorstellung einiger Tausend in allen vier Welt-Thei-*

len gewachsener Bäume, Stauden, Kräuter, Blumen, Früchte und Schwämme, published by Johann Wilhelm Weinmann at Ratisbon between 1735 and 1745. A porcelain tankard in the Hamburg Museum with figures of a man, woman, and two children is attributed to him, but examples of his work are rare (see Pazaurek, *Deutsche Fayence- und Porzellan-Hausmaler*, I, pl. 7, fig. 82).

44

Jean-Charles Sioux, or **Siou**, known as **Sioux aîné** (born about 1716), was born in Paris and served as a flower painter and in other capacities at Vincennes-Sèvres from 1752 until 1792. He was formerly a fan painter. His mark is either a misshapen Roman letter R or a circlet of dots with a single dot at the center.

95 A TO FF

Johann Ehrenfried Stadtler, or **Stadler** (1701–June 3, 1741) was born at Dresden and was active briefly at the Meissen faïence factory. From 1723/1724 onward he decorated Meissen porcelain, and from 1731 he was listed as a flower painter. A small covered tureen and stand in the Royal Saxon Collection, Dresden, painted with Oriental flowers and birds, bears his signature (see Pazaurek, *Meissner Porzellanmalerei des 18. Jahrhunderts*, fig. 9). A very similar decoration was on a pair of vases with the royal monogram AR (for Augustus Rex) in the Erich von Goldschmidt-Rothschild Collection, while other attributed pieces are in the collection of Ernst Schneider, Düsseldorf.

50

Vincent Taillandier, or **Taillandiez** (born about 1737), was employed at Sèvres as a painter of flowers from 1753 to 1790. Before he entered the factory, he had been associated with the factory at Sceaux. His mark is a fleur de lys.

83, 87, 94 A and B, 95 A TO FF

Charles Tandart, known as **Tandart jeune** (born 1736), was employed as a flower painter at Sèvres from

1756 to 1760. He had earlier been employed by the mirror maker Deslandes. Apparently because of family affiliation, he shared the three-dot mark of Jean-Baptiste Tandart (*q.v.*), who preceded him at the factory (see Dauterman, Parker, and Standen, *Decorative Art from the Samuel H. Kress Collection at The Metropolitan Museum of Art*, pp. 190, 191).

97

Jean-Baptiste Tandart, known as **Tandart aîné** (born 1729/1731), was a former fan painter, and was employed at Sèvres as a painter of flowers from 1754 to 1803. Among objects decorated by him were plaques for furniture, displaying bouquets and wreaths of flowers. His mark consists of three dots in a horizontal row. See also Charles Tandart.

● ● ●

105 A to O

Claude-Antoine Tardy, or **Tardi** (born 1733), was employed at Sèvres from 1757 to 1795 as a painter of flowers. His mark resembles a square letter D with serifs and with a dot at the center.

95 A to FF, 97

Théodore, a painter and gilder at Sèvres, worked there from 1765 to 1779/1780. His mark consists of four dots in a horizontal row.

● ● ● ●

95 A to FF, 97, 107

Thevenet père (1708–1765) was employed at Vincennes-Sèvres from 1741 to 1777. Formerly a fanmaker, he at first painted the porcelain flowers modeled in the studio of François Gravant (working about 1738–1765) at Vincennes, and later painted flowers on Sèvres porcelain. His mark resembles a pin or an inverted baton (although Chavagnac illustrates it as a comma or musical note).

76 A and B, 95 A to FF

Vandé père (born 1727) was employed at Sèvres from 1753 to 1779. In his capacity as a gilder he rose to chief burnisher. Chavagnac describes him as also a painter in oil. His mark consists of the Roman letters VD, conjoined.

97, 110

Vavasseur aîné (born 1731) was employed at Vincennes-Sèvres as a flower painter from 1753 to 1770. His mark is a Roman letter W.

97

Vieillard (born 1718) was a decorator at Sèvres, where he was employed as a painter of flowers, attributes, and landscapes from 1752 to 1790. Jacquemart and Le Blant (*Histoire Artistique, Industrielle et Commerciale de la Porcelaine*, II, p. 511) classify him among figure painters of the second class. His mark consists of three dots above a horizontal line (interpreted by Chavagnac as the heraldic device known as a label of three points).

101, 109

Johann Abraham Winckler (died 1768), a goldsmith of Augsburg, became a master in 1736. A set of knives, forks, and spoons in a parcel-gilt toilet service dating from 1757/1759 in the Germanisches Museum, Nuremberg, are by him. His mark consists of the Roman letters AW, conjoined, in an oval.

73 A to JJ

Philippe Xhrouet, or **Xhrouuet**, **Xrowet**, known as **Xhrouet père**, also as **Croix**, or **Secroix** (born about 1730*), was employed at Sèvres as a landscape painter from 1750 to 1775. Before entering Sèvres, he painted decorative borders for fans. His greatest contribution to the evolution of porcelain painting at Sèvres was the creation, about 1757, of the fresh rose tint that in modern times is called *rose Pompadour*. For this, he received a reward of 150 livres. His mark, an allusion to his nickname, is a cross.

92, 105 A to O

GLOSSARY

T HE TERMS in this glossary relating to Sèvres porcelain have been confirmed as to their eighteenth century usage by reference to the unpublished sales records of the Sèvres manufactory.

Altozier   literally, old osier, a molded pattern in low relief, simulating basketwork of fine weave, with radial ribs. It was used at Meissen at least as early as 1735, especially as a border design for plates.

anchor marks   devices painted or molded to represent anchors and used as factory marks on Chelsea and other porcelain. The term applies in this catalogue only to the products of Sprimont's Chelsea Porcelain Manufactory. Each type of mark indicates, approximately, a phase in the history of Sprimont's factory, viz.: raised anchor, 1749–1752; red anchor, 1752–1758; gold anchor, 1758–1769.

arcanist   a craftsman who possessed the *arcanum*, or secret, of the materials and processes used in the manufacture of ceramic pastes and glazes. The arcanist in many instances was also familiar with the essentials of building and operating kilns.

Arita   a Japanese place name associated with the production of several types of Japanese porcelain, including that of the school of Kakiemon (*q.v.*).

assiette à potage   a soup plate

beurrier   a butter dish, usually tub-shaped and fitted with a flat cover. Often it is affixed to a saucer-like stand.

blanc de chine   the mellow white porcelain made at Tê-hua, in Fukien province, during the Ming and Ch'ing dynasties. It is regarded technically as the acme of hard-paste porcelain in its blending of body and glaze.

bleu céleste   literally, sky-blue, the name given in the Sèvres eighteenth century factory records to a bright greenish blue of the hue called turquoise-blue today.

bleu du roi   literally, king's blue, the term for a deep blue made from cobalt and introduced at Sèvres in 1763. This color was used extensively as a ground color, or field, from that date through the balance of the reign of Louis XV and that of Louis XVI. In the early records of the Sèvres factory it is sometimes referred to as *bleu nouveau*.

Blind Earl   a motif employing flower stems, leaves, and buds in relief, found on Chelsea and Worcester porcelain. The name is taken from George William, 6th Earl of Coventry, but is anachronistic because he did not become blind until 1780, well after the pattern had been established.

boîte à éponge   a vessel, usually spherical and in two parts, for holding a sponge. The walls were pierced, usually in a decorative pattern, to permit evaporation.

bougeoir   a candlestick. In Sèvres porcelain the usual type was that known, in silver, as a chamber candlestick, which has a short stem set into a dished base fitted with a ring handle.

broc et sa jatte   a ewer or pitcher, and the bowl in which it rests.

cachepôt   see *seau à bouteille*.

cailllouté literally, pebbled. In Sèvres porcelain it means a type of gilded decoration consisting of ovals interspersed with irregular smaller circles, outlined on a colored ground.

caisse a term with a variety of meanings, here used to designate a small vessel in the form of an orange tub. The Sèvres sale records for the period from December 20, 1753, to December 24, 1761, reveal that porcelain *caisses* were usually sold in pairs. Although size, color, and decoration are usually mentioned, these records contain no specific references to the tub shape. See also *cuvette*.

cavetto a concave molding, as at the inner border of a dinner plate.

celadon a porcelain of Oriental origin, coated with a glaze of muted gray-green or blue-green; also, a term for such colors.

Ch'ien Lung a period in Chinese history named after the emperor who reigned from 1736 to 1795, during the Ch'ing Dynasty.

Ch'ing a Chinese dynasty dating from 1644 to 1912.

compotier a dish, sometimes on a low foot, for serving compote, a preparation of fruit in syrup. Special varieties are the *compotier à coquille*, *compotier carré*, *compotier ovale*, and *compotier rond*, allusions to their shapes.

coquetier an egg cup. Its usual shape is ovoid, with a molded lip and ring foot. An alternative term, probably not used before the nineteenth century, is *tasse à oeuf*. The phrase *coquetier sans pieds* was used in the sale records of Sèvres (where it appears first about 1759) to designate a type of egg cup that rests on a molded ring base.

coupe a cup. The term appears to be used interchangeably with *tasse* (*q.v.*) in the Sèvres sale records.

crossed L's the royal cipher, in script, used by Louis XIV, Louis XV, and Louis XVI. Under the latter two, it was employed as a factory mark on Vincennes and Sèvres porcelain.

crossed swords the principal mark of Meissen porcelain for the last two and a half centuries, derived from the arms of Saxony. From time to time the appearance of the mark was altered, and dots, stars, or numerals were added. These changes may be assigned to various periods. For example, a dot (sometimes two) between the hilts was used from 1763 to 1774. Other marks were placed below the swords: an asterisk or star, from 1774 to 1814; a Roman numeral I from about 1814 to 1818; and a numeral II in 1818. Such dots or stars are, however, occasionally found on earlier pieces. A dot between the tips of the swords was used in 1924 and later. The crossed swords were characteristically painted in blue under the glaze, although they are found occasionally over the glaze, as in examples with Kakiemon decoration, usually not dating later than 1730.

cuvette sometimes used in referring to a platter or stand (as for a tureen), but more generally applied to an oval basin of the type that accompanied a ewer in eighteenth century French silver and porcelain. When modified, however, the word may designate an oblong flower holder, as in *cuvette à fleurs*, a term that appears in the Sèvres sale records as early as 1753. A *cuvette Mahon* is a type of flower holder of exaggerated, rococo boat shape, with *bombé* sides and ribbed ends, resting on four elaborately scrolled feet (see Eriksen, *Waddesdon Manor: Sèvres Porcelain*, p. 88, no. 29). See also *caisse*.

date-letter a letter either single or double, a usual component of a Sèvres porcelain mark, that indicates the year in which a given piece was decorated. It may be either upper or lower case, and placed either within or outside the crossed L's (*q.v.*). The first series began with A in 1753 and continued through Z in 1777. A new series, begun with AA in 1778, continued through PP (1793), although porcelains carrying the rare marks QQ and RR are not unknown. These latter two are freakish and unofficial.

decorators' marks letters or symbols abundantly used on Sèvres porcelain to identify the painters and gilders who contributed the decoration for individual pieces. They are characteristically painted outside the crossed L's (*q.v.*). The practice was discouraged at the Meissen factory, although the prohibition was not completely effective. Decorators' marks are not commonly found on English porcelain.

déjeuner   a breakfast set. In its simplest form it consisted only of a small tray, and a cup and saucer. The composition of larger sets varied, and additional items found include plates, egg cups, butter dishes, pots for coffee, tea, or chocolate, a cream or milk jug, a sugar bowl, a conserve jar, and a salt. The term was sometimes modified, alluding to the shape of the cup (although the precise shape is not always documented), e.g., *déjeuner Bouret* (cylindrical; see Eriksen, *Waddesdon Manor: Sèvres Porcelain*, p. 62, no. 14), *déjeuner carré* (square), *déjeuner Dauphin*, *Duvaux*, or *Hébert* (of squat, inverted pear shape; Eriksen, p. 38, no. 2).

dot period   in Meissen porcelain, the years 1763 to 1774, when the factory mark was a pair of crossed swords with a dot between the hilts. A similar mark is occasionally found on pieces dating from about 1740.

Dulong   a pattern in low relief introduced at Meissen in 1743. It employed cartouches, scrolls, and floral motifs, and was generally used on the borders of plates. The name honors Dulong, Godefroy, and Dulong, Amsterdam dealers in Meissen porcelain.

écritoire   an inkstand or standish. Elaborate examples consist of an inkwell and a pounce pot flanking an ornament or bell, either wholly of porcelain or partly mounted with gilt bronze. An example of the former is a Sèvres *écritoire* in the Wallace Collection, London (illustrated in Verlet, *Sèvres*, pl. 56), in which the inkwell and pounce pot are fashioned in the form of terrestrial and celestial globes, respectively.

écuelle   a deep bowl, usually with two handles, a cover, and stand, for serving individual portions of liquid foods such as bouillons. During the Middle Ages and Renaissance, *écuelles* of wood, pewter, enamel, silver, and gold were shared by two persons at family meals and banquets.

en briques d'or   a type of gilded decoration simulating the flakes of gold found on certain kinds of Oriental lacquer, in which the flakes are rectangular and arranged like brickwork.

famille verte   a French term applied to a specific type of Chinese porcelain and by extension to corresponding European porcelains. The type is characterized by a combination of enamel colors introduced during the K'ang Hsi period (*q.v.*), consisting of green, yellow, red, blue, and manganese purple.

flying dog pattern   a decorative motif introduced at Meissen about 1730 or a little later, in imitation of Kakiemon (*q.v.*) porcelain. "Flying fox" and "flying squirrel" are alternative names resulting from variations in the depiction of the principal motif, which is usually highly stylized. Of all these names, flying squirrel seems most nearly to convey the original intention of the Japanese artists from whose porcelains the motif was adopted.

fu-lion   a combination of Chinese and English words rendered literally as "lion of happiness." The term is commonly applied in English writings to the lion represented in Chinese art as a guardian of Buddhist images and temples. Thus it appears to be a corruption of the Chinese expression for "dog of Fo [Buddha]." Small versions of *fu*-lions for altars in Chinese homes often support tubes to hold sticks of incense.

Fukien   a province in China noted for its creamy white porcelain called *blanc de chine* (*q.v.*), made principally at Tê-hua. Hence, the term is also used to designate the porcelain itself.

gilders' marks   see decorators' marks.

girandole   in French usage a candelabrum usually hung with crystal drops or pendants, and in the eighteenth century, by extension, a chandelier. In England, the term applies to a wall mirror with candle arms. The name derives from the Italian *girandola*, a pyrotechnical term, and is described more fully in Volume II of this catalogue, pp. 584–585.

Girl-in-a-Swing   a type of porcelain made at Chelsea about 1749–1752, but differing in character from that made at Sprimont's Chelsea Porcelain Manufactory and therefore taken to be the product of a rival enterprise. It takes its name from a porcelain group now in the Victoria and Albert Museum, London (see Introduction, p. 317).

gobelet   generally, a tall cup. In the Sèvres records, however, the term was used with various modifiers to denote cups of special shape rather than unusual size. A *gobelet Bouillard*, a cylindrical cup with a rounded base resting on a contracted ring foot, is named after the *fermier-général* Antoine-Augustin Bouillard, a shareholder in the Vincennes-Sèvres enterprise. Other variants are the *gobelet Bouret* (cylindrical, rounding inward toward the base); *gobelet Duplessis; gobelet à cuvier* (a general term for conical cups); and the *gobelet Hébert* (of inverted pear shape).

gold anchor   see *anchor marks*.

Hausmaler   literally, "home-painter," i.e., a freelance artist who decorated porcelain to his own taste, independent of factory supervision. In many instances the work of these artists was of the highest quality. Such a considerable amount of white porcelain fell into their hands that Meissen and Vienna took strenuous steps to discourage their competition.

incised marks or *marques en creux*   letters or symbols scratched into the clay before firing to identify the sculptor, *répareur*, *tourneur*, or other artisan responsible for the several processes required in finishing a piece of porcelain before it is glazed and decorated.

Indianische Blumen   (Indian flowers), stylized flower motifs introduced at Meissen about 1725 to 1730, in the form of Europeanized versions of Chinese and Japanese motifs. Those deriving from Chinese sources are sometimes found on vases made to the order of Augustus II.

jatte   a bowl or dish, as in *jatte à punch* or *ponch*, a punch bowl, or *jatte ovale*, an oval serving dish.

Johanneum inventory marks   a variety of eighteenth century marks found on porcelain formerly in the Royal Saxon Collection. The name derives from the Johanneum, a building in Dresden where the collection was housed during the nineteenth century. The marks, cut into the glaze or body and colored black, are those of an inventory begun in 1721 and extended several times during the eighteenth century. It has been suggested that one purpose they served was to discourage the stealing of porcelains while they were on exhibition at the Japanese Palace.

Kakiemon   a school of Japanese potters and porcelain painters. During the late seventeenth and eighteenth centuries, the Kakiemon developed a distinctive, almost sketchy manner of painting vignettes. Hence, in European porcelain Kakiemon is a style of decoration derived from Japanese prototypes, seen in the work of Chantilly, Meissen, and several English porcelain factories.

K'ang Hsi   a period within the Ch'ing Dynasty, dating from 1662 to 1722.

Laub und Bandelwerk   (foliage and scrollwork), a combination of motifs much used at Meissen as a border decoration for chinoiseries during the early period of J. G. Herold (*q.v.*), i.e., from the early 1720s to the mid-1730s. Iron-red, puce, and gold were characteristic colors. It was also used as a decorative scheme on the earlier Böttger stoneware, in which the foliations, engraved with a wheel, were less feathery than in the painted versions.

litron   a cylindrical cup that apparently takes its name from a type of measuring vessel for liquids. Saucers for such cups were customarily designed with sharply sloping, straight walls. The Sèvres sale records often use the term *tasse forme litron*.

lorgnette monoculaire   a small telescope or spyglass with an extendable tube of porcelain or enamel; a species of opera glass.

magot   a grotesque, tail-less monkey and thus applied to ugly men, particularly dwarfs. Louis XIV applied it to the peasants in Teniers's paintings. Hence a statuette of an Oriental in porcelain, often of a grotesque character.

Merkurstab a "caduceus" mark, so called from its loose resemblance to the herald's staff used by Mercury. Meissen used it briefly as a factory mark, painted in blue, beginning about 1723.

marques en creux see incised marks.

mouleur a craftsman responsible for preparing molds and/or making casts of vessels and figures.

Ming a Chinese dynasty dating from 1368 to 1644.

navette a shuttle, sometimes used for winding gold and silver thread obtained by unraveling braids, tassels, and galloons, as in *parfilage* (for an account of this, see Groves, *Country Life*, February 6, 1953, pp. 338, 339).

Neuozier literally, new osier, a molded pattern in low relief simulating a basket weave of spiral pattern. It was introduced at Meissen in 1742. See also *Altozier*.

oeil de perdrix a type of decoration employing an allover "partridge-eye" pattern, used at Sèvres to break up the too-even appearance of large areas of uniform ground color. At least two types exist: in one, dots of gold (as in *fond bleu pointillé d'or*) make up a pattern of circlets with a larger dot at the center, and sometimes dots of enamel color alternate with the gold; in the other, tiny dotted reserves (cells) in the colored glaze produce a textured surface relief not unlike that of a honeycomb; the cells may be bordered with gold dots forming circles.

patchmarks irregular scars about a half-inch in diameter occurring on the underside of certain porcelains and representing the points on which the pieces rested, on pellets of clay, while being fired. The glaze is accordingly damaged or missing at these points, and in consequence the porcelain may become discolored there.

plateau a tray, platter, or stand for other porcelain vessels, such as a tureen or the articles of a tea or coffee service. A *plateau Bouret* was a tray or oversized saucer for accommodating an ice cup. It was evidently named for N. Bouret, a high tax official (*fermier-général*) under Louis XV, who was a notorious gourmand. Eight such trays were in the service made in 1772 for the Prince de Rohan. A *plateau carré* was a small, square tray with pierced, sloping sides, used in a breakfast service. The name seems also to have been applied in the Sèvres records to oblong trays with openwork sides. A *plateau Hébert* was a tray for a *déjeuner Hébert* (in which the cups are of inverted pear shape, and there is no milk jug).

pointillé d'or spangled with small dots of gold. See *sablé d'or*.

pois d'or gold decoration consisting primarily of round dots about the size of a pea.

Pokal a cup or goblet on a high stem. The term is usually reserved for a goblet of some distinction, suitable for ceremonial purposes or presentation, and fitted with a cover.

porte-fleurs a pierced device for holding in place a flower arrangement with stems of different length; it stands within a container.

pot a term applied to several types of ceramic vessels, and modified as follows, with reference to this catalogue: *pot à crème*, *pot à lait*, jugs for cream and milk, respectively; *pot à jus*, a cup, often slightly bulbous, with a cover and handle, for serving hot sauce or the juices of meat; *pot à pommade*, a small jar for holding pomade, a perfumed preparation for the toilette. An entry in the *Livre-Journal* of Lazare Duvaux for March 16, 1754, records:

Mme la Marq. de Pompadour. Un petit pot à pommade, blanc & or, de Vincennes, 24 l.

(no. 1711)

A *pot à confiture* held jam or other preserves. It was usually a small jar or cup fitted with a cover. Although lacking a handle, it had at times two small horizontal loops at one side to hold a porcelain spoon.

pot à sucre see *sucrier*.

pot à thé see *théière*.

pot-pourri a vessel designed to hold aromatic leaves and flowers for perfuming a room; accordingly, its cover and/or walls were pierced with patterns of openwork to permit the fragrance to escape. Various entries in Lazare Duvaux's *Livre-Journal* reveal that such vessels were available in 1748–1749 in Meissen porcelain and Chinese pottery and porcelain. An entry for August 8, 1752, reads:

Mme de Pompadour, pour le bosquet et l'Ermitage; deux pots-pourris de Vincennes, forme d'urne, en blanc & bleu, 168 l.

(*Livre-Journal*, no. 1193)

A *pot-pourri gondole* was a deep, boat-shaped vessel with pierced shoulders and a high, pierced cover; specifically, it is a rare form of Sèvres vase introduced about 1757.

raised anchor see anchor marks.

red anchor see anchor marks.

répareur a craftsman who worked with unfired clay. He assembled parts that were separately molded and removed the seams left by the plaster molds. He also carved openwork patterns and in general perfected the surface detail with fine tools. Those who worked on complicated pieces at Sèvres were called *répareurs en ornements*. Liance (*q.v.*), was one of these.

rose Pompadour a name applied to a fresh rose-pink introduced at Sèvres in 1757, but not released for sale until 1758, possibly by order of the king (see p. 207). Made from a compound of gold, the color was invented by the Sèvres artist Xhrouet (*q.v.*), who was rewarded for his success. In the eighteenth century archives of Sèvres, it is referred to only as *rose* or *roze*. Although the term *rose Pompadour* may not have been in use during the lifetime of the marquise, who died in 1764, the color was then at its finest.

sablé d'or literally, "sanded with gold," i.e., spangled with minute dots of gold. The term seems to be interchangeable with *pointillé d'or*.

saladier a salad bowl. At Sèvres it was influenced in size and shape by prototypes in silver, which made their appearance during the Régence. Its form was that of a deep, round bowl not unlike a punchbowl, but occasionally it was modeled in low relief both inside and out with panels shaped like stylized leaves, as in a service made for Christian VII of Denmark in 1768.

salière a salt cellar or condiment holder, usually a vessel of trencher type. This is in all probability the type referred to in the *Livre-Journal* of Lazare Duvaux for March 1757, item 2736:

Mme d'Egmont, douairière: Quatre Salières de Vincennes, 48 l.

A *salière à corbeille* was an open salt in the form of an oval basket with an arched (bail) handle. In this catalogue, the term is extended, in the absence of specific documentation, to include a cluster of three condiment baskets, with bowknotted ribbons linking the arched handles. The Sèvres archives also mention a *salière à paniers ozier tortillé*.

scolopendrium a genus of plants with lance-shaped leaves, the veinings of which resemble centipedes. It is found occasionally as a decoration on Chelsea and Worcester porcelain.

sculpteur a craftsman who modeled figures or decorative objects of clay. Various combinations of the term occur, such as *sculpteur-modeleur*.

seau a category of vessel of which several specialized forms were made, especially in the porcelain of Sèvres. The following are represented in this catalogue: *Seau à bouteille*, a deep, tub-shaped vessel with a constricted base and two small handles in the form of scrolled brackets. Its purpose was to keep a bottle of wine cool during a meal. The size varied according to the type of bottle; for instance, a *seau à demi-bouteille* was intended for a half bottle. In the nineteenth century the name *cachepôt* was applied to this form. *Seau ovale à liqueurs*, a term employed at Sèvres to designate a boat-shaped container used for chilling one or two bottles of liqueur. The vessel was frequently fitted across the middle with a pierced, removable partition, presumably to separate the bottles or to retain the ice at one end. *Seau à verre*, a small version of the *seau à bouteille*. Its purpose was to hold an inverted wine glass for chilling. *Seau crenélé*, also called a *verrière*, an oval vessel with a deeply rippled rim, which was used for chilling or warming inverted wine glasses, the stems of which rested in the troughs of the rim. The English term is monteith.

soucoupe   a saucer. A *soucoupe à pied* was a dish mounted on a low foot, for holding ice cups.

sucrier   a sugar bowl. Both this and *pot à sucre* are found in the eighteenth century records of Sèvres. The distinction made by Havard (*Dictionnaire de l'Ameublement*, IV, pp. 1087–1089), in which the former is a sugar caster (with threaded lid) and the latter a sugar bowl (with flanged lid), did not apply at Sèvres.

tasse   a cup. The following varieties are represented in this catalogue: *tasse à thé*, a teacup; *tasse à café*, a coffee cup, usually larger and deeper than a teacup; *tasse à chocolat*, a chocolate cup; *tasse à glace*, a small cup used for serving ices. Rococo versions of the last-mentioned were characteristically of tulip shape, with a scroll handle and short stem. Later (neoclassical) ones were urn-shaped with two handles.

tasse à oeuf   see *coquetier*.

tasse forme litron   see *litron*.

théière   a teapot.

thrower   see *tourneur*.

tourneur   literally, a turner. As the term is used by potters, a thrower: one who gives form to objects by turning the moist clay on a wheel and shaping it with his hands or with a template called a jigger.

trigram   an Oriental motif that consists of three lines variously grouped in horizontal and vertical combinations, each group suggesting a solution to some metaphysical problem. Since eight of these groups comprise the usual composition, they are known as the "Eight Mystic Trigrams" (*pa-kua*).

truité   a type of crackle found on porcelain glazes in which the pattern suggests the scales of a trout (*truite*).

vase à cartels   probably a general term applied to vases of irregular outline or with variously shaped panels of painted decoration. One form reasonably well established by means of a label on a plaster model at Sèvres is the *vase à cartels, modèle d'Hébert*. It has a bold, inverted pear shape, and is oval in section, resting on a spreading round foot. The cover is pierced with fan-shaped openings so that the vessel could be used as a *pot-pourri* (*q.v.*).

vase à Dauphins   a vase in two parts, of a similar character to a *vase hollandais* (*q.v.*), but of oval section. The upper portion has a rippled and fluted rim; the lower is boat-shaped, with dolphin handles at the ends and panels of open trelliswork along the shoulders.

vase à éléphants   a descriptive name for a type of vase designed (or claimed to have been designed) by J.-C. Duplessis (*q.v.*). It refers to a vase of baluster form, with an elephant head molded in relief applied at each side of the neck. The upturned trunks support candle sockets of porcelain or gilt bronze, thereby giving the vase a second function, that of a candelabrum. The use of elephants' heads as handles may have derived from Chinese porcelain of the Ming Dynasty, for example, the *san ts'ai* (three-color) ware of the sixteenth century. Such motifs, however, were also employed by Meissen about 1730 to serve as tripods for porcelain candelabra.

vase à oreilles   a vase with a body of inverted pear shape, resting on a round foot with a low stem. The name derives from the shape of the handles, which are ear-like scrolls that spring from the foliated mouth of the vessel. The name occurs in the Sèvres records as early as 1754, according to Eriksen (*Waddesdon Manor: Sèvres Porcelain*, p. 58, no. 13).

vase à têtes de bouc   a name given to several types of pot-pourri vases decorated with handles in the form of goats' heads. An example of its most elaborate form is illustrated by Eriksen (*Waddesdon Manor: Sèvres Porcelain*, p. 57, no. 12); another, without a cover, is in the Henry E. Huntington Collection and Art Gallery, San Marino (see Wark, *French Decorative Art in the Huntington Collection*, fig. 102).

vase antique ferré an ovoid vase, with a beaded rim and stem and a cover with an artichoke finial. Its sides are modeled with four oval plaquettes suspended from simulated cords and eyelets, the plaquettes painted, alternately, with miniature scenes and with trophies or other ornament.

vase Fontenoy according to tradition, a vase made to commemorate the Battle of Fontenoy (1745). There is, however, little to support this idea, since the model does not seem to date from earlier than 1758. The vase is shaped as a round tower, with the muzzles of cannon projecting from buttressed windows; the cover is a high dome, with a cupola and dormer windows.

vase hollandais a type of flower vase introduced by Sèvres shortly before 1760. The origin of the name is unknown. It consists of a fan-shaped upper portion set into a separate reservoir that serves as a base and holds the water, or water and moss. The bottom of the vase descends into the base and is pierced to permit water to enter. The base may have openwork along its upper surface to accommodate narcissus bulbs or short-stemmed flowers.

vase hollandais nouveau a modification of the preceding type, in which the upper portion is trumpet-like, having walls that flare out in a curve rather than the straight line of the *vase hollandais*.

vase Montcalm the name alludes to the Marquis de Montcalm, who died in defending Quebec on September 14, 1759 (see Eriksen, *Waddesdon Manor: Sèvres Porcelain*, p. 104, no. 36).

vase pot-pourri see *pot-pourri*.

vase Tesniers a term rather frequently used in the Sèvres sale records, apparently in reference to vases decorated with scenes in the manner of David Teniers the younger.

vase vaisseau à mât a type of porcelain pot-pourri (*q.v.*) vase in the form of a ship, introduced at Sèvres. Its design is credited to J.-C. Duplessis (*q.v.*). From its resemblance to the sailing vessel in the heraldic arms of Paris, some relationship to that city has been assumed. However, this is uncertain, as a very similar vessel appears in the arms of the medieval guild of the *marchands d'eau*. A closely related form in silver may have been the prototype, as in a cruet stand by François-Thomas Germain dated 1757/ 1758 in the Museu Nacional de Arte Antiga, Lisbon (illustrated in *Catálogo da Exposição de Obras de Arte Francesas Existentes em Portugal*, no. 106, pl. 34).

vermiculé a type of openwork gilding much used at Sèvres during the eighteenth century. It assumes various patterns, sometimes resembling the "worm-eaten" effect of architectural rustication, though more often suggestive of lacework or netting. The patterns are almost always filled with minute dots, sometimes interspersed with ovals, circles, and other outlines resembling *caillouté* decoration (*q.v.*).

yellow tiger pattern a decorative motif introduced at Meissen about 1728, where it was first used on a service ordered by Augustus II. The essential element is a yellow tiger that curls around a truncated bamboo stalk. The design is decidedly Japanese in flavor and is sometimes, though erroneously, called the yellow lion pattern.

yin-yang a Chinese motif consisting of a circle bisected by an S-shaped line. It represents the duality of nature, as, for example, male and female. It is sometimes found in combination with the Eight Mystic Trigrams (see trigram).

BIBLIOGRAPHY

The titles listed here represent only those used in the preparation of Volume IV. For a more general bibliography on ceramics, the reader is recommended to consult William B. Honey, *European Ceramic Art*, I, London, 1949, pp. 17–27, and Robert J. Charleston, ed., *World Ceramics*, New York, 1968, p. 8.

Books and Periodical Articles

A

Albiker, Carl. *Die Meissner Porzellantiere im 18. Jahrhundert.* Berlin: Deutscher Verein für Kunstwissenschaft, 1935.

Die Meissner Porzellantiere im 18. Jahrhundert. Berlin: Deutscher Verein für Kunstwissenschaft, 1959.

Alembert, J. le R. d', *see under* Diderot, Denis.

Alfassa, Paul, and Guérin, Jacques. *Porcelaine Française du XVIIe au Milieu du XIXe Siècle.* Paris: Les Éditions Albert Lévy, n.d.

B

Bachelier, Jean-Jacques. *Mémoire Historique sur la Manufacture Nationale de Porcelaine de France, rédigé en 1781, . . . réédité avec préface et notes par Gustave Gouellain.* Paris: Raphael Simon, 1878.

Barber, Edwin Atlee. *Artificial Soft Paste Porcelain.* Philadelphia: Museum and School of Industrial Art, 1907.

Barrett, Franklin A. *Worcester Porcelain.* London: Faber & Faber, Ltd., 1953.

Basil, Guy, *see under* Besterman, Theodore.

Belevitch-Stankevitch, H. *Le Goût Chinois en France au Temps de Louis XIV.* Paris: J. Schemit, 1910.

Bemrose, William. *Bow, Chelsea and Derby Porcelain.* London: Bemrose & Sons, Ltd., 1898.

Berling, Karl. *Das Meissner Porzellan und seine Geschichte.* Leipzig: F. A. Brockhaus, 1900.

Berling, Karl, ed. *Dissertation-programme de la Plus Ancienne Manufacture de Porcelaine d'Europe, à l'occasion de son deux-centième anniversaire Meissen, 1910.* Leipzig: F. A. Brockhaus, 1912.

Berry, Mary. *Extracts of the Journals and Correspondence of Miss Berry from the Year 1783 to 1852,* ed. Lady Theresa Lewis. 3 volumes. London: Longmans & Co., 1865.

Besterman, Theodore, ed. *Studies on Voltaire and the Eighteenth Century.* Volume XXI: *The French Image of China before and after Voltaire,* by Guy Basil. Volume I—. Geneva: Institut et Musée Voltaire, 1955 to date.

Birioukova, N. *Figurines et Groupes en Porcelaine des Manufactures Françaises du XVIIIe Siècle.* Leningrad: Édition de l'Ermitage, 1962.

Blunt, Reginald, ed. *The Cheyne Book of Chelsea China and Pottery.* London: Geoffrey Bles, 1924.

Bourgeois, Émile, and Lechevallier-Chevignard, Georges. *Le Biscuit de Sèvres, Recueil des Modèles de la Manufacture de Sèvres au XVIIIe Siècle.* Paris: Pierre Lafitte, n.d.

Braun-Troppau, Edmund Wilhelm. "Die Sammlung Porzellanflakons der Frau Cahn-Speyer in Wien," *Kunst und Kunsthandwerk,* XVIII, 1915, pp. 57–77.

Brébisson, R. *La Porcelaine Tendre de Rouen.* Evreux: 1895.

Britton, John. *Graphical and Literary Illustrations of Fonthill Abbey, Wiltshire . . . .* London: privately printed, 1823.

Brongniart, Alexandre. *Traité des Arts Céramiques ou des Poteries Considérées dans leur Histoire, leur Pratique et leur Théorie. Deuxième édition, revue, corrigée et augmentée de notes et d'additions, par Alphonse Salvétat.* 3 volumes. Paris: Béchet jeunc, 1854.

Brunet, Marcelle, *see under* Verlet, Pierre.

Bryant, G. E. *The Chelsea Porcelain Toys.* London—Boston: The Medici Society, 1925.

C

Chaffers, William. *Marks and Monograms on European and Oriental Pottery and Porcelain.* London: Reeves & Turner, 1912.

Charles, Rollo. *Continental Porcelain of the Eighteenth Century.* London: Ernest Benn, Ltd., 1964.

Charleston, Robert J., ed. *World Ceramics.* New York: McGraw-Hill Book Company, 1968.

See also under Lane, Arthur.

Chavagnac, Xavier-Roger-Marie, Comte de. *Catalogue des Porcelaines Françaises de M. J. Pierpont Morgan.* Paris: Imprimerie Nationale, 1910.

Chavagnac, Xavier-Roger-Marie, Comte de, and Grollier, Gaston-Antoine, Marquis de. *Histoire des Manufactures Françaises de Porcelaine . . . .* 2 volumes. Paris: A. Picard et fils, 1906.

Clarke, T. H. "A Remarkable Group in the Royal Collection," *The Burlington Magazine,* CIV, August 1962, pp. 348–351.

Clerc, Nicolas-Gabriel. *Yu le Grand et Confucius. Histoire Chinoise.* 3 volumes. Soissons: P. Courtois, 1769.

Climenson, Emily J. *Elizabeth Montagu, the Queen of the Blue-Stockings: Her Correspondence from 1720 to 1761.* 2 volumes. New York: E. P. Dutton & Co., 1906.

Cohen, Henry. *Guide de l'Amateur de Livres à Gravures du XVIIIᵉ Siècle. Sixième édition, revue, corrigée et considérablement augmentée par Seymour de Ricci.* Paris: A. Rouquette, 1912.

Cole, Rev. William. *A Journal of My Journey to Paris in the Year 1765,* ed. Francis Griffin Stokes. London: Constable & Co., Ltd., 1931.

Connaissance des Arts. Le XVIIIᵉ Siècle Français, ed. Stéphane Faniel. ("Collection Connaissance des Arts.") Paris: Hachette, 1958.

Les Porcelainiers du XVIIIᵉ Siècle Français. ("Collection Connaissance des Arts.") Paris: Hachette, 1964.

"La Collection Mannheimer," no. 10, December 1952, pp. 64–65.

"Bronzes Dorés pour Vases de Chine," no. 86, April 1959, pp. 52–57.

Connell, Brian. *Portrait of a Whig Peer. Compiled from the Papers of the Second Viscount Palmerston, 1739–1802.* London: André Deutsch, 1957.

Connolly, Cyril. "Style Rococo—The Wrightsman Collection," *Art News* (Annual Christmas Edition), 1957, pp. 108–125.

Cooper, Douglas, ed. *Great Family Collections.* New York: The Macmillan Company, 1965.

Cordey, Jean. *Inventaire des Biens de Madame de Pompadour, rédigé après son décès.* Paris: Société des Bibliophiles Français, 1939.

Cordier, Henri. *Bibliotheca Sinica.* 2nd ed. 4 volumes. Paris: E. Guilmoto, 1904–1908.

Courajod, Louis, *see* Duvaux, Lazare.

Cradock, Anna Francesca. *La Vie Française à la Veille de la Révolution, 1783–1786. Journal inédit . . . Traduit de l'anglais par Mme. O.-Delphin Balleyguier.* Paris: Perrin et Cie, 1911.

D

Dacier, Émile. *Catalogue de Ventes et Livrets de Salons Illustrés par Gabriel de Saint-Aubin.* 6 volumes. Paris: Société de Reproduction des Dessins de Maîtres, 1909–1921.

Danes, Robert. *La Première Maison Royale de Trianon, 1670–1687.* Paris: Albert Morancé, 1927.

Dauterman, Carl Christian. "Chinoiserie Motifs and Sèvres: Some Fresh Evidence," *Apollo,* LXXXIV, December 1966, pp. 476–481.

"Porcelain in the Forsyth Wickes Collection," *Antiques,* XCIV, September 1968, pp. 344–354.

"Sèvres Incised Marks and the Computer," in *Computers and their Potential Applications in Museums, a Conference sponsored by The Metropolitan Museum of Art.* New York: Arno Press, 1968.

Dauterman, Carl Christian, Parker, James, and Standen, Edith Appleton. *Decorative Art from the Samuel Kress Collection at The Metropolitan Museum of Art.* London: Phaidon Press, 1964.

Davis, Charles. *A Description of the Works of Art forming the Collection of Alfred de Rothschild.* Volume II: *Sèvres China, Furniture, Metal Work and Objets de Vitrine.* 2 volumes. London: C. Whittingham, 1884.

Defoe, Daniel. *A Tour thro' the Whole Island of Great Britain, divided into circuits or journeys. Giving a particular and diverting account of whatever is curious and worth observation . . . By a gentleman [i.e. D. Defoe]. 4th edition. With very great additions, improvements and corrections which bring it down to the year 1748*. 4 volumes. London: S. Birt, etc., 1748.

Dennis, Jessie McNab. "J. G. Herold and Company: The Art of Meissen Chinoiserie," *Metropolitan Museum of Art Bulletin*, Summer 1963, pp. 10–21.

Diderot, Denis, and Alembert, J. le R. d'. *Encyclopédie, ou Dictionnaire Raisonné des Sciences, des Arts et des Métiers, par une Société de Gens de Lettres*. A–Z, 17 volumes; supplement, 4 volumes; plates, 11 volumes; supplement with plates, 1 volume. Paris—Amsterdam: 1751–1777. Table, 2 volumes, 1780.

Dingwall, Kenneth. *The Derivation of Some Kakiemon Designs on Porcelain*. London: Ernest Benn, Ltd., 1926.

Doenges, Willy. *Meissner Porzellan. Seine Geschichte und Künstlerische Entwicklung*. Dresden: Wolfgang Jess, 1921.

Dreyfus, Carle. *Musée National du Louvre: Catalogue Sommaire du Mobilier et des Objets d'Art du XVIIe et du XVIIIe Siècle*. 2nd ed. Paris: Musées Nationaux, 1922.

Ducret, Siegfried. "Weltberühmte Papageien," *Die Weltkunst*, XXII, April 1953, pp. 7–8.

"Die Arbeitsmethoden Johann Gregor Höroldts," *Keramik-Freunde der Schweiz*, July 1957, pp. 38–40.

German Porcelain and Faience. Translated by Diana Imber. New York: Universe Books, 1962.

"Augsburger Hausmalerei," *Keramos*, July 1967, pp. 3–62.

Duesbury, William. *William Duesbury's London Account Book, 1751–1753*. With a Foreword by R. L. Hobson, C. B., and an Introduction by Mrs. Donald Macalister. London: Herbert Jenkins, Ltd., 1931.

Du Halde, Jean-Baptiste. *Description Géographique, Historique, Chronologique, Politique, et Physique de l'Empire de la Chine et de la Tartarie Chinoise. . . .* 4 volumes. Paris: P. G. Le Mercier, 1735.

Duvaux, Lazare. *Livre-Journal de Lazare Duvaux, Marchand-Bijoutier, 1748–1758*, ed. Louis Courajod. 2 volumes. Paris: Société des Bibliophiles Français, 1873.

E

Edwards, George. *A Natural History of Uncommon Birds, and of Some Other Rare and Undescribed Animals . . . To Which is Added a . . . General Idea of Drawing and Painting in Water Colours; with Instructions for Etching on Cop-* *per with Aqua Fortis; Likewise Some Thoughts on the Passage of Birds; etc.* 4 volumes. London: 1743–1751.

Eriksen, Svend. "Ducal Acquisitions of Vincennes and Sèvres," *Apollo*, LXXXII, December 1965, pp. 484–491.

"Rare Pieces of Vincennes and Sèvres Porcelain," *Apollo*, LXXXVII, January 1968, pp. 34–39.

The James A. de Rothschild Collection at Waddesdon Manor: Sèvres Porcelain. Fribourg: Office du Livre, 1968.

See also under Waddesdon Manor.

F

Falke, Otto von. *Die Kunstsammlung von Pannwitz*. Munich: F. Bruckmann, 1925.

Finer, Ann, and Savage, George. *The Selected Letters of Josiah Wedgwood*. London: Cory, Adams, and Mackay, 1965.

Fisher, the Lord. "Some Notes on the 1743 Chelsea Jug," *Apollo*, XL, December 1944, pp. 138–139.

Foster, Kate. *Scent Bottles*. London: Connoisseur and M. Joseph, 1966.

The Frick Collection. An Illustrated Catalogue of the Works of Art in the Collection of Henry Clay Frick. Volume III: *Paintings*. Introduction by Sir Osbert Sitwell. Volume VIII: *Potteries and Porcelains* by Walter Read Hovey. 12 volumes. New York: Frick Art Reference Library, 1949–1955.

G

Gallo, R. *Il Tesoro di S. Marco e la Sua Storia*. Venice—Rome: Istituto per la Collaborazione Culturale, 1967.

Gardner, Bellamy. "Further History of the Chelsea Porcelain Manufactory," *The English Ceramic Circle Transactions*, II, no. 8, 1942, pp. 136–141.

Garnier, Édouard. *The Soft Porcelain of Sèvres*. London: John C. Nimmo, 1892.

Gilhespy, F. Brayshaw. *Derby Porcelain*. London: MacGibbon & Kee, 1961.

Gimpel, René. *Journal d'un Collectionneur, Marchand de Tableaux*. Paris: Calmann–Lévy, 1963.

Giraudy, Marguerite. "European Porcelain from the Tuck Bequest at the Petit Palais," *The Connoisseur*, CLXIII, October 1966, pp. 77–82.

Gouellain, Gustave, *see under* Bachelier, Jean-Jacques.

Grandjean, Serge, *see under* Verlet, Pierre.

Gröger, Helmuth. *Johann Joachim Kaendler: der Meister des Porzellans, zur zweihundertfünfzigsten Wiederkehr seines Geburtsjahres*. Dresden: W. Jess, 1956.

Grollier, Marquis de, *see under* Chavagnac, Xavier-Roger-Marie.

Groves, S. M. "The Practice of Parfilage," *Country Life*, February 6, 1953, pp. 338–339.

Guérin, Jacques. *La Chinoiserie en Europe au XVIIIe Siècle; Tapisseries . . . .* Paris: Librairie Centrale des Beaux-Arts, 1911.

See also under Alfassa, Paul.

Guiffrey, Jules. *Inventaire Général du Mobilier de la Couronne sous Louis XIV (1663–1715)*. 2 volumes. Paris: Au Siège de la Société d'Encouragement pour la Propagation des Livres d'Art, 1885.

H

Hackenbroch, Yvonne. "Chinese Porcelain in European Silver Mounts," *The Connoisseur*, Antique Dealers' Fair Issue, June 1955, pp. 22–29.

Meissen and Other Continental Porcelain, Faience, and Enamel in the Irwin Untermyer Collection. Cambridge, Mass.: Harvard University Press, 1956.

Chelsea and Other English Porcelain, Pottery, and Enamel in the Irwin Untermyer Collection. Cambridge, Mass.: Harvard University Press, 1957.

"Meissen Porcelain Sculpture from Kirchner to Kaendler," *Keramik-Freunde der Schweiz*, April 1960, pp. 51–54.

English and Other Silver in the Irwin Untermyer Collection. 2nd ed. New York: The Metropolitan Museum of Art, 1969.

Handt, Ingelore, and Rakebrand, Hilde. *Meissner Porzellan des Achtzehnten Jahrhunderts, 1710–1750*. Dresden: Verlag der Kunst, 1956.

Hannover, Emil. *Pottery & Porcelain, a Handbook for Collectors. Volume III: European Porcelain*. Translated from the Danish by W. W. Worster. 3 volumes. New York: Charles Scribner's Sons, 1925.

Haslem, John. *The Old Derby China Factory: The Workmen and Their Productions*. London: George Bell & Sons, 1876.

Hastings, Reginald Rawdon, *see* Rawdon-Hastings, Reginald.

Havard, Henry. *Dictionnaire de l'Ameublement et de la Décoration depuis le XIIIe Siècle jusqu'à Nos Jours*. 4 volumes. Paris: Quantin [1887–1890].

Hayden, Arthur. *Old English Porcelain. The Lady Ludlow Collection*. London: John Murray, 1932.

Hébert. *Dictionnaire Pittoresque et Historique, ou description d'architecture, peinture, sculpture, etc., etc., . . . des Établissmens et Monumens de Paris, Versailles, Marly, etc.* 2 volumes. Paris: Claude Herissant, 1766.

Hernmarck, C. *Opuscula in Honorem C. Hernmarck 27.12. 1966*. Stockholm: Nationalmuseum, 1966.

Héziques, Comte d', ed. *Souvenirs d'un Page de la Cour de Louis XVI par Félix d'Héziques, Comte de France*. Paris: Didier et Cie, 1873.

Hobson, R. L. *Catalogue of the Collection of English Porcelain in the Department of British and Mediaeval Antiquities and Ethnography of the British Museum*. London: Printed by order of the Trustees, 1905.

Worcester Porcelain. A Description of the Ware from the Wall Period to the Present Day. Illustrated by Ninety-two Collotypes and Seventeen Chromo-Lithographs. London: Bernard Quaritch, 1910.

Hodgkins, E. M., Catalogue of an Important Collection of Old Sèvres Porcelain, Louis XV and Louis XVI Period, belonging to. Paris: n.d.

See also under Ricci, Seymour de.

Hofmann, Friedrich H. *Das Europäische Porzellan des Bayerischen Nationalmuseums*. Munich: Verlag des Bayerischen Nationalmuseums, 1908.

Das Porzellan der Europäischen Manufakturen im XVIII. Jahrhundert. Berlin: Propyläen-Verlag, 1932.

Honey, William Bowyer. *Dresden China. An Introduction to the Study of Meissen Porcelain, etc.* London: A. & C. Black, Ltd., 1934.

The Ceramic Art of China and Other Countries of the Far East. London: Faber & Faber, Ltd., and The Hyperion Press, Ltd., 1945.

Old English Porcelain. London: Faber & Faber, Ltd., 1948.

European Ceramic Art from the End of the Middle Ages to about 1815. 2 volumes. London: Faber & Faber, Ltd., 1949–1952.

Honour, Hugh. *Chinoiserie: the Vision of Cathay*. New York: E. P. Dutton & Co., Inc., 1962.

Hood, Graham. "French Porcelain from the J. P. Morgan Collection at the Wadsworth Atheneum," *The Connoisseur*, CLVIII, February 1965, pp. 131–137.

"European Ceramic Masterpieces of the Eighteenth Century," *Apollo*, LXXXVIII, December 1968, pp. 440–445.

Hovey, Walter Read, *see under Frick Collection*.

J

Jacquemart, Albert, and Le Blant, Edmond. *Histoire Artistique, Industrielle et Commerciale de la Porcelaine* . . . . Paris: J. Techener, 1862.

Jallut, Marguerite. "Marie Leczinska et la Peinture," *Gazette des Beaux-Arts*, sixth series, LXXIII, 1969, pp. 305–322.

Jenyns, Soame. *Japanese Porcelain*. New York: Frederick A. Praeger, 1965.

Jewitt, Llewellyn. *The Ceramic Art of Great Britain from prehistoric times down to the present day; being a history of the ancient and modern pottery and porcelain works . . . and of their productions of every class*. 2 volumes. New York: Scribner, Welford, and Armstrong, 1878.

Jones, E. Alfred. "The Prices Paid for the Sèvres Porcelain at Windsor Castle," *The Burlington Magazine*, LXIV, July 1908, pp. 220–221.

K

Kaogu Xuebao (Chinese Journal of Archaeology), "Excavations of Two Western Chou Tombs at T'un Ch'i, Southern Anhui," no. 4, 1959, pp. 59–90.

Kimball, Fiske. "French Soft Paste Porcelain of the Louis XV and Louis XVI Periods," *Philadelphia Museum Bulletin*, March 1944, pp. 69–111.

King, William. *Chelsea Porcelain*, London: Benn Bros. Ltd., 1922.

L

Laking, Sir Guy Francis. *Sèvres Porcelain of Buckingham Palace and Windsor Castle*. London: Bradbury, Agnew and Company, 1907.

Lane, Arthur. "Queen Mary II's Porcelain Collection at Hampton Court," *Transactions of the Oriental Ceramic Society*, 1949–1950, pp. 13–21.

"The Porcelain Collection at Waddesdon," *Gazette des Beaux-Arts*, sixth series, LIV, 1959, pp. 37–48.

English Porcelain Figures of the Eighteenth Century. London: Faber & Faber, Ltd., 1961.

"The Gaignières-Fonthill Vase; A Chinese Porcelain of about 1300," *The Burlington Magazine*, CIII, April 1961, pp. 124–132.

Lane, Arthur, and Charleston, Robert J. "Girl in a Swing Porcelain and Chelsea," *The English Ceramic Circle Transactions*, V, Part 3, 1962, pp. 111–144.

LeBlant, Edmond, *see under* Jacquemart, Albert.

Lechevallier-Chevignard, Georges, and Savreux, Maurice. *Le Biscuit de Sèvres. Directoire, Consulat et Premier Empire*. ("Documents d'Art.") Paris: Albert Morancé, 1923.

See also under Bourgeois, Émile.

Lee, Sherman E. "The Celadon Tradition," *Bulletin of the Cleveland Museum of Art*, March 1956, pp. 46–52.

Levallet, Geneviève. "Jean-Claude Duplessis, Orfèvre du Roi," *La Renaissance de l'Art Français et des Industries de Luxe*, February 1922, pp. 60–67.

Lewis, Lady Theresa, *see under* Berry, Mary.

Lister, Martin. *A Journey to Paris in the Year 1698*, ed. Raymond Phineas Stearns. Urbana: University of Illinois Press, 1967.

Little, Nina Fletcher. "Early Ceramic Flower Containers," *Antiques*, XXXV, June 1939, pp. 281–283.

Louvre, *see under* Dreyfus, Carle.

Lugt, Frits. *Répertoire des Catalogues de Ventes Publiques Intéressant l'Art ou la Curiosité, Tableaux, Estampes . . . Tapisseries, Céramiques, Objets d'Art, Antiquités &c.* Volume I: *Première Période (vers 1600–1825)*, 1938. Volume II: *Deuxième Période (1826–1860)*, 1953. Volume III: *Troisième Période (1861–1900)*, 1964. 3 volumes. The Hague: Martinus Nijhoff.

Luynes, Charles-Philippe d'Albert, Duc de. *Mémoires du Duc de Luynes sur la Cour de Louis XV*. 17 volumes. Paris: Firmin Didot Frères, Fils et Cie, 1860–1865.

M

Mackenna, F. Severne. *Worcester Porcelain. The Wall Period and its Antecedents.* Leigh-on-Sea: F. Lewis, Ltd., 1950.

Chelsea Porcelain. The Red Anchor Wares. Leigh-on-Sea: F. Lewis, Ltd., 1951.

Mackenna, F. Severne, and Scot, F. S. A. "English Porcelain: A Chelsea Rarity," *Apollo*, XL, December 1944, pp. 136–137.

Marik, Klára Tasnádi. "Zwei Walzenkrüge von J. G. Höroldt," *Keramik-Freunde der Schweiz*, May 1965, pp. 5–7.

Marryat, Joseph. *A History of Pottery and Porcelain, Mediaeval and Modern.* 3rd ed. London: John Murray, 1868.

Marshall, H. Rissik. *Coloured Worcester Porcelain of the First Period (1751–1783).* Newport, Monmouthshire: Ceramic Book Company, 1954.

Meiss, Millard. *French Painting in the Time of Jean de Berry.* 2 volumes, London: Phaidon Press, 1967–1968.

Melton, James. "XVIIIth-Century Porcelain in Ormolu Mounts," *Apollo*, LXV, February 1957, pp. 61–63.

Menzhausen, Ingelore. "Eine neue kryptische Signatur von Höroldt," *Keramik-Freunde der Schweiz*, May 1965, pp. 3–4.

Meyer, Erich. *Festschrift für Erich Meyer zum Sechzigsten Geburtstag, 29. Oktober 1957.* Hamburg: E. Hausewedell, 1959.

Miller, Philip. *Figures of the Most Beautiful, Useful and Uncommon Plants described in the Gardeners Dictionary ... To which are added their descriptions, and an account of the classes to which they belong, etc.* 2 volumes. London: 1760.

Montagu, Elizabeth, *see under* Climenson, Emily J.

Morassi, Antonio. *Art Treasures of the Medici: Jewellry, Silverware, Hard-stone.* London: Oldbourne Press [1964].

Morse, Hosea Ballou. *The Chronicles of the East India Company Trading to China, 1635–1834.* 5 volumes. Oxford: Clarendon Press, 1926–1929.

N

Nocq, Henry. "L'Orfèvrerie au Dix-Huitième Siècle: Quelques Marques: Le C. Couronné," *Le Figaro Artistique*, no. 31, April 17, 1924, pp. 2–4.

Nolhac, Pierre de. *Madame de Pompadour et la Politique, d'après des documents nouveaux.* Paris: Calmann-Lévy, 1928.

O

Oppenheim, Michel. "Die Porzellane in den Neuen Räumen des Rijksmuseums in Amsterdam," *Keramos*, April 1963, pp. 34–38.

P

Palmer, M. A. "Meissen Porcelain in the Cecil Higgins Museum, Bedford," *Apollo*, LI, February 1950, pp. 39–42.

Parker, James, *see under* Dauterman, Carl Christian.

Pazaurek, Gustave E. *Deutsche Fayence- und Porzellan-Hausmaler.* 2 volumes. Leipzig: Karl W. Hiersemann, 1925.

Meissner Porzellanmalerei des 18. Jahrhunderts. Stuttgart: Hugo Matthaes, 1929.

R

Rackham, Bernard, *see under* Victoria and Albert Museum.

Rakebrand, Hilde. *Meissener Tafelgeschirre des 18. Jahrhunderts.* Darmstadt: Schneekluth, 1958.

See also under Handt, Ingelore.

Rawdon-Hastings, Reginald. Historical Manuscripts Commission. *Report on the Manuscripts of the late Reginald Rawdon Hastings, Esq., of the Manor House, Ashby de la Zouche.* 4 volumes. London: Her Majesty's Stationery Office, 1928–1947.

Réau, Louis, *Étienne-Maurice Falconet.* 2 volumes. Paris: Demotte, 1922.

"Jean-Baptiste Defernex, Sculpteur du Duc d'Orléans (1729–1783)," *Gazette des Beaux-Arts*, sixth series, V, 1931, pp. 349–365.

Reichwein, Adolf. *China and Europe: Intellectual and Artistic Contacts in the Eighteenth Century.* 2nd ed. London: Routledge and Kegan Paul, 1969.

Reitlinger, Gerald. *The Economics of Taste.* 2 volumes. London: Barrie and Rockliff [1961–1963].

Ricci, Seymour de. *Catalogue of a Collection of Mounted Porcelain Belonging to E. M. Hodgkins.* Paris: P. Renouard, 1911.

See also under Cohen, Henry.

Rice, Howard C., Jr. "A Pair of Sèvres Vases," *Bulletin of the Museum of Fine Arts*, LV, Summer 1957, pp. 31–37.

Rienaecker, Victor. "Fantasies of Chinese Ceramic Art," *Country Life Annual*, 1956, pp. 52–61.

Rosenberg, Marc. *Der Goldschmiede Merkzeichen.* 4 volumes. Frankfurt am Main: Frankfurter Verlags-Anstalt A.-G., 1922–1928.

Rubinstein-Bloch, Stella. *Catalogue of the Collection of George and Florence Blumenthal, New York.* 6 volumes. Paris: Éditions Albert Lévy, 1926–1930.

Rückert, Rainer. *Meissener Porzellan 1710–1810.* Munich: Hirmer Verlag, 1966.

Rüdt von Collenburg, Ludwig. *La Porcelaine en Europe.* Geneva: C.A.D.M.U.S. [1962?].

S

Sainsbury, Wilfred J. "Soft-paste Biscuit of Vincennes-Sèvres," *Antiques*, LXIX, January 1956, pp. 46–51.

"Large Groups and Figures in the Soft-paste Biscuit of Vincennes-Sèvres," *Antiques*, LXXXVII, April 1965, pp. 430–433.

"Small Figures and Groups in the Soft-paste Biscuit of Vincennes-Sèvres, *Antiques*, LXXXVIII, December 1965, pp. 824–828.

Salvétat, Alphonse, *see under* Brongniart, Alexandre.

Savage, George. *18th-Century English Porcelain.* London: Rockliff, 1952.

See also under Finer, Ann.

Savreux, Maurice, *see under* Lechevallier-Chevignard, Georges.

Schmidt, Robert. *Porcelain as an Art and a Mirror of Fashion.* London: George C. Harrap & Co., Ltd., 1932.

Schmitz, Hermann. *Generaldirektør Ole Olsens Kunstsamlinger. Ole Olsens Art Collections. Ole Olsens Kunstsammlungen.* Text in Norwegian, English, and German. Munich: F. Bruckmann, 1924.

Schnorr von Carolsfeld, Ludwig. *Porzellansammlung Gustav von Klemperer.* Dresden: 1928.

Schönberger, Arno. *Meissener Porzellan mit Höroldt-Malerei.* Darmstadt: Franz Schneekluth, n.d.

Scot, F. S. A., *see under* Mackenna, F. Severne.

Sédillot, René. *Toutes les Monnaies du Monde: Dictionnaire des Changes.* Paris: Libraire du Recueil Sirey, 1955.

Sponsel, Jean-Louis. *Kabinettstücke der Meissner Porzellan-Manufaktur von Johann Joachim Kändler.* Leipzig: Herman Seemann, Nachfolger, 1900.

Standen, Edith Appleton, *see under* Dauterman, Carl Christian.

Stokes, Francis Griffin, *see under* Cole, Rev. William.

Synge-Hutchinson, Patrick. "G. D. Ehret's Botanical Designs on Chelsea Porcelain," *The Connoisseur*, CXLII, November 1958, pp. 88–94.

Syz, Hans. "Distinctive Features of Löwenfinck's Painting," *Antiques*, LXXVII, June 1960, pp. 567–571.

T

Tait, Hugh. "Sèvres Porcelain in the Collection of the Earl of Harewood. Part I: The Early Period: 1750–60," *Apollo*, LXXIX, June 1964, pp. 474–478.

"Sèvres Porcelain in the Collection of the Earl of Harewood. Part II: The Middle Period: 1760–75," *Apollo*, LXXXI, January 1965, pp. 21–27.

"Sèvres Porcelain in the Collection of the Earl of Harewood. Part III: The Louis XVI Period: 1775–93," *Apollo*, LXXXIII, June 1966, pp. 437–443.

Tapp, W. H. "Thomas Hughes, First Enameller of English China, of Clerkenwell," *The English Ceramic Circle Transactions*, II, no. 6, 1939, pp. 53–65.

Thoma, Hans, ed. *Schatzkammer der Residenz München, Katalog, hrsg. und bearbeitet von Hans Thoma und Herbert Brunner.* Munich: Bayerische Verwaltung der Staatlichen Schlösser, Gärten und Seen, 1964.

Tilley, Frank. *Teapots and Tea.* Newport, Monmouthshire: Ceramic Book Company, 1957.

Tilmans, Émile. *Porcelains de France.* Paris: Éditions Mondes, 1953.

Toynbee, Mrs. Paget, *see under* Walpole, Horace.

Troïnitsky, S. "Galerie de Porcelaines à l'Ermitage Impérial," *Starye-Gody*, May 1911, pp. 3–27.

Troude, Albert. *Choix de Modèles de la Manufacture Nationale de Porcelaines de Sèvres appartenant au Musée Céramique.* Paris: Librairie des Arts Décoratifs, n.d.

V

Verlet, Pierre. "A Note on the 'Poinçon' of the Crowned 'C,'" *Apollo*, XXVI, July 1937, pp. 22–23.

"Le Grand Service de Sèvres du Roi Louis XVI," *Faenza*, XXXIV, 1948, pp. 120–121.

Versailles. Les Grandes Études Historiques: Villes et Pays. Paris: Librairie Arthème Fayard, 1961.

"Les Gemmes du Dauphin," *Art de France, Revue Annuelle de l'Art Ancien et Moderne*, III, 1963, pp. 135–151.

"Homage to the Dix-Huitième," *Apollo*, LXXXV, March 1967, pp. 208–213.

Verlet, Pierre, Grandjean, Serge, and Brunet, Marcelle. *Sèvres. Le XVIIIᵉ Siècle par Pierre Verlet; les XIXᵉ & XXᵉ Siècles par Serge Grandjean; les Marques de Sèvres par Marcelle Brunet.* 2 volumes. Paris: Gérard Le Prat, 1953.

Victoria and Albert Museum. *Catalogue of English Porcelain, Earthenware, Enamels, etc. Collected by Charles Schreiber, Esq., M.P., and the Lady Charlotte Elizabeth Schreiber and Presented to the Museum in 1884.* Volume I: *Porcelain*, by Bernard Rackham. 3 volumes. London: His Majesty's Stationery Office, 1915.

Catalogue of the Herbert Allen Collection of English Porcelain, by Bernard Rackham. London: His Majesty's Stationery Office, 1917.

Catalogue of the Jones Collection. Part II: *Ceramics, Ormolu, Goldsmiths' Work, Enamels, Sculpture, Tapestry, Books and Prints.* London: Board of Education, 1924.

Volker, T. *The Japanese Porcelain Trade of the Dutch East India Company after 1683.* Leiden: E. J. Brill, 1959.

W

Waddesdon Manor. The James A. de Rothschild Bequest to the National Trust, by Svend Eriksen. Aylesbury, Buckinghamshire: 1965.

Wallace Collection. *Catalogue of the Oil Paintings and Water Colours in the Wallace Collection with Short Notices of the Painters, and Sixty-one Illustrations.* 11th ed. London: His Majesty's Stationery Office, 1910.

Provisional Catalogue of the Furniture, Marbles, Bronzes, Clocks, Candelabra, Majolica, Porcelain, Jewellery, Goldsmiths' and Silversmiths' Work, Ivories, Medals, Illumina-

tions, and objects generally in the Wallace Collection . . . London: 1902.

Walpole, Horace. *The Works of Hora[ce] Walpole, Earl of Orford.* 5 volumes. London: G. G. and J. Robinson [etc.], 1798.

The Letters of Horace Walpole, fourth earl of Orford, chronologically arranged and edited with notes and indices by Mrs. Paget Toynbee. 16 volumes. Oxford: Clarendon Press, 1903–1905.

Wark, Ralph. "Adam Friedrich von Löwenfinck einer der bedeutendsten deutschen Porzellan und Fayencemaler des 18. Jahrhunderts," *Keramik-Freunde der Schweiz*, April 1956, pp. 11–19.

Wark, Robert Roger. *French Decorative Art in the Huntington Collection.* San Marino, California: The Huntington Library, 1968.

Watney, Bernard. *Longton Hall Porcelain.* London: Faber & Faber, Ltd., 1957.

Watson, F. J. B. *Wallace Collection Catalogues: Furniture.* London: W. Clowes & Sons for the Trustees, 1956.

Wills, Geoffrey. "Some French and English Porcelain at Woburn Abbey," *Apollo*, LXIII, January 1956, pp. 14–17.

Winternitz, Emanuel. "Bagpipes and Hurdy-Gurdies in Their Social Setting," *Metropolitan Museum of Art Bulletin*, Summer 1943, pp. 56–83.

Z

Zick, Gisela. "D'Après Boucher," *Keramos*, July 1965, pp. 3–47.

Zimmerman, Ernst Albert. *Meissner Porzellan.* Leipzig: Karl W. Hiersemann, 1926.

Exhibition Catalogues

1862

London, South Kensington Museum. Special Exhibition of Works of Art of the Mediaeval, Renaissance, and More Recent Periods. Catalogue edited by J. C. Robinson. London: Eyre & Spottiswoode for Her Majesty's Stationery Office, 1862.

1934

Lisbon, Museu Nacional de Arte Antiga. Catálogo da Exposição de Obras de Arte Francesas Existentes em Portugal. Catalogue introduction by José de Figueiredo. Lisbon: Libânio da Silva, 1934.

1948

London, Victoria and Albert Museum. English Pottery and Porcelain. Commemorative catalogue of The English Ceramic Circle, London: Routledge and Kegan Paul Ltd., 1949.

1949

New York, The Metropolitan Museum of Art. Masterpieces of European Porcelain. Catalogue by C. Louise Avery. New York: 1949.

1951

London, The Antique Porcelain Co., Ltd. English and Continental Porcelain of the 18th Century. Illustrated catalogue, London: The Antique Porcelain Co., Ltd., 1951.

1951

Sèvres, Musée National de Céramique. Les Grands Services de Sèvres. Catalogue edited by Serge Grandjean and Marcelle Brunet with an introduction by Pierre Verlet. Paris: Éditions des Musées Nationaux, 1951.

1953

London, The Antique Porcelain Co., Ltd. Coronation Exhibition, 1953. Illustrated catalogue, London: The Antique Porcelain Co., Ltd., 1953.

1963–1964

Frankfurt am Main, Museum für Kunsthandwerk. Figürliche Keramik aus Zwei Jahrtausenden. Illustrated catalogue, Frankfurt am Main, 1963.

1966

London, Buckingham Palace, Royal Gallery. George IV and the Arts of France. Catalogue, London: William Clowes and Sons, Ltd., 1966.

1966

Munich, Bayerisches Nationalmuseum. Meissener Porzellan 1710–1810. Catalogue by Rainer Rückert. Munich: Hirmer Verlag, 1966.

1968

New York, À la Vieille Russie. The Art of the Goldsmith & the Jeweler. A Loan Exhibition for the Benefit of the Young Women's Christian Association of the City of New York. Catalogue, New York: À la Vieille Russie, Inc., 1968.

INDEXES

Craftsmen and Artists

This includes the names of all artists and craftsmen who receive mention in the text, including those about whom fuller particulars are given in the Biographies of Craftsmen.

A

Albrecht, modeler 438

Aloncle, François-Joseph, porcelain painter 171, 175, 192, 220, 253, 260, 262, 265, 266, 272, 274, 276, 429

B

Bachelier, Jean-Jacques, painter, sculptor, and art director 154, 155, 156, 160, 163, 170, 171, 222, 285, 430

Barbin, François, faïencier 151

Barlow, Francis, engraver 317

Basan, Pierre-François, engraver 165

Baudouin père, gilder 238, 429

Belanger, François-Joseph, architect 391

Bequet, Charles-François, porcelain painter 170

Bienfait, Jean-Baptiste, porcelain painter 229, 429

Binet, porcelain painter 234, 236, 429

Blondeau, Pierre, sculptor 280, 383, 429

Boizot, Louis-Simon, sculptor 156, 172, 282

Bono, répareur 177, 178

Böttger, Johann Friedrich, alchemist, arcanist, and porcelain maker 3, 4, 5, 149, 152, 437, 438, 444

Bouchardon, Edme, sculptor 172, 290

Boucher, François, painter 165, 170, 171, 172, 182, 203, 204, 280, 282, 283, 285, 294, 295, 317, 333, 386, 387, 390, 391, 432

Bougon, family of potters VI, 285, 429, 430

Bouillat père, porcelain painter 231, 234, 430

Boulanger, Jean-Pierre, père, gilder and porcelain painter 229, 235, 239, 248, 272, 274, 276, 430

Boulle, André-Charles, ébéniste 381

Bourdois, sculptor 285, 430

Brachard, Jean-Charles-Nicolas, sculptor 285, 430
   Jean-Nicolas-Alexandre, sculptor 285
   Nicolas, sculptor 285

Bradley, Samuel, goldsmith 315

Briand, Thomas, potter 314, 315

Brongniart, Alexandre, factory director 176, 178, 180

Buffon, Georges-Louis, naturalist and artist 185

Bulidon, porcelain painter 175, 231, 236, 237, 272, 274, 430

Bulidon, sculptor VI

Busch, Christian Daniel, chemist 179

Buteux, Charles, aîné, porcelain painter 229, 242, 243, 430

C

Callot, Jacques, engraver and etcher 438

Cardin, porcelain painter 277, 430

Carlin, Martin, ébéniste 157, 167

Caton, porcelain painter 215

Censier, Charles, jeune, répareur VI

Chabry, Étienne-Jean, fils, porcelain painter and sculptor 169, 274, 430

Chambelan, Claude-Thomas, see Duplessis, Jean-Claude, père

Chappuis, Antoine-Joseph, aîné, porcelain painter 171, 261, 262, 265, 272, 274, 430

Chauveaux (or Chauvaux), Michel-Barnabé, aîné, gilder and porcelain painter 175, 272, 274, 430

Chicaneau, Pierre, porcelain maker 150
   family 150

Ciamberlano, see Duplessis, Jean-Claude, père

Cirou, Ciquaire (or Sicaire, Cicaire), porcelain maker 151

Clodion, Claude Michel, known as, sculptor 172

General Index

C

D

F

I

J

K

N

T

W

Photography by Taylor & Dull. Designed by Peter Oldenburg and Anne Preuss. Composed in English Monotype Bembo and printed on Warren's Cumberland Dull by Clarke & Way, Inc.; color separations by Edmund Loper; color and monochrome plates by Publicity Engravers, Inc.; endleaves and map printed by The Meriden Gravure Company; binding by Tapley-Rutter Co., Inc.

First printing, 1970: 2500 copies

N
5220
W95   Wrightsman, Charles B
            The Wrightsman collection, by F.J.B. Watson.
         [New York] Metropolitan Museum of Art; distributed
         by New York Graphic Society, Greenwich, Conn.
         [1966-1973]
            5v. illus., col. plates. 29cm.

            "Catalogue of the collection of Mr and Mrs.
         Charles B. Wrighsman."
            Bibliography: v.2, p.596-635.

            Contents.-v.1. Furniture.-v.2. Furniture.
         Gilt bronze and mounted porcelain. Carpets.
                                (Continued on next card)

N
5220   (card 2)
W95   Wrightsman, Charles B   The Wrightsman col-
            lection. [1966-1973]
                     Contents - Continued
         v.3. Furniture, gold boxes, by F.J. B. Watson.
         Porcelain boxes, silver, by C.C. Dauterman.-v.4.
         Porcelain, by C.C. Dauterman.-v.5. Paintings,
         drawings, by E. Fahy. Sculpture, by F.J.B.Watson.

         1.Art-Private collections. 2.Art, French-Catalogs. I.
         Wrightsman, Jayne. II.Watson, Francis John Bagott, 1907-
             III.Dauterman, Carl Christian, 1908-   IV.Fahy,
         Everett, 1941-   V.Title.

OVERLEAF: View of a potter's workshop, taken from Diderot and d'Alembert's *Encyclopédie*, Supplément, volume V of plates, 1777. The Metropolitan Museum of Art, Harris Brisbane Dick Fund, 33.23

A Firing the decoration in a muffle kiln

B Modelers' shop

C Grinding the colors and preparing them for drying

D Painting the porcelain